Accounting and Emancipation

'Accounting' and 'emancipation' have typically been seen as contradicting each other. Yet, as a social practice, accounting is deeply implicated in social concerns and should be evaluated in terms of its contribution to social well-being. Social analysis, seeing accounting intertwined in a wider social context, has reached a deepened appreciation of accounting's problematic character. This book presents a critique of accounting that emphasises it's emancipatory and enabling potential.

Accounting and Emancipation adopts an interdisciplinary and supradisciplinary perspective that draws upon debates from the social sciences and humanities, embraces a radical questioning of existing traditions, conventions and practices and engages with multiple accountings and agencies in differing modern contexts in an exploration of how emancipation can be positively aligned with accounting. Major focuses of the book include the accounting of Jeremy Bentham, accounting and socialist agitation in the late nineteenth century, the recent 'social accounting' phenomenon and a reflection upon accounting and praxis.

Essential reading for academics and advanced students in accounting research, this book will also be invaluable for policy-makers and practitioners with an interest in accounting.

Sonja Gallhofer is Professor of Critical Accounting at Glasgow Caledonian University and has published numerous critical, including feminist, historical, pedagogical and cultural, analyses of accounting. **Jim Haslam** is Professor of Accountancy and Head of Accountancy and Finance at Heriot-Watt University, Edinburgh. He has published numerous articles contributing to the critical social analysis of accounting.

Routledge Studies in Accounting

Accounting and Emancipation

Some critical interventions

Sonja Gallhofer and Jim Haslam

Routledge
Taylor & Francis Group

LONDON AND NEW YORK

First published 2003
by Routledge
11 New Fetter Lane, London EC4P 4EE

Simultaneously published in the USA and Canada
by Routledge
29 West 35th Street, New York, NY 10001

Routledge is an imprint of the Taylor & Francis Group

© 2003 Sonja Gallhofer and Jim Haslam

Typeset in Garamond by
Newgen Imaging Systems (P) Ltd, Chennai, India
Printed and bound in Great Britain by
MPG Books Ltd, Bodmin

British Library Cataloguing in Publication Data
A catalogue record for this book is available from the British Library

Library of Congress Cataloging in Publication Data
A catalog record for this book has been requested

ISBN 0-415-22014-9

To our parents
Wir widmen dieses Buch unseren Eltern

Contents

Preface

Ours is an age devoid of emancipatory vision.

Best (1995: 270)

Rather than concretizing history in narrative and popular memory, culture, in its degraded, commodified form, serves to induce amnesia and thwart collective action.

Best (1995: xii)

... remembrance keeps open both the past and the utopian future ... [it] ... is the womb of freedom and justice.

O'Neil (1976: 4)

Yes! This book focuses upon accounting and emancipation – and argues that they can be more closely aligned. The key accounting focus of our study is external disclosure in the public realm, understood as an element of the communicative structure of society. We hope that the book finds a broad readership amongst those with an interest in emancipatory endeavour.

In our on-going work, we are concerned to extend and enhance a mode of social analysis that is broadly critical in orientation. We aim to develop critical theoretical argumentation that elaborates and responds to a sense of crisis, that is critical of present forms of social repression and injustice and that aspires to individual and societal emancipation. We seek in this context to add further to the literature constituting social analysis of accounting in action, an area in which there have been major advances since the mid-twentieth century. Our critical theoretical approach is open to refinement through engagement with alternative modes of social theorising and is informed by relatively recent debates over theory in the social sciences and humanities. We share the view that critical social and historical analysis can be developed and refined, in some ways advancing its critical possibilities, through engaging with postmodern theorising (Best and Kellner 1991, Best 1995; in accounting see, for example, Arrington and Watkins 2002). Such engagement opens up, through its problematisation of seemingly fixed and certain positions and its loosening of the grip of established modes of thought, new avenues for social and historical analysis and facilitates radical re-interpretations of past discourses, including, if the logic of postmodern interventions is to pull back from avoidable contradiction, historical discourse delineating the modern (see Critchley 2001: 123, Arrington and Watkins 2002: 155). Some of these possibilities are reflected in this book, which is especially inspired by the view that some of the 'old' positive critical themes and notions – not least, emancipation – can be seen in new and radical ways whilst remaining worthy of our regard and our commitment. This is a view consistent with Critchley's (2001: 51) suggestion that '[t]he way one moves forward philosophically is by looking backwards in a fresh manner'. Thus, within the book we reflect our concern to continue to develop a rescuing critique of modernity and to advance the theme that a radical democratic polity can be facilitated by openness in the communicative structure of society. Relatedly, we indicate the continuing actual and potential significance of labour in the realm of social praxis. Yet, in both cases we reflect a recognition of the social actor's decidedly compromised and problematic location. Further, we recognise labour's location amongst a range of agencies and institutions and the impact of contextual dynamics upon the nature of its significance. We also acknowledge a multiplicity of interests and the need to embrace an ethics of difference as well as solidarity and to go beyond the problematic stance of a privileged knower (Ross 1988, Best and Kellner 1991, Benhabib 1994). That is, in reflecting upon how to better align accounting and emancipation in today's context, we acknowledge the complex, embedded character of and the uncertainties facing a critical holistic praxis and the relevance of postmodern insights for this praxis.

Our work has reflected a concern to challenge the emphasis in much social analysis of accounting in action upon the negative and repressive dimensions of accounting in society. To counter this emphasis, we have sought to contribute to an appreciation of accounting's mutability, including in terms of how it has been variously envisioned in society (cf. Best 1995). We have attempted to elaborate some of the ambiguities of accounting's social positioning, including indicating that it has no necessary class belongingness and that it exhibits a contradictory character as a communicative and strategic practice (cf. Benhabib 1986). And we have tried to promote and advance the envisioning and realisation of accounting as an accounting beyond convention, including an accounting taking on the radical potential of art (Critchley 2001: 66). Furthermore, in more direct and explicit terms, we have sought to indicate and to move towards the realisation of the 'enabling' and 'emancipatory' potentialities of accounting, a concern and interest that indeed led to our involvement in the editing of a special issue of *Accounting, Auditing and Accountability Journal* upon the theme of 'Enabling Accounting' (Gallhofer and Haslam 1991, 1993, 1994b, 1996a, Broadbent *et al.* 1997). In relation to the notion of an accounting at the service of society, the promotion and development of the view that accounting has emancipatory possibilities that can be advanced through critical social analysis provided specific motivation for this book. We were especially motivated to seek theoretical justification for our aim to better align accounting and emancipation and to engage in and develop socio-historical analyses and theorisings geared to the promotion of social change (Wolin 1960). We were particularly concerned to promote ways of seeing accounting as emancipatory and to articulate insights for the realisation of accounting's emancipatory possibilities. Such thematisation came to dominate the book. Given the vastness of its scope, we saw ourselves as making a number of interventions in this area. The title of our book thus emerged as *Accounting and Emancipation: Some Critical Interventions*.

Chapter 1, our first substantive intervention, addresses theoretical issues in respect of accounting and emancipation's actual and potential alignment. We engage with dominant ways of seeing and interacting with accounting which constrain recognition of accounting's emancipatory potential, and with theoretical and philosophical discourse that has put into question the very possibility of an emancipatory project. Here we reflect that philosophy belongs to the sphere of the political (Butler *et al.* 2000). We suggest that acknowledgment of the subject as embedded and embodied, and appreciation of a range of insights emerging in contemporary theoretical discourse (including recognition of the flux and instability of theoretical concepts), still allows us to mobilise emancipation as a social goal. Further, we indicate that the concerns of the philosophical critique of emancipation actually provide an impetus to critical accounting research and radical accounting mobilisation by emphasising the value of a radical democracy. Chapters 2–4 are offered here as interventions constituting contributions to social analysis as praxis. The analyses give recognition to the view that as contextually situated social actors we can find radical potential in the contingent particular (Leonard 1990). We elaborate critical theoretical analyses of a broad if clearly not exhaustive range of manifestations of accounting as idea and practice, these being selected from the vast field of such manifestations in history. We bring out progressive and regressive features of these historical manifestations and point to dimensions of continuity and discontinuity. Chapter 2 offers a radical interpretation of the writings upon accounting of the English philosopher Jeremy Bentham, a theoretical extension and deepening of work that has been and remains one of our major interests. Bentham reflected a key modern discourse and wrote prior to the establishment of a formally organised accountancy profession. Reflecting his own particular concern to move from 'is' to 'should be' (see Mack 1962), Bentham is understood to have held a vision of an emancipatory accounting that can still inspire us today and encourage us to acknowledge and emphasise the longevity of calls for social and radical accounting. At the same time, we elaborate how Bentham's intervention is problematic in a number of ways and suggest that an appreciation of these problematics ought to inform a radical praxis mobilising an emancipatory accounting. If Bentham's texts can themselves be considered an accounting in action, we pursue the latter notion more evidently in Chapters 3 and 4 of the book. In Chapter 3, we focus upon the mobilisation of alternative 'counter' accountings by radical social activists aligned to labour. We undertake case studies of the work primarily of Henry Hyde Champion in the late nineteenth century and explore his strategy of mobilising accounting in the context of industrial disputes, notably involving the companies *Brunner, Mond and Co.* and *Bryant and May*. Champion mobilises accounting, including existing accountings, as part of a concern, echoing Bentham's radical vision through the lens of a basically Marxist praxis, to engender a transformation of society in the name of emancipation. Our study points to dimensions of the sense in which accounting has no necessary class belongingness. In Chapter 4, we focus upon episodes and interventions of more recent times by turning our attention to a 'social accounting' phenomenon. We broadly explore dimensions of a social accounting that took off in the late 1960s and through the 1970s and that has pursued an interesting trajectory in thought and practice through to today. Calls for social accounting here have ostensibly again reflected mobilisations of accounting beyond the conventional that, especially in more radical discourse and action, have been formulated in the name of emancipatory progress. We analyse positive and regressive dimensions of social accounting interventions that prominently involved counter information systems type activists, business organisations, the government, the accountancy profession and academics and point to the relevance of contextual dynamics for an appreciation of these interventions. Our focuses are substantively on UK manifestations of accounting, reflecting our geographical location. Nevertheless, we do hold that our focuses are key and in some ways illustrative of more global developments. And, we broaden out to consider these more global developments in giving recognition to the contextual dynamics in the cases focused upon. In Chapter 5, our epilogue, we reflect further, in general terms, upon accounting, emancipation and praxis today. This includes reflecting on the various analyses of the book and upon how, in broad terms, accounting can be better aligned to emancipation in today's context. We hope that our book can help more people to see the emancipatory potentialities of accounting and that it stimulates further work, including in the form of more social and historical analyses, motivated by the aim of realising these potentialities through praxis. In our view, through engagement with interactive elements or dimensions of the sociopolitical order, including through setting one's focus on accounting in this regard, people can make a difference. We are hoping the book can encourage and stimulate further engagement towards the realisation of a more emancipatory accounting in a more emancipated world.

Sonja Gallhofer and Jim Haslam
Edinburgh, June 2002

Acknowledgements

In offering acknowledgments here, it is appropriate to make reference to the large number of people who have helped to shape our interest in the critical social analysis of accounting and encouraged us to pursue it. Those who have contributed to the development of the area of critical and historical social analyses of accounting in action are of particular note here. They prominently include those who have given journal space to such analyses, especially those who have established and run successful international journals largely devoted to this area. For us, the editors of *Accounting, Auditing and Accountability Journal* (James Guthrie and Lee Parker), *Accounting Forum* (Glen Lehman and Tony Tinker), *Accounting, Organisations and Society* (Anthony Howood), *Advances in Public Interest Accounting* (Cheryl Lehman) and *Critical Perspectives on Accounting* (David Cooper and Tony Tinker), including for their related work in the organising of successful conferences that have further stimulated activity throughout the world, deserve a special mention. The influence of Tony Lowe and the 'Sheffield School' on our work is of particular note. Our thinking on accounting and emancipation has been inspired by Ernesto Laclau who was Director of the *Centre for Theoretical Studies in the Humanities and Social Sciences* during our time at the University of Essex. He shared our view, and the view of others in the area of the social analysis of accounting, that a focus on accounting is of general interest and relevance in the social sciences and humanities. Our many colleagues and students, past and present, both in the institutions we have worked at and beyond, have helped encourage our work over the years. There are many who have helped us specifically during the period of writing this book. We would like to thank the following who have all kindly read and commented encouragingly on various drafts of material helping constitute this book: Jane Broadbent, Pat Devlin, Richard Laughlin, Tony Lowe, Christopher Napier, Prem Sikka, Tony Tinker, Stephen Walker and Hugh Willmott. We would like to especially thank Alan Godfrey, Paul Hare and John Fernie who have helped provide an environment facilitative to the task of writing this book. Your great encouragement and support mattered. We are particularly indebted to Robina Kelly, Joyce Nicol, Claire Taylor and Alison Wilson for their general administrative support. Our work for this book has been facilitated and has been rendered very enjoyable by the help and welcome received from staff of the various libraries and archives we visited and consulted. We would like to particularly mention in this respect the Archive at the London School of Economics, the Bentham Archive as well as members of the Bentham Project at University College London, the British Library, the Cheshire County Archive and Record Office, the Hackney Archive Department, the Library of the Institute of Chartered Accountants in England and Wales and the National Library of Scotland. We would like to thank the Bentham Archive at University College London and the Hackney Archive Department for permission to cite from their material. Our families have been patient during our work on this book, as well as 'concerned'. We hope they like its positive message.

When engaged in a project such as writing a book there is always a special person whose encouragement and friendship helps one to see it through. For us, this person has been Gabi Schendl who has understood so well the challenges involved in writing this book and whose support and wisdom knew no bounds. Danke Gabi!

1 Accounting and emancipation

Developing and promoting an alignment

A ray of courage to the oppressed and poor;
A spark, though gleaming on the hovel's hearth;
Which through the tyrants' gilded domes shall
roar;
A beacon in the darkness of the Earth;
A sun which, o'er the renovated scene,
Shall dart like Truth where falsehood yet has been.
(From Shelley 1812, *To a Balloon Laden with Knowledge*)

Accounting and emancipation: how can one possibly link these things together? At the time of writing there remain, no doubt, many who would find the very idea of juxtaposing accounting and emancipation to be somewhat absurd or ill conceived. Linkages between accounting and emancipation have for some time readily been displaced from perception. Rather, views suggesting that accounting has nothing to do with notions such as emancipation are prevalent.

It seems to us that one can today all too easily come to take on board ways of seeing accounting and the accountant that delimit both. A widely held current perception of accounting almost reduces it to a taken for granted, somewhat unexciting and unappealing mechanical practice that records and reports the 'facts' that are simply to be recorded and reported, a technical practice that almost just is. Accounting is apparently taken in this view to be virtually an asocial and apolitical practice. Such a perception is in part shaped and fostered by the portrayal of accounting and the accountant in literature, film and the media and seems to us to be of some weight at least in the public realm of the West (Amernic *et al.* 1979, Tinker 1985, Power and Laughlin 1992: 115, Beard 1994, Bougen 1994, Hopwood 1994, Fraser *et al.* 1999, 2000, Tew 1999). This view is consistent with a perception of accounting that also appears to us to be in effect quite widely held, namely that accounting is not something that needs especially to be probed into by anyone outside of the apparently separable sphere of the accounting expert. As Tinker (1985) has suggested, such a conception not only fails to question accounting, it also fuses with and is integral to views that legitimise accounting in the public realm. Such views lend themselves to a conservative rhetoric that legitimises much else besides. Attention in this respect is displaced almost as much from the notion of emancipation as from accounting's linkage to this concept. This amounts to a way of seeing accounting that is bound up with a way of seeing society. In this way of seeing, the current socio-political order is taken to be at least legitimate, perhaps even the best of all possible worlds, and accounting practice can be justified in this context (see Tinker 1984c, 1988, Lehman and Tinker 1987, Richardson 1987, Gallhofer and Haslam 1991).

The view that accounting is an asocial and apolitical practice is one that scarcely survives close examination. A serious probing of accounting quite readily debunks rhetoric that equates to a bracketing of accounting from the social and thus can foster the problematisation of positions legitimising accounting. In formal academic and philosophical discourse, such a serious probing has manifested historically in a worrying about accounting through numerous critical lenses, giving rise to texts of varying degrees of radicalism that are suggestive of the need for both accounting and social change (see, e.g., Lowe and Tinker 1977, Briloff 1986, 1993, Gallhofer and Haslam 1993). Indeed, the history here is a long one. Notably, accounting did not escape a critical Enlightenment questioning that crystallised in the late eighteenth and early nineteenth centuries, a questioning exemplified in the writings of Jeremy Bentham for whom accounting was a major focus of critique (Gallhofer and Haslam 1993, 1994a,b, 1995). While we acknowledge that radical modernist discourses have come to be variously distorted and problematised (see Arrington 1990: 2, Gallhofer and Haslam 1995), an interpretive analysis of Bentham's writings can indicate the sense in which they are both a substantial critique of accounting and a critique that can still be relevant today. In relatively recent times, a critical discourse on account-ing has emerged especially in the adoption of a systems approach to the analysis of accounting and the mobilisation of a variety of forms of critical social analysis, some of which accentuate the case for radical change in accounting and society (see in this regard, e.g. Lowe and Tinker 1977, Willmott 1983, Puxty 1993). Such critical analy-ses have not only had to struggle against widely held perceptions of accounting in society but also against mainstream perspectives of accounting in academia, which, masking their own problematic political philosophy, would similarly see account-ing, as well as accounting research and education, as at least potentially apolitical (see Gambling 1974, Merino and Neimark 1982, Tinker *et al.* 1982, Tinker 1985, 1988, 1991, Neimark 1986, 1990b, Arrington and Francis 1989, Arrington 1990, Solomons 1991a,b).

Views of accounting that go beyond the prevalent perception and at least have begun to indicate accounting's social location and the relevance of social deliberation over it have not only manifested in academia but have gained some purchase in society more generally. In short, these views equate to the construal of accounting in negative terms, even though the practice is scarcely explicitly challenged. Accounting is not uncommonly associated with the like of fiddling the books, fraud and a general lack of humanity. Again, this negative construal comes through and is in part constituted in literature, film and media in the West (Beard 1994, Fisher and Murphy 1995). A way of seeing accounting that perceives it as negative logically indicates a linkage between accounting and emancipation in the sense that, at a limit, accounting and emancipation appear to be opposites. The notion of an emancipatory accounting here comes to express a contradiction: accounting at this point is taken to be repressive.

Seeing accounting as the other of emancipation may constitute a positioning of accounting in an emancipatory discourse but, unreasonably, it is a very one-sided one that suppresses much of the possible envisioning of what is at stake in linking accounting and emancipation. The logical implications of seeing accounting as repressive amount at a limit to a serious problematisation of a project concerned to positively align accounting and emancipation. On the one hand, if we assume we cannot be rid of such an accounting we would logically have to tolerate it. Such a logic can lend itself to a conservative rhetoric. On the other hand, if we assume we can rid ourselves of this accounting, then logically we would seek to rid ourselves of it. At the envisaged extreme, ridding ourselves of accounting would logically constitute an emancipatory act, albeit that any notion of pursuing this logic can be heavily and variously suppressed in society. Here, all positive associations of accounting would have been lost.

The practice of accounting is not, however, doomed to the status of an evil to be rid of. The view that equates accounting to a pure repression is very problematic. A negative, one-sided construal of accounting is a perspective that once more does not survive close attention when viewed through a critical lens. The negative and one-sided construal has been countered by argumentation that has developed out of that critical academic discourse on accounting, briefly introduced above, which has made accounting the focus of critical social analysis. Admittedly, much of the latter discourse portrays accounting as negatively repressive in a way that overlaps with the more general negative perception of accounting in society outlined earlier (see Arrington 1990: 2). Yet the way of seeing accounting that is integral to and informs this critical academic discourse, namely the cognition of accounting as a social and communicative practice, encourages in that critique a going beyond simply taking accounting to be repressive. In a branch of this critique, at least, the possibility of a practice that has even been termed 'emancipatory accounting' has been envisaged (see Tinker 1984a,b, 1985). This positive linking of accounting and emancipation, consistent with an understanding of accounting as a social and communicative practice of broad potentiality, constitutes a dimension of the critical academic discourse over accounting referred to that renders this discourse more balanced and comprehensive. As we shall suggest here, it is a step beyond a philosophy of despair, whether that philosophy be constituted in something like a 'radical nonidentity between the truth of reason and any existing practice' or in something like a continual deferral or evasion of the task of formulating and seeking to realise a political vision implicating social betterment (Leonard 1990: 259, see Critchley 1997: 357).

In relatively recent times, a challenging philosophical discourse on modernity has arisen that has again raised questions for a project concerned to develop and promote an alignment between accounting and emancipation. Critical thought has problematised or worried about the very idea of emancipation. Strands of this discourse have even appeared to join with conservative rhetoric in deeming it appropriate to throw out the idea of emancipation altogether. In these trajectories of philosophical engagement, one can locate the view that notions such as emancipation – and emancipatory accounting – are what we ought to be emancipated from. For us, again, this critique is countered by further close exploration and questioning. Engagement with this philosophical critique of emancipation does yield substantial insights that ought properly to lead us to seriously re-think emancipation but it does not in our view lead reasonably to abandoning emancipation or to jettisoning a project seeking to positively align accounting and emancipation. Rather, engagement with this philosophical critique suggests new possible dimensions and resonances for such a project. It turns out that engaging with views that at least imply that a positive linking of accounting and emancipation is problematic actually allows us to develop this alignment through clarification if also through refinement. Indeed, notions that a practice such as accounting could come to secure a better alignment with emancipation are even thus further promoted: we can promote accounting as an emancipatory force.

Here, our concern is to elaborate key dimensions of the above argumentation. There are a number of good reasons for doing this. We believe that a stance such as it being deemed worthy to secure positive alignment between accounting and emancipation is very prone to undermining and appropriation by counter progressive forces. Thus, the progressive stance needs to be critically appraised and re-invigorated. This factor seems to us to be of some import given the manifestations of the various perspectives, delineated above, that risk countering a positive discourse of accounting and emancipation. Indeed, the notion that accounting can be positively aligned with emancipation is one that at least has come to be somewhat muted in even the critical accounting literature (Broadbent *et al.* 1997: 265). Furthermore, it appears to us that, consistent with this near silence and helping to sustain it, the promotion of emancipation as an idea more generally has become less common in recent times. In this respect, emancipation has in some cases been displaced by a variety of other related terms – such as enablement and empowerment – that are more easily appropriated by those who would wish to overly water down what can for us be envisaged in the mobilising of the idea of emancipation (see Inglis 1997). In the accounting literature, if terms such as enablement and empowerment can still be used to connote a more substantial emancipatory project (see Broadbent *et al.* 1997, Broadbent 1998), it is also the case that there are usages in this literature that at least are more problematically ambiguous (see the various contributions to the special issue of the *Accounting, Auditing and Accountability Journal* on 'Enabling Accounting' 1997). Lather (1991: 3), in contributing to the critical feminist education literature, felt the need to point out that her usage of empowerment went beyond 'the reduction of the term as it is used in the current fashion of individual self-assertion, upward mobility and the psychological experience of feeling powerful'. Emancipation itself has come to be problematically appropriated, being largely restricted to usage in an overly limited sense equating, for instance, to moving forward within current structures. Aside from the need to counter a conservative rhetoric, there are other reasons for elaborating argumentation that would foster a renewed positive alignment between accounting and emancipation. In our view, the notion of positively aligning accounting and emancipation is a complex and fluid one that is properly shaped or influenced multifariously in society. It needs to be thus assessed on an on-going basis. We also hold that it needs to be kept under review and explicitly re-appraised if there is to be hope of extending appreciation of it and retaining and enhancing its import. While there are fragments of a rationale for developing and promoting anew the positive link between accounting and emancipation in the critical accounting literature (e.g. Broadbent *et al.* 1997) there is a need to attempt this in a more explicit and fuller way in the terms we have suggested.[1]

We initially explore here critical appreciation of accounting in academic discourse. We elaborate how this critical appreciation develops out of a way of seeing account- ing that takes it to be a social and political practice, a way of seeing that goes beyond prevalent perspectives of accounting as apolitical. The predominant understanding of this critique is that accounting functions repressively in society. We delineate how a branch of this critique goes on to envisage the possibility of an accounting that can play an emancipatory role as part of a broader critical praxis. Having traced these basic linkages between accounting and emancipation in the literature, we go on to engage with the worrying about emancipation in relatively recent philosophical discourse. We elaborate the sense in which engaging with this discourse allows us, through clar- ification and refinement, to develop and promote a project concerned to further mobilise a positive alignment between accounting and emancipation.

Accounting and emancipation in critical academic discourse: elaborating key linkages

> ... subjects like accounting must be invented or
> created ...
>
> (Tinker 1985: 206)

Basic linkages between accounting and emancipation are discernible, sometimes quite explicitly, in a significant critical academic discourse on accounting that has long been in a process of development. This discourse has challenged an influential orthodoxy that has advanced or laboured under the delusion that accounting – along with accounting research and accounting education – can be abstracted from the social context of which it is part to accrue the status of a 'merely' technical and purely neutral practice. The critics have been concerned to problematise the orthodoxy's stance by bringing out its political and far from purely neutral dimensions. The influential orthodoxy in question typically reduces accounting to the role of 'merely' depicting, in various degrees of sophistication, the income and wealth of entities in neo-classical financial economistic terms. It clearly sees this as the legitimate role for accounting in society. As critical analysis has properly brought out, these views are value laden and not purely neutral. They are bound up in a contestable view of what is in the public interest. The influential orthodoxy, as rhetoric and as practice, has thus been understood to be politically aligned and to engender a variety of political consequences (see Burchell *et al.* 1980, Cooper 1980, Tinker 1980, 1984a,b, 1985, 1991, Tinker *et al.* 1982, Hopwood 1983, Cooper and Sherer 1984, Hines 1988, 1989, Arrington 1990, Solomons 1991a,b, Puxty 1993, Roslender 1992, Jones 1995). The critical academic discourse on accounting goes beyond the narrow and problematic conception of accounting that would allude to a purely neutral status and theorises accounting explicitly as a social and political and thus, contextually situated practice. Understanding accounting explicitly as a social and dynamic practice, we can come to better and more clearly appreciate the forces that shape accounting and put it in motion and the various consequences that accounting has in society (Burchell *et al*. 1980, Cooper and Sherer 1984, Roslender 1992, Puxty 1993, Jones 1995).

Such a way of seeing accounting, as the above suggests, opens out to more critically appreciative understandings (see, e.g. Hopper *et al*. 1987, Cooper and Hopper 1990, Puxty 1993). Accounting has been theorised critically, interpretively and contextually as a social practice that is problematically constituted and has problematic consequences. The perspective that accounting functions repressively in society has thus for some time been a key and predominant theme in a critical academic discourse on accounting. For instance, rather than unambiguously serve the whole community or the 'public interest', in accordance with the claim of the accountancy profession on behalf of the state, critical researchers have brought out how accounting has been captured by repressive hegemonic forces. Through what it informs about and brings attention to and through what it fails to inform about and displaces from attention, accounting has been understood to impact upon people's attitudes, ways of thinking and behaviour so as to help sustain and enhance a problematic social order. The content, form, aura[2] and social usage of accounting have been understood to be problematic and repressive in terms of their consequences in wider problematic contexts.[3] These negative consequences have been theorised as being enhanced or basically supported by problematic functionings of wider contextual phenomena, including the state and practices more closely associated with accounting such as accounting education, the deliberations of the accountancy profession and accounting research (Cooper and Sherer 1984, Tinker 1984b, 1988, Lehman and Tinker 1987, Tinker and Neimark 1987, Willmott 1990, Gallhofer and Haslam 1991, Lehman, 1992).

While some critical perspectives on accounting virtually imply, unreasonably, that we would be better off rid of the practice, the adoption of a critical vision and critical engagement with accounting through social analysis, coupled to understanding accounting as a social practice, has led some critical researchers to see accounting against the grain as an at least potentially emancipatory practice. As Tinker puts it:

> ... social philosophers will help us to see accountants in a different light: not as harmless bookkeepers but as arbiters in social conflict, as architects of unequal exchange, as instruments of alienation, and as accomplices in the expropriation of the life experiences of others. More than this though, these voices ... teach us that this dismal picture of accounting need not be so. There is no absolute necessity that accounting be rapacious or exploitative ... a constructive, emancipatory role for accounting is quite possible.
>
> (Tinker 1985)

Critical writers on accounting who see the possibility of something akin to an emancipatory accounting, a construct which is explicitly used by Tinker (1984a,b, 1985) (see also Cherns 1978, Sotto 1983, Gallhofer and Haslam 1996a), have theorised accounting in relation to dialectical tension. Accounting can function repressively overall but through social interaction it can come to function in accordance with an emancipatory role. An erstwhile repressive or alienating accounting can be transformed into an emancipatory accounting. Accounting is theorised as being constituted in such a way that it is never fully captured by repressive forces and is viewed as engendering countervailing or what might be termed contradictory forces through social interaction. Contradiction in society is viewed here as an engine of social change (see Neimark and Tinker 1986: 377–8). Countervailing forces might be heightened in particular contexts such as contexts involving social systemic crisis or intense social struggle. With their vision of accounting's emancipatory possibilities, critical researchers indicate the case for the capture of accounting by the repressed through social struggle. And they have come to envision this capture as positively aiding the repressed rather than simply mitigating the effects of a repressive functioning. That accounting has no necessary class belongingness is thus given a significant emphasis (Tinker 1985, Lehman and Tinker 1987, Gallhofer and Haslam 1991).

An appreciation of accounting's emancipatory possibilities implies seeing accounting as at least potentially aiding (and being integral to) or giving further help to an emancipatory project. Critical researchers thus envisage accounting as functioning to help overcome repressive obstacles so that a better state is realised. That is to say, they envisage accounting as functioning to contribute to the elimination of a gap between an actual experience of alienation and a potential state envisaged beyond this problematic experience. A vision of accounting as an emancipatory force is consistent with seeing accounting as a communicative social practice that functions as a system of informing that renders transparent and enlightens with the effect of social betterment. It is a vision in which a progressive community comes to control accounting rather than be controlled by it, a reflection of a proper accountability. This is to foresee an accounting that does not function to repress. It can also be understood as an emancipated view of accounting, at least relative to many mainstream views: new visions of accounting, translating into new practices of accounting, here throw off the constraints of past accountings in terms of their content, form, aura and usage. And connotations of accounting that see it as negative are transformed through praxis into connotations that see it as positive.

Critical writers envisioning accounting's emancipatory possibilities have recognised the significance of intervention by human agency in bringing about the realisation of these possibilities and have at least in effect advocated such intervention. In this regard, that people can come to see accounting differently, in terms of its emancipatory dimensions, is itself understood and fostered as an element of praxis. A number of other dimensions of praxis are recognised in critical discourse. Supported is action to pressurise for change in accounting and its context that would constitute the realisation of accounting's emancipatory possibilities. This can involve mobilising a counter information system or what one might call a counter accounting. It can include pressurising government and the accountancy profession towards change in respect of accounting, for instance by reminding these institutions of their claim to function in the public interest and attempting to get them to face up to that challenge more seriously (see Willmott 1990, Cousins and Sikka 1993, Mitchell and Sikka 1993, Sikka and Willmott 1995, Sikka 2000). Also supported is praxis in and through accounting education (see Tinker 1985, Gallhofer and Haslam 1996b). And research is advocated as a form of praxis (cf. Lather 1991) that can help stimulate emancipatory engagement in and through accounting and suggest insights for such engagement. Critical, interpretive and contextual analysis is especially put forward here (see Cooper and Sherer 1984).

Aligning accounting and emancipation: development and promotion through engagement with a challenging philosophical discourse

> ... at a juncture such as the present one ... the question of
> what conceptions of emancipation are remaining or
> emerging seems particularly pertinent.
>
> (Doornbos 1992: 1)

A philosophical critique of modernity has in relatively recent times come to pose critical questions to the very idea of emancipation and thus is yet a further challenge for a project aiming to secure an alignment of accounting and emancipation. Indeed, the poststructuralist and postmodern interventions that have helped shape this critique have come to be influential in social analyses of accounting and a dimension of this influence has led a number of texts to indicate some debilitating effects of the critique for a notion of positively aligning accounting with ideas such as emancipation (see Neimark 1990a, Moore 1991, Roslender 1992, Puxty 1993, especially chapter 5).[4] Yet our contention is that, again, through engaging with and responding to this worrying about emancipation we can continue to mobilise the project of developing and promoting the alignment of accounting and emancipation.[5]

The debate in respect of modernity has problematised the credibility of grand narratives of legitimation (Lyotard 1984, Fraser and Nicholson 1988, Garnham 2000). As Lather well summarises:

> ... [the critique of modernity has proposed] a break with totalizing, universalizing "metanarratives" and the humanist view of the subject ... as an autonomous individual capable of full consciousness and endowed with a stable "self" ... Such a subject has been at the heart of the Enlightenment project of progress via education, reflexive rationality and human agency ... Such a subject has been de-centered, refashioned as a site of disarray and conflict inscribed by multiple contestatory discourses. "Grand narratives" are displaced by "the contingent, messy, boundless, infinitely particular and endlessly still to be explained".
>
> (Lather 1991: 5–6)

This challenging discourse thus impacts upon the concept of emancipation, constituting a worrying about the concept in various ways (Lather 1991: 4). At the very least it expresses concern about some particular ways of seeing emancipation.

An extreme view that has come out of the challenging discourse, namely that emancipation has dissolved as a goal we might reasonably desire altogether, is a view that in our opinion must be countered. We have to overcome the overly debilitating dimension of a critique that has rendered a discourse of emancipation more anxious. We have to resist being silenced by the tendency in the critique to paralysis through the deconstruction of 'principled positions' (Benhabib 1992, Squires 1993: 1), to a celebration of undecidability (see here Alvesson and Willmott 1992: 440),[6] to the abandonment of all substantive support for solidarity, community, direction and co-ordination in favour of notions of absolute difference (Biesta 1995) and to excessive problematisation of efforts to justify emancipatory projects theoretically (Norris 1993: 186).

One way of countering the extreme view is to recognise its own totalitarian and contradictory character. Lyotard's engagement with totalising thought has in this regard been viewed as totalitarian:

> Postmodern sensibilities are plural, protean, not reducing to a single view – not even to [an] 'incredulity towards metanarratives' … Postmodernism cannot simply be presented as the refutation of modernity's 'grand recite', without in turn exposing itself as a total theory of postmodernity.
>
> (Nederveen Pieterse 1992: 26)

For us, there is indeed a sense in which a fear of the totalitarian can ironically foster the totalitarian (see Kellner 1988). And against the dangers of pursuing a positive interventionism that risks the totalitarian one has to balance the negative implications of not intervening in our problematic context (see Arendt 1958, Bronner 1994). Not unrelatedly, Alvesson and Willmott (1992) maintain that there is a danger in contemporary theoretical currents of leaving the social totality unexamined and unrepresented – and in this sense failing to make it the subject of an intervention – thus going on to leave 'virtually undisturbed' wider social structural conditions (pp. 448–9). These authors specifically warn that we should not trade totalising thinking for myopia (Alvesson and Willmott 1992: 449). Relatedly, if a dogmatic and problematic universalism can displace recognition of the many ways in which emancipation might be realised, we should also be aware that 'skepticism closes off the possibility of taking up solidarity with those who are oppressed' (Leonard 1990: 258). Since a critique assumes at least implicitly 'a possible superior state or an emancipatory change of direction', the extreme view can be equated to a contradictory position (Alvesson and Willmott 1992: 450).

Another way of countering the extreme view is thus to appeal to our values beyond skepticism, which can include giving a high status to political and ethical solidarity (Harvey 1993, Benhabib 1994), to justify a critical emancipatory project today. For Alvesson and Willmott (1992: 446, drawing from Rorty 1989):

> … the idea of emancipation must be retained and reconstructed if social science is not to become a nihilistic enterprise in which the generation of knowledge is completely divorced from the values that inspire and guide its production. Even if the idea of emancipation cannot be justified by appealing to rationality as a universal, it can be defended pragmatically by appealing to values that resonate with its concerns.
>
> (Alvesson and Willmott 1992: 446)

For Nederveen Pieterse (1992: 32): '... emancipation refers to collective actions which seek to level and disperse power, or seek to instil more inclusive values than the prevailing ones. This means that emancipation, postmodern turn or not, involves a moral horizon'. Our values can continue to both persuade and allow us to mobilise emancipation as a positive goal today. The more extreme postmodern positions that would abandon emancipation as a positive term in discourse in effect reflect values that typically cannot be reconciled to ours (see Hudson 1989, Nederveen Pieterse 1992: 26). A neo-conservative view might approach the notion that we are all emancipated already or, à la Pangloss (see Tinker 1988), that we are as emancipated as possible, thus displacing emancipation as stimulus. Our view is that, while we should not see our current social state in absolutely negative terms, there is a problematic to address and a great deal of potential yet to be realised. Views that amount, at least in effect, to embracing and celebrating repression we regard to be too cynical, pessimistic or otherwise excessively or problematically negative.[7]

While the above suggests that we can, in response to the critique, still mobilise and foster alignment between accounting and emancipation, we still need to give consideration to how the critique problematises emancipation and alters the way we should see it, even where emancipation is deemed to be a surviving goal. It turns out that engaging with the critique on these terms allows for the clarification and refinement of how we can properly see and approach the task of enhancing an alignment between accounting and emancipation. The critique here can actually aid the development and promotion of an emancipatory praxis in and through accounting.

Reflecting the thrust of the critique of modernity, concerns have been expressed about what amount to over-simplifying conceptions of emancipation and the notion of an emancipatory project. For instance, tendencies in theorising emancipation to crudely fit phenomena into the interpretive powers of single integrated frameworks have been problematised. In this respect, the need to explore such phenomena in their complexity and ambiguity and to thus go beyond overly broad-brush approaches has been emphasised. Related to and overlapping with worries about over-simplification, concerns have arisen about presumption, dogmatism and even authoritarianism in respect of particular conceptions of emancipation. For instance, due to a re-thinking of real world events coupled to developments in theorising, major visions of an alternative future society have bleakened (Doornbos 1992) and logics of necessity, various rational pretensions whereby rationality comes to embrace the real, and the idea of a single foundational revolutionary act that would be emancipation constitutive have been problematised (see Kolb 1986, Aronowitz 1988, Mouffe 1993b, Gabardi 2001). Similarly, the notion that a pure and unmediated knowledge or absolute truth can or will render all transparent and radically break a repressive power has come to be seriously questioned. How, it has been asked, can a pure emancipatory knowledge or any pure emancipatory act emerge out of a problematic language system or context? As Leonard (1990: 258–9) suggests, theory is not politically innocent and we should thus go beyond theory, whether modern or postmodern, that tends to 'make it appear that emancipation in practice and theoretical reflections on emancipatory ideals have little, if anything, to do with each other'. For Laclau (1992: 122), in this regard, 'the assertion of the classical notion of emancipation in its variants has involved the advancement of incompatible logical claims'. For example, emancipation, to be radical, must be its own ground. The order it rejects must be radically other and be constituted by evil or irrationality. If 'there is a deeper ground which establishes ... rational connections between the pre-emancipatory order, the new "emancipated" one and the transition between both ... emancipation cannot be considered as a true *radical* foundation' (Laclau 1992: 124). Similarly Laclau (1992: 124) points out that if the founding act of a truly rational society has no truck with the irrational order, this act cannot be rational. It is contingent and depends on a relation of power along with the new social order which cannot be considered as the liberation of a true human essence. Conversely 'if we want to insert the rationality and permanence of the new social order that we are establishing we have to extend that rationality to the founding act itself and, as a result, to the social order which is to be overthrown – but in that case the radicalism of the dichotomic dimension vanishes' (Laclau 1992: 124).[8] Views associated with the critique of modernity have emphasised that any structure of social relations inevitably both enables and constrains subject autonomy, that emancipation does not boil down to a single overthrow of a dominant, single and unified force and that power is thus exercised in the context of a complex network of relations and struggles (Foucault 1980, Rorty 1989, Biesta 1995). Gabardi here elaborates relevant insights from Foucault:

> Networks of power relations are permeated with multiple "points, knots, or focuses of resistance" that "are spread over time and space at varying densities" and that "are inscribed in the latter (power) as an irreducible opposite" ... Every power relation contains within it an element that cannot be controlled, integrated, or fully assimilated. This element, or cluster of elements, creates a tension within the social power environment. It is this tensional effect within the power relation that opens up the possibility of changing this relation ... What makes resistance possible is the very nature of power itself. For the very power techniques and matrices that seek to achieve control over individuals and environments of action can be employed by subjects to resist this control ...
>
> (Gabardi 2001: 74–5)

We thus need to go beyond seeing a dichotomy of repression/emancipation. Associated with all the worryings discussed so far is something of a loss of confidence and a cognition of our uncertainty in respect of emancipation together with a related recognition of the pervasiveness of power relations. These concerns suggest the need for a more modest epistemology and eschatology in respect of the emancipatory project. A cautious pragmatism has been promoted.

Consistent with the above, the philosophical critique has – in keeping with a theme in neo-Marxist and Habermasian discourse (see Habermas 1982) – problematised the notion of a privileged emancipatory agent in possession of knowledge with a privileged status, an agent such as the working class in some theoretical formulations, necessarily identifying or even having the capacity to identify with the interests of humanity as a whole in a pristine articulation. This problematisation can be read as a specific instance of a more general concern related to and consistent with the worrying about oversimplified, dogmatic and over confident conceptions of emancipation: a concern about the tendency to a problematic bluntness in the articulation of universalism and particularism. Questions have been raised about even the possibility of concurrently aligning a myriad of diverse emancipatory interests. Laclau (1990: 215) points in this respect to a disintegration of the dimension of globality inherent to what he sees as classical emancipatory discourses. For Laclau, something has gone into crisis and this is 'the idea that the whole of [the specific demands of the emancipatory projects formulated since the Enlightenment] constituted a unified whole and would be realised in a single foundational act by a privileged agent of historical change' (Laclau 1990: 215). Questioning the universalising character, strategy and rhetoric of many mobilisations of emancipation has led to a concern that some interests are being marginalised or excluded in the process of such mobilisations in what amounts to an excessively dogmatic way. For Weeks (1993: 205), such 'universalising' often masks and in effect reduces to what is a narrow particularism rather than an inclusive universalist stance: 'More often than not ... emancipatory movements have succeeded in making their voices heard in so far as they represent the militant particularism of some, rather than a social emancipation of all'.[9] Concerns have arisen in this context that particular emancipatory interventions run the risk of speaking for the other with one voice so as to ironically actually repress even while aiming to emancipate the other (see Derrida 1978a, Alvesson and Willmott 1992: 440, Biesta 1995, Gallhofer *et al.* 1999, 2000a). Debates in critical pedagogy have likewise highlighted worries about overly dominant and 'all-knowing' educators in effect repressing those they seek to emancipate (see Gore 1993: 73–4, *subter*). It is not unrelated to such worries that, often under the influence of some reception of Heidegger's critique of modernity, there have been concerns about contradictory possibilities in so-called emancipatory drives, including about overly authoritarian and totalitarian dimensions of narratives of justification or legitimation which have been universalising, totalising and 'grand'. Indeed, the very idea of progressive development has been thought of as totalitarian (see Lyotard 1984, Kolb 1986, Ross 1988, Alvesson and Willmott 1992: 444, Ray 1993). Such issues in respect of articulating universalism and particularism are further deepened by the heightened awareness of uncertainty and complexity. In respect of uncertainty and complexity, Laclau (1990, 1992) calls for the recognition that interests, identities and rationalities are not fixed but change in social interaction. To take them as fixed carries with it totalitarian dangers when moves are made to adopt the social order to these identities.

How do these concerns properly impact upon the way in which we should see and approach the task of aligning accounting and emancipation? The philosophical critique of emancipation points to the insight that, in theorising the linkages between accounting and emancipation, one ought to take a critical step beyond the adoption of an over-simplifying and over-totalising perspective by more explicitly delving into the complexity and ambiguity of accounting in action in the context of which it is part. Such a move can be assisted, it seems to us, by the adoption and development of a way of seeing accounting that goes beyond a dichotomous *either/or* thinking whereby accounting is deemed to be either an instance of absolute repression or an instance of absolute emancipation. Rather, as a communicative social practice, accounting can properly be viewed as having *both* emancipatory *and* repressive effects at any instant of time [see Lather 1991, Gabardi 2001, cf. Prokhovnik's (1999) articulation of relational thinking]. For us, it is such an appreciation of accounting's ambiguity that helps to justify much of what is involved in the very act of delving into accounting in action. If one seriously held the view that the task was to throw out accounting *in toto*, that is, that accounting was a completely repressive practice, the justification for engaging in very detailed analysis would be substantially constrained in scope. The argumentation here has a more general application, beyond the accounting focus. Laclau (2000b: 304) holds in this context that 'the universality obtainable through equivalential logics will always be a universality contaminated by particularity'. Leonard's (1990) concern to reconstruct critical theory resonates well here. While challenging the extreme normative skepticism of some postmodern positions, he works through a tension in critical approaches between on the one hand an emphasis on the historicity/contextuality of knowledge and on the other a particular promotion of a principle of universalisability. While we still deem it appropriate to summarily assess whether the repressive effects of accounting's functioning outweigh the emancipatory in terms of their significance, or vice versa, it is important for the task of developing an appropriately informed emancipatory praxis to value and recognise the more complex and comprehensive picture summarised in terms of appreciating both repressive and emancipatory effects in a given context. This also points to the need to theorise the detailed specificities of accounting in context. Alvesson and Willmott (1992: 437) advocate an increased sensitivity to such specificities and thus the avoidance of 'a cavalier and dismissive attitude toward mundane detail of key institutions and features of modern society'.[10] The call here to theorise the detailed specificities of accounting is a call for a renewal and extension of an emphasis that is already significant in critical accounting research, where detailed social analysis of accounting in context has to some extent flourished.

Introducing dynamics to the above way of seeing a relation between accounting and emancipation, we can appropriately recognise a continuum along which accounting can move in the direction of greater emancipatory or greater repressive force. To recognise a continuum is to focus upon these movements and to go beyond the dichotomous envisaging of repression/emancipation. This notion of a continuum is consistent with the idea of a summary assessment of the relative weights of both accounting's repressive and emancipatory impacts. It thus can be consistent with understanding the complexity and ambiguity of accounting in a dynamic context. The theorising of emancipatory movement here as complex movement along a continuum is an appropriate response to the philosophical critique in that it goes beyond understanding emancipatory change in terms of a radical break (e.g. through a single foundational revolutionary act implicating an enlightenment through accounting) that suddenly constitutes an absolute emancipation. A move beyond dichotomous thinking leads us to suggest that accounting 'as it is', which from a critical and situated perspective we take to be problematic, is in part retained in the process of radicalisation to a more 'emancipatory accounting'.[11] For Wertheim (1992: 260), emancipation in this regard is a process that 'remains open ended ... with ups and downs' while Alvesson and Willmott (1992: 447) formulate the emancipatory project as a 'precarious, endless enterprise'. This way of seeing goes beyond an all or nothing conception of accounting as either an emancipatory or repressive force in favour of delineating a balanced sense of progress or regress along a continuum. Nederveen Pieterse (1992: 5) elaborates such a balanced perspective as 'a sense of [emancipatory] direction far more subtle, multiple and modest than the "modern" views'. A concern to appreciate complexity, reflective of the philosophical critique, extends properly to maintaining a heightened sensibility to 'instability, indeterminacy and transience' (Nederveen Pieterse 1992: 26). This concern extends to recognising in assessing change that interests, identities and rationalities are not fixed and 'simply repressed' but change in social interaction, thus suggesting a critical reflexivity vis-à-vis the very notion of emancipation (Laclau 1990, 1992). The move beyond dichotomous thinking that can be preserved in theorising the dynamics of accounting in relation to emancipation is also consistent with perceiving power as never absolutely and simply held by one group over another, an implication of the philosophical critique.[12] To further an emancipatory praxis implicating accounting it would again be important to undertake contextual analysis of detailed specificities, here detailed specificities of a changing accounting in action. Such a call is again one that supports re-invigorating and extending an emphasis already significant in critical accounting research.

The modesty referred to above by Nederveen Pieterse can be taken to reflect the calls for a modest eschatology and epistemology that emerge from the philosophical critique. Such calls have implications for how we can properly link accounting and emancipation. In respect of eschatological modesty we need to take, as a deliberative act, a step beyond presumption, dogmatism and over-confidence. The philosophical critique points rather to a cautious approach that, for instance, would appreciate how problematic dimensions of prior contexts leave their mark upon interventions in and through accounting intended to be emancipatory and upon apparently emancipatory social trajectories implicating accounting (cf. Laclau and Mouffe 1985, Nederveen Pieterse 1992: 5). At the same time if, consistent with a cautious pragmatism, we give further recognition to the need to respond contextually and strategically to shifting frameworks of power and resistance, we can, to the extent that we reflect what is here valuable in postmodern insight, actually further radicalise and incorporate critical gains into our praxis (see Squires 1993: 1–2). In respect of epistemological modesty we need to act with a heightened awareness of uncertainty, lack of assurance and the pervasiveness of power. Neither accounting in itself, nor understandings of its repressive and emancipatory dimensions, nor appreciations of how these dimensions might be mobilised, can be taken to be pure unmediated knowledge (cf. Laclau and Mouffe 1985).[13] The pertinence of the above notion of a continuum constituted by a complexity and ambiguity follows from the adoption of such eschatological and epistemological modesty.

The philosophical critique indicates the need to seek a new articulation between universalism and particularism that is reflective of a heightened sensitivity to as well as awareness of the dogmatic excesses of Western universalism. This seems to us to be especially of import in respect of accounting, a practice captured by a Western universalism which, for instance, in various historical projects concerned to foster global accounting principles and practices, has at the very least threatened valued particularities integral to local accountings that reflect local cultural perspectives. The concern to better articulate universalism and particularism seriously enhances the complexity involved in the emancipatory project, albeit that, as Squires (1993: 2) argues, poststructuralist and postmodern insights appropriately bring refinement and new emphases to a critical project by taking on board 'a fuller reflection of multiplicity and differences' relative to previous approaches. An implication is that in seeking to foster an alignment between accounting and emancipation we need to acknowledge a notion of emancipations plural as Nederveen Pieterse (1992: 32) puts it (see also Laclau 1996), and ought to also recognise the existence of a variety of relevant agencies. Such acknowledgement and recognition can properly lead us to contemplate a variety of accountings linked to various agencies and emancipations and appropriately encourage us to see diverse ways in which these differing accountings might be acted upon and mobilised. In this regard, the challenging philosophical discourse implies, in the case of projects intervening in and through accounting, that we should go beyond a problematic Western-centricity and universality that is reflective of a problematic power (see Arrington 1990) and allow and make possible the recognition of other voices (see Fraser 1986, Young 1993).

We should stress here that, drawing insights from the philosophical critique, we can conceive of a way forward that seeks to arrive at a better articulation between particularism and universalism rather than abandon the latter for the former. We can still aim to mobilise a universalist stance but one that gives due recognition to valued particularities. We can still appeal to the goal of emancipation and to an appreciation of general social dynamics whilst being concerned about the particular and the local (see McNay 1992, Humphries 1997). As far as a universalist stance is concerned, we cannot avoid it in our sphere of politics. As Laclau (2000b: 305) suggests: 'There is no politics of pure particularity ... Even the most particularistic of demands will be made in terms of something transcending it' (see Butler 2000: 166). There are, however, different universalities (Butler 2000, Laclau 2000b: 305). An open and sensitive universalist stance here can, on the one hand, be concerned to gain insights from other particulars that will help refine universal (as well as local particular) accounting principles and practices (Gallhofer and Chew 2000, Gallhofer *et al.* 2000a). On the other hand, such a stance, one still amenable to an articulation that preserves the sort of universalism in ethics and politics defended by Benhabib (1994), can aim to recognise what might be valued particularities of dimensions of accounting in differentiated domains. Lister (1997: 28), in this regard, in her work on citizenship, has elaborated a construct of 'differentiated universalism' that expresses a concern to 'reconcile the universalism which lies at the heart of citizenship with the demands of a politics of difference'. Many of those who have engaged with the challenging discourse on emancipation have come to adopt views that at least have an affinity with a differentiated universalist stance as understood here. Nederveen Pieterse (1992: 15) holds that it is important to historicise and recognise the plural character of emancipations and also to look for ways in which these emancipations may be correlated, coordinated or articulated rather than be conceived of and treated as 'simply isolated processes' (see also p. 32). For Mouffe (1993a: 79) what is at stake in the present juncture is 'not a rejection of universalism in favour of particularism, but the need for a new type of articulation between the universal and the particular'. One can thus call for a differentiated universalism that involves sensitively engaging in the very difficult task of aligning emancipations plural to emancipation in general. The task is consistent with steering a path between an authoritarian ethnocentrism and an absolute cultural relativism. It appropriately implicates various mobilisations of and interventions in accounting, including an alignment of accountings plural to accounting in general.

Cognisant of multiple sites of repression and of the importance of difference and particularity, a differentiated universalist approach can seek to articulate and respond to this complex multiplicity through an open negotiation that still recognises its positioning in a universalist stance. Laclau and Mouffe (1985), influenced by Gramsci, refer in this respect to the need to seek 'hegemonic articulations' of various particular emancipatory demands while Laclau (1990: 211) envisages 'an open-contingent hegemonic-articulatory process'. According to Laclau, if the notion of the essential unification of emancipatory demands around a global transforming act is today weakened this:

> ... does not mean that the various demands are doomed to isolation and fragmentation, but rather that their forms of overdetermination and partial unification will stem from hegemonic articulations forming part of 'historic blocks' or 'collective wills', and not from the apriori ontological privilege of a particular class or social group.[14]

(Laclau 1990: 215–6)

Thus, formulating an alignment between various emancipatory interests, identities and rationalities, with the various accounting implications,[15] constitutes a terrain of social struggle today (cf. Laclau and Mouffe 1985). Creating new power around a hegemonic centre can emancipate a constellation of social forces that can be brought into relative universalisation by the expansion of a chain of equivalences around the particularistic in terms of some form of anti-systemic alignment (Laclau 2000a: 208, 2000b: 302). Laclau (2000a: 209) thus calls for the 'construction of languages providing that element of universality which makes possible the establishment of equivalential links', constituting the construction of a new social imaginary (Laclau 2000a: 211). These languages can include languages of and about accounting. Aligning emancipations plural involves co-ordination and a prioritisation not inconsistent with pursuing various projects concurrently – indeed, this multidimensionality is encouraged by the critique. We can here posit an ethics of both solidarity on the one hand and openness to difference on the other that can inform our understanding of accounting, our theory constructions and our praxis in general (Leonard 1990: 261, see Fraser 1986, Arrington 1990, see also Arrington and Puxty 1991).

Understanding the way forward in the above terms, and thus aiming to better articulate universalism and particularism in the context of a praxis seeking to mobilise a positive alignment between accounting and emancipation, one comes to properly appreciate the complexity involved, more especially if giving cognition to social dynamics.[16] Such awareness ought to deepen the concern to adopt a modest epistemology and eschatology and aptly encourages a self-questioning approach. The more global the vision of an alignment between emancipation and accounting, the greater the weight that appropriately accrues to such modesties and cautions. The notion of continuum is important in respect of an ethical position of openness to difference: Laclau (2000a: 209) refers to a 'protracted war of position tending towards more global aims' and maintains that universality should be considered as a horizon (Laclau 2000a: 211). He thus maintains: 'There is no universality ... except through an equivalence between particularities, and such equivalences are always contingent and context-dependent' (Laclau 2000a: 211). In relation to such awareness, further support must be given to a critical, contextual and interpretive mode of analysing accounting in action, here especially emphasising an interest in gaining an appreciation of valued particularities and in critically assessing their articulation in relation to universalism.

In recognising that the critique requires us to clarify and refine our way of seeing emancipation, we should emphasise that, consistent with this, the critique suggests we need to look at more 'traditional' critical concerns differently rather than not look at them altogether. For instance, previously 'privileged' agents such as the working class in Marxist discourse are still appropriately recognised as agents in new conceptions and can be constituted as social entities to be emancipated, if this very constitution has to be constructed through political action (Laclau 2000b: 306). Abandoning the idea of a particular agent being privileged does not imply the irrelevance of that particular agent, albeit that we do have to worry about the precise meaning of, for instance, the term 'class' in discourse and recognise its instability (Laclau 2000b: 297–301, 306). Accepting the absence of a privileged subject for radical change, Nederveen Pieterse (1992: 21–2) notes that this only indicates the changing significance of class: it 'does not mean that class loses relevance but that it is no longer necessarily the single overriding dimension'. On class, while one must guard against anchoring the moment of struggle in the sectorial identity of a group and transcend that identity towards a 'complexly articulated' collective will (Laclau 2000a: 210), Žižek (2000a) has recently declared: 'Class Struggle or Postmodernism? Yes, please!' and has gone on to stress that postmodernism does not negate a concern to engage in praxis aimed at intervention towards global structural change (Žižek 2000b, cf. Derrida 1978b, see also Gallhofer and Haslam 1995 on the possibilities of modernity in respect of accounting).

Further, the above hints at ways in which the philosophical critique, rather than challenge the idea of a project concerned to promote and develop an alignment between accounting and emancipation, can actually function as a stimulus to an emancipatory praxis in and through accounting. This includes adding new dimensions to or suggesting new emphases for such praxis. On the one hand, the critique can be read as a spur to emancipatory praxis in general, this praxis including the project concerned to better align accounting and emancipation. On the other hand, the critique can be read as encouraging more specifically the mobilisation of and intervention in accounting in the context of broader emancipatory praxis.

In respect of its stimulus to emancipatory praxis in general, the critique points more emphatically to a role for human agency in social change, highlighting people's responsibilities even if offering no guarantees in going beyond past dogmatism. Accepting the non-inevitability thesis of social change and that there is no clear-cut logic of necessity, we can more clearly recognise ourselves as agents who can make a difference within our context.[17] With a less re-assuring discourse about emancipation and with no obvious easy and pristine solutions, life may in some ways be more difficult, messy and awkward, but we are encouraged and motivated to face up to the challenge. Laclau (1990: 216, see also pp. 210–1) suggests that it is:

> ... precisely this decline in the great myths ... which is leading to freer societies: where human beings see themselves as the builders and agents of change of their own world, and thus come to realise that they are not tied by the objective necessity of history to any institutions or ways of life – either in the present or in the future.[18]
>
> (Laclau 1990: 216)

According to Laclau and Mouffe (cited in Laclau 1990: 98, Nederveen Pieterse 1992: 26), the present juncture is:

> ... a moment in which new generations, without the prejudices of the past, without theories presenting themselves as "absolute truths" of history, are constructing new emancipatory discourses, more human, diversified and democratic. The eschatological and epistemological ambitions are more modest, but the liberating assumptions are wider and deeper.
>
> (Laclau 1990: 98)

For Laclau (1992), opportunities are opened up in this regard for the radical critique of multifarious forms of domination and the possibility for more democratic societies (see Laclau 2000a: 208–9). Nederveen Pieterse (1992: 33), in reviewing Melucci (1992), accentuates the positive here by suggesting that the loss of certainties brought about by the critique can engender a new awareness translateable into co-operative solidarity: '... if we can accept that in social relations everything is not subject to the calculus of an absolute rationality, diversity and uncertainty can become the basis for a new solidarity. From this condition of conscious frugality could come the changes in ethical values that form the basis for coexistence' (Nederveen Pieterse 1992: 53).[19] That the critique opens up space for radicality can also be read specifically as a stimulus to the development of various 'emancipatory accountings' in respect of the diverse agendas. More generally, an implication of the critique is that we should acknowledge a *responsibility* to positively align accounting and emancipation, albeit in the face of complexity, uncertainty, instability and contingency. We should also accept responsibility for the content of the concept of emancipation itself. In this regard one can sketch out, across a range of identities, desiderata for well-being, that can be an impetus in a radical democratic negotiation. Through this process, the narrow, inappropriate, dogmatic and unbalanced character of instrumental goals that often manifest in society, can be problematised: an emancipation from problematic ends is an element in a broader emancipatory praxis. The philosophical critique of modernity thus at least need not dissuade one from the view that emancipatory projects can be concerned to create something rather than just prevent something. We agree with Nederveen Pieterse's (1992: 13) view that 'emancipation is not simply about saying no, reacting, refusing, resisting, but also and primarily about social creativity, introducing new values and aims, new forms of cooperation and actions'. This is to go beyond Alvesson and Willmott's (1992: 450) view that the anti-authoritarian emphasis of a critical theoretical perspective leads it only to counter ideologies and arrangements 'that obstruct human freedom, not filling the latter with particular contents'. In our view, one can appropriately construct a more positive vision or sketch of a future society, if recognising it as such and acknowledging its instability (Bronner 1994).[20]

In respect of providing a stimulus more specifically to projects giving greater attention to accounting in the context of a broader emancipatory praxis, the philosophical critique of emancipation points to the relevance of analysing detailed specificities of the social and places emphasis upon the potentiality of democratic forces. The emphasis upon the relevance of analysing detailed specificities is arguably especially an encouragement to focused social analysis of accounting in action, albeit that critical accounting researchers have engaged in such analysis for some time. The emphasis upon the potentiality of democratic forces is for us very important. If we accept that accounting is a communicative social practice that can function as a system of informing including in respect of concerns to render accountable, then the emphasis upon radical democratic forces implies that greater attention be placed upon accounting in terms of its potentiality to function positively vis-à-vis radical democracy. Communication, information and accountability are key terms in a discourse of democracy (see Bronner 1994). The philosophical critique of modernity can be understood to emphasise and promote democratic forces in a number of ways. For example, Laclau holds that a going beyond totalising perspectives can implicate the unleashing of positive forces in terms of a radical democracy:

> The central obstacle preventing the democratisation of emancipatory discourses is the fact that ... while ambiguity and indeterminacy are central features of democracy, emancipatory discourses tend to manifest themselves as total ideologies which seek to define and master the foundations of the social.[21]

(Laclau 1990: 169)

And, Laclau suggests that the challenges to the rationalist and foundationalist pretensions of emancipatory discourse allow a more democratic vision of social demands:

> People do not now have to justify their demands before a tribunal of history and can directly assert their legitimacy on their own terms. Social struggles can thus be seen as "wars of interpretations" in which the very meaning of demands is discursively constructed through struggle.[22]
>
> (Laclau 1990: 216)

For Nederveen Pieterse (1992: 31), democracy is a 'recurrent theme in the contemporary re-orientation of emancipatory thought'. Several texts emerging out of the philosophical critique have placed a particular significance on the critique's positive implications for a praxis emphasising democracy (see Laclau and Mouffe 1985, Laclau 1990: 98, 196, Nederveen Pieterse 1992: 26).[23]

What then, in brief, does the philosophical critique imply for the range of elements that can constitute an emancipatory praxis in and through accounting? We have seen that the critique aptly modifies aspects of a praxis concerned to better align accounting and emancipation. It appropriately shapes the envisioning of accounting in relation to emancipation, this envisioning constituting an element of praxis. And it duly transforms how we can develop an understanding of accounting's emancipatory dimensions through the contextual analysis of accounting in action, a further element of praxis that is constitutive of accounting research. In respect of research, critical, contextual and interpretive analysis is further promoted by the challenging philosophical discourse which especially emphasises the case for paying attention to detail and reflecting awareness of the dangers of an excessive and problematic dogmatism and universalism. Accounting education, also an element of praxis, has not been specifically highlighted in the above but the critique duly impacts in this sphere in a way similar to its impact upon accounting. For instance, the 'educator', *inter alia*, needs to put more emphasis on giving a voice to those with whom s/he interacts in the context of educational activity (see, e.g. Gore 1993). Praxis concerned to pressurise for accounting change can also properly respond to the philosophical critique, for instance, by going beyond a crude dichotomous thinking, adopting the more modest epistemological and eschatological ambitions and relatedly reflecting a heightened awareness of and sensitivity to the problematics of universalism. Thus the philosophical critique implies modification to various elements of an emancipatory praxis in and through accounting. We should stress, however, that this is far from implying the abandoning of the project aimed at positively aligning accounting and emancipation. Indeed, we can still have our theories about emancipatory possibilities, practices and processes and we can still sketch our vision of a better accounting in a better society – an accounting for emancipation (see Bronner 1994). We have also indicated that, albeit that we need to appreciate the difficulties of the task, aligning accounting positively with emancipation today is a task that can be given further emphasis in a broader critical praxis. The philosophical critique considered can engender, through clarification and refinement, the development and promotion of a positive positioning of accounting in relation to emancipation.

We have indicated how the philosophical critique actually re-invigorates and re-vitalises the project concerned to foster an alignment between accounting and emancipation, notably by, in emphasising radical democracy, suggesting the need to give greater attention to accounting in terms of its potentiality to function positively. Or, with appropriate awareness and sensitivity, forward accounting!

2   Jeremy Bentham, accountant[1]

A radical vision of an emancipatory modern accounting

> From the art of Pauper Economy, studied with any attention, the transition is
> unavoidable to the ministering art of book-keeping ... book-keeping was one of
> the arts which I should have to learn ... the cries of the poor called aloud and
> accelerated the demands for it ...
>
> (Jeremy Bentham UC, cliiia: 33–4)

> Philosophy requires both critical and logical destruction and patient hermeneutic
> reconstruction.
>
> (Critchley 2001: 47–8)

In seeking to develop and promote an alignment between accounting and emancipation,
we are here concerned to critically explore the extensive writings upon accounting of
Jeremy Bentham (1748–1832), the British philosopher, social reformer and social
visionary.

This choice of focus might surprise some. Why, especially in a project concerned
to develop and promote an alignment between accounting and emancipation, would
one focus upon Bentham on accounting? The question seems all the more pertinent
given how Bentham is perceived by many critics, including a number in the accounting literature. Is it not the case that Bentham can to all intents and purposes be dismissed as a purveyor of narrow and even basically negative and repressive ideas? By
now, have not a large number of critics properly and easily summarised these ideas and
located them in the trajectories of modern institutions and practices? How, it might
be asked, can any detailed critical exploration of Bentham's writings on accounting
be justified today? What is there to add now from a close review of Bentham's work?
These are questions reflecting serious concerns.

Given these concerns, we initially put quite an emphasis here upon developing
argumentation supporting the case for an analysis of Bentham's accounting writings,
elaborating at length in order to clear a path for a more balanced and imaginative
appreciation of these texts than has been apparent hitherto. Various general and
specific arguments in support of our analysis are thus presented and we indicate how
a critical and interpretive approach allows us to gain substantial insights and stimulus from the exploration of Bentham's accounting texts. We challenge treatments of
Bentham that have portrayed him simply as crudely narrow and worryingly problematic and that, we suggest, in various ways encourage us to be overly dismissive of

his texts. We point to argumentation in the literature that counters the reception of Bentham as crudely negative and that encourages us to explore his work more closely and in a more balanced way. Critical theoretical argumentation suggesting that Bentham's texts might be rescued as texts of radical and emancipatory character is elaborated. In our analysis of Bentham's writings on accounting that follows our extensive rationale, we explore and interpret Bentham's accounting texts as developing and promoting the alignment of accounting with emancipation. We delineate how Bentham sought to 'liberate' and mobilise accounting so that it could better contribute to progressive and emancipatory social change. We go on to critically reflect upon Bentham's accounting texts and in the light of this consider what can go wrong in the operationalisation today of a project to advance, like Bentham, an accounting that would be emancipatory. We emphasise in this context the relevance of our analysis for a project concerned to better align accounting with emancipation today.

Our argument, then, will be that not only can one gain insights for praxis from a critical theoretical engagement with the negative in Bentham, but also from a more balanced critical theoretical appreciation of the positive. Indeed our view is that Bentham's mobilising of accounting – some two hundred years ago – can still serve as a basic model, albeit one that needs refining and one that we ought to use with caution, for praxis in and through accounting. We ought especially to recognise the ways in which Bentham's vision continues to constitute an unrealised positive potential for an accounting that would be emancipatory today.

Why Bentham? Accounting and the voice of reason: Bentham's significant place

Since Bentham wrote around two hundred years ago, what is the relevance of analysing his accounting texts today? A general rationale can be briefly elaborated for such an analysis consistent with the adoption of a critical approach. The comparison and contrast of a past with a present accounting and the tracing of continuities and discontinuities in accounting's trajectory can indicate ways of aligning accounting and emancipation. Historical analysis can facilitate a deeper appreciation of both repressive and emancipatory dimensions of accounting today. Past ways of seeing and rationales for accounting can be unearthed and can inspire and stimulate. We can unearth or clarify, through analysis of the constitution and consequences of discourses and practices in terms of a broad and complex social field, the problematic biases of current ways, including biases reflective of problematic hegemonic forces that continue. One can locate a more emancipatory potential of accounting of relevance for a rescuing critique. In this regard, one can consider how the past can indicate better ways for us and explore paths laid down that were subsequently scarcely taken up or largely abandoned, becoming covered under layers of history. This can in our realm stimulate an awakening to new visions and their articulation. In the above respects, substantial insights can be gained from critical, interpretive and contextual analysis. Bracketing the particularities of accounting's current location, thus escaping being too wedded to current perspectives on accounting (see Gallhofer and Haslam

1996a: 263, n. 6) – or going beyond an excessive chronocentrism[2] – can facilitate the gaining of greater insights (see Haslam 1991, Gallhofer *et al*. 1991, 1993, 1994a,b, Miller and Napier 1993, Fraser *et al*. 1999).[3] Historical analysis, we should emphasise here, can also help us to appreciate the historical longevity of current radical argumentation in respect of accounting. Discourses and practices of today with much emancipatory potential that are commonly imagined to be of more recent vintage may be shown, at least in some ways, to have had a much longer history. Such insight can add its own weight to dimensions of current praxis. With an appreciation of the historical longevity of a radical discourse, one can argue that radical proposals in circulation today are now long overdue.[4]

There are a number of reasons in our view why an analysis of Bentham's accounting texts are of more particular interest and relevance and it is appropriate to give these more emphasis here. It is noteworthy, for example, that Bentham, a significant philosopher, was a prominent exemplar amongst those modern philosophers, Enlightenment writers on administration and modern reformers concerned to engage in practice, who variously turned their attention to accounting with a view to advancing social progress.[5] In what we may call 'modern' contexts (see Calinescu 1986, 1987, Osborne 1992, Gallhofer and Haslam 1995: 204–6) we can locate major philosophers who have included a broadly conceived accounting within the ambit of their work in some significant way. Consistent with modern reasoning, typically they have done this in elaborating designs for new and better ordered worlds. For example, in England traces of such an approach can be found in the works of Bacon and Locke and a close reading of Hobbes indicates the weight he, in effect, placed on what can be termed accounting controls (see Bacon 1944, Hobbes 1991, Munday 1992). In a context constituting a significant crystallisation of modernity,[6] a number of Enlightenment texts on administration were produced that claimed to elaborate a better way of administering the state. Many of these at least implied accounting's role, often as reformed, in the order of things they envisaged. For instance, the works of von Bielfeld, Necker, Turgot, Bonvallet des Brosses, many of the Cameralists and indeed the adaptations and contributions of Catherine the Great are of note here.[7] In Continental European philosophy, Kant's writings begin to especially indicate the potential of reporting systems in the public domain: the significance of informed public opinion and thus transparency is emphasised for the progressive, emancipatory and utopian construction of social relations through rational communicative interaction (see Laursen 1986, de Lucas 1987, Holub 1991: 41, Davis 1992, Habermas 1992: 102, see also Oncina 1994 on Fichte, Goodman 1995, La Vopa 1995 on Herder).[8] Bentham, intervening with his accounting texts in the late eighteenth and early nineteenth century context, was influenced by many of the philosophical currents delineated above, and notably and in various ways by the texts of Bacon, Locke, Hobbes, Hutcheson, Hartley, Beccaria, Hume, Priestley, D'Alembert, Condillac, Condorcet, Montesquieu, Voltaire, Diderot and Helvétius (see Kayser 1932, Mack 1962, Russell 1962, Rosen 1983, Boralevi 1984).

The context in which Bentham intervened in respect of accounting – for the radical Saint Simonians in France a context in which the old world was dissolving and a new world crystallising (Anonymous 1832) – was of especially great import for the forming and shaping of many modern institutions and practices. Albeit that this modern context is in significant ways discontinuous with our context today – in any case suggesting historical difference that we are concerned to explore – there is also a continuity to which we can relate. In reading Bentham as modern, one can, as well as exploring negative dimensions of his work, conceive of his modernity and his modern accounting as worthy of rescue as well as what we need to work through and with in order to progress (see Bronner 1994). Bentham's mobilising of accounting can, for example, be interpreted in terms of seeking to better align accounting with progressive and emancipatory social change. And through the historical analysis of Bentham's writings one might discover potentialities of modernity more generally, consistent with an approach that sees value in attempting to rescue the modern. As well as being a context of import in the formation of many modern institutions and practices, the context in which Bentham intervened was also an environment in which the professional accountancy bodies of today had not yet formally manifested. It was thus an environment that in some ways can be understood to have facilitated a discourse upon accounting differing from later discourses in respect, for instance, of its relative openness and radicalism.[9] Analysis of Bentham's writings on accounting, given the context in which they are located, therefore promises to be insightful for our purposes.

If the context in which Bentham, the 'great questioner of things established' (Anonymous 1838), wrote on accounting was indeed significant, it is also the case that Bentham wrote extensively on accounting and generally gave a great amount of attention to it over many years (*subter*, see also Munday 1992). Bentham was prominent among those who subjected accounting, in the context of a substantive crystallisation of modernity, to a critical questioning and anti-traditionalist discourse. He saw accounting as a practice of the utmost importance in the rationalised modern system of governance he envisaged and promoted (*subter*). Few major contributors to philosophy since Bentham as well as before have as yet come even close to granting to accounting – in the more everyday as well as in a broader and more holistic sense – as much critical attention and significance as did Bentham. Many have overlooked the importance Bentham attributed to accounting. When Cumming (1961) mocks Bentham's chrestomathic education programme, adding for good measure, to emphasise his point, that it ends with book-keeping, he looks at book-keeping through the typical spectacles of today. He overlooks the particular resonance of book-keeping to Bentham and the sense in which book-keeping is in many ways the culmination of Bentham's project.

For those concerned to elaborate a critique of modern accounting, including those who are engaged in projects to construct and promote a more emancipatory accounting, Bentham thus constitutes a significant focus. Yet surprisingly, beyond our own previous studies (see Gallhofer and Haslam 1993, 1994a,b, 1995, 1996b, 2000a,b), little immediate attention in the way of detailed critical interpretive analysis has been paid to Bentham's writings on accounting to date. It is all the more surprising because the few works published prior to our own that have at least touched upon aspects of Bentham's writings upon accounting [e.g. in the accounting literature the largely descriptive texts of Goldberg (1957) and Hume (1970), and in the broader social sciences and humanities literature the texts of Hume (1981) and Bahmueller (1981)] very much stimulate further research (see also Hoskin and Macve 1986, Loft 1988). There are, it appears, obstacles to the analysis of Bentham's accounting writings. These include obstacles constituted by the impact of interpretations of Bentham as crudely narrow by a number of writers over many years and in more recent times the impact of the critique of Bentham as a contributor to or an exemplar of a negative side of modernity by especially postmodern writers. Such ways of seeing equate to a profound pessimism about the potentialities of modern accounting that we need to surmount. We now turn to consider some key aspects of the negative reception of Bentham with a view to helping clear the path towards a more balanced and positive appreciation. In attempting to overcome the obstacles we can search out dimensions of Bentham that are suggestive of a radical and emancipatory project that remains meaningful. Such a search leads one to glimpse not only a Bentham that merits a closer reading but also at least reminds us of a 'Radical Bentham' that ought to be critically explored in a more balanced way including in terms of critical and emancipatory possibilities.

Why Bentham? Challenging displacements of the possibility of a more balanced and positive view of Bentham

The limited research that has generally been done into Bentham's writings on accounting may in part reflect an accessibility problem. It is only in relatively recent times, through the work of the Bentham project at University College, London (UCL), that Bentham's texts have become more readily and publicly available in an extensive form and in a form less affected by an editing that has variously distorted and displaced earlier manifestations of Bentham's work (albeit that the task of assembling Bentham's manuscripts is an enormous one and historically the issue of censorship loomed large, see Bowring 1877: 339). And the handwritten original texts, accessible in a few archives (mainly at UCL), are not easy to read. Further, many attempting to engage in a close reading of Bentham conclude that his texts are far from straightforward. Overcoming these obstacles may be difficult but they are not insurmountable, being obstacles that present themselves in many historical analyses. There are other obstacles to an analysis of Bentham's writings that we wish to particularly engage with here. Numerous critical assessments of Bentham as negative, from the nineteenth century through to today, have arguably discouraged many from a close and balanced reading of Bentham's works. Receptions of Foucault's intervention, including in the accounting literature, are noteworthy in relatively recent times in this respect. We need to clear a path to a more balanced and positive appreciation. By challenging interventions that are dismissive of Bentham we can see more of the possibilities of an analysis of Bentham's texts upon accounting.

Bentham has long provoked negative and dismissive commentaries that arguably have displaced the possibilities of a balanced view and discouraged close readings of his work.[10] John Stuart Mill although flattering Bentham in referring to his genius and although emphasising Bentham's progressiveness (Critchley 2001) portrays him in significant ways as very narrow and simplistic. For instance, Bentham is depicted as someone overly reducing well-being to a narrow and crude materialism. Mill's views have been very influential on others (see, e.g. Williams 1987). Mack (1962) elaborates some of the indicative and more well-known commentaries upon Bentham that caricature him negatively, citing from Marx, Nietzsche, Keynes and Schumpeter. Marx's well-known commentary is particularly sharp: '... the arch-philistine, Jeremy Bentham, the insipid pedantic leather-tongued oracle of the commonplace bourgeois intelligence of the nineteenth century ... I should call Mr Jeremy a genius in the way of bourgeois stupidity' (cited in Mack 1962: 2).[11] This strand of critique of Bentham, identifying Bentham with narrowly conceived bourgeois interests, is reflected in the accounting literature (e.g. Gray 1989). Such views may indeed have discouraged many, including many critical scholars, from a close reading of Bentham's works. Writing in the late 1960s, Himmelfarb (1968: 32) did suggest that many critics were ignoring Bentham, putting forward the view that Bentham 'might ... legitimately complain of a conspiracy of silence'. Early negative views are, however, being re-interpreted these days. The early views were based on a very limited picture of Bentham in terms of texts readily available – and what was readily available was in part a distortion of Bentham's writings – and were much shaped by John Stuart Mill's intervention. The latter intervention, whether it reflected a grudge against Bentham on the part of Mill or not, is a reading of Bentham that displaces the latter's deeper radicalism (Mack 1962, Pitkin 1990, Lyons 1991, Gallhofer and Haslam 1993, 1994a,b, Semple 1993, Crimmins 1996, Harrison 1996, Blake 1997).

In relatively recent times, what we can call a 'Foucault effect' may have dampened enthusiasm amongst especially critical researchers for the analysis of Bentham's writings on accounting. For the French philosopher–historian Michel Foucault, most obviously in *Discipline and Punish* (1977b), a reading or mobilisation of Bentham's Panopticon project – Bentham's attempt to use architectural and organisational design to increase transparency – occupies a crucial place in an articulation of how the Enlightenment project transformed into a disciplinary society that one might worry about (see Foucault 1977a,b, Gaonkar and McCarthy 1994). Receptions of Foucault's intervention and of work paralleling this has arguably in some quarters – ironically, to some extent (*subter*) – fuelled a prejudice against a close and balanced critical and interpretive analysis of Bentham's writings on accounting. In this respect, Semple (1992) has suggested that many critics in general now see Bentham through a reading of Foucault that is prejudicial to and dismissive of Bentham.

It is not surprising that the reception of Bentham through Foucault is basically *contra* Bentham. While it is possible to trace more balance in Foucault's 'treatment' of Bentham than many critics suggest – and also substantial complexity – the basic thrust of Foucault (Foucault 1977a,b), influencing a number of critical commentators (see Donzelot 1979, Bahmueller 1981, Miller 1987, Jay 1993, Deleuze 1995, Boyne 2000), tends towards projecting a very unfavourable view of Bentham.[12] Panopticism, as Foucault's 'Panoptisme' has been translated, has often been portrayed by those receiving Foucault as a highly negative form of intervention both in principle and – to the extent that it is seen as applying[13] – in practice (see Sullivan 1996). Thus Bentham's Enlightenment project has been portrayed, especially by those influenced by Foucault's characterisation, as widely eccentric and negatively influential, being suggestive of a highly problematic disciplinary control. It even appears as exemplary of just about the very worst of modern projects.

This negative image of the Panopticon could well have dissuaded many from seeking out a more positive potentiality in Bentham. Further, many critics may have been dissuaded from engaging with Bentham's writings in general, even so as to clarify appreciation of the negative dimensions of the Panopticon. As Semple (1992) in effect suggests, many may take Foucault's characterisation of the Panopticon in terms of Panopticism to be a good and comprehensive summary of Bentham's intervention, albeit that Foucault was much more interested in constructing and mobilising Panopticism as a metaphor of disciplinary power than he was in elaborating a critical interpretive analysis of Bentham's work. After Foucault's intervention it has typically been a problematic, negative Panopticism – as constructed in the works of analysts influenced to various degrees by Foucault – that has emerged as a major constituent in analyses (see Boyne 2000), rather than Bentham's texts more immediately.

Social analysts captured by appreciations of Panopticism, including in relation to the study of management and accounting, have not been overly concerned to engage directly with Bentham's texts. Theorists of organisations have tended rather to critically explore 'Panopticism' in practice in recent organisational and social manifestations.[14] Social analysts of accounting influenced to varying degrees by Foucault have linked accounting to such organisational manifestations or constructions. Such researchers have thus come at least implicitly to mark accounting down as an instrument of modernity's negative trajectory or possibilities (see Burchell *et al.* 1980, Hoskin and Macve 1986, 1988, Loft 1986, 1988, Miller and O'Leary 1987, Walsh and Stewart 1988, 1993, Laughlin 1992, Power 1997, see also Bahmueller 1981 and, for a review, see Roslender 1992).[15] Emphases of these social analyses have arguably helped displace detailed critical analysis of Bentham's writings on accounting, albeit on the face of it unintentionally. Bentham, usually implicitly, is more often than not equated to the constructed 'Panopticism' and typically dismissed or silenced. Foucault's metaphor, and related envisioning, has had a much more powerful appeal to critical analysts than has a critical exploration of Bentham's accounting texts.[16] Thus, from the above, even if one might be open to glimpsing at least something of broad interest and relevance in an analysis of Bentham's writings on accounting, there are in effect many sirens that can dissuade one from such analysis.

Of the social analyses of accounting referred to above, Loft (1988) does explore some of Bentham's accounting texts. Yet her analysis, although stimulating, is consumed by a Foucault-inspired interpretation that construes Bentham in overly negative terms.[17] Loft (1988: 23) makes reference to individuals being under the constant watchful eye of an authority that is apparently alien to them. Her analysis presents citations from Bentham as if self-evidently indicating Bentham's negativity, irrespective of the positive and very particular insights Bentham may have been concerned to mobilise (see, e.g. Loft 1988: 24, 30, *subter*). Bentham is seen by Loft (1988: 23–9) in terms of intensifying a negative disciplinary control. She places stress on the Panopticon as a means for the few to control the many (e.g. the poor and the prisoners) – a means of bringing the many under a 'single gaze'. Loft especially emphasises how the Panopticon and its 'interested' record keeping practices can facilitate the control and domination of the workers by interested owners and managers (Loft 1988: 27–37, 53). She relatedly places emphasis upon how the Panopticon controls individuals in institutions (Loft 1988: 28). Reference is made to a 'fetishistic' type of control exercised through Bentham's way of making visible (Loft 1988: 33). Loft (1988) promisingly follows Bahmueller (1981) in beginning to draw attention to the quite distinctive emphasis Bentham places on record-keeping (see here the brief comments of Hoskin and Macve 1986: 128). Many might be persuaded by her analysis, however, as we have suggested above, to opt out of a closer and especially out of a more balanced reading of Bentham's writings on accounting.

We should stress that for us useful insights are gained by mobilising Panopticism or some modification of it (see Boyne 2000) in critical analysis. The social analyses of accounting discussed above are indeed, we should emphasise, thought provoking, reflecting at least some of what is insightful in Foucault. The stress in these analyses on pointing to the link between Bentham's Panopticon and accounting must in itself be acknowledged. While Bentham himself makes this link quite explicitly clear in his texts (see e.g. Bentham 1797: 104–5, Gallhofer and Haslam 1993, 1994a,b, Fraser *et al.* 1999, cf. Bahmueller 1981: 192, e.g. Giddens 1981, Hume 1981, who links publicity appropriately to both the Panopticon and the Constitutional Code, Gandy 1993, Boyne 2000), this and even more obvious parallel links have been overlooked until relatively recently, as suggested by Gaonkar and McCarthy's (1994) stimulating work. Nevertheless, our point of critique is that these social analyses have generally contributed to displacing a balanced critical analysis of Bentham's writings on accounting, adding to previous dismissals of Bentham. A consequence is the overlooking of radically progressive dimensions of Bentham's interventions in respect of accounting.

The downside of this overlooking is underlined by the many readings of Bentham that indicate the potentiality of a critical and interpretive analysis of his writings on accounting. Controversies over Bentham flourish as new ways of seeing his work have become possible and manifest and as new texts of Bentham have come to be more readily accessible in the public realm. Further, some writers have suggested that, in spite of what many acknowledge to be Bentham's great influence, much of the radical vision that can be read from his text has scarcely impacted.[18] Review of these various contributions motivate one towards seeing that a balanced reading of Bentham is possible whereby one might learn not only from the negative, but also from the positive possibilities in his formulations.

Foucault's work itself, we should point out, can be read as providing some indications as to why a close reading of Bentham on accounting could be insightful.[19] Foucault indicates the sense in which analysis of Bentham's projects can help us appreciate a negative side of practices of modern governance: he makes the Panopticon an ideal typical metaphor for such negativity (see Foucault 1977a,b, Boyne 2000). A closer critical and interpretive analysis can thus aim to provide further relevant insights into the negativities of modern practices of governance and organisation along these lines [a path pursued to some extent by Loft (1988) and Gallhofer and Haslam (1994a,b, 1995, 1996b)]. Further, consistent with a number of perspectives labelled postmodern, Foucault suggests the case for a closer reading of interventions such as those of Bentham, a reading more open to the complexities, ambiguities and possibilities in Bentham's texts. Pitkin (1990: 107), in this respect, actually highlights some of the ambiguities in Bentham: '... what most characterises Bentham's theorising is a recurrent pattern of unacknowledged ambiguity ... We are used to charges of ambiguity against allusive thinkers like Hegel and Heidegger – but Bentham'?[20] More generally, academic battles continue to be fought between differing philosophical perspectives on modernity. Foucault is a key protagonist in these debates, a significant figure of controversy. Thus, that Foucault uses Bentham as a kind of exemplar might properly alert us to the need to look at Bentham more rather than less closely to gain an appreciation of various dimensions of his work.

Why Bentham? Habermas' more positive appreciation of Bentham and Bentham's principle of publicity

In this regard, amongst those encouraging us to take a closer look at Bentham, including in effect Bentham on accounting (as we shall see), is Jürgen Habermas, the German Critical Theorist who has elaborated a substantial critique of Foucault (see Habermas 1987a,b). Habermas, furthermore, emphasises a positive radicalism and potentiality in Bentham. Habermas' different emphasis upon Bentham to that of Foucault delineates, on reflection, an important dimension of the wider Foucault–Habermas debate. Habermas' (1992, originally 1961) position on Bentham is bound up with his own concern to rescue the potentiality of modernity which he perceives as an unfinished project, a concern that can also be read into the nevertheless more pessimistic perspective of the Frankfurt School (Peters 1993). A concern more specific to Habermas is to perceive significance in this respect in characteristics of the bourgeois Enlightenment with its universal, utopian and emancipatory spirit (see Jameson 1989: 376, Gallhofer and Haslam 1995, cf. Horkheimer and Adorno 1972). It is in this context that Habermas focuses upon Bentham. Again, it is worthwhile to explore this here to further advance the case for and clarify the potentiality of an analysis of Bentham's writings on accounting.

Especially in earlier work of continuing relevance that also expresses strong continuities with his later work (see Peters 1993), Habermas does much to provide a useful counter in helping us to rescue Bentham from those who might be tempted to dismiss his texts entirely and in particular to overlook, through a one-sided and distorted view, its more positive potentialities (see also Peters 1995: 658). If viewing some dimensions of Bentham through a critical theoretical lens to gain a positive appreciation of these dimensions or to deem them worthy of a rescuing critique may appear somewhat misguided to a number of critical researchers today, exploring aspects of Bentham in this way is actually a task already stimulated by critical theory.

In his critical appreciation, Habermas locates a key focus of Bentham that turns out, as we discuss later, to have an especially strong relation to accounting: Bentham's mobilisation of publicity. Focusing upon Bentham's *Of Publicity* (1843a), Habermas (1992) portrays Bentham's concept of publicity in favourable terms, associating it with his own construct of the public sphere (see Habermas 1974, 1992) and seeing

Bentham as an architect of that sphere. Habermas reconstructs aspects of Bentham's theorising in terms of his own project (Peters 1993). He locates Bentham's text *Of Publicity* in a genealogy of the idea of the bourgeois public sphere from the work of Hobbes to that of Kant (Gaonkar and McCarthy 1994: 548, see also Hohendahl 1979, Keane 1984, Calhoun 1992). Gaonkar and McCarthy (1994: 549) point out that for Habermas it was Bentham who 'recognised the importance of publicity as a separate and distinct category – a social formation – that stands in a complex and enabling relationship to both public opinion and the doctrine of popular sovereignty. He even speaks of the "regime of publicity"'. Of significance for the genealogical construction here is Habermas' perception of Bentham as producing the first mono-graphical explication of 'the connection between public opinion and the principle of publicity' (Habermas 1992: 99). As understood by Habermas, for Bentham, public-ity transforms opinion into public opinion through rational discussion (Gaonkar and McCarthy 1994: 554). This is the case so long as it is possible to engage in open and critical communication respecting all manifest forms of publicity including official ones. This also permits the mobilising of alternative or counter publicities to any official publicities (see Bentham 1843a: 592, Mack 1962: 182, cf. Bronner 1994). Habermas' appreciation of Bentham's conceptualisation of the link between public opinion and publicity is significant. This is because the principle of publicity is understood by Habermas to be the crucial element in Kant's elaboration of the bour-geois public sphere, which for Habermas is the most theoretically developed form of this construct (Habermas 1992: 102). And, in turn, Kant is understood by Habermas to place the public sphere, with some optimism, at the centre of his Enlightenment project (Holub 1991: 41).

Positioning Bentham in this way, Habermas clearly associates him with the poten-tialities of the bourgeois public sphere (Gaonkar and McCarthy 1994). And, more particularly, Habermas understands Bentham to mobilise his principle of publicity in the context of seeking to better the usage of reason in the public sphere, a position very much consistent with his own (Holub 1991). For Habermas, the potential of the public sphere in this regard includes that communicative interaction might better approximate to communication free of domination by particular factions and be more rational, emancipatory and enabling in character. It thus could help engender and sustain a critique of society based on democratic principles (Holub 1991: 3). Habermas' understanding here is consistent with the view that publicity, as well as being indicative of openness in general and an integral element of an enabling communicative interaction, also constitutes an enabling element for the promotion of better – emancipatory – communicative praxis for democracy (see Peters 1993). Publicity can thus be envisaged to function as a condition for facilitating rational and critical discourse. Gaonkar and McCarthy (1994: 550) acknowledge that this is also a reading of Bentham. In this regard, following the positioning of a legitimate sys-tem of publicity in open social communication, Bentham (1843a, p. 583) envisaged that 'sound opinions will be more common – hateful prejudices, publicly combated. The multitude will be more secure from the tricks of demagogues, and the cheats of impostors ... A habit of reasoning and discussion will penetrate all classes of society'. The same text of Bentham suggests that this positive potential exists so long as manifest forms of publicity do not over determine opinion but rather communicative possibilities remain open (Bentham 1843a, cf. Mack 1962, Bronner 1994). Habermas thus finds in Bentham, alongside and consistent with Kant, a positive element in a visionary sketch of social communication (Holub 1991).

Habermas places emphasis in his text upon forms of publicity akin to those equating to the idea of a 'free press' with relative autonomy from the state (see Peters 1993). Nevertheless, his argumentation also applies in principle to publicity as generally envisaged by Bentham. This is publicity ranging from the 'free press', which indeed Bentham was much concerned to defend, promote and extend (see Mack 1962: 182), to a publicity prescribed and validated by experts, for example, by 'experts' such as civil servants or 'independent' professionals, including, for Bentham (1843a), the short-hand writers, and/or by the state. Thus, there is affinity between Habermas and Bentham in respect of publicity of a broad scope. Prescribed publicity is envisaged by Bentham to be ideally controlled by a principle of popular sovereignty combined with the possibility of active engagement in rational and critical debate *pro* or *contra* the position that might be deemed integral to any such publicity (cf. Bronner 1994). In principle, for Bentham, manifest forms of publicity – such as journalist reports or official reports of parliamentary activity (the latter being the focus of Bentham in his *Of Publicity*) – can facilitate greater openness and transparency in society. They can thus constitute manifestations of rational and critical discourse as well as instruments thereof, more especially if constituted in a spirit of openness and democracy, which Bentham sought to ensure would be the case (Mack 1962). Bentham (1843a: 592) was especially concerned to stress that non-authentic or unauthorised publications should be tolerated, thus expressly allowing for and encouraging counter information type reports. He was very much aware that official publications were very prone to capture by what today we might call a problematic hegemony (see Mack 1962: 182). Publicities are envisaged by Bentham as giving rise to other publicities, constituting a network of mutual enlightenment and communicative interaction in a way that can gain the positive appreciation of a critical theoretical approach. If struggles are no doubt envisaged, the aim is that the project of rational democratic governance is strengthened. Habermas' theoretical argumentation, if it has become more complex, has retained key strands of the above argumentation and thus has continued to have some affinity with Bentham (see Peters 1993, Bronner 1994). The potential of critical communication continues to be envisaged. In relation to Foucault's intervention in respect of Bentham, Habermas (see Habermas 1987a,b) later in effect perceives this to dismiss the progressive potentiality in Bentham's publicity and to threaten his own project. The later engagement of Habermas with Foucault on the Enlightenment and its unfinished project of modernity is already anticipated in their earlier differing approach to Bentham (Gaonkar and McCarthy 1994: 550). If Habermas' concerns in respect of Bentham overlap with those of Foucault (see Habermas 1987a,b), Habermas takes a different stance in giving greater emphasis to the relevance of a more balanced and even positive appreciation of Bentham, especially on publicity, in the articulation of a historically informed social and political theoretical perspective that bears critically upon the present.

Bentham's publicity constitutes an unrealised potentiality of modernity in terms of Habermas' analysis.

Reflecting this Bentham–Habermas alignment, a positive appreciation of Bentham is also discernible, albeit typically embedded rather than explicit, in other critical theoretical interventions influenced by Habermas and the wide-ranging critical philosophical heritage that informs Habermas' work. For us, one can especially find this positive appreciation embedded in the work of Stephen Eric Bronner (1994) in respect of openness in the public realm, accountability and regulation. Bronner (1994) is informed much by that dimension of Habermas that has affinity with Bentham. Bentham's optimistic beliefs about the possibilities of openness, beliefs that he shares with Kant and that continue to have their echo in Habermas, are in effect embedded in Bronner's (1994) concern that we need to work through the existing institutions of modernity if the problems of modernity are to be overcome. In particular, Bronner's (1994: 137) critical theoretical emphasis upon the positive role of an accountability regulated so that it better support democratic and rational social governance – together with the promotion of counter-information systems – is consistent with Bentham's emphases and themes in respect of publicity. For Bronner (1994: 336), emancipation or empowerment 'generates a concern with the accountability of all social, political and economic institutions'. And:

> Empowerment ... is always the product of strategic action even if its aim involves the creation of institutions capable of reproducing norms consonant with an ongoing discourse among equals ... *Accountability* is the lynchpin for any institutional notion of empowerment ... It reflects a concern not only with the reproduction of relations empowering the disempowered ... It recognizes the positive role bureaucracies can play in furthering democracy and insists on confronting their petrifying tendencies ... Formulating standards of accountability for differing institutional systems and sub-systems, illuminating repressed contradictions within the "autopoetic" processes of a complex bureaucratic society, can alone make empowerment concrete.
>
> (Bronner 1994: 337)

Bronner's (1994) work thus, with Habermas, particularly stimulates us to engage more closely with Bentham, more especially with Bentham on publicity.

We shall hold back, for the moment, our elaboration of how Bentham fused accounting and publicity such that they became virtually interchangeable in his rhetoric. And thus we shall delay our analysis of how Bentham's engagement with this 'accounting publicity' constituted a radical emancipatory intervention that intertwined with precisely those dimensions of his work that critical theory can positively evaluate.[21] Rather, to better introduce this elaboration and analysis and to justify our focus more we attempt to further clarify a 'Radical Bentham'. As well as paralleling and re-enforcing the positive appreciation of Habermas, our delineation of Bentham's radicalism permits us to elaborate Bentham's wider radical affiliations. We do this at some length here (even if we are only offering a cursory interpretive review of a vast enterprise), reflecting in part our view that, albeit there is a downside to Bentham's intervention, it is important not to lose sight of the potentiality of his progressive radicalism. Furthermore, our review gives us access to a greater context-sensitive awareness of Bentham's writings on publicity and accounting. These texts can be located in relation to Bentham's broader radical approach and framework and can thus be better understood and interpreted.

Further insights into a 'Radical Bentham': towards an understanding of the location of publicity in Bentham's wider radical envisioning

To elaborate what Bentham sought to achieve is to also relate Bentham's own way of seeing emancipation. We provide here a basic overview for our purposes.[22] Briefly, Bentham wanted to advance the happiness of the community, ultimately the whole global community (Mack 1962: 174, 397, Pitkin 1990: 105). He wrote that the 'right and proper end of government in every political community, is the greatest happiness of all the individuals of which it is composed ... ' (Bowring 1843, IX: 5, see Pitkin 1990: 108).[23] For a while, Bentham borrowed a phrase that had been in currency for some time to express this goal – the greatest happiness of the greatest number – but his reflections upon the need to try to avoid suppression of and indeed his concern to respect minorities led him to articulate his envisaged social goal in terms he felt more comprehensive. Bentham also indicated that his vision was to take into account future generations in holding that the sacrifice of the present to the future was the common basis of all the virtues, a stance that if not always attributed to Bentham would later appeal to environmentalists (Mack 1962: 110, 418–19).

It is a distortion to view Bentham as having an especially narrow and crude conception of what constitutes happiness. Suggestions that Bentham was 'simply' concerned to apply science to help preserve material progress already achieved or that he reduced happiness to a crude materialistic ability to consume (see Anonymous 1838, Williams 1987, Gray 1989) are distorted and very partial readings. If we ought to be concerned to appreciate the downside of his way of seeing, we should also be receptive to the more positive and radical visions he opens up to us. It is reasonable to argue that Bentham put a lot of emphasis upon security as a constituent of happiness (Russell 1962: 742, Hart 1982: 25). Yet, as Boralevi (1984: 97) points out, security was deemed to be so important (e.g. relative to equality) because without security other constituents of happiness could not last. They might dissolve in a breakdown of the social order. Bentham did experiment in some particular trajectories of his work with ways of roughly approximating well-being by reference to the ability to consume and what can be read as a crudely quantitative and narrowly materialistic approach. Yet his vision of what constitutes happiness when discerned from his writings taken as a whole is more evidently holistic. We have already mentioned Bentham's concern to serve future generations. Further, Bentham flatly denied that people were moved only by 'worldly' interests (Mack 1962: 11). Relatedly, materialistic concerns were seen by Bentham as means to better ends rather than as ends in themselves (Boralevi 1984: 103). And he believed that the greatest happiness ensued from the act of benevolence, the key word in his moral dictionary (Mack 1962: 310). Bentham thus went beyond overly simple and crude understandings of what motivated people (Pitkin 1990: 106). In short, he understood happiness to be derived from a multiplicity of phenomena, that we can consider 'non-material' as well as 'material'. For instance, Bentham appreciated and emphasised that the satisfaction people had from feeling that they were making a good contribution to society positively helped constitute their well-being. Thus, the industrious could feel happier than the idle and the benevolent could feel happier than the selfish (see Mack 1962: 310, Pitkin 1990: 306). Bentham did have an appreciation that some goals that might equate to happiness for individuals might in principle be socially unattainable. Subject to such practical constraints that we all have to live with, if happiness in principle could be advanced he sought to advance it. Perfect happiness was considered a somewhat fanciful notion but the task was to advance towards it. Similarly with equality: perfect equality was a 'chimera'. All we can hope to do is to diminish inequality (Boralevi 1984: 97). At the same time, Bentham saw a reduction in inequality as very much desirable and strove to diminish it, a stance that merits further elaboration here.

Subject again to the practical constraints referred to, Bentham envisaged, at least in the more enlightened society he strived for, a basic harmony between the happiness of the individual and the happiness of the community, the latter being understood as all the individuals in society. His vision here implied the desirability of equality, as well as security, subsistence and abundance, in advancing happiness. He made explicit his view that equality was a positive constituent of social happiness (Dinwiddy 1989). A number of writers have basically acknowledged Bentham's concern to push for equality in relation to his general happiness principle. Boralevi (1984: 97) suggests that for Bentham: ' ... the closer the distribution of wealth approached equality the greater the sum of happiness; a poor man would gain more from the transfer than a rich man would lose'.[24] Grasping the detail of Bentham's position is not straightforwardly discerned from his texts. Going beyond Boralevi here, and taking into account his more holistic notion of well-being, Bentham's stance can be read as suggesting that in an enlightened state it is possible to reconcile the interests of all the individuals in a community to achieve maximum social happiness. Bentham believed that the feeling that one was contributing in a positive way in society (e.g. being helpfully industrious or being benevolent) was a constituent of happiness so that it is possible to envisage a transfer of material wealth from rich to poor actually leaving the rich better off from a more holistic standpoint. Bentham's anti-elitism coupled to such reasoning may be taken to suggest that, subject to practical constraints, if the constituents of happiness come to be more equal between individuals then this is consistent with happiness reaching its zenith for all the individuals constituting the community. Bentham, then, can be considered to be strongly community orientated in the sense that for him the happiness of an individual is strongly linked to the happiness of others. Bentham's view is at least consistent here with Hume: the civilised human being is one denuded of all parochialisms who considers all people members of the same family (Mack 1962: 180). In the same vein, Boralevi (1984: 102) holds that Bentham saw humanity as the first of virtues.

At the same time, Bentham held to the long standing view of the ultimate alignment of knowledge and wisdom (see Critchley 2001). As for Socrates, knowledge – including knowledge of what constitutes happiness – is virtue for Bentham. Virtue is constituted by insight and wisdom: it is not only good to be virtuous, but wise. Virtue is a constituent of happiness (Mack 1962: 249, 323).

Bentham's concern to strive for equality, consistent with the general happiness principle, shapes his concern to come to the aid of the (relatively) poor and oppressed. Bentham recognised that many of his fellow human beings were oppressed in significant ways, including being disadvantaged and abused. He favoured or was concerned to especially protect particular oppressed groups (so long as they remained oppressed), such as women (Williford 1975, Boralevi 1980, 1984: 11). Boralevi (1984) places emphasis upon and elaborates Bentham's concern for the oppressed, making the point, in terms consistent with the above, that an advance for the oppressed adds to aggregate happiness (Boralevi 1984: 97, see also Dinwiddy 1989). She stresses: 'The greatest happiness principle, particularly, appears as a dynamic element, insofar as its egalitarian premises open wider horizons and provide appropriate justification for Bentham's consideration of and concern for the oppressed' (Boralevi 1984: 186). Boralevi (1984) articulates Bentham's concern for the oppressed explicitly in terms of emancipation.[25] For Bentham, all the oppressed are united by a suffering which restricts their possibilities. Bentham understood that those less repressed than others would benefit themselves as well as others if they helped the relatively more repressed. He saw himself and those he considered part of his movement as among the enlightened. And he did not see his work involving any real sacrifice. In his position, helping people was not a burden. Rather, it was a pleasure. He might refer to his efforts in this context as his 'amusements'. More emphatically, one can suggest that for Bentham the pleasure to be gained from helping others was intense and deep.

Bentham's radicalism, as the above indicates, opens the way to forms of socialistic development.[26] Russell (1962: 740) suggests that this opening up was unintentional on Bentham's part. Yet Bentham himself was open to and enthusiastic about socialistic plans and experiments and there is much that can be read already as socialistic in Bentham. We have seen how Bentham was concerned to act for the abused and oppressed and valued movement towards greater equality (*supra*). Mack (1962: 438) describes Bentham as 'equalitarian' (see also Mack 1962: 178, Postema 1988). Bentham thus sought a more equitable distribution of the social product. Concerned to diminish inequality, he also supported tax systems that would tax the rich more than the poor. Relatedly, he thought wages were too low relative to other incomes. He sought to look for ways in which inheritances could be distributed to the community at large. And he held that excessive profits made by business organisations should be distributed to those working in the organisations. He advocated profit ceilings. Further, he advocated guaranteed job security and minimum wages, pensions, health insurance and a welfare system (Mack 1962: e.g. 207–8, 427, Russell 1962: 742). Bentham also problematised the distinction between the private and the public sphere. In his later years, disturbing Himmelfarb's (1968) thesis that Bentham sought to personally gain in a crude materialistic sense from the poor, he proposed to transfer the *National Charity Company* into an *Indigence Relief Ministry*. He more and more saw the possibility of setting up an efficient system of state administration, and was in any case always concerned to compare whether 'public' or 'private' systems were better in terms of effects on well-being (see Boralevi 1984: 103, Gallhofer and Haslam 1993).

Bentham had a number of links with active socialists. Boralevi (1984: 24–33) notes Bentham's friendship with William Thompson, the Irish co-operative socialist (a friend of the feminist Anne Wheeler) who stands alongside Robert Owen as the most significant of advocates of co-operative socialism in the context. Thompson was a guest of Bentham in London for 4 months and always maintained a personal admiration for Bentham (Boralevi 1984: 37). Russell (1962: 747) points out that Bentham was also a friend of Owen, investing a considerable sum of money in Owen's *New Lanark* project. Bentham, as Russell (1962) suggests, did also inspire and influence later socialists. French socialists in the 1830s especially emphasised the potential role of a Benthamite publicity in enhancing their campaign. Laski, writing with a socialistic emphasis, understood Bentham to have made a significant contribution to political thought (Mack 1962: 196). Many locate Bentham in a movement leading to Fabian socialism (e.g. Letwin 1965). Mack (1962: 2) even informs us that the young Trotsky was for a short time an enthusiast of Bentham. Russell (1962) indicates how Bentham anticipated Marx in a number of ways and suggests that Bentham's rationalism overlaps strongly with that of Marx (e.g. Russell 1962: 743). Several writers offer comparisons and contrasts of Bentham and Marx that indicate affinities in their projects. As more texts have gone beyond the problematic and narrow interpretations of Bentham that have become so influential it has been possible to see more affinities with a critical school (see Mack 1962: 421, Russell 1962, Rostenreich 1974, Hart 1982, Boralevi 1984, Almond 1994).

More generally, as different interpretive schema have emerged, so have more possibilities to read Bentham with a view to gaining inspiration and insights for a radical and emancipatory praxis. A range of writers have stressed that influential commentaries on Bentham such as those of J. S. Mill and Marx have for a variety of reasons overlooked much of the radicalism of Bentham. A more radical, progressive and emancipatory Bentham is glimpsed by a number of critics, including an array of broadly critical writers. Crimmins (1994) points to Bentham's early and continuing radicalism (see also Hart 1982, Boralevi 1984, Long 1987, Crimmins 1996, Akinkummi and Murray 1997). Writers elaborate on, for instance, his anti-war stance, his advocacy of an extensive democracy, his concern about the oppression of women (following Helvétius), his liberalism on sexuality (for Semple 1993, ironic in the light of Foucault's usage of Bentham)[27] and his highlighting of forms of ideological oppression. Bentham is now understood by many to have perceived numerous abuses of power in terms of the social relations of his time that he was concerned to rectify. Boralevi (1984: 4), in relation to the oppression of women, cites a Bentham text of the 1780s as follows: ' ... the strongest have had all the preference. Why? Because the strongest have made the laws'. Further, she cites Bentham as maintaining: 'For the benefit of the ruling few ... the minds of all women are castrated' (Boralevi 1984: 8).

Aside from a widening of interpretive schema, the appreciation of Bentham's radicalism has been fostered by an increased accessibility of Bentham's texts. Further, one needs to recognise that the writings he published in his own time were highly restricted by censorship laws, his own pragmatism and his concern to gain purchase with a variety of social groups (see Boralevi 1980, 1984: 105). Bowring (1877: 339) in this regard commented as follows:

> So much was Bentham in advance of his age, that Sir Samuel Romilly recommended him not to publish several of his works, as he felt assured that printing them would lead to prosecution and imprisonment. Many ... I have not deemed it safe to give to the world ... they remain in the archives ...
>
> (Bowring 1877: 339)

Bentham himself came to develop different criteria for his published and non-published writings and justified this by his context. Mack (1962) makes the point that, especially in the very oppressive British regime of the late eighteenth and early nineteenth centuries, Bentham was very careful about what he wrote in public. For her, Bentham's unpublished material was much more radical as well as more carefully argued and theoretically developed. Given that Britain was a tyrannical regime in the late eighteenth and early nineteenth century, one can see why many of his views scarcely entered the public realm in his own life time (see Mack 1962, Foot 1984). In this regard, Harrison (1983: 131) notes that when Leigh Hunt, the radical journalist and publisher, was imprisoned for publishing work critical of the authorities, Bentham visited him in prison to offer his support.

Bentham's basic radicalism can be summarised thus: he was critical of the world as it was and sought a better world. This is evident in his focus on the law from his earliest writings. Like Beccaria, Bentham continually stressed a distinction between what the law is and what it ought to be, or, as Bentham sometimes put it, between 'expository' and 'censorial' jurisprudence (Hart 1982: 41). By at least the same extensive measure by which he came to see the scope of the law he was concerned to critically appraise and question it in his concern to rationalise it: the institution of accounting, as we shall see, came within his ambit in these respects. Mack (1962: 67) summarises the extensiveness of Bentham's critical or 'rationalising' approach as follows: ' ... to cleanse the Augean stable to any purpose there was no other way than to pour in a body of severe and steady criticism and to spread it over the whole extent of the subject in one comprehensive unbroken tide ... '. Through a rationalisation of the law, as broadly envisaged, well-being would be enhanced.

Viewing society in his own day and with the expectation that this would be the case for many ages to come, Bentham held that people had to be helped towards happiness. The concern to help others thus leads Bentham to embrace an interventionist stance – particularly on behalf of the oppressed – that would be evaluated in terms of its effects. Bentham's concern to intervene, which some see as threatening liberty, can rather be interpreted as a dimension of his radicalism reflecting a critical understanding of his socio-political context that has affinity with many later critical positions. What Bentham is concerned to achieve he calls general happiness rather than liberty. In one sense, however, Bentham strives for liberty in his pursuit of general happiness. The logic of his position is that he is concerned to secure a very general freedom: the freedom to actually realise one's potential happiness, viewed holistically. When Russell (1962) and others suggest that Bentham cared little for liberty they typically meant liberty in a narrow sense. Even, however, in respect of particular liberties, Bentham did actually care about striving for these (rather than seeing them as 'natural rights' – although he did use the language of rights and duties) to the extent they were congruent with general happiness.[28] Bentham had an awareness that, for instance, progress in respect of a particular emancipatory campaign was likely only to be a step on the road and might actually lead to countervailing repressions elsewhere. More generally, influenced by Helvétius, he stressed the importance of contextual factors that might be managed to impact upon people (Boralevi 1984: 7–10, Smith 1989). Bentham has a sense of obstacles to progress in his context. These include that people might seriously misconceive what constituted their happiness.[29] For instance, consistent with the above argumentation, Bentham understood that people might come to adopt an instrumental and narrow reasoning. Rather than keep the goal of happiness in mind they might get obsessed about a goal that could easily become incongruent with it. Thus, the interventionism which in some ways creates its own constraints is motivated by radical aims and a radical understanding of the context.

Consistent with his stance on the importance of context, Bentham therefore appears to have acknowledged that people could fall into illusions. This is another dimension of his radicalism worth elaborating upon here. Hart suggests:

> Bentham had as vivid an appreciation as Karl Marx of the ways in which mysteries and illusions, often profitable to interested parties, have clustered round social institutions, concealing the fact that they with their defects are human artefacts, and encouraging the belief that the injustices and exploitation which they permit must be ascribed to nature and are beyond the power of men to change. 'Law' says Bentham 'shows itself in a mask', and much that he wrote was designed to remove it.
>
> (Hart 1982: 2)

For Bentham as well as Marx:

> ... human society and its legal structure which had worked so much human misery, had been protected from criticism by myths, mysteries and illusions, not all of them intentionally generated, yet all of them profitable to interested parties.
>
> (Hart 1982: 25–6, see Boralevi 1984: 176).

Boralevi (1984: 176) suggests in this regard that Bentham had an appreciation of the concept of ideology not far from the sense of Marx in his *The German Ideology* and that he in effect attacked the institutions of the status quo in terms of ideology (see also Russell 1962: 743). He saw the establishment of his own time as corrupt in many ways. For Bentham 'the avaricious ... calumniate the poor, to cover their refusal ... [to help the poor] ... with a varnish of system and of reason' (Boralevi 1984: 102). Sinister interests delude the people and instil prejudice, adding to the oppression. The people are in effect corrupted by ideological forces. The character of the people is debased and their sensitivity to suffering diminished. These developments, however, can inspire a desire for counter actions on the part of the oppressed (Boralevi 1984: 176). Thus, Bentham advocated a counter discourse aimed at enlightening or educating people away from the forms of ideology that could capture them towards wisdom and an appreciation of what was the best way forward. More generally, he sought to arrive at an educated and wise governance. Bentham envisaged that the rationalisation of the law, albeit not straightforward, was to involve the attainment of an understanding, involving foresight – beyond the illusions – as to the consequences of a law for general happiness, on the part of the governors and its application: the adoption of critical elements of jurisprudence (Mack 1962).

Another radical aspect of Bentham's intervention in respect of social practices and institutions is its extensiveness. If we consider his work on law we can attain a good appreciation of this. Influenced by Helvétius, who wrote about the great significance of creative legislation (as well as education) for the progress of humanity, Bentham held that changes in the law extensive in character constituted the most promising mode of intervening for human betterment (every change in the law had to be supported by a rationale in terms of the general happiness principle). In keeping with his holism, Bentham came to see anything – systems of governance, rules, practices, institutions and knowledges (elements in the order of things) – that might be mobilised so as to regulate matters in society as a branch of law. The law was inseparable from the whole social structure and included political economy as a branch (Mack 1962: 97, 420, Postema 1989). It thus could be conceived of as including practices of education and management.[30] The mobilisation of the law as thus broadly conceived – as a system of governance, regulation, management and administration – had a key part to play in engendering happiness. Relatedly, everyone was to be looked after by a benevolent and caring system of government and moved towards their potential (Mack 1962: 69, Boralevi 1984). Bentham not only thought it unreasonable to see the inhabitants of the Panopticon as, unaided, the best judges of their own interests but also thought it reasonable to seek to help those much better off in the community, aiding their will to do good (Mack 1962).[31]

Bentham's somewhat pragmatic and pedestrian interventionism (see Hart 1982: 25) initially does not appear especially radical. Nevertheless, his appeal to caution and his concern to understand context and experience (Boralevi 1984: 17, 190) may be considered to have some affinity with a critical approach informed by more recent debates in respect of theory and praxis. Boralevi (1984) points to a number of dimensions of pragmatism but still links his work to the goal of emancipation. Bentham viewed his Panopticon as a less than ideal system but one practically suited for the purposes he envisaged in his context. Many of his peers were against relieving the indigent in any way (Boralevi 1984: 103–4). Some might view Bentham's pragmatism as pedantic (p. 10) yet Bentham 'never forgot to be concerned with the people living in a period of transition' (p. 11). He held that major ruptures to the sociopolitical order were likely to bring about serious problems and so preferred gradual and pragmatic change if possible (Mack 1962: 403, 411). He conceived that progress in one area might mean regression in another and sought to proceed cautiously so as to assess the situation and modify the trajectory as appropriate. He did not like the idea of initiating 'wars and storms' (Russell 1962: 742). This depended on the context, however. Bentham could embrace the more obviously radical position of seeking a more revolutionary action. Schemes that excluded people from participation in social activities for no good reason harvested this. An especially extreme censorial government (one can presume even more extreme than the government of his own day) ought to be overthrown, even by more revolutionary ways (Mack 1962: 182).

Bentham was also, radically, an advocate of democracy. He came to the view that if government was in the hands of an elite, the propensity to act in accordance with their own misguided (and sinister) conception of their interests would typically dominate their potential susceptibility to a wisdom promoting the general interest (and their own genuine interests). It was such reasoning, combined with a view that the very act of participation in formal governance by an individual could enhance that individual's well-being (*supra*), that led Bentham to the radical advocacy of democracy. Bentham, with Frances Place, James Mill and other radicals, looked forward to the day when an enlightened populace rather than an elite would control the system of governance (see Boralevi 1984: 107, Gallhofer and Haslam 1996b). He was an advocate of an extensive democracy in the sense of governance by the people with equal voting rights, including for women, frequent elections, secret ballots and an overthrow of property qualifications (Russell 1962: 742). As early as 1773, he declared under the heading 'Public Virtue in the Body of the People' that the people were his Caesar, a Caesar he sought to render better informed and enlightened (Mack 1962). From 1789 he held that women should be given the vote and educated: women had to be given an equal dignity (Boralevi 1984: 14, 21). A key democratic emphasis of Bentham's polity is his emphasis upon participatory inclusion. Bentham stood against any schemes that shut out categories of people from participation in any social activity without any good reason. Griffin–Collart (1982) points to the irony of accusing Bentham of authoritarianism – as many studies viewing Bentham through 'Panopticism' tend to do – and stresses how much he was concerned in his work to give equal consideration to the interests of all of the people and involve them in governance to this effect. William Thompson, one of Bentham's socialist friends, emphasised Bentham's radical democratic view in elaborating upon him: ' ... the philosophy of that enlightened and benevolent man, embraces in his grasp every sentient human being, and acknowledges the claim of every rational adult, without distinction of sex or colour, to equal political rights' (cited in Boralevi 1984: 24). In the future 'Age of Prevention' that Bentham envisaged – an age in which the people would foresee the conditions that lead to crime, or more generally would foresee the obstacles that stand in the way of the realisation of happiness, and intercept or counter these negatives (Mack 1962: 77, 171–3) – the people would be able to take control, look after themselves and hence, in Bentham's view, look after each other. Everyone would be their own legislator: the only control was self-control, for well-being. The people would not see the system of governance as something alien from them and oppression would thus be countered (Mack 1962, Boralevi 1984).

Clearly, to educate a democracy might be more difficult than to educate an elite, but a democracy, albeit its problems (and Bentham understood that it could still abuse minorities), would in Bentham's view be more likely to make decisions in accord with the general interest because of the numbers that would in effect be required to support policies. He believed extensive democracy and popular sovereignty would best reinforce the commitment to general happiness and best ensure that the associated benevolence and insight would manifest effectively. He appreciated in this regard that governance was not a matter of a precise and certain science but that it involved judgment and given the aim of general happiness he deemed it appropriate to involve everyone in the process of governance. He feared that the smaller the group of governors the more likely that more narrowly selfish, less benevolent or less wise dimensions of their perceived interests would dominate or counter their will to benevolence and wisdom to the detriment of general happiness. Bentham's reliance upon the masses, in effect, has some affinity with, even if differing from, Marx (Mack 1962, Hart 1982).[32] A democracy would be more likely to be wise and virtuous. His concerns to enlighten and educate the public, which he again shared with Helvétius, in this context were emphasised all the more.

The radical Bentham promotes enlightenment and education (Mack 1962: 249, 323). In the 1770s he declared that political evil was the product of ignorance and that an enlightened democracy would reconcile the will and understanding in favour of benevolent and progressive action (Mack 1962: 412–3). Bentham was a supporter of education for all (Mack 1962: 207). UCL, which Bentham fostered, was the first English university open to students without distinction of class, religion or sex (Boralevi 1984: 15). Bentham sought to contribute to an overcoming of the 'failure on the part of ordinary men to realize that the forms of law and human society were at bottom merely human artefacts, not natural necessities but things actually made by men, and hence things which could be unmade and remade ... ' (Hart 1982: 25–6). Educating people as well as enhancing their material welfare was understood here as making popular sovereignty more effective. Education itself was to be democratised. These processes were understood to enhance positive movement towards the general happiness criterion. It is in the context of his broad concern to educate and enlighten, including to make transparent, and more generally in his concern to mobilise mechanisms for a radical social regulation, that we can locate Bentham's mobilising of publicity. And here we find Bentham's accounting. Thus, publicity and accounting are very much integral to Bentham's radical progressivism. We turn to publicity, and accounting publicity, next.

Accounting publicity: a cornerstone of Bentham's vision and a key instrument for social happiness

> ... embedded ... [in Bentham's work] ... there are bold and provocative reaffirmations of the general principles which gain in clarity and in a sense reveal more of their meaning.
>
> (Hart 1982: 5)

Publicity, or the instrument to engender openness and transparency in the public realm, is a key mechanism for Bentham in his concern to bring about social happiness. Habermas, as we have seen, understands Bentham's mobilisation of publicity to be significant in relation to the constitution of the public sphere. In our earlier elaboration of Habermas on Bentham we already picked up some key aspects of Bentham's appreciation of publicity. Yet, it is now worthwhile extending this appreciation and bringing out more explicitly the link to accounting, thus helping to locate Bentham's accounting texts firmly in his radical project. For Bentham, publicity could function in a number of ways to further emancipation and happiness. We have noted that Bentham appreciated how people could come to be captured by illusions. They could fall into ways that were neither in their own nor in the general interest: they could come to behave in ways that were unwise and lacking in virtue or morality. Bentham saw publicity as helping here. It could 'aid the will' of the person or group of people exposed and re-inforce and enhance an orientation towards sympathy, benevolence and the general well-being (Mack 1962). Under the public gaze, people would act more in a general interest that was also consistent with their own and less in accordance with some other wayward path. Publicity was also envisaged to function as a system of informing in a more general sense. It could help people to make good decisions so that they could stay in control and steer themselves so as to align their own interests with the general interest. Further, publicity could aid the people in terms of stimulating them to political action and making democracy work better. Bentham promoted official publicity or disclosure but also what we might call 'counter information systems' or unofficial disclosures that were critical of the official government operations. He sought very strongly an open communication for the same reason as he supported an extensive democracy. He advocated openness to as many people as possible so that governance would come to operate in the general interest.

Boralevi (1984: 178) explicitly interprets Bentham's project of extended disclosure and reform to be a project of emancipation: Bentham can be read as an advocate and proponent of an emancipatory praxis to which publicity was an integral and indeed important element. His concerns about oppression and abuse in society influenced his emphasis in mobilising his principle of publicity. He was especially concerned to make visible social abuses, including the kind of abuses that some versions of Panopticism in the literature associate with his Panopticon. Boralevi (1984: 176) interprets Bentham as being concerned to unmask sinister interests through enlightened reason and education or the diffusion of knowledge, this having a strong affinity to publicity. She also delineates how Bentham's advocacy of a public opinion tribunal was a dimension of his concern to bring about the radical reform of social institutions, indicating the significance of publicity in his writings on codification (see Rosen 1983). Bentham was especially concerned to render the relatively powerful few – those running the state and powerful organisations in general – visible and accountable to the relatively repressed many. Hence the irony of views of commentators such as those reviewed in Boyne (2000: 299) which suggest that Bentham was interested in the opposite. Some of these commentators have even constructed terms such as 'Synopticon' to denote a system whereby disclosure goes from few to many, suggesting that this is an alternative to the Panopticon (Mathiesen 1997, adopts the term from Henriksen, see Boyne 2000: 301). They may be alternatives to Panopticism but not so much to Bentham: indeed, in *Panopticon* and *Pauper Management* Bentham is concerned that the experiences of the prisoners and the paupers in the poor houses – and thus the impact of the powerful upon them – be rendered visible to many (see Loft 1988: 26, Gallhofer and Haslam 1993). As Harrison (1983: 131) suggests, for Bentham the guards had to be guarded – 'the eye of the public makes the statesmen virtuous' (see also Boralevi 1984: 191). According to Bentham, cited in Harrison (1983: 131): '... publicity is the very soul of justice. It is the keenest spur to exertion, the surest of all guards against improbity. It keeps the judge himself, while trying, under trial' (cf. Laursen 1986, Davis 1992). Boralevi (1984: 7) sees Bentham's view of knowledge as a way of mediating the power of the strong – bettering the conditions of life and above all social relations. It is possible and indeed likely that Bentham's concern to promote publicity – the 'soul of justice' – and to make as many things visible as he could reasonably do, constitutes a pragmatic way in which developments equating to the socialistic might be encouraged and evaluated. In this regard, Bentham specifically linked his advocacy of a statistic/accounting society to the aim of 'promoting the condition of the labouring classes' (UC, cxlix: 237).[33]

Although Bentham at times was so enthusiastic about publicity that he appeared to believe in a total surveillance society, a reading of his texts as a whole indicates a more sensitive perspective. Bentham also valued privacy, for instance. Nor was he in favour of a secret surveillance. He was against those mixtures of openness and secrecy that operated to the benefit of what he called sinister interests and stood for those mixtures that operated to the benefit of the community in terms of general happiness. He advocated as much publicity as possible about a whole range of social activities – but he was at the same time concerned only to disclose as much as was reasonable in terms of limits determined by an enlightened and sensitive community. A further sensitivity of Bentham can be articulated in terms of a caution about universality. While much of what he advocated was in the form of universal principles – his schemes even often suggesting an extensive uniformity – he did recognise that the general happiness criterion could be served by respecting difference and not pushing, as he put it, uniformity too far. This recognition extended to his project to mobilise publicity (see Gallhofer and Haslam 1993). His emphasis on the need to respect difference follows Locke: toleration of difference is an important principle (Boralevi 1984: 181).

If we understand accounting as a system of informing, including an informing that would enhance transparency, openness and accountability, then it appears to follow logically from what we have put forward so far that accounting would be a form of publicity for Bentham. Given the associations between accounting and accountability, Bronner's (1994) work gives emphasis to and encourages such a logic in the reading of Bentham: influenced by Habermas' (1992) appreciation of the publicity advocated by Bentham, Bronner prefers to use the word accountability rather than publicity and thus suggests a strong overlap between a Bentham-like publicity and accounting. It is indeed very much possible to infer from Bentham's mobilising of accounting and book-keeping that the overlap between those terms in Bentham's discourse is strong. For instance, Bentham sees publicity as key to governance and management which helps to locate accounting as a form of publicity given its association in administrative discourse with the term management especially. This link to management is evident in the naming of the principle of publicity: for Bentham, alternative names for the principle were the 'open-management-principle', the 'transparent-management-principle' as well as the 'all-above-board-principle' (Gallhofer and Haslam 1994a: 256). With regard to accounting, Bentham understands it as a practice he wishes to rationalise and extend in its limits. Rather than setting artificial boundaries upon it, he makes no clear demarcation of accounting from a broader publicity and his work is thus suggestive of an accounting that would tend towards such publicity.[34]

While it is possible to make these strong inferences in seeking to link accounting and publicity in Bentham's discourse, it is not so necessary here as Bentham makes the overlap between accounting and publicity much more explicit in his texts. At times he uses accounting and publicity interchangeably (Gallhofer and Haslam 1994a,b, Fraser *et al.* 1999). And he makes use of the construct 'accounting publicity' (Gallhofer and Haslam 1993, Fraser *et al.* 1999), a construct that was indeed quite commonly used in the early to mid-nineteenth century beyond Bentham's discourse, typically to refer to tables with a financial accounting emphasis, in his text (see Haslam 1991). Bentham used the term 'book-keeping' very frequently. This term, which is strongly associated with accounting, Bentham again used interchangeably with publicity. Thus, again, accounting and publicity are intertwined in Bentham's discourse. An illustration of where book-keeping and publicity are linked by Bentham is when he describes his 'tabular-statement-principle', his principle of summarising accounting and statistical information in clear and tidy tables (alternative names for which where the 'tabular principle' and the 'bird's-eye-view principle', UC, cliib: 360), as 'an instrument in the hand of the principle of publicity. It is book-keeping reduced to quintessence' (UC, cliib: 360, 360n, Bahmueller 1981: 192). Book-keeping also has a very broad scope in Bentham's discourse, not being constrained to the financial and numerical and again equating to a broader notion of publicity (see Bentham 1797: 101). Bentham makes the overlap between book-keeping and a broader publicity quite explicit in his *Chrestomathia* (Gallhofer and Haslam 1996b). Book-keeping, including in micro-organisational settings (see Bentham 1797: 61), was closely aligned to a notion of stat(e)istics (see Burchell *et al.* 1980) that was also broader in scope than was later to be the case, a notion equating to knowledge of the state (see Cullen 1975, Haslam 1991, Gallhofer and Haslam 1994a,b, 1995, 1996b, see also Bentham's Constitutional Codification writings, e.g. Rosen 1983). Bentham was a great promoter of collecting records and statistics that would then be made visible (see Mack 1962: 237).

So strong are the interlinkages between book-keeping, accounting and publicity in Bentham that any suggestion that Bentham's publicity might be differentiated absolutely from his accounting or book-keeping arguably betrays an excessive chronocentrism, as well as a narrow way of seeing. If we look today beyond the British context, it can also be argued that it betrays a British ethnocentrism too: reference to publicity or something very similar to that has been apparent in the 'accounting legislation' of some continental European countries, such as that of Germany and Sweden (Haslam 1991, Lowe *et al.* 1991), for some time, indicating a strong overlap between accounting and publicity, or at least echoing a strong relation. Bentham's rationale for accounting and book-keeping thus fuses with his rationale for publicity: accounting is for Bentham an instrument for the enhancement of social happiness. Hume (1970: 24–5) indicates how Bentham understood accounting publicity functioning as publicity in a broad sense to produce its positive attitudinal, behavioural and thus social effects. In a myriad of ways, through the particular exposures and the enlightenment that it constitutes, accounting, as publicity, is envisaged as coming to impact upon people's attitudes and behaviour to further well-being.

Bentham goes further than the act of relating accounting to his emancipatory social goal. He gives accounting a very key role in this regard. 'Accounting publicity' is promoted by Bentham as a very important principle of management for his radical progressive project. Bentham's central principle of management or governance by which a whole manner of things were to be ordered to facilitate social progress and the realisation of human goals was the Panopticon or inspection-architecture principle. Bentham's principle of publicity was integral to this and Bentham states explicitly that the principle of publicity was second only to his inspection-architecture principle (Gallhofer and Haslam 1993). Accounting publicity was an 'indispensable basis to good management' and 'of peculiar extent and importance' (UC, clivb: 406, Bahmueller 1981: 91). Book-keeping, was to be 'one of the main pillars' of his system (UC, cliv: 34). The concern was to render visible, open and transparent, to inform, in respect of whatever social activities were to be a worthy focus of attention, on what was happening or on what had been going on. This was to be a most extensive application, with publicity also given a place in the final master plan for Bentham's complete administrative state (see Hume 1981: 242, 283, for an indication of its general applicability in Bentham, see also Harrison 1983: 131).

Aside from the explicit statement by Bentham that the principle of publicity was second only to that of the Panopticon itself, Bentham's writings indicate the significance he gave to publicity in a number of ways. Specifically, he places importance upon what we can recognise as accounting publicity and book-keeping. For instance, in the context of elaborating his Chrestomatic educational schema (see Gallhofer and Haslam 1996b), Bentham stresses his concern that everyone must strive to be a perfect bookkeeper, and, if possible, pass on their understanding of this 'most universally useful art':

> In the Chrestomathic school, the principle thereby indicated will of course be pursued; but, proportioned to the superior extent of the *field* assumed by it, will necessarily be the extent and variety of the *application* made of it. In the practice of this most universally useful art, all those Scholars, who, from the lowest up to the highest Stages, in the character of *Teachers*, *Private Tutors*, or *Monitors*, bear any part in the management of the School, will gradually be initiated, and insensibly perfected ... [35]

(Bentham 1816: 62)

In his associated table of knowledges for well-being, as well as in this educational schema more particularly, book-keeping is considered a sub-division of ethics. Moreover it is considered to be of great significance and occupies a prominent place therein (Bentham 1817, table V). Bentham (1816: 61) refers to the 'proportionable importance' of accounting or book-keeping. Everything was possible with the aid of book-keeping it seems, given the praise Bentham affords to it in the following citation from his work on *Pauper Management*:

> In a system of poor-houses of the proposed extent and magnitude, good book-keeping is the hinge on which good management will turn: the demand rises to the highest pitch; and so (it will be seen) does the sufficiency of the means at command for satisfying it. With the instruction, and under the check, of an adequate system of book-keeping, the management may be better conducted by the most ordinary hand, than by the ablest hand without that advantage; and the good management accidentally introduced by an able hand, would vanish with the hand that introduced it. *Without* this advantage, every thing would be too much; *with* it, nothing would be too much. *Without* it, any single one of the collateral benefits ... proposed, might be deemed visionary; *with* it, all of them together would be found practicable, easy and secure.
>
> (Bentham 1797: 100–1, cf. Bowring 1843, viii: 391–2,
> fragments thereof being cited in Hume 1981: 157)

In a draft of a letter to his friend the scientific agriculturist Arthur Young, himself a promoter of rationalised book-keeping in agriculture, Bentham's praise of accounting publicity and the significance he gave to it reaches a grand height:

> ... [I]f the season were not over for the manufacture of Heathen Deities, a Goddess, a Muse at the least thus ought to be for agricultural book-keeping ... your President should canonise her – you should be her High-Priest – and her place – should be at ... [?] ... right-hand ... and these two Tables you may consider as so many exercises, the production of a learner ... in simple truth a learner ... laid with all fear and trembling ... awe and reverence ... at the feet of a master ... I had all along said to myself, that while the Penitentiary House was building ... [?] ... book-keeping was one of the arts which I should have to learn ... the cries of the poor called aloud and accelerated the demand for it ... accept accordingly some anticipations ... [at this stage] ... mere crudities ... on book-keeping.[36]
>
> (UC, cliiia: 33–4)

Bentham's radical questioning of accounting and some characteristics of the accounting publicity that Bentham deemed would be emancipatory

Bentham sought to intervene in the name of a better accounting in a better society. He promoted a radical questioning of accounting. And reflecting his own radical questioning, he proposed that accounting ought to be changed in a number of ways so that it be aligned with more emancipatory development. He thus advocated an emancipation of accounting for emancipatory purposes. He sought changes in the scope, content, form, aura and usage of accounting. The changes he advocated reflected his concern to serve the oppressed, disadvantaged and abused (Boralevi 1984) and more generally his wider radical vision and strategies.[37] We elaborate here a critical review of Bentham's interventions in respect of accounting. We have already elaborated on publicity as discussed in Habermas' and then in Bentham's writings, and we have also elaborated on the overlap between accounting, book-keeping and publicity in Bentham's texts. Nevertheless, we consider that it is worthwhile to bring together the fuller array of insights into the various emancipatory possibilities of Bentham in respect of accounting more specifically.

In reviewing Bentham's focus on accounting, let us begin with his call for a radical questioning of it, a call reflecting his opposition to tradition for tradition's sake (see Gallhofer and Haslam 1993). Bentham held that accounting should be radically questioned in the name of emancipation or well-being. In relation to accounting he was concerned to keep his social happiness goal in focus.[38] Bentham stresses, consistent with a basically modern way of seeing accounting, that in 'book-keeping the heads – as in management, the principles of the system – will be governed by the objects or ends which it has in view ...' (see also Hume 1981: 154–5, Bowring 1843, vol. viii 393, UC, cxxxiii, 61, 62, 65). Book-keeping was to be properly adopted to particular purposes – linked to social happiness – from which he suggested may also be derived 'the *qualities* desirable in a system of this kind' (Bentham 1816: 61–2, see also Hume 1970: 27). What was to be made visible through accounting, that is the particular social activities it was to cast light on, what form, in the broadest sense, accounting was to take, what was to be its aura and what was to constitute its social usage, were for Bentham radically open questions to be answered for him by reference to the likely impacts upon the emancipatory progression he sought. For Bentham, questioning accounting opened it up to change. In this respect, he sought to change accounting consistent with his general radicalism. He sought greater openness and transparency and an alignment of accounting with socialistic and democratic progress.

For Bentham, an accounting that would be emancipatory would reflect a concern to serve the oppressed and more broadly a concern to fulfil what Bentham called a 'duty' to humanity. In the context of poor house management, Bentham sees accounting publicity as coming to the aid of the oppressed, consistent with his emancipatory project. One can thus radically interpret the text of the letter drafted by Bentham to the scientific agriculturist Arthur Young:

> From the art of Pauper Economy, studied with any attention, the transition is unavoidable to the ministering art of book-keeping. ... book-keeping was one of the arts which I should have to learn ... the cries of the poor called aloud and accelerated the demands for it ...
>
> (UC, cliiia: 33–4)

In keeping with his aim to aid the 'subject many' and his call for an extensive democracy, Bentham thus places great stress on the need to render open to view those he perceives to have relative power in society – such as those leading significant organisations or administering the state (*supra*). Further, Bentham relatedly sought to make visible to the world the conditions and experiences of the poor and disadvantaged in order to stimulate action directed at the improvement of these conditions and experiences. This is consistent with Bentham's declaration that publicity is the soul of justice.

Consistent with a practical and interventionist emancipatory stance, Bentham especially did not trust those he envisaged to have relative power in the community. He was not prepared to accept without questioning, for instance, the 'prerogatives of some corporations' (to use Foucault's 1980: 152, words). For Bentham (1843a: 589): 'Whom ought we to distrust, if not those to whom is committed great authority, with great temptations to abuse?' Bentham's concern to question the relatively powerful extends to his promoting counter publicity systems to challenge official systems of publicity (Bentham 1843a: 583).[39] In advocating accounting publicity, Bentham maintains that 'the eye of the public is drawn upon the subject' to operate 'as a check ... [upon] ... personal interest and favouritism' and other abuses, especially of the relatively powerful vis-à-vis the relatively oppressed (UC, cliiib: 281, Bahmueller 1981: 190). Thus, an accounting publicity that would serve the oppressed would make visible the relatively powerful and facilitate an assessment in the public realm of whether their behaviour fulfilled standards acceptable to the community. Bentham is optimistic about publicity 'disciplining' the relatively powerful, an optimism reflected in his opinion that 'the publicity of debates has ruined more demagogues than it has made' (Bentham 1843a: 588).[40] Accounting publicity was therefore to be geared towards aiding the will of those exposed to realise their most benevolent possibilities or stimulating them to fulfil their duty to humanity, a very general duty – including or encompassing a duty to serve the oppressed. Analysis of Bentham's writings on the duty of humanity brings out how he was concerned to expose moral behaviour (in his terms) and indicates how important publicity was for him in securing this duty. Bentham refers in *Pauper Management* to the appropriateness on the part of those running The National Charity Company of embracing two 'duties': the duty to economy and the duty to humanity. As Boralevi (1984) suggests, the duty to economy is a 'means' while the duty to humanity is an 'end'. To better gear social practices to the duty of humanity and the concerns of the oppressed, accounts were to make visible the moral as well as the economic. Harrison (1983: 130) points out that in his pauper management and Panopticon projects the chief sanction designed to align the interests of the managers with their duty to be humane in general was publicity. For Bentham:

The duty of the manager of an industry house has two main branches: duty towards those under his care, resolvable into *humanity* – and duty to his principals (the company), resolvable into *economy*. *Publicity*, the most effectual means of applying the forces of moral motives, in a direction tending to strengthen the

union between his interest and the *humane* branch of his duty; by bringing to
light, and thus exposing to the censure of the law and of public opinion, or at
any rate of public opinion, every instance of contravention.

(Bentham 1797: 51–2)

Elsewhere, Bentham clarifies that this vision of accounting publicity is more
generally applicable, beyond this particular micro-organisational Panopticon project
(UC, cliiia: 154, cliib: 282, Bentham 1797: 13, full title of work, Bahmueller 1981:
157, Hume 1981: 157, Gallhofer and Haslam, 1993, 1994b).[41] In elaborating his
plans for pauper management, Bentham was concerned to pursue the duty to humanity by recommending that paupers be encouraged to make complaints about
management in a complaint book that would be disclosed to the world (cf. UC,
clii: 312). His concern here is basically consistent with giving the oppressed a voice
in accounting. He sought in this and other respects that the experience of paupers be
made visible to the public.[42] His aim in general to render visible the experiences and
conditions of the relatively disadvantaged shows his concern about them and the
positive role he envisaged for accounting publicity in coming to their aid.

Related to and consistent with the above line of reasoning, the accounting that
Bentham proposed would be aligned to an attempt to reflect a holistic appreciation
of what matters to people, beyond an appreciation in accord with a narrowly problematic instrumental reasoning or an unthinking technical orientation. Thus, the
accounting that Bentham envisioned – especially given that he sought to extensively
apply his principle of accounting publicity – would have a broad scope and content, as
is also suggested in Bentham's mobilising of accounting publicity in relation to
a duty to humanity that goes beyond the duty to economy. The concern to emancipate
accounting beyond the duty to economy, so that it might play a more emancipatory
role in society, is well illustrated in the following citation from Bentham:

Pecuniary economy, usually regarded as the sole object of book-keeping, will
here be but as one out of a number; for the system of book-keeping will be neither more nor less than the history of the system of management in all its points.

(Bentham 1797: 101; see UC, clii: 360, Hume 1981: 52)

This is a remarkable citation that illustrates Bentham's radical envisioning of
book-keeping. For Bentham, the basic principle in general was that anything that
might conceivably be useful for governance should be recorded in the books: 'The
supposition to be set out upon is – that everything is to be registered ... for ...
which ... any use can be found' (UC, clivb: 406, Bahmueller 1981: 192–3). In his
proposed pauper management system, given its size, complexity and the uncertainties it faced, Bentham felt that record keeping should be extensive because 'the
minutest article may swell into importance' (Bowring 1843, viii: 392, see also
Bentham 1797: 102–3). This extensive collecting of records was linked to Bentham's
concern to try to understand dimensions of social functioning in order to then better
regulate these for well-being. The equation of book-keeping with the 'history of the
system of management in all its points' is to broaden significantly the scope and content

of book-keeping relative to the book-keeping now regarded as conventional (see Hoskin and Macve 1986: 128). For Bahmueller (1981: 193), Bentham wanted to capture every moment (see also Loft 1988). Hume (1970: 30) acknowledges that the set of books and accounts generally advocated by Bentham covered financial transactions and the handling of money but did not give primacy thereto. In aggregate, the accounts of Bentham constituted not so much accounting 'in the conventional sense' but, as we have already suggested, a comprehensive set of records, returns and statistics which managers or administrators could make use of (Hume 1970: 30).[43] Hume (1970: e.g. p. 5) indicates that Bentham equates accounts with statistics or information generally, reflecting the earlier connotation of statistics as knowledge of the state (*supra*, see Cullen 1975, Burchell *et al.* 1980, Haslam 1991). And in Bentham notions of accounting and statistics are closely intertwined (*supra*, cf. UC, cxlix, 237–53, 19, 149; Bentham 1816, 1817, see Cullen 1975, Burchell *et al.* 1980), his approach clearly challenging a reduction of the focus of accounting publicity to an entity's narrow financial dimensions.[44] He aimed to go beyond, if also to include, a focus upon the financial (Bentham's book-keeping-at-large, Bentham 1816, notes to tables, Bahmueller 1981: 193, cf. Bentham 1797, British Parliamentary Papers, 1825 (522), IV, 321, 1826–7 (558), III, 869, Davidoff and Hall 1987, Haslam 1991). Understanding financial such as commercial accounts to be conventional, Bentham sought to extend accounting 'in its limits' as he wrote to Arthur Young. This was consistent with his concern to 'rationalise' it (Bahmueller 1981: 193). There are numerous illustrations of this principle at work throughout his texts. In his *Pauper Management*, Bentham advocated, as we have touched upon above, a 'moral book-keeping' which would record various aspects of the behaviour of those focused upon (see Bahmueller 1981: 192, cf. Bowring 1843, vol. viii: 392–3, see also Davidoff and Hall 1987, Walsh and Stewart 1988)[45]: again, he believed this beneficial for those being observed as well as for society more generally. Amongst what Bentham referred to as the elementary population books would be a personal book or diary for each poorhouse occupant. In this would be noted daily the state of health, meals, conduct and subject-matter worked upon, utensils worked with, quantity of work done, time employed for that quantity, place of work and encouragement money (bonus) earned (Bowring 1843, vol. viii: 393). These books would be used for accountings geared to an array of objects reflective of the duty to economy and, more broadly, humanity. This broadening of the content of accounting fuses with the broadening of the scope of accounting towards the broader duty to humanity. Thus accounts might reflect a concern to play a part in the management of the 'health' and 'comfort' of people (cf. British Museum Manuscript MS 33541, f. 203, note drafted by Bentham, 23 January 1791, Bowring 1843, viii, pp. 392–3, UC, clii, 312, cf. Bahmueller 1981: 192).

More generally, Bentham envisaged accounting publicity as a mechanism for moving people towards the realisation of their goals: emancipation towards well-being. He sought that accounting reflect this and reflect an overcoming of obstacles and deficiencies constituted by or functioning in past accounting. Bentham sought to render visible the individual (see his 'distinction' or 'separate-exhibition' principle, UC, cliiia: 165),[46] the group (intersecting with the organisation) and the social in the name of well-being. He argued (for instance in his *Constitutional Code*) for the need for limits to exposure (see Semple 1993) but the presumption was, in the absence of what he took to be such legitimate exceptions, for as much exposure as possible. Social activities to be made visible included the activities of business organisations but went beyond these. And to fully appreciate the activities of business organisations, it was appropriate to take into account the interaction of these with other activities. Further, disaggregated information that could render open to view the local effects of local activities was within the ambit of this vision. Hume (1970: 28) places some stress on the open-ended character of Bentham's scheme, such as its allowing for or facilitating of the unlimited multiplication of accounting categories and books including through sub-division. Such radical possibilities respecting the form and content of accounting found in Bentham can be interpreted as consistent with calls for rational and critical social communication with a broad scope, including in respect of micro-organisational manifestations and activities. In *Chrestomathia*, Bentham's programme of education for useful learning (Bentham, 1816, 1817), book-keeping was to be taught on the curriculum at the final and highest stage (see Gallhofer and Haslam 1994b, 1996b), and Bentham's broader view of accounting is again reflected here. According to the Chrestomathic plan, two types of book-keeping were to be taught: the more narrowly and (including in Bentham's context) conventionally conceived 'mercantile' or commercial book-keeping (which he was also concerned to question) and the wider notion of 'book-keeping at large' or general book-keeping for society. The latter is briefly described as the 'art of Registration or Recordation' (Bentham 1816: Chrestomathic Instruction Table, table I):

> The *commercial* process or operation, on the subject of which, under the name of Book-keeping, works in such multitude have been published, is but a branch – a particular application – of an art, of the most extensive range, and proportionable importance: viz. the art of *Book-keeping at large* – the art of *Registration* – of Recordation – the art of securing and perpetuating *Evidence*.
>
> (Bentham 1816: 61)

In respect of Bentham's appreciation of a broader, more holistic, type of book-keeping, Hoskin and Macve (1986) begin to recognise and acknowledge that this aspect of Bentham's writings on accounting opens up a new insight into accounting's history. This is beyond, indeed, any narrow focus upon an overly restrictive notion of calculation. Hoskin and Macve (1986: 128) refer here to Bentham's intervention as 'a startling reversal of accounting's specific history', a comment that begins to problematise some dismissive treatments of Bentham in the accounting literature.

These interventions of Bentham to broaden accounting's scope and its content, which amount to a relatively early advocacy of what latterly came to be typically known as social accounting, are interpreted differently by Loft (1988). She sees the text in which Bentham advocates going beyond 'Pecuniary economy' (Bentham 1797: 101), for instance, as illustrating the intensity of disciplinary control in Bentham's project. In contrast, we wish to stress that Bentham promoted a broad understanding of what constituted book-keeping facts and accounting publicity and their scope. He was concerned to go beyond – if still to at least in some respects encompass – accounting as more narrowly conceived towards wider conceptions of accounting publicity consistent with a more enabling and emancipatory vision (*supra*, Bentham 1797: 101, 103). The only constraint upon accounting was that it be geared towards the generation of well-being: this implied that book-keeping be corrected 'in its limits' (*supra*).

Bentham's accounting would also reflect a concern to advance or fuse with a democracy consistent with his radicalism. In the push for democracy, and with a view towards reflecting more democratic practice, Bentham sought that accounting should be mobilised to inform the people at large, a very broad audience. This, he understood, was a way of advancing emancipatory change. Accounting in this respect could be educational and enlightening. Consequently, it follows from this that accounting itself had to be more accountable. The language of accounting had to be more comprehensible to the public so that they could better control it and make use of it in the name of emancipation. Alternative scenarios, such as the public being problematically controlled by accounting and an expertise distant from them, had to be countered.

Bentham virtually advocated the disclosure of as much as possible to as many as possible (see UC, cl: 147, cliv: 33, Hume 1981: 155, cf. Bentham 1830: 46 and PRO, T64/388, 1841). In *Pauper Management* we can discern his concern to widen the audience or potential usage of accounting publicity. Bentham sometimes, as in *Pauper Management*, construes the public, to whom accounting was addressed, in terms of various groups that might be deemed to have an evident interest in particular social or organisational focuses. He was concerned to set up information including information-for-accountability systems in respect of organisations and activities that would inform a number of groups. These groups went beyond, if they included, the particular group deemed by the prevailing law formally governing ownership to be the owners. Again, the key criterion for Bentham is development towards well-being or emancipation, and existing arrangements were to be radically questioned against this criterion. He suggested that the management of an organisation or social practice, whether formally and legally owned by shareholders or not, had a duty to the public at large (UC, cliiia: 153). In elaborating upon envisaged users of the accounting of a micro-organisation with shareholders, Bentham's writing reflects the aforesaid underlying concern to decide this by reference to the overall emancipatory impact for the people. He translates this into a proposal in his context that would go beyond an emphasis upon the capitalistic property rights recognised by the law to develop a system of book-keeping as a basis for publicity that would serve various groups in his context and ultimately the public at large. In the context of The National Charity Company, with its 250 poor-houses, such a system would be:

> ... an indispensable security for the due discharge of the several obligations, which the direction of the company will have ... to the various parties interested – viz. the paupers ... the rateable parishioners ... the stock-holders ... government – and the public at large ...
>
> (Bentham 1797: 99–100)

This approach is suggestive of what is referred to as a stakeholder approach today (see Gray *et al.* 1996), although the ultimate emphasis in Bentham is the public-at-large. Bentham was also supportive of a kind of audit/consultancy whereby groups with alternative viewpoints could observe and report on organisational practices. According to his 'concourse-attraction principle' one was, in 'the contrivance of buildings, and the whole system of management' to 'neglect no circumstance that can contribute to engage attention to the management, and attract to the spot a *concourse* of such visitors, whose remarks may afford instruction, and their scrutiny a spur to improvement, and a check to abuse' (Bentham 1797: 56–7, cf. chapters 10, 12). This latter stance, as well as reflecting Bentham's commitment to openness and transparency so as to achieve a practical emancipation of the people, also particularly emphasises his commitment to rational and critical deliberation including in micro-organisational settings.[47] More generally, Bentham held that the wider the audience able to access accounting and accounting language, the more effective the accounting publicity in securing its aims. As is evident in his *Constitutional Code* – but not restricted thereto – Bentham promoted his principle of accounting publicity in the context of calling for a radically extensive democracy in an open and enlightened society (see Bowring 1843: viii, 343, UC, cxxxiii: 61–2, 65).[48] Accounting publicity was thus integral to calls for extensive education and democracy, considered by Bentham to be means for promoting radical emancipatory change towards social betterment.[49] The usage of the construct accounting publicity, suggestive of accounting for and to the public, in itself indicates the link to democracy (see Lowe *et al.* 1991). Accounting is envisaged as an instrument for facilitating and a manifestation of rational and critical communication in a democratic society (Bentham 1797: 101–3). Bentham saw accounting as an emancipatory instrument that multifariously both reflects and helps constitute public opinion and popular sovereignty (Holub 1991, Habermas 1992, Gaonkar and McCarthy 1994: 549). He also wished to see the manifestation of alternative publicities to those mobilised by the state, so that the people might have some hope of bringing their will and understanding to bear on the democratic process (Bentham 1843a: 592, cf. Holub 1991: 3, Peters 1993, cf. Bronner 1994, see also Power 1991).

Bentham was concerned in the above respects that accounting be comprehensible in the public realm. He understood accounting to be an indispensable practice that ought to be open to all and that could be challenged and changed through a democratic process (see Bentham 1816: Chresthomathic Instruction Tables, table I, Gallhofer and Haslam 1994b: 450). Bentham's texts express a concern to critique accounting language and render accounting itself accountable, this being motivated by his aim to render accounting more comprehensible and clearer as well as more open to challenge by the public at large. Accounting publicity was to be comprehensible as well as comprehensive (UC, cxxxiii, 65). Bentham sees his proposed accounting as contributing to an inclusive and open communication that would transform mystifying expert language (see Bentham 1797: 105).[50] This would make it more an instrument of the people, an instrument of their emancipation. In a letter to the scientific agriculturist Arthur Young (cited in Bahmueller 1981: 193),

Bentham expressed the intention of correcting book-keeping 'in its language'. Bentham sought to make accounting publicity, serving in part as an instrument of accountability, itself more accountable, open and comprehensive to the non-expert. Accounting (as writing, see Gaonkar and McCarthy 1994: 567) was to be an object for regulation. Accounting publicity and book-keeping had to be 'inspective or information-elicitative': 'natural' (or commonly understood) were to replace 'technical' expressions, the latter potentially being envisaged as an instrument of fraud rather than a protection from it (Bentham 1797: 50, 1993, chapter 9, section 7, statistic function, V.I.: 274, Bentham 1830: 49n, Bowring 1843, ix: 219–26, 252, 253n, UC, cxxxv: 141–94, 6 November, 1831, Goldberg 1957, Hume 1981: 51).[51] Such interventions amounted for Bentham to correcting accounting in its language so that it could be grasped by the people for emancipatory development. Much of Bentham's critique of the accounting of his own time focused in this regard upon that shaped by or equating to double-entry book-keeping. Bentham criticised the technicality of the double-entry of his day, and problematised its universality, in his work on *Pauper Management*: 'In the form called the Italian, book-keeping is a science of itself, and a most intensely difficult one. Happily it is not here a necessary one' (Bentham 1797: 105n). In his *Official Aptitude Maximized: Expense Minimised* he also wrote opposing (at the stage he was writing) the introduction of the Italian mode into public account keeping – due to the difficulty of its language (Bowring 1843, vol. V: 383, Goldberg 1957: 219). In developing a more general critique of the Italian mode of double-entry book-keeping towards the end of his life, Bentham studied thoroughly Robert Hamilton's (1788) *An Introduction to Merchandise*, including taking time to complete some book-keeping exercises therefrom (Goldberg 1957, Hume 1981: 152, UC, cviii: 109). In notes from the 1830s analysed by Goldberg (1957) (UC, cxxxv: 141–94), Bentham particularly aimed at the 'substitution of natural to technical equivalences' or the substitution of 'vulgar [i.e. commonly understood] to the Italian nomenclature' in book-keeping, a project which he held to be of some value. He suggested that, if the keeping of accounts of transactions in the 'technical language of [an overly complex] double-entry system' be employed, 'the accounts are ... unintelligible to all ... to whom that language is not familiar', and could be the instrument of fraud (UC, cxxxv: 141–94, 6 November 1831). Bentham conveys some of his critical stance in respect of double entry book-keeping in the following citation, which also indicates the location of his critique of accounting in his general critique of fictions (see Mack 1962).

> The *Italian method*, or method of *Double Entry*, is the name given to that system of Book-keeping, which is commonly employed in establishments of superior importance. Unfortunately, old established as it is, the *obscurity* of this method is still more conspicuous than its *utility*; and in consequence, *generation*, instead of *correction* of Error, is but too frequent a result. The obscurity has for its sole *cause*, the *fictitiousness*, – and thence the *inexpressiveness*, or rather the *misexpressiveness*, – of the language.[52]

> (Bentham 1816: 63–4)

Bentham argues in this context that proper book-keeping should be portrayed in his planned educational instruction as:

> *Correct, complete, clear, concise, easy to consult* – in case of *error*, so framed as not to *cover* it, but to *afford indication* of it – *appropriate*, i.e. adapted to the particular practical purpose it has in view – the purpose, for the sake of which the labour thus bestowed is expended – in these epithets may be seen the *qualities* desirable in a system of this kind.
>
> (Bentham 1816: 61–2)

To improve comprehensibility and facilitate comparison, Bentham advocated uniformity in method in general for all joint stock companies and beyond into other bodies. This included an attempt by Bentham to integrate accounting in accordance with a 'uniform-management-principle' (UC, cliiia: 154, cliib: 281, 363–4; Bahmueller 1981: 187, see also UC, cliib: 361–2).[53] In this regard, facilitating a 'management-selection principle', the system of book-keeping in The National Charity Company was to be 'reduced ... to the form of a table, inspectable in one view' (Bentham 1797: 50).[54] These stipulations reflect Bentham's concern to arrive at and promote a comprehensible and widely accessible accounting – here, in respect of the case of the business organisation. His concern was to correct 'error having for its ultimate effect diminution of happiness' (UC, cxxxv: 141–94, Goldberg 1957). If much of his critique focused upon that accounting shaped by double-entry book-keeping, his critique had a wider pertinence.[55] It is important to recognise that Bentham's emphasis here was motivated by a concern to better inform people so as to engender positive emancipatory development.

We have noted that Bentham did not restrict accounting to an accounting reflecting the structure of an organisation as delineated by the factor of ownership under existing formal laws. He aimed to render social activities in general open to view to engender socially desirable effects and was thus not constrained by any proprietary or related entity concept.[56] Bentham's looking to the people behind the structures is a dimension of his concern to challenge problematic fictions or fictitious entities, abstract terms that in his view served to confuse people (sometimes, he believed, purposefully) rather than to enlighten them. Bentham held that the mobilisation of fictitious entities such as law and property and the corporate entity, instead of personalised terms (such as 'the rich'), served as a kind of propaganda supporting and venerating what one may call today the existing hegemonic forces (see Peardon 1974: 125). Bentham's critique of fictions and de-personalisation finds some echoes in more recent critical theoretical work in accounting that has challenged the corporate entity principle (see Haslam 1991, Power and Laughlin 1992, Gallhofer and Haslam 1993, 1995).

In effect, Bentham recognises that accounting is not a straightforwardly neutral device. Bentham is thus concerned that the accounting publicity system become and then remain a system for people that they feel comfortable using. This is consistent with and follows from his view that an extensive democracy that practices openness and transparency would deliver emancipation and social betterment. Bentham's view that accounting could manifest and function as mystifying fuses with what Boralevi (1984) terms Bentham's appreciation of ideology. One further dimension of such an appreciation is that Bentham explicitly recognised that accounting could become shrouded in a language of mystifying expertise and be captured by an interested expertocracy. Indeed he understood that the accounting of his own time was at least partially captured in this way. He sought to counter the threat of the problematic influence of an expertocracy that might remain accountable to virtually nobody in practical terms and aimed to render accounting an instrument of the people in their pursuit of emancipatory development. Accounting as a practical social activity had to be accountable itself. Bentham explicitly suggests that the real reasons for the existence of a mystifying accounting expert practice – implying that they are interested reasons – constituted an issue worthy of investigation:

> ... [The Italian mode of accounting, i.e. based on double-entry book-keeping, is a] ... language composed entirely of fictions, and understood by nobody but the higher clan of merchants and their clerks ... The real use of the particularities which characterize the Italian mode, might be a subject well worthy of investigation.
>
> (Bentham 1797: 106n)

He suggests more openly elsewhere that 'sinister interest in a pecuniary shape' is one factor in explaining the 'real use of the particularities' referred to, along with the interest of the expert in preserving self-esteem after spending so much time on the cultivation of a peculiar talent (Bowring 1843, vol. ix: 253n, cited in Goldberg 1957: 220, see also UC, cxxxv).[57] Habermas (1992) does not acknowledge this dimension of Bentham, a dimension that is scarcely present in Bentham (1843a). Yet elsewhere Habermas does express concern about the eroding impact of problematic and interested expertocracy upon the potentialities of the public sphere.[58]

Although at times Bentham embraces universality and even uniformity in his social vision,[59] he elsewhere values particularity and difference. This sensitivity can be located to some extent in his texts on accounting. His system of accounting publicity can indeed be considered to reflect a balance between openness and confidentiality and universality and particularism. This adds a new dimension to his emancipatory projects. Bentham's proposed accounting would reflect a sensitivity to and an awareness of particularities, including valued particularities. He positively valued privacy and confidentiality (see his *Constitutional Code*, Rosen 1983, Semple 1993). In some ways, his approach is consistent with a contingency perspective. He applied a broad cost–benefit analysis in terms of the general happiness principle to proposed disclosures, thus attempting to take into account the economic and social cost of disclosure including the impact upon valued privacy (Bentham 1797: 56, 100, 105, chapter 3, *Constitutional Code*, Gallhofer and Haslam 1993). There are various suggestions that the particular nature of the accounting system ought to depend on the character of the institution (see Hume 1970: 30, 1981: 154, Bentham 1797: 56, 100, 105, chapter 3, Bowring 1843, vol. viii: 393, UC, cxxxiii: 61, 62, 65).[60] In other ways, as well as being deemed appropriately flexible and open to change (from the point of view of their purpose) accounts might be appropriately modified by a 'local-consideration' or 'local-modification' principle (UC, cli: 363–4, Bentham 1797):

> Frame for this purpose at the outset, a set of blank books or forms to be observed in all, improving them from time to time … [and a] local-consideration observing principle – not to push the principle of uniformity too far.[61]
> (Bentham 1797: 50, cf. 103, see also his *Constitutional Code*)

In summary, Bentham's texts on book-keeping and accounting publicity are, as we have indicated, reflective and consistent with his broader radical envisioning. The texts are suggestive of a number of insights into the accounting that Bentham envisaged to be emancipatory. Such an accounting reflects a radical questioning. It is shaped by a concern to serve the oppressed and more broadly to fulfil a duty to humanity, thus making visible the conditions and experiences of the disadvantaged rendering open to view the activities of the relatively powerful and exposing the latter's practices in relation to a broadly understood duty to humanity. The oppressed are given a voice in Bentham's accounting. It is an accounting influenced by a critical appreciation of people and their needs and wants. Thus, it was to be extended 'in its limits' as part of its rationalisation and to be an accounting of broad scope and content. Bentham's accounting also is aimed at advancing or being consistent with his radically conceived democracy. It would be an accounting for the people and be comprehensible rather than alien to them. Bentham hinted at an accounting that reflected valued particularities and went beyond a crude universality, suggesting an opening up of a further emancipatory dimension to his work on accounting publicity.

On mobilising an accounting that would be emancipatory: some critical reflections on reading Bentham on accounting

In seeking to mobilise an accounting that would be emancipatory today where should we locate Bentham? The above review suggests that Bentham's texts provide a number of insights in terms of visions and strategies. Yet one can also properly suggest that, if one is to positively position Bentham in relation to such an emancipatory project, one ought to refine and transform Bentham's model in a number of ways. This includes notably being especially aware of and sensitive to a number of possible problems and potential pitfalls in mobilising a project that draws insights from or has important overlaps with Bentham. Analysis of Bentham's texts already suggests a number of problems in our view: as we have acknowledged, there is something of substance in those critical receptions of Bentham referred to earlier, and this substance is also manifest in respect of Bentham's accounting visions. In spite of Bentham's own quite pragmatic and context-aware cautions and sensitivities – cautions and sensitivities that critical actors today can evaluate in positive terms – it is possible to elaborate a number of dimensions of Bentham's envisioning and mobilising of accounting publicity as problematic and negative. More generally, one can envisage how projects at least ostensibly drawing from Bentham can come to accrue yet more problematic dimensions in their conception and application. In what follows we highlight some problems of Bentham's proposals in respect of accounting and some difficulties with possible interpretations and applications thereof that would continue to be problematic in the event of their manifestation or promotion today. Yet at the same time we also suggest ways in which we can nevertheless attempt to learn from and overcome these problematics and go forward in a way that still reflects Bentham's basic vision of an alignment between accounting and emancipation.

Let us begin with a citation from one of Bentham's critics. Letwin maintains that Bentham can be seen as:

> ... the hermit of Queen Square Place, sitting on his platform in the dining room, dreaming of a world that had adopted his code and canonized him as High Codifier and Grand Benefactor of all mankind. ... Whatever community adopted his constitutional code, he was confident, would have no further need of any of its former institutions, and whoever opposed the code was an enemy of the people. For the good produced would be pure from evil, and the government perfectly directed to the interests of the governed. In the end the very precision on which Bentham rested his faith defeated his purpose. ... By ruthlessly ignoring the refractions of ideas and emotions, he produced devices of a monstrous efficiency that left no room for humanity.
>
> (Letwin 1965)

This reading of Bentham can be related to tensions in his work. He seeks that the people be in control, but wants to direct them first. He wants their views to be reflected in their complexity and diversity but seeks a cost-efficient and universal way of understanding, educating and enlightening them that threatens such intricacies. Such tensions may be located in any radical progressive work, and Bentham actually did show an awareness of these tensions and a sensitivity towards the issues involved (Letwin 1965, acknowledges as much) – yet the case can be made that he slips too often into a mode of intervention equating to an excessive over-confidence and an overly insensitive dogmatism. He saw himself and his band of disciples as privileged knowers with little time to listen directly, it seems, to the views of the repressed and relatedly with little time to respect diversity and difference. Here Bentham is influenced by his own reading of his context – a context which, to be fair, many saw as being a poor one for the establishment of effective democratic practice – and his location in a confident Enlightenment school of thought. Letwin (1965: 183) suggests that Bentham sometimes acted as if he need only declare that things be so in order for them to happen. He was also somewhat naively optimistic about the progressiveness of a democratic government (see Bowring 1843, vol. x: 66). Boyne (2000: 289) cites Bentham writing in 1786 of the compelling potential accomplishments of the Panopticon so that 'wonder is not only that this plan should never ... [hitherto have been]... put into practice, but how any other should ever have been thought of'.

Such excessive confidence can lead to a simple laying down of instructions for better-ment. And more sophisticated and participatory political strategies can be displaced.

Another way of seeing this, or another dimension of it, is to suggest that Bentham has very little faith in people who are undirected and indeed unsupervised. Bentham explicitly advocated or at least strongly endorsed a lack of trust, albeit that his emphasis was upon recommending that the people as a whole should not trust those who are relatively powerful in society. While he refers to his principle of benevolence in the following citation, he also appears to endorse and encourage a more problem-atically distrustful practice: 'Here accounts must be kept, must be published ... regularly – and will be scrutinized ... by many a benevolent ... suspicious ... envious eye ...' (UC, cli: 322, Bahmueller 1981: 187). If it is ironic in the light of Bentham's concerns to enhance morality and counter corruption, Himmelfarb (1968) could thus link Panopticon to corruption and moral decay (following Keynes, see Mack 1962). The over-confidence of Bentham in his own position and his associated bluntness might translate in some instances into a tendency to see all too little good worthy of rescue in the existing practices and institutions of a society that the radical interven-tion is seeking to change.[62]

Again reflecting the tendency of his work to an insensitive dogmatism Bentham's texts are suggestive at times, in spite of his professed sensitivity to difference and the particular or local, of a crude universality and overly extensive uniformity. The following citation is striking in this respect, suggesting an obsessive uniformity:

> I have a machine put together these many years for answering all such questions: give me an hour or two to wind it up, you shall have the pro and con in its full extent any time you please ... To make the thing the easier to talk of, and enquire after at the Bookseller's, I have given it a particular name in a single word, viz.: Panopticon or the Inspection-House. Panopticon is already in use as a name for I forget what optical instrument ... in or by means of which you may see everything as the name imports ... You had the goodness to offer me some papers relative to some of the establishments to which the idea promises to be applicable ... Houses of Industry ... Jails ... Hospitals ... Schools && ... Do you happen to want a plan of Education just now, or a plan of anything else? These are my amusements. One thing pretty much the same to me as another.[63]
>
> (Letter to the Right Hon John Parnell, Buxton, Derbyshire from Jeremy Bentham, 2 September 1790, British Museum Manuscript, MS 33541, f. 160, see also Boyne 2000: 288–9)

Bentham sees book-keeping as a system of uniformity that will itself engender uniformity in this regard. He also appears to look favourably upon a notion whereby book-keeping would help produce and reflect a uniform and robotic order: ' ... let it be a rule to render the management the same as to each point in every branch of the management ... the general advantage depends on uniformity of which uniformity is productive ... Refer to book-keeping' (UC, cliib: 363).

He reasons that tabular statements that were 'methodical, uniform, distinct, all comprehensive' would engender 'methodical' and 'uniform' behaviour (UC, cliib: 360n,

361, Bahmueller 1981: 192, Hume 1981: 160–1). According to Bahmueller (1981: 193), this is a 'utilitarian' victory over the messy 'disorderliness' of social reality for Bentham (see Loft 1988), for whom book-keeping was: ' ... an integral part ... a sine qua non of the inspection system itself; and as such it was a powerful vehicle for the removal of the last vestiges of contingency from the ...[whole]... company' (Bahmueller 1981: 192, Bowring 1843, viii: 414).

Bentham maintained that business practice in his own time fell down because it was 'not consigned to any fixed and written general rules' (UC, cli: 309–10, Bahmueller 1981: 188). This is suggestive of an accounting that could engender excessive and stifling uniformity that would constitute a form of repression.

Analysis of such tendencies towards excessive confidence and dogmatism in Bentham suggests that, if the intentions are good, the approach is problematic. Bentham is dogmatic and elitist in spite of himself, or in danger of stimulating an overly dogmatic and elitist approach. And as Letwin (1965) suggests, Bentham's 'colourless treatises were interpreted by disciples moved by different experiences and aims' to be yet more problematic. There may be a failure to appreciate the ambiguity of the concepts, constructs and practices of Bentham in their mobilisation in an ostensibly progressive intervention. All these potential pitfalls would continue to loom large today in relation to a mobilisation of accounting publicity akin to Bentham's project.

The way forward here has to be to reflect an awareness of the tensions we have elaborated. It would be an awareness consistent with a view of change as reflecting both progressive and regressive trajectories, an approach consistent with a more balanced view of the complex and multifarious functionings of existing practices and institutions. In some ways this is to emphasise Bentham's professed sensitivities and cautions yet further. For instance, appreciation of the ambiguities and differing meanings of concepts, constructs and practices *in situ* is an important consideration, as is the need to consciously seek to communicate interactively with and take guidance from people. Further, a deliberative attempt to listen to the other voices of diversity and difference and to act upon this in terms of a differentiated universalism would constitute an appropriate extension of Bentham's local-consideration principle.

Bentham's text is suggestive of an extensive surveillance and social control that would also continue to pose a repressive threat today. In respect of surveillance and the Panopticon ' ... a single room the inspection lodge, is all one need set foot in: for from that one can command every nook and cranny of the rest' (UC, cliiia: 312). Further, in this system 'every person and every thing' were to be 'within reach at the same instant' (Bentham 1797: 104–5). Accounts were to be 'kept, must be published ... regularly ... under heads previously arranged with the declared purpose of giving the most perfect transparency to the whole management in every point of view imaginable' (UC, cli: 322, Bahmueller 1981: 187, see also 193). And Bentham stated: 'In the instance of each [poor-house] establishment give to the whole system of management both as to plan and execution – every degree of publicity possible – neglecting no means that can contribute to this effect' (UC, cliiia: 154, management principles and rules). Such citations emphasise Bentham's enthusiasm for openness and transparency. Nevertheless, there is at least a potential downside. Hume (1981) stresses how a rigorous surveillance that focuses on the individual in the way Bentham's schema threatens to do can displace forms of collective solidarity. A negative potential that counters emancipatory possibilities was in effect envisaged by a number of Bentham's contemporaries (Semple 1993: 311–2). The objectives of mobilising accounting publicity systems can come to be lost or forgotten in these trajectories of an obsessive surveillance.

Bentham in effect provides mechanisms that while never neutral or innocent can come to be taken up in different ways to different political effect. Radical possibilities can be appropriated for different, more conservative or 'sinister' purposes. Bentham's prescriptions increase and deepen significantly the possibilities for managers to control subordinates (Hume 1981: 163).[64] Bentham himself could classify people in a problematically hierarchical way in this respect as where he noted, with biological analogy, that some of his principles applied 'to the situation of the working hands, others to that of the superintending eyes' (UC, cliiia: 143, cf. Bentham 1797: chapter 12, 1816, longer title of work). This is a departure from Bentham's concern elsewhere (including in Bentham 1797) to render the public as a whole the 'superintending eyes'. The Panopticon principle can be viewed in part as a device by which the powerful few can exploit the powerless many and as a social experiment involving the control of some people over others (Hobsbawm 1962, Himmelfarb 1965).[65] If, as we have suggested, accounting publicity might come to be misinterpreted, misapplied or otherwise problematically used by those forces ostensibly radical and progressive, Bentham's visions also run a high risk of capture by problematic hegemonic forces. Pragmatism in relation to accounting and related change might easily fall back into conservatism and reaction. This may especially be the case where there is a failure to adequately understand the context. Adapted versions of Bentham's plans for the prison, poor-house and school as well as factory can be mobilised in an effort to manage the disadvantaged and the oppressed in effect for the benefit of the more wealthy and powerful to whom the poor are to remain subordinate. Instead of openness to all, Bentham's schemes can in this context come to be distorted so that it is openness to the relatively powerful that applies in practice. At the time Bentham was extending his elaboration of the Panopticon principle from prison to poor-house, while poverty was coming to be the most significant issue of the age this was to some substantial extent because of the perceived expense of coping with the poor and the threat of revolution.[66] There is a suggestion in Bentham's writings, as we have seen, of forcing order and uniformity on to a chaotic, disorderly, dynamic and threatening context, thus providing for a greater certainty that could additionally re-assure and enhance already prevailing and problematic hegemonic forces (see Bahmueller 1981: 193).[67]

Bentham's texts can lend considerable support to an oppressive capitalistic activity. Much of Bentham's work in practice might easily be mobilised narrowly and problematically to a simple profit seeking focus. Its implying of a primarily secular 'rationalism' can still in some ways help today to foster a crude individualism. It can help support bourgeois capitalist activity and the control of labour from a narrow capitalist perspective (Hobsbawm 1962, Berg 1985). Hobsbawm (1962) reasonably suggests in reference to Bentham's context that if the development of

Enlightenment reasoning in general cannot be taken simply as a conscious strategy exercised by bourgeois interests, the bourgeoisie in particular could come to see it as serving their perceived interests through its anticipated effects.[68] The Panopticon accounting of Bentham – an accounting eye concerned to render 'all things visible' – can in practice still be channelled to narrow capitalistic or financial economistic property interests. Accounts might thus come to be governed by a narrow notion of hierarchy, whereby employed agents are accountable to capitalist principals, a 'higher' but not necessarily a socially legitimate authority. Further and relatedly, if Bentham alludes to a holistic vision of well-being, his rhetoric slips at times into a narrow economicism that threatens to enhance such tendencies. In delineating a 'duty to economy' seemingly separate from a 'duty to humanity' he ironically distances somewhat the economic from the social. Surely, a duty to economy is part of a deeper duty to humanity? In what reasonable sense can one separate the duty to economy from the duty to humanity in this way?[69] Bentham refers again relatedly to commercial book-keeping as a subset of book-keeping-at-large in a way that is problematic. He appears at times to be insufficiently critical of commercial book-keeping as a system geared to what Bentham referred to as the management of pecuniary economy, but also seems to unreasonably separate out commercial book-keeping from book-keeping in general. His concern that accounting publicity reports be easily inspectable and comprehensible also runs the risk of simplification and again a narrowing of accounting's possibilities – including accounting's emancipatory possibilities – typically in terms again of narrowing to a focus upon the management of a capitalistic pecuniary economy. Book-keeping could be conceived of as reducing things and events to categories which could be displayed in their condensed form and be visible at a glance but in the process convey a problematically simplified and biased image of reality (Bowring 1843, viii: 392, Bahmueller 1981: 193). At times Bentham also re-inforces a narrower notion of accounting as a capitalistic instrument that is distant from social democratic control (Gallhofer and Haslam 1994a,b). This could at the very least encourage others more interested in, for instance, the aggrandizement of narrow capitalistic property interests than in Bentham's vision of social well-being. Bentham himself in his work on pauper management could classify the poor as personal stock, the 'stock of working hands' to be surveyed, superintended and directed by the management, a thing-like commodity (UC, cliiia: 144, cf. Hume 1970: 29). And Bentham's proposed prison plan was a commercial proposal and the 250 poor-houses of his proposed National Charity Company were initially to be operated as factories of a commercial and industrial character (Hume 1970, see the critique of Himmelfarb 1984: 78–80). Himmelfarb (1965) stresses Bentham's own commercial interests in such ventures (Boyne 2000).[70]

Such problematically narrow usages of Bentham's accounting or an accounting akin to this would again threaten to be negatively influential today. It is clearly important that those seeking to mobilise accounting publicity to serve a radical project should not only be sensitive and cautious – including in relation to the potential negative effects of an excessive surveillance – but should also recognise the constant tendency for the trajectories of their endeavours to equate to a capture by problematic hegemonic forces. Awareness of this and insights into past endeavours are in themselves helpful. They suggest a constant struggle to seek to ensure a radically engaged accounting, a situation unlikely to equate to a smooth transformation.

Further examples of tensions in Bentham's mobilising of accounting publicity that continue to be of potential significance today are his handlings of expertise and facticity. While he advocates a challenging of expertise and seeks to ensure that expert practices are accountable to the people, his very own advocacy of accounting is ironically consistent with the promotion of a mystifying expertise that is distant from the public. His excessive praise of book-keeping can be taken to help grant it a status and position in society from which it might be distanced from the control of the people at large, including through displacing any popular critical questioning of accounting (see UC, cliiia: 33–4). Bentham's location of accounting in a scientific materialistic philosophic reasoning and in a scientifically derived legislation could have helped contribute to the notion of accounting as an expertise distant from the people (cf. Hume 1970, 1981, Bahmueller 1981, Baskin 1988, Gallhofer and Haslam 1991, 1994a: 269–70, note 39, see Bentham 1993).[71] Bentham held in *Chrestomathia* that those following the Chrestomathic programme, which prominently included book-keeping as a difficult, high-level, subject, would secure the 'possessor a proportion-able share of general respect' (Bentham 1816, Chrestomathic Instruction Tables: table I) in this regard. If Bentham's texts on accounting in part ironically encourage the enveloping of accounting by a cloud of mystifying expertise, this nevertheless is also accompanied by the giving to accounting of an aura of facticity. The latter as well as the former constitute forces that help alienate many people from accounting, displacing democratic possibilities in and through accounting and diluting or dissolving accounting's emancipatory possibilities. Contradicting himself elsewhere, Bentham in some texts portrays accounting as uncontroversial and factual (see Bentham 1816, 1817: table V), portrayals which could still displace critical attention from accounting and its functioning today (cf. Gallhofer and Haslam 1991). It is sometimes as if accounting is beyond the political. Letwin (1965: 188) emphasises such a tendency in Bentham's work more generally, a tendency to reduce politics to an 'impersonal, foolproof system … [to] … supposed … science'. Bentham expressed at times especially strong preferences that accounts be what he termed 'facts' rather than 'opinions' and that accounts be in numerical and tabular form (consistent with the 'tabular-statement principle') (see Davidoff and Hall 1987, Gallhofer and Haslam 1994a: 251–4). He here arguably contributes to a displacement of alternative accountings that were less restricted by such a matter of form and were relatively more emancipated (see Edwards 1989 on the varieties of form in the historical context). Bentham may also here again facilitate the domination of a narrow financial as well as quantitative accounting over alternative possibilities. The danger of further embracing the narrower possibilities remains today. As ways forward here we should take Bentham's concerns to place accounting under the control of the people more seriously. A struggle to overcome mystical expertise and to problematise and see beyond an often narrow facticity can be given greater emphasis on an agenda seeking to push forward an accounting that would be emancipatory.

In our view, one can learn from an analysis of the deficiencies of Bentham's accounting project, reflect on what can go wrong and seek to develop Bentham's way of seeing and strategies in ways cognisant of more recent theoretical developments. Yet, it is also our view that one can embrace a way of seeing Bentham on accounting that is cognisant of the positive potentialities beyond the grasp of those critical interventions that in effect displace such potentialities from our attention: Bentham's envisioning of an accounting publicity that would be emancipatory, an envisioning that is very much integral to his wider radical project, can still serve as a basic source of insight, inspiration and stimulus today, a radical model, as our main analysis here has brought out. Bentham's vision, as others, has no necessary class belongingness in its practical articulation. It is a locus of struggle. Bentham's modern vision of a radical accounting that would be emancipatory constitutes a key historical intervention but one of continuing relevance. It should inspire us in the struggle to align accounting and emancipation as well as remind us of its historical longevity. In brief, Bentham identified basic social problems and posed ways forward that included giving a high profile to accounting publicity, some two centuries ago. In effect, the basics of his vision and its radical possibilities have been resisted by problematic hegemonic forces for some time now. The negative image of Bentham has in some ways served those forces well, albeit often unintentionally. We hold that a more balanced vision and radical interpretation of Bentham can better serve a radical project in and through accounting, one that aligns accounting and emancipation in more positive terms.

3 Accounting and emancipatory practice

The mobilising of accounting by socialist agitators of the late nineteenth century

> ... public attention will be drawn to the subject, and, when all is said, public opinion is a force which cannot be defied even by the greatest capitalist.
> (*The Labour Elector*, 22 June 1889: 12)

Critical analyses have typically emphasised how accounting is shaped and captured by hegemonic forces, thus serving the relatively powerful. Accounting has often been portrayed as serving capitalistic forces in tensions between capital and labour (see discussions in Ogden and Bougen 1985, Lehman and Tinker 1987, Gallhofer and Haslam 1991). In such analyses, however, there is a danger that accounting is simply appreciated as a crude reflection of the interests of prevailing and basically repressive forces. Our concern here is to emphasise that accounting is more ambiguously located. It has emancipatory dimensions and possibilities. Even the conventional 'actually existing' accounting of practice has emancipatory dimensions and/can, in particular contexts, come to function as a more emancipatory force. Exploring accounting's actual functioning in historical contexts can indicate an emancipatory potential. Such analysis can foster encouragement to those engaged with accounting as praxis and yield insights for such praxis. Here, we focus upon accounting's mobilisation by socialist agitators in the context of industrial and socio-political tensions in late nineteenth century Britain, particularly focusing upon the work of the prominent activist Henry Hyde Champion but also giving some attention to a campaign of Annie Besant that Champion helped inspire. In our analysis we indicate accounting's potential to function more on behalf of the relatively oppressed and to serve an emancipatory project.

Britain in the mid-1880s: some key contextual dimensions

The social, political, economic and cultural landscape of Britain in the mid-1880s was a context of turmoil and crisis. It constituted a context ridden by conflicts and tensions that were, in significant ways, becoming more manifest. Britain, beginning to lose some of its domination of world markets while also effected by serious economic cycles, experienced an economic downturn from the early 1870s that continued through to the end of the century. Debates about the end of Victorian progress were fuelled. Prices and profits were generally depressed and production restrained.

According to Callaghan (1990: 4), the 1880s was a decade 'when ... unemployment became a problem ... when the modern idea of "unemployment" and "unemployed" came into common usage'. For labour, if generally wages rose slightly during the late nineteenth century, a benefit for those in work, they remained extremely low, scarcely changing from the 1870s. And any rise, given the context, was often offset in terms of labour experience by longer hours under enhanced disciplinary management and bad conditions (Daunton 2000). The 1880s was a decade of serious industrial unrest in Britain (Beaver 1985: 64). Trades Councils often negotiated on behalf of workers in disputes, mainly in support of relatively skilled working men. Senior labour activists such as Keir Hardie sought the establishment of tribunals for the settlement of labour disputes (see *Common Sense*, 15 July 1887: 54). The trade union movement, struggling for better wages and conditions, gathered pace. This was a period of mass unions – the 'Match Girls' strike', which helps constitute one of our case studies here, is often seen as the harbinger of new model unions for unskilled workers (Soldon 1978, Beaver 1985). Protest against poverty and unemployment was evident on the streets. Riots were increasingly manifest, especially in London (Clayton 1926: 26–8, Callaghan 1990: 5, Hopkins 1995: 143).

In the 1880s, a growing concern about poverty and poor conditions manifested and went beyond those immediately effected by it. According to Beatrice Webb 'mass poverty' had become one of the burning issues of the 1880s and 1890s (Callaghan 1990: 4). Indeed, as Hopkins (1995: 141) points out, by the late 1880s the middle classes had come to recognise poverty as a social problem to address. The growing concern was reflected in attempts to investigate poverty and depravation if these also helped constitute the concern. Mass poverty as well as labour experience were exposed by numerous social investigators, many of whom, whether social reformers, political agitators, religious activists or journalists, were motivated by a concern to see some social change. Andrew Mearns' *The Bitter Cry of Outcast London* (1883), to be followed by Charles Booth's *Life and Labour of the People of London* (17 volumes, 1889–1903) and William Booth's *In Darkest England and the Way Out* (1890),[1] are notable texts documenting the extent of deprivation in London (Hopkins 1995: 140–1, cf. Preston and Oakes 2001). The first volume of Charles Booth's study could document that '35 per cent of Tower Hamlet's 900,000 residents were in a condition of "poverty sinking into want"' (Callaghan 1990: 7).[2] On the same theme, Engels commented: 'The East End of London is an ever spreading pool of stagnant misery and desolation, of starvation when out of work, and degradation, physical and moral, when in work' (*Commonweal*, 1 March 1885; cited in Jacobs 1950: 48).

Such were the general concerns with poverty that, according to Callaghan (1990: 5), 'a significant body of opinion within the intelligentsia ... moved towards advocacy of greater state intervention'.[3] In this context a Liberal government and administration philosophically having an anti-interventionist rhetoric and much occupied with affairs in Ireland was at least moved to appoint a Royal Commission to investigate the depression in trade and industry in 1886 (Hopkins 1995: 138–41).[4] The government also came to appoint a House of Lords Select Committee (sitting between 1888 and 1890) to inquire into 'sweating', the term used to express work involving excessive hours of severe toil for low wages. The committee was particularly to highlight the low wages paid, wages insufficient to sustain a life outside poverty.

According to Meacham (1987: ix), a social reform movement sought to address the 'increasingly complex social problems generated by advanced capitalism. International competition, industrial obsolescence and technological change, chronic under-employment, and urban decay were forcing social critics and reformers to rethink older attitudes and prepare new solutions'. Charitable and related activity grew with the unemployment and the growing concern about poverty (Callaghan 1990: 4). Several bodies arose to have distinct social and political missions. One instance is Toynbee Hall (after the Victorian social reformer Arnold Toynbee), the educational and investigative institution founded in the East End by the Reverend Barnett, vicar of St Jude's, Whitechapel (Pimlott 1985), to establish a link between university people and London's East End poor (Briggs and Macartney 1984: 1). As a promotional pamphlet of 1888 put it:

> Toynbee Hall ... was the outcome of a series of meetings and discussions in Oxford on the condition of the labouring classes, and the remedies which lay more especially within the grasp of university men. It is therefore neither a purely charitable, a purely social, a purely educational, nor, we may add, a purely disinterested institution. It is rather a ... [body seeking] ... friendship and co-operation between the universities and the so-called masses, and an attempt to place such leisure and knowledge as we may possess at the service of those who need them, while by practical association with the life of a working city, we obtain some of the necessary data for dealing with the great social questions of the day.
>
> (Toynbee Hall 1888: 3)

In 1888, in a speech reflecting upon the achievements of the previous four years, Barnett could report as Warden that 'Toynbee Hall was now inhabited by twenty men, and was a centre of education to which some 1,000 learners were drawn every week' (*East London Observer*, 23 June 1888: 7). Beyond facilitating education, including through making available lecture theatres and class rooms and providing lodgings for students, Toynbee Hall was keen to support labour in 'industrial disputes resulting from the first attempts by previously unorganised workers in ... [unskilled] ... trades, to achieve acceptable working conditions.' Workers and trade unionists were given rooms to help them 'to shape their strategies, and to appeal to a sympathetic public' (Briggs and Macartney 1984: 45, Meacham 1987: 67).

Also increasingly evident was the growth of more formally organised political movements aimed at seeking better conditions for the poor and the working class. There was a revival in the 1880s of socialist movements in Britain. Many of the middle classes were receptive. 1884 was a significant year with the adoption of a socialist programme by the Christian Socialists of the Anglican Guild (Clayton 1926: 9) and the formation of several other socialist bodies, which apart from the middle classes also attracted prominent working class unionists. These socialist groups shared a general concern with the interrelationship between the capitalistic system, poverty and exploitation. They differed, however, in their goals and objectives and strategies for overcoming the negative impact of capitalism. The Social Democratic Federation (SDF), set up in 1884 under the leadership of H. M. Hyndman, had clearly socialistic objectives such as 'the Socialisation of the Means of Production, Distribution, and Exchange to be controlled by a Democratic State in the interests of the entire community, and the complete Emancipation of Labour from the domination of Capitalism and Landlordism, with the establishment of Social and Economic Equality between the Sexes' (cited in Clayton 1926: 22).[5] The Socialist League, which was set up under the leadership of William Morris in 1884 out of a discontent of former SDF members with SDF policies, was more international, revolutionary and anti-State in orientation and, as Tzusuki (1961: 57) put it, aimed at a 'genuine revolution in the future'. The Fabian Society, also established in 1884, aimed to work for a reconstruction of the social system by placing wealth in the hands of the community for general well-being (Cole 1961). Although the Fabian Society propagated socialism, it differed in its emphasis and strategies. Strongly opposed to violent revolution, it pursued, especially after 1886, a policy of gradual democratic reform (Hulse 1970: 115). It did not advocate forming a socialist political party on the grounds that its work would change the thinking and policies of the then main political parties (Hopkins 1995: 142, 2000: 106).

The 1880s also witnessed a concern – in the context of a growing women's movement – with the working and living conditions of women. The women's movement, attempting to overcome class barriers, drew particular attention to the problems experienced by paid working class women (Bolt 1993: 174–5). Recognising that in the sphere of work women's interests were not represented by the exclusionary policies of the male trade unions, attempts were made to organise women. Women trade unionism was coming to be increasingly active with women very prominent amongst the poorest paid workers. The Women's Protective and Provident League (WPPL), founded in 1874 by Emma Paterson as a response to the exclusionary policies in existence and motivated by feminist principles and a concern to effect cross-class co-operation, was concerned to fight for the establishment of female trade unions through journalistic and strike activity. It had a strong belief that women would gain in confidence while organising themselves (Boston 1987: 30–5, Bolt 1993: 174–5).

The strategies employed by those wanting to overcome poverty, whether motivated by Christian ethics, socialist principles, feminist concerns or philanthropic leaning, show one striking similarity: the concern to make visible, through the detailed provision of 'facts', the extent of poverty and depravation. The social investigations of the late nineteenth century, such as for example Charles Booth's *Life and Labour of the People of England* (*supra*), as in the case of Dickens' fiction and journalism (Fraser *et al.* 1999), were to some extent inspired by the belief, a belief promoted in Bentham's philosophy and in the nineteenth century statistical movement (see Cullen 1975), that a proper knowledge of the 'facts' would help the process of overcoming poverty and poor conditions. People would begin to see that environmental factors were influential to social outcomes, whatever be the need to improve people's morals.[6] The work of the Fabian Society was very much influenced by this way of thinking.

For Callaghan (1990: 39), 'the Fabians depended on the simple proposition that "facts were facts" and could be recognised by all rational politicians of good faith whatever their ideological allegiances'.[7] The body especially emphasised engendering debate through educational activity and making things visible in the public sphere through journalism, public debate and education, involving collecting and disseminating information on social questions. It organised lectures and printed essays on socialism and current social issues in its *Fabian Tracts*. Its strong commitment to publicity indicate the Benthamite as well as Marxist roots of the socialist movement of the time. According to Hulse (1970: 115) this reflects especially Sidney Webb's influence for he had 'brought to Fabianism the moderation and the respectability of the Benthamite Utilitarian tradition, which in the previous 50 years had been substantially modified in the person and work of Mill'. Whilst this praxis of publicity was an emphasis of the Fabians, it was also supported and practised by other socialists. Socialists mobilised newspapers in their attempt to increase visibility of the injustices of capitalism. Many socialist bodies had their own newspapers and journals attempting to increase visibility of the injustices of capitalism. These papers included *Justice* (of the SDF) and *Commonweal* (of the Socialist League). Other newspapers and journals with a socialist orientation included the *Christian Socialist*, *Common Sense*, *The Labour Elector* (all three edited by H. H. Champion), *Our Corner* and *The Link* (both edited by Annie Besant) and Belfort Bax's *Today* (Callaghan 1990: 45). The WPPL was concerned to mobilise facts in their attempt to make visible and draw attention to the plight of working women.

Established accounting practice in this context functioned substantively as a capitalistic artefact. Although the Liberal, Laissez-Faire polity and rhetoric that was of some influence in late nineteenth century Britain helped to shape the particular form of accounting regulation in the 1880s, there were forces at work providing key incentives favourable to accounting disclosure and publicity (see Parker 1990, Edwards, 1992, Jones and Aiken 1995, Walker 1996). A firm that had gone public, especially if listed on the stock exchange, often deemed it easier to attract capital if publishing accounts. Further, it would often be felt that any progress in a company's economic position would more easily translate into an increased share price with the appropriate accounting publicity. In this regard, key dimensions of disclosure content of interest to shareholders included whether assets exceeded liabilities, the size of the profit and how much of the profit was to be paid out as a dividend. Often much of it was. Late nineteenth century shareholders liked to receive tangible benefits in the form of dividend income from their shareholdings (see Edwards 1989, 1992 cf. Toms 1998). Such recognition of the importance of accounting publicity has a long history (Haslam 1991, Gallhofer and Haslam 1995). Accounting reports, more especially of listed companies, would thus often be published at shareholder general meetings and find their way into the financial pages of the press.

Such accounts may have been regulated largely by imperfect market forces but they had attained an aura of facticity giving them a particular weight in the context. Further, by the 1880s, auditors signing off these business facts or accounts, who denoted themselves chartered accountants, were likely indicating their status as members of a formally organised profession (see Edwards 1989: 277), a status that would impact upon the status of the accounts. And while the law did not require even limited liability companies, of the general form, to publish accounts, many companies did include provisions to publish accounts of some sort, often in connection with shareholder general meetings. Such provisions could have attained a legal-like status, enhancing a noble aura of substance in the context (Gallhofer and Haslam 1991). This latter factor was enhanced by the significance of the Companies Act of 1862, still in force in the 1880s, which contained model articles of association specifying that companies were to present a balance sheet in a prescribed format to the annual general meeting (AGM) (to be circulated to members a week before the AGM), to present an income and expenditure account distinguishing between sources of income and categories of expenditure to the AGM, to open their books to inspection by members,[8] and to undergo an annual audit by an auditor, appointed by the members, who was not to be a director of the concern (if they could be a member) and who was to have a right of access to the books and directors and a duty to examine and report on whether the balance sheet was 'full and fair' and gave a 'true and correct view' of the firm's state (Edwards 1989: 192). Such a buttressing through association with the law as well as with the notion of business facts could have held even if in practice many companies, including the larger ones (e.g. listed on the stock exchange), did not adopt the model articles, tending to prefer as much flexibility over disclosure as the law allowed, especially in respect of the accounting (as distinct from the auditing) provisions (see Edwards 1989, 1992, Parker 1990, Toms 1998).

Henry Hyde Champion, common sense and the match girls

Herbert Hyde Champion was amongst the most prominent socialist activists of the 1880s. The son of a Major-General, Champion had initially attended Marlborough College and pursued a distinguished military career but factors such as his disgust at the British imperialism he witnessed (Hyndman 1911: 308, Pelling 1953: Tsuzuki 1961, Thompson 1976: 299), and his reading of the works of Henry George, John Stuart Mill, Marx and Engels, led him to socialist activism. In addition, that he was shown around deprived areas of London by a friend left a particularly deep impression on Champion as he later stresses in his autobiography:

> What I saw in London during those few weeks completely changed the course of my life. Whatever I have done that seems to me, in the retrospect, to have been worth doing – that was the beginning of it.
>
> (Champion 1983: 23)

From the early 1880s he emerged as a key figure in the socialist and labour movements, initially rising to prominence in Christian Socialism and the SDF. He came to work closely with union and labour leaders to campaign for improvements in wages and working conditions and to promote socialism (Whitehead 1983: 17). After his experience of being arrested (along with Hyndman, John Burns and the radical MP Cunnighame Graham) for his involvement in the 'Bloody Sunday' anti-capitalist demonstration about unemployment, he became committed to independent labour representation. Like Engels, he envisaged the latter to be achievable through an alliance of socialists and existing working class organisations (Callaghan 1990: 49, Hopkins 1995: 3). His vision was that radical change towards socialism was achievable through democracy and non-violent action. One of his main themes was to advocate socialistic government action to counter what he saw as the anarchy of market forces (see *Brotherhood*, 24 June 1887: 118–9). Although involved in the SDF and the Fabian Society, Champion was a strong and independent character who in many respects pursued his own projects in the cause of socialist struggle – eventually becoming alienated from the faction-ridden socialist associations of his time (Tsuzuki 1961).

Key to Champion's socialist activism was his communicative ability, something acknowledged by contemporary socialist agitators (Hyndman 1911: 308, 345, Mann 1923, Tillett 1931).[9] He perceived a particular value in exposing through publicity to create awareness of the need for action and to stimulate that action. An article in *Brotherhood* (reprinted from the *Christian World*) puts it as follows:

> Personally Mr. Champion is not one of the "masses" whose cause he advocates. He is a well-to-do employer of labour, who from being convinced of the selfishness and injustice of the system under which honest and industrious men and women are ground to the point of starvation, and too often are pushed over the border-line, has devoted his life to endeavouring to arouse the conscience of the country, and to induce it to re-place the existing system by some better one.
>
> (*Brotherhood*, 24 June 1887: 119)

He threw himself into socialist journalism, becoming editor of the *Christian Socialist* and the SDF's *Justice*. Champion's obituary in *The Times* (2 May 1928) maintained he was 'an exceedingly able writer and the wielder of a caustic pen'.

In May 1887, Champion pursued one of his own projects in founding a journal, *Common Sense*, 'For People with Brains and Hearts'. Not only was its socialist emphasis clear but also the influence of Bentham's advocacy of exposure and publicity. While not formally an organ of any particular political association, the journal's embeddedness in the major socialist currents of the time is reflected in its advertisement of socialist literature[10] and its suggestion to its readers that, if they were interested in joining a political association, they should consider the SDF, the Socialist League, the Fabian Society and the Land Restoration League (see *Common Sense*, 15 July 1887: 56). Citations from philosophers published in the journal also reflected its key socialistic themes. These were to publicise the injustices of the gulf between rich and poor, principally between capitalists and labour/the poor – including emphatically women in these latter categories,[11] and to support state intervention to counter the anarchy of the market place[12] and address social problems. The Benthamite influence upon publicity and exposure as a steer to action is particularly evident in *Common Sense*. This includes the Benthamite facticity and preference for comprehensiveness (see Gallhofer and Haslam 1994a,b).[13] The statistical movement and affiliated currents are drawn upon to support the journal's socialist themes and campaigns so that argument could be communicated as 'undeniable facts' to be received by the reader and society in general as such (*Common Sense*, 15 May 1887).[14] Sismondi's 1826 view that 'political economy is lost in abstraction and enveloped in calculation' is favourably cited in relation to the case for a popular language of science that would be more comprehensive amongst the people. Champion's emphasis on 'facts and figures' and clarity in *Common Sense* echoes the content of his speeches, according to the following report on one of his orations:

> No better champion of the cause – the name and the man fit each other as the hand the glove – could have been found. He is well educated, and does not indulge in random declamation and vituperation. He deals largely in facts and figures, which he leaves to a considerable extent to tell their own tale …
>
> (*Brotherhood*, 24 June 1887: 118–9)

The very first issue of *Common Sense* contrasted experiences of the financially rich and poor in a prominent and striking way, pointing to the injustices involved. Two distinct columns were presented in a format echoing the dichotomous logic integral to conventional financial accounting. The left-hand side depicted 'national wealth' and the right-hand side 'national poverty'. This format was used to contrast an extravagant restaurant bill run up by a wealthy citizen in Paris (£4 0s 6d) with the weekly expenses of a farm labourer and family (14s 9¼d), a report that every fifteenth person in England then accepted relief for poverty and, reflecting one of the journal's strongest themes, reports that female labour was 'wretchedly paid' (*Common Sense*, 15 July 1887: 19).

Champion was very keen to bring out a contrast between high profits/dividends and poor wages/conditions in the case of specific companies and to indicate in such analyses the injustices of the capitalistic system more generally. In doing this he used material already published (e.g. in newspapers) and his own investigative journalism. This included making use of accounting disclosures, typically assembled from reports of AGMs. Aspects of his usage of published accounts are similar to usages by some other labour activists of his time, such as notably Benjamin Jones.[15] Champion's usage was an instance of the usage of accounts in the name of a radical socialist praxis by a prominent figure in the socialist movement. The company he focused most of his attention on in *Common Sense* was that of Bryant and May Limited.

An historical overview of the rise of Bryant and May (a name continuing as a company brand today) is here useful. The rise was remarkable. From a mid-nineteenth century general merchandising partnership, founded by the Quakers that gave it its name, arose a notable match-making concern centred in East London.[16] Bryant's sons came to dominate an aggressively expanding firm that was incorporated in 1884 under the Companies Acts 1862 to 1883 and listed on the stock exchange very shortly thereafter (MDM, 12 June 1884).[17] The Bryant brothers stood to benefit greatly from the company's financial success. They had significant ownership stakes in the company and their remuneration was linked to company profits.[18] Bryant and May was run so as to protect the company's financial position, and also to aggressively expand where possible.[19] Within only a few years the share price soared. From 1885 the share price fluctuated around £15 through to the time Champion made Bryant and May a focus of his analysis, for a period rising to £22 (see the retrospective in *The Statist*, 5 November 1887: 513–4). Dividends of between 20 and 30 per cent on initial nominal capital were being paid in the mid-1880s. Table 3.1 comprises some figures for Bryant and May for the 1880s, the table indicating the close correspondence between accounting profits and dividends.

By the time Champion was turning his attention to Bryant and May, financial commentators were still congratulating the firm on its success. Wilberforce eulogised the company in the 1880s at AGMs, using accounting disclosure – a balance sheet with a summary statement providing information about dividends and transfers to reserves certified as 'a true statement of the Liabilities and Assets' by the auditor, accountant Richard Rabbidge – there presented. Champion brought a different perspective.

Champion's attention was drawn to Bryant and May by its having risen from humble origins – so that the wealth of its founders and their inheritors could be attributed to capitalistic business practice, its continuing to have remarkable financial success in spite of the depressed trade and his view that, in spite of the firm's Quaker origins, modern factory and financial wealth, the firm paid very poor wages in return for work in poor conditions. The majority of employees were women (the 'match girls') coming predominantly from what were the poorer districts of East London, where unemployment was high (see Collett 1889). In any case, match-making in general had long been associated with poor wages and conditions (Lowell 1982). In the early 1860s, the *Commission on the Employment of Children in Industry* had found horrendous employment practices and working conditions in match-making, linking the industry to crude exploitation and serious illness. Some of the negative practices involved home working and, although there is a suggestion that due to automation the numbers involved at Bryant and May had dramatically fallen (Beaver 1985), the company still continued to employ a number of home workers to make match boxes in the mid-1880s.[20] If the accounting disclosure was fairly minimal and investigative journalism was needed to bring to light wages and conditions – these were not subjects of disclosure in the same way as the high shareholder returns! – Champion was determined to elaborate the contrast between those receiving high dividends, capital gains and, in the case of the Bryants, high remuneration, and those who from the same business operations were receiving barely survival wages for their difficult toil.

The first exposé on Bryant and May in *Common Sense* comes under a heading 'Questions that Require Answers' (15 May 1887: 11). The 1886 dividend of £80,000, or 20 per cent of the nominal value of share capital, is highlighted[21] as is the company's high reserve fund,[22] invested in sound securities. The figures are taken from accounts referenced at the AGM of 10 February 1887. The article ends with a question alerting readers to the contrast that is to be exposed: 'What is the average wage of the workers who produced this 20%?' *Common Sense* returns to where it left off on 15 June 1887 (27). An investigator for the paper is reported as having 'made

Table 3.1 Some financial figures for Bryant and May Limited in the 1880s

Six-month ending	Dividend	% on nominal value of issued capital	Dividend per share (s and d)	Income tax rate (%)	Dividend net of tax	Accounting profits	Accounting profits/opening balance of nominal value of shares issued (%)
31/12/84[a]	£18,000	12	6/0	2.5	£17,550	£33,044 6s 0d[c]	22
30/06/85[a]	£22,500	15	7/6	2.917	£21,843.75		
31/12/85[a]	£45,000	30 (221/2)[b]	15	3.333	£43,500	£67,712 5s 0d	22.6
30/06/86	£35,000	171/2	8/9	3.333	£33,833.34		
31/12/86	£45,000	221/2 (20)	11/3	3.333	£43,500	£80,217 12s 8d	20.1
30/07/87	£35,000	171/2	8/9	3.125	£33,906.25		
31/12/87	£45,000	221/2 (20)	11/3	2.917	£43,687.50	£80,136 13s 3d	20
30/06/88	£30,000	15	7/6	2.708	£29,187.50		
31/12/88	£40,000	20 (171/2)	10	2.5	£39,000	£69,714 3s 5d	17.4
30/06/89	£30,000	15	7/6	2.5	£29,250		
31/12/89	£40,000	20 (171/2)	10	2.5	£39,000	£69,648 15s 3d	17.4

Notes

a Shares issued: 60,000. By 31 December 1885, 80,000 shares had been issued but the table calculates accounting profits/opening balance of the nominal value of shares issued.

b Figure in brackets = % return for year. With the exception of 1884, note the similarity between the figures in this column and the last column of the table, indicating that typically a high proportion of the accounting profit is distributed as a dividend.

c Prior to writing off preliminary expenses £1,187 10s 0d; New Building a/c £1,396 19s 8d; to reserve fund (invested in consuls) £10,000.

inquiries at Bow' and there having uncovered insights into the wages and experiences of a Bryant and May match-box maker. He indicates sweating, finding:

> ... a woman who earns a living by making on the piece-work system, the boxes in which the "Ruby" matches are placed. The name and address of the woman in question are very much at the service of anyone who might like to verify the statements[23]... The firm supplies the thin slips of wood out of which the tray and the outside is made; also the paper and labels. The women supply labour, paste, firing to dry the finished boxes and the hemp wherewith to tie them up in a bundle of 24. They are paid for 6 bundles of 24 or 144 boxes, if delivered without any flaw (the work is carefully examined), twopence-farthing. A woman can earn at this work, if she is quick and works uninterruptedly, about 9d in 11 hours or 3 farthings an hour, which, as our readers will know, is the usual rate of wages for female labour on the sweating system ... Illustrations of the hardships entailed by this inhuman wage-slavery can hardly be required. But our informant had in the week previous to our representative's enquiry been able to complete only 3 gross of boxes. This was owing to her youngest child requiring her care. It was dying, and the mother could not neglect it even to keep up the 20%. It died and the dead body was lying in the single room while these facts were being narrated. The mother took her poor 6³/₄d worth of work to the factory, and was sent back with 4¹/₂d because in one of the gross a single matchbox had its label slightly torn.
>
> (*Common Sense*, 15 June 1887: 27)

This state of affairs is sharply contrasted with the returns to the shareholders. If the company had so far managed to avoid having the typical image of sweaters[24] they were sweaters, nonetheless:

> The peculiarly infamous feature of this case is, that it is not a struggling middleman who grinds down this helpless women but a company returning 20% on an enormous and presumably partly fictitious capital.[25]
>
> (*Common Sense*, 15 June 1887: 27)

The terms offered to Bryant and May employees are reported as comparing unfavourably with those offered by other firms: 'The woman who informed our representative states that other firms give better terms to their employé.' At the same time, the difficulties of accessing information were stressed. It was especially difficult to access the girls working in the factory:

> While some of the girls who work inside the factory on weekly wages were being interviewed at the gate in Fairfield Road, a man named Robertson, a foreman or overseer of some sort, came out: "Here, get inside out of this" and the girls went in humbly. We can therefore not give in this issue any information as to the weekly wages paid to regular hands.
>
> (*Common Sense*, 15 June 1887: 27)

The article reports that the journal was considering mobilising the publicity for a boycott on Bryant and May's products – a call for an ethical consumerism: 'Enquiries on the subject are being made with a view to organising a boycott on the goods of Bryant and May, and the purchase instead of the matches of manufacturers who pay better wages.' A comment on the matchbox maker helps to bring out the journal's preference for state regulation with a note of irony: 'The woman, in conversation, did not appear to have fears of her *liberty* being further curtailed by the interference of the State.' The journal also promises to bring further pressure to bear through its analysis by stating a commitment to expose more, including names of the company's financiers: 'We shall be glad to have the name and address of any persons, known to be shareholders, profiting by this system of torture, also any genuine information as to the earlier history of the firm' (*Common Sense*, 15 June 1887: 27).

Common Sense indeed returns to the story on 15 July 1887 (42) under the heading 'Who are the shareholders of Bryant and May?' and a citation from *Proverbs*, XXII, 1, 2: 'A good name is rather to be chosen than great riches and loving favour rather than silver and gold. The rich and the poor meet together: the Lord is the maker of them all.' A particular concern here is to highlight the hypocrisy of ministers of religion owning shares in Bryant and May. Fourteen ministers sharing 'in the 20% and 22½% dividends' are listed. Again, the journal calls for greater and increased exposure:

> We trust that any readers who have the opportunity will, on every possible occasion, advertise the fact that these persons who preach on Sunday "Come unto me, all ye that labour and are heavy laden, and I will give you rest", in their weekday practice countenance a form of industrial tyranny which alters the text into: "Come unto us, ye who labour, and we will pay you three farthing an hour."
>
> (*Common Sense*, 15 June 1887: 42)

The readers are promised that a copy of the issue in which this article appeared would be sent to the address of the ministers listed. After listing other shareholders the article attacks the capitalistic financiers:

> Judging them even by the conventional standards of fair dealing these gentlemen are sucking profit in a manner every bit as dirty as a money lender, who extorts 30% from the necessitous, or promoter of bubble companies. It is allowed by law, and they do not scruple to take advantage of the power they have to oppress the widow and orphan, in order to swell their dividends. If they have any scruples they will, now the matter is directly before them, clear their names of the reproach of grinding the faces of the poor.
>
> (*Common Sense*, 15 June 1887: 42)

Champion added to the publicity about Bryant and May by including the case in a speech he delivered by invitation to the annual Church (of England) Congress, a significant arena, at Wolverhampton on 5 October 1887.[26] During his speech, Champion again exposes the stark contrast between the high financial returns to the shareholders and the poor returns to the workers, again using accounting publicity. He also pointedly refers to the shareholdings of Church ministers.[27] According to *The Record's* account of the speech, described as a fair representation and reprinted by *Common Sense* (15 October 1887), Champion introduced his focus upon Bryant and May in the context of contrasting the experiences of the materially rich and poor more generally and through an exchange with his audience:

> Many of his points were most heartily taken up by the meeting, particularly where he contrasted great riches with extreme poverty ... Another little episode arose when he touched the Bryant and May incident. There were a number of clergymen, he said, who were shareholders in that match-making company and the dividends on the capital were as high as 20%. "Hear, hear", exclaimed a voice on the platform, and the meeting interpreting it as coming from one of the clerical shareholders laughed heartily. "That gentleman seems to think it a capital joke", said Mr Champion, with some severity, "but let him wait a moment. The employés are paid at the rate of one penny an hour. Now he may have his joke".[28]
>
> (*Common Sense*, 15 October 1887: 90)

The publicity concerning Bryant and May was also taken up through other media, especially after the Church Congress speech (*Common Sense*, 15 September 1887 evidences earlier take up). Church newspapers published articles sympathetic to the match girls. *The Christian* of 28 October 1887 (12, notes and comments) cites an article in the *Birmingham Weekly Post* regarding 'the firm of match-makers alluded to at the Church Congress.' After repeating the story, the paper declares: 'If these assertions are not true, let ... Bryant and May ... nail them to the counter at once; if they are facts, the time is come for another Wilberforce to emancipate another race of slaves ...' (*The Christian*, 28 October 1887: 12).

In relation to a similar case, *The Christian* advocates a form of ethical consumerism based on publicity and suggests that shareholders ought to 'at least have the satisfaction of knowing that their profits were not being made at the expense of worn out human bodies and minds' (14 October 1887: 6–7). Amongst those encouraged to add to the discourse was the Reverend J. Wright. *The Family Churchman* published an article on 2 November 1887 by Wright, 'Christ's Poor; and their claim on Christ's People', which also calls for ethical consumerism (22). The article was very much in the style of Champion, exposing the contrasts between the situations of rich and poor. In the case of Bryant and May the same figures as in Champion's analysis are used, except that the piece rate for 144 boxes is upped to 2½d (since typical hourly rate of pay is estimated, this may be a printing error). The same contrast with the 20 per cent dividend is made. Additionally, Wright suggests that we can only begin to appreciate the 'abject wretchedness of unskilled workers in large towns' (221) if consideration is given to the rent they have to pay. In the East End this was from 3s to 3s 6d a week (the matchbox makers' weekly pay having been estimated at 3s per week) (221).

Others were taking notice. The campaign started, it seems, to have some impact. Champion, perhaps to encourage others, is keen to cite evidence of his publicity having some effect and he prints a letter pointing to an 'ethical investment' concern engendered by campaigns such as his in respect of Bryant and May:

> M. H. writes – "you would be interested to hear that a stockbroker tells me that no less than six people had recently been to him to enquire whether their money was invested in undertakings which would bear the scrutiny of humane persons".
>
> (*Common Sense*, 15 August 1887: 59)

It was doubtless publicity engendered by the council speech that brought the criticism to the attention of the Bryant and May board. Carkeet recorded the publicity in his diary. Had he not been aware of it through his own reading of the papers, he would have found out soon enough. Several people wrote in to Bryant and May as a result of the publicity. Mr F. Abbot 'asks whether a statement made more than once in the church he attended with regards to wages paid to box makers and the dividend paid to share holders is true' (SD 24 October 1887). Charles McComas writes regarding 'statements made at the recent Church Congress at Wolverhampton which he thinks should be answered, the wages paid per hour and per gross to the matchbox makers' (26 October 1887). Stephen Bourne of the *Central Vigilance Society for the Repression of Immorality* (a body concerned to explore all ways in which prostitution might be eradicated and in this connection concerned about reports of the sweating of female labour) wrote to the chairman 'in reference to the statements made at the late Church Congress' (SD 28 October 1887). Mrs Mary Allen 'further discusses the Dividend and Wages question' (29 October 1887). A letter from George Ireland specifically 'calls our attention to an article in *The Family Churchman* contributed by the Reverend J. Wright … the poverty and wages of the East End of London' (10 November 1887). And a shareholder was prompted after the Church Congress to request of the company that they calculate the average wage paid to the workers.[29] Letters expressing concern continued into 1888. On 26 May 1888, the company received a letter from Reverend M. J. Baugh, Salcombe Regis, that expressed an ethical investment concern. He hesitated '… [to invest] … in the company in consequence of unpleasant statements about the ill payment of match-making children and would like to be assured'.[30]

The Fabian Society, the boycott of Bryant and May and a further investigation

> … comfortable people object to the veil being torn off the putrefying wounds of society.
>
> (*The Link*, 30 June 1888: 1)

Champion sought to enhance his campaign by bringing it to the attention of the Fabian Society. Champion attended a Fabian Society meeting, held on 15 June 1888, at which Clementina Black, campaigner for women's emancipation, gave a lecture on the plight of female labour and advocated a form of ethical consumerism. She sought the formation of a Consumers' league pledged only to buy from shops certified 'clean' from unfair wages (Besant 1938: 334). According to Besant:[31]

> At a meeting of the Fabian Society, Miss Clementina Black gave a special lecture on Female labour, and urged the formation of a Consumers' League, pledged only to buy from shops certified "clean" from unfair wages. H. H. Champion in the discussion that followed, drew attention to the wages paid by Bryant & May (limited), while paying an enormous dividend to their shareholders, so that the value of the original £5 shares was quoted at £18 7s 6d.[32]
>
> (Besant 1938: 334)

Champion took the opportunity to propose a boycott of Bryant and May. The resolution was seconded by Herbert Burrows, another leading Fabian, and carried by the meeting. Annie Besant, already a Fabian socialist, was asked by the meeting to investigate the case further.[33] If, like Champion's investigator, finding access difficult, Besant with Burrows did interview some of the factory girls. New material for publicity emerged. On 23 June 1888 Besant published an article in *The Link* (2), a radical half penny weekly she edited and had established with W. T. Stead[34] with the objective of serving and giving voice to the poor.[35] Its motto, from Victor Hugo, reflected a pro-active concern to change debilitating environments and an Enlightenment concern to make visible to promote change for betterment, a concern that Besant, as a leading Fabian, identified with as a matter of praxis and struggle:

> The people are silence. I will be the advocate of this silence. I will speak for the dumb. I will speak of the small to the great, and of the feeble to the strong ... I will speak for all the despairing silent ones. I will interpret this stammering; I will interpret the grumblings, the murmurs, the tumults of crowds, the complaints ill-pronounced, and all these creeds of beasts that, through ignorance and through suffering, man is forced to utter ... I will be the Word of the People. I will be the bleeding mouth whence the gag is snatched out. I will say everything.
>
> (*The Link*, 30 June 1888: 1)

Besant follows Champion in being concerned to use accounting disclosure to emphasise the exploitation. Printing a version of the resolution calling for a boycott of Bryant and May, she begins by elaborating on the sharp and unacceptable contrast between the high accounting profits/dividends and the poor terms of the match girls. By reference to the factory work, Besant explores 'how the money is made with which the monstrous dividends are paid'. She detailed out the dangers of the various tasks carried out, the poor wages and the fines and deductions applied in case of mistakes. She puts the contrast in terms she believed would have an impact:

> Such is a bald account of one form of white slavery as it exists in London. With chattel slaves Mr. Bryant could not have made his huge fortune, for he could not

have fed, clothed, and housed them for 4s a week each, and they would have had a definite money value which would have served as a protection. But who cares for the fate of these white wage slaves? Born in slums, driven to work while still children, undersized because underfed, oppressed because helpless, flung aside as soon as worked out, who cares if they die or go on the streets, provided only that the Bryant and May shareholders get their 23 per cent, and Mr. Theodore Bryant can erect statues and buy parks?[36]

(*The Link*, 23 June 1888: 2)

Besant closes with a further call to boycott Bryant and May: '... let us strive to touch their consciences, that is, their pockets, and let us at least avoid being "partakers of their sins", by abstaining from using their commodities' (*The Link*, 23 June 1888). Pro-actively, Besant distributed her article to the workers as they left the factory. In a subsequent article 'White and Black Lists' (*The Link*, 30 June 1888: 1), Besant called for the boycott of all companies engaged in unethical practices, more specifically paying unfair wages and providing poor working conditions. She advocated publishing lists of companies that 'ought to be severely encouraged or discountenanced'. An interesting refinement of this advocacy was that she wanted the lists constructed by reference to localities. Thus, recognising that local operations of companies would resonate with local populations, the lists would at least emphasise different companies to different local populations. This was understood as exerting more pressure:

If such a list could be published for each locality public opinion might be brought to bear very effectively on the manufacturers and sellers of goods, for a premium would be put on honesty and fair dealing, while grasping avarice and tyranny would cease "to pay".

(*The Link*, 30 June 1888: 1)

Besant also called for comprehensive disclosure of wages and working conditions. This had to be backed by force of law because, while Besant suggested in her article that companies more appropriately on the white list would be more forthcoming and furnish the publicity, the construction of a black list would be a difficult struggle. Workers would not be very willing to talk for fear of the sack and authors would be restricted by the fear of being taken to court under the libel law, the operation of which, under the jury system, was captured by capitalistic interests:

Now an exposure of the way in which successful firms make their fortunes is not likely to be popular among the class from which juries are drawn; it is the very poor who are the victims of the oppression, and these do not find their way on to juries ...

(*The Link*, 30 June 1888: 1)

And she adds, in an expression with clear affinity to Bentham: '... comfortable people object to the veil being torn off the putrefying wounds of society' (*The Link*,

30 June 1888: 1). In early July 1888, Besant and Burrows tried to increase exposure of the Bryant and May case by writing letters to the press. These letters reported allegations that the company had located two workers who were key to giving information to Besant, about such matters as wages, fines and breaches of the Truck Act,[37] and sacked them. Three papers published the letter (*The Pall Mall Gazette*, *The Star* and *The Echo*, 3 July 1888).[38]

Bryant and May continued to monitor the publicity. The article was noted in the secretary's diary at Bryant and May soon after publication: 'See "The Link" of this date – No. 21 – published at ¹⁄2d – containing reference to "The Fabian Society" and Miss Clementina Black. Also scurrilous article by Annie Besant' (SD 23 June 1888).[39] The government also monitored, in a context of more general industrial unrest, a potential disturbance, encouraged by socialists, threatening disruption of a sizeable business. The Inspector of Factories, Bowling, visited Bryant and May on 27 June 1888 very shortly after the article's publication. Bowling is reported as being concerned to see 'by himself as to the Trash or otherwise of certain statements made in articles in *The Link*' (SD 23 June 1888). Unhappy about the disclosure of wages and fines in Besant's article of 23 June 1888, Bryant and May threatened legal action, confirming an aspect of Besant's concern expressed in her later article of 30 June (*supra*) (see *The Link*, 7 July 1888: 3). Bryant and May noted the three letters published reporting the allegations concerning the sackings. The secretary sent letters the following day denying the allegations and claiming that other factors were involved in the sackings (SD 3, 4 July 1888).

Accounting disclosure, the match girls' strike, unionisation and reflections upon accounting as praxis

Tensions at Bryant and May were mounting, culminating in a strike of the match girls on 5 July 1888. At first the 'box fillers in Victoria Factory had struck work' but this led to 'the hands in all other Factories going out' (MDM, 5 July 1888, see also SD of the same date). The strikers and the political activists supporting them maintained that the sackings were the final straw giving rise to the strike, thus indicating that 'White Slavery in London' had significant consequences. According to some reports the sackings were also after the girls 'refused to sign a declaration that the information given in Besant's article was false' (*The Link*, 7 July 1888: 3).[40] The role of Besant and related agitation in contributing to the tension at Bryant and May is confirmed by the way Besant was subsequently asked to support the strike. Between one and two hundred strikers marched to the office of *The Link* in Fleet Street and sent a deputation to see Besant. The day after the strike commenced, the government revealed its interest. The factory inspector called again at Bryant and May requesting that information in respect of the strike be passed on to the Home Office.[41]

Besant, with Burrows, responded to the call from the strikers. They sought to produce further visibility to pressurise Bryant and May.[42] Public meetings were organised, attempts made to enlist the support of MPs and *The Link* was mobilised for the cause. With expanding interest, Bryant and May's industrial strife now being a significant news item, including the particular interest in the case of a group from Toynbee Hall, further and more widespread publicity was thus to be given to the discrepancy between the dividends/accounting profits and the wages/conditions. Agitators continued to mobilise accounting in the dispute. At a public meeting at Mile End Waste, the following resolution was carried:

> That this meeting affirms the truth of the statements in the articles by Annie Besant, entitled "White Slavery in London", in the Link of 23rd; that it protests against the falsehoods circulated by the Bryant and May Company, and against the shamefully low wages and the shamefully high dividends paid by them. That this meeting calls on the Home Secretary to enforce the Law against the Bryant and May Company, and requests him to receive a deputation of work girls on the subject. That a union be found by the match makers.[43]
>
> (Besant and Burrows in *The Link*, 7 July 1888: 3)

Besant is reported as declaring at the meeting that 'the girls get from 4s to 13s weekly while the firm paid 38½% dividend' (*St. James' Gazette*, 9 July 1888: 11). Consistent with this, according to Beaver (1985: 66) a giant matchbox was paraded at one of the demonstrations carrying the words '38% dividend'. In this regard, the theme of ministers of religion investing in Bryant and May apparently featured in the demonstrations. According to *The Globe* of Thursday 19 July 1888: 1, a large matchbox carried on demonstrations beared 'on top a dummy clergyman in an attitude of supplication'. It seems initially difficult to locate where the figure of 38.5 per cent, or 38 per cent, came from, these not being reconcilable to the accounting profits disclosed or the reported dividend as a percentage of the nominal value of shares issued. While it is possible it was misreported or arrived at in some especially eccentric way, it is likely that the figure was computed by taking into account capital gains as well as dividends. Besant publicised the high capital gain as well as the high dividend in seeking to expose the company (*supra*).[44] Besant is reported as again calling for an ethical consumerism at the meeting and as underlining her high valuation of publicity by claiming 'to have stopped the fines inflicted on the girls by giving publicity to them' (*St. James's Gazette*, 9 July 1888: 11).

As resolved by the Mile End Waste meeting, a deputation of girls accompanied by Besant and Burrows went to the House of Commons 'to lay some of their grievances before Messrs. Cunninghame Graham[45] and Coneybeare' (*The Link*, 7 July 1988: 4) (a meeting reported more widely by its inclusion in *The Star*, 11 July 1888). Bradlaugh was persuaded to table a question in Parliament to the Secretary of State for the Home Department asking whether the East London Inspector of Factories had investigated complaints about Bryant and May breaking the Truck Act, whether he was aware that some employees had been sacked after disclosing information of breaches of the law and whether, if this be true 'he will give directions to the Public Prosecutor to take proceedings in order to punish such an attempt to defeat the ends of justice by terrorising witnesses' (*The Star*, 11 July 1888).

In a letter 'To the Shareholders of the Bryant and May Company, Limited', published in *The Link* on 14 July 1888, Besant drew the attention of shareholders in general as well as the shareholding directors in particular to the unethical and exploitative means by which their dividends had been earned.

> I do not know whether Mr. Theodore H. Bryant, with his 3,000 shares in '84; Mr. William Carkeet, with his 1,250 shares in '84; Mr. G. Bartholomew with his 500 qualifying shares; Mr. G. B. Rix[46], with his 180 shares last year and his 85 this; whether any or all of these, have special guilt on their consciences. To-day I am concerned with you, ordinary shareholders, whose names do not appear, as a rule, in public; you who are quiet and unobtrusive persons, going about in society as decent respectable folk, honored as good citizens by your neighbours ... Do you know that the women and girls whose labor made the 22 1/2 per cent. dividend paid in February last are living, or dying, in Old Ford, Bromley, Tiger Bay, and other districts of East London, on wages varying from 4s. to about 13s. a week?'
>
> (*The Link*, 14 July 1888: 1)

She was particularly concerned to expose the double-morality of the clergy, using Bryant and May's own figures. Promising to print more shareholder names in the next issue, and declaring that the shareholders should give back some of the money unjustly and illegally taken from the match girls, she suggests that shareholders sought to repress their own awareness of company practices:

> But let us take the "average wage"; how would you like, wife of a clerical share-holder in Bryant and May's, to keep house for a week on 11s. 2d.? How would you like to start for your work at half-past five a.m., reach home again at seven :p.m., having been on your feet nearly all the time, and after doing this for five days, with an additional half-day on the Saturday, to take home 11s. 2d. as a reward?"... Are you not ashamed, you priests, who read out Sunday after Sunday "Thou shalt not steal", and then pocket the results of thefts carried out for your profit?... And of what avail, after all, to tell it to you, who if you cared to know might have known long ago how high dividends are earned. You do not want to know and you do not care to know. ... Your anger is against me who have exposed the wrong, instead of against those who have wrought it ...
>
> (*The Link*, 14 July 1888: 1)

The interest of Toynbee Hall was reflected in the media on 12 July 1888 when *The Times* and *St. James's Gazette* published a letter 'signed by ... gentlemen who have investigated the grievances or alleged grievances of the young women employed in Bryant and May ... [and who have conducted]... a careful examination of consider-able numbers of the girls and other people employed' (*St. James's Gazette*: 4).[47] *St. James's Gazette*, highlighting the Toynbee findings, commented upon the Bryant and May case repeating the contrast between the high dividends and the poor wages and conditions and promoting ethical investment to counter problematic company practice:

> To these statements the representatives of the match factory must now reply; and we hope for the sake of all concerned, that they will be able to make a clear and satisfactory answer to them. According to all accounts, theirs is a very prosperous business indeed, paying dividends at an unusually high rate, while, on the other hand, we know that their work people belong to a very poor and wretched class; so poor and so wretched, that we utterly refuse to believe that any considerable number of the shareholders in the company are willing to earn enormous profits by rendering these poor creatures yet more miserable than under any circumstances they must be.
>
> (*St. James's Gazette*, 12 July 1888: 4)

The Toynbee Hall letter brought out that demands that the sacked be re-instated and that the Truck Act be followed had been joined by demands to address the poor wages and conditions. They added more detail to the publicity. The Toynbee team reported that there were general grievances in this respect but also grievances specific to three categories of girls. The fillers complained they used to receive 1s 11d for filling 100 'frames' but in the time it had taken them to do this they could not now earn 1s 11d using new machinery, given a rate of pay of 10d for filling 100 'coils' and frequent machine breakdown. They also complained they had to pay for their own brushes (roughly 1d to 1 1/4d per week). The cutters down complained that their rate of pay had fallen from 3d to 2 3/4d for three gross of boxes. A farthing had been deducted to pay for children to bring work but the children had since been removed without restoration of the farthing so a 'penny in the shilling' was lost. The packers complained of various deductions to their wages, including payments for stamps to stamp the packages. All the girls were concerned about the levying of fines, such as when they were late – the gates were then closed and 6d deducted. And they complained that sometimes fines were deducted without explanation. While acknowledging it was a slack period, the girls were reported as reckoning that recent wages were as low as between 4s to 6s a week and that earnings were in any case never more than 13s a week. The concern to bring more light to the wages leads the Toynbee Hall investigators to call for a disaggregated 'wages accounting':

> Statements of average wages are meaningless unless – (1) they are calculated for the whole year instead of for the winter months or for a few weeks when the girls have possibly been in full work; unless (2) they are calculated on net, not on gross, wages [ie. after the deductions and fines]; unless (3) they differentiate the girls who get especially high wages, such as those employed in the wax-match department, and unless (4) the larger number of girls under 21 are included as well as the adults in the estimate.
>
> (*St. James's Gazette*, 12 July 1888: 4)

The Toynbee Hall delegation was granted an interview with Theodore and Frederick Bryant. They did not manage to reflect this in their letter of 12 July but

the directors' counter claims were published the day after. They clearly felt it important
to engage over the disclosures. The directors maintained that the average wage had
not fallen in the immediate past to around 4–6s, if they admitted that wages were
lower due to the bad summer, many girls staying in the factory rather than doing
summer jobs. They tried to justify their average figure of 11s 2d suggesting it was
based on a period of some months 'including part of the summer'. Two forewomen
were produced to support the view that there were no legitimate grievances, one of
these pointing out that 'her niece, 14, had earned 13s in a recent week'. The Toynbee
Hall team were left largely unmoved. That wages were poor remained clear and the
firm had not denied that the average wage was based on a sample excluding children
(they indeed referred to the 'average adult wage') and including the wax-match
makers.[48] On 17 July 1888 *St. James's Gazette* reported a further statement from the
Toynbee Hall team following a further investigation. While admitting that fines had
recently diminished they maintained that the girls' complaints were substantially
correct. The directors had had to admit 'after reference to their books' that the practice of deducting three pence per week from the packers' wages did in fact happen.[49]
The team confirmed that the average wage was not estimated to their satisfaction,
again returning to the contrast between accounting profit/dividends and the poor
wages and conditions. And they added further themes, giving further weight to the
role of publicity.

> We are convinced that even the question of low wages, important as it is, is but
> a part of the wide question of the whole relation between employers and
> employed. To say nothing of the want of sympathy which we have observed
> on the part of the directors and the dislike and fear on the part of the girls, the
> present strike provides unanswerable evidence of the deplorable relations
> which exist ... They receive during the greater part of the year a wage so small
> as to be totally insufficient to maintain decent existence ... No evidence ...
> [was] ... offered of attempts to improve material and social conditions. All this
> time the company is dividing among its shareholders a phenomenally high div-
> idend ... This dividend has hitherto been accepted without question; but among
> the shareholders there must surely be many who will now insist that the present
> dispute should be made the beginning of a better state of things.
>
> (*St. James's Gazette*, 17 July 1888: 12)

Such was the stark contrast being exposed (even accepting Bryant and May's own
figures), newspapers in general were bringing pressure on Bryant and May, even to
some extent *The Times*, which was more clearly one of the leading papers aligned to
the directors' view.[50] Accounting's aura of facticity was serving labour and the socialistic rather than the capitalistic even here. Socialists too could see a value in emphasising the 'factual'. The liberal *St. James's Gazette* expressed concern that the stark
contrast, in a context when Bryant and May had no valid excuses for paying such low
wages, could lead to unrest and encourage socialist praxis, making an earnest plea to
Bryant and May and all companies in their position:

> Messrs. Bryant and May have not so suffered from depression of trade as to
> be unable to be generous without a too severe strain on their resources. On the

contrary, it seems pretty certain that their profits have been very great, and that their shares were a desirable possession. We think – we say again, that they, and others in their position, would do well to reflect on the effect likely to be produced by the spectacle of a company making 25 or 30 per cent. out of the labour of girls who earn, taking the year all round, eleven shillings a week: not very much. The effect of such a spectacle can only be to greatly encourage that mischievous interference of the Socialists which has been complained of in the present case. No reasonable man desires to see the State, and still less the agitator, interfere largely in the relations of employer or employed; but it is useless and foolish to shut our eyes to acknowledged facts. There is nothing more certain at this time than that "grinding the faces of the poor" – to use the old and expressive phrase – would be considered by many, if not to justify, at least to excuse interferences even of a very rough kind.

(*St. James Gazette* cited in *The Link*, 28 July 1888: 1)

Thus, Bryant and May struggled to mobilise counter publicity.[51] Aside from the Toynbee Hall team (see MDM 12 July 1888) and the numerous reporters, negotiations were held with the London Trades Council (deputations being received on 16 and 17 July).[52] The latter were crucial to the ending of the strike on 19 July 1888 (MDM 17 July 1888). It was unusual that the Council had seen fit to negotiate on behalf of this relatively unskilled female group of workers. The strike clearly had assumed significance for this body.[53] The match girls agreed to return to work having achieved quite a bit more than the 'full surrender' of their position.[54] Indeed they and their allies could in many ways – and this is the view of the bulk of labour and union history – claim victory in respect of this particular struggle. Some saw it in these terms at the time, notably the *Liberal Radical* of 28 July 1888, which reported:

'The workers of Bryant and May's factory have reason to thank Mrs. Besant for her disinterested efforts on their behalf... The Directors have made a number of concessions which will very considerably improve the conditions of the girls... The emancipation of the workers is no party question; it should be subservient to no political or religious creed; the welfare of humanity is surely the desire of every honest man and woman. All praise to those who dare to be *practical* as well as theoretical.'

(cutting kept in SD)

The sacked girls were re-instated. No one involved in the strike was to be discriminated against. The system of fines was withdrawn (although the directors felt this constrained their disciplinary weapons to more severe ones). Increases in wages, admittedly small, were granted. And the Board promised to look into the provision of a canteen (one was subsequently provided – previously the match girls had to eat in the factory, amongst all its fumes). Finally the Board agreed to welcome the founding of a match-maker's union. The union was established, with Besant as the first secretary overseeing strong early participation. Bryant and May gave it an official welcome, suggesting that thereafter any grievances could be directly communicated to management. This was seen as a step forward relative to the alternative of exposure to the public via external publicity! Wilberforce Bryant was still feeling the need to engage in a counter publicity at Bryant and May's AGM of 29 January 1889:

> '... in moving the adoption of the report [Wilberforce Bryant] stated that in the middle of the year they [ie. the board] were annoyed by outsiders with reference to their work-people, which for a time disorganised the works, involving extra worry to the management, and causing a slight diminution of business ... the women employed by them received 15 to 25% more wages than the same class of hands could earn in other factories in East London engaged in similar works. He had been told by a gentleman who was acquainted with the operatives of the North of England that the money Bryant and May's hands received was at least 10% higher than the same class of hands got in several of the large towns in the North of England. The report was adopted.'
>
> (reported in *St. James's Gazette*, 30 January 1889 and filed in SD)

Given the seemingly successful mobilisation of accounting publicity in the match girls' case, more negative publicity for the company was stimulated. The need for counter publicity at Bryant and May was strongly felt. Champion's journal, *The Labour Elector*, the paper he edited after his *Common Sense* project, attacked the level of directors' pay under the heading of 'Bryant and May converted':

> About the last people one would expect to find advocating increased pay are the Directors of Bryant and May Limited. Yet at the external meeting of the share-holders on August 12th, all the discourse was about increased remuneration, and Mr. Wilberforce Bryant was warmly in favour of it. Our readers will not be much surprised when they learn that the increase proposed was in the pay of the Directors themselves who are to get a miserable £8,000 a year between them. And it was carried.[55]
>
> (*The Labour Elector*, 24 August 1889, cutting filed in SD, same date)

Our suggests that the socialist agitators and those aligned with them refined to some extent their usage and appreciation of accounting during the strike. The Toynbee Hall investigators, for example, called for additional, more disaggregated, disclosure in respect of wages as a result of their investigations. There were other calls for more and better disclosures, including from Besant. The strike's outcome con-fined for the agitators that accounting publicity was something that could be usefully mobilised in industrial conflict. Besant had been encouraged in her view, consistent with that of Champion, that publicity of 'facts' could help rectify social injustices. This was reflected in her 'Labour Statistics' published in the *Pall Mall Gazette* (23 February 1889), an article actually prompted by the match girls' dispute in that it followed a request made of Besant by Burnett, Labour correspondent of the Board of Trade, for more information about the strike. Besant supported Burnett's concern to gather and publish social information. If publicity was not a panacea, it was a helpful force:

> Knowledge of the amount of wages paid in different trades, of the cost of living, and so on, will not solve the social problem, nor render to the workman his due; but they will guide him in many a perplexity, throw light on many a wrong, and supply the material for solid arguments.
>
> (*Pall Mall Gazette*, 23 February 1889)

She praised Burnett's statistical reports and his papers in the *Board of Trade Journal* for having 'attracted much public attention' and 'given rise to comments in the press'. Besant lamented the poor response to Burnett's various surveys. She declared that she would like to see 'reliable returns of wages in various staple industries disclosed to the public' and 'a record of cost of living over a long enough period (at least a century)'. She wanted such information readily accessible, indeed pro-actively disclosed, to the public:

> Much of this information is ... already discoverable in Blue-books; but facts contained in Blue-books are buried rather than published so far as the "man on the 'bus" is concerned ... nothing but good can come from throwing on the many problems of our social system the dry, cold light of facts.'
>
> (*Pall Mall Gazette*, 23 February 1889)

Besant was motivated by a desire to see publicity linked to social well-being and in this regard problematised conventional distinctions between company accounting disclosures and social statistics, echoing an earlier blurring of such distinctions (Burchell *et al.*, 1980, Gallhofer and Haslam, 1993, 1995). Besant also developed a contextual, contingency, perspective in suggesting that the strategy of publicity had a greater chance of success in some cases than it did in others. In her 'The Next Point of Attack' (*The Link*, 4 August 1888: 1), Besant elaborates on the conditions under which an action can lead to victory. Firstly, there needs to be a case 'where there are wrongs glaring enough to compel universal admission as to the injustice with which the workers are treated'. And:

> Secondly, the industry in which they are employed must be prosperous. That which fetched the public in the case of Bryant and May was the contrast between the fat dividend of the shareholder and the lean allowance of the match-maker. If Bryant and May had only been earning two or three per cent., our appeal would have been fallen on death ears. ... Therefore the dividend of the concern against whom our next operations are to be undertaken must be over five per cent.
>
> (*The Link*, 4 August 1888: 1)

Accounting disclosure was a focus of the strategy. Besant stressed the importance of giving further publicity to more typically suppressed voices, principally the voices of the poor and the workers (and working women especially):

> In the case of the Match Girls it voiced their complaints, and forced them on the attention of the public, and what it has done for this one class of the oppressed it must do, one after the other for every such class ...[56]
>
> (*The Link*, 4 August 1888: 1)

Henry Hyde Champion, The Labour Elector and Brunner, Mond and Co: a case of critical financial analysis

After proposing the resolution regarding the match girls at the Fabian Society, Champion switched from his *Common Sense* and founded *The Labour Elector* (subtitled, to reflect Champion's emphasis, 'Organ of Practical Socialism'). Union leaders and socialist agitators, such as for example John Burns and Tom Mann, contributed to the journal. The objectives of *The Labour Elector* were to advance the cause of independent labour representation, to support the campaign for the eight-hour-day[57] and, as in *Common Sense*, to make visible the practices of bad employers (Whitehead 1983: 17–19). These campaign focuses were explicitly informed by the view that capitalism was unethical:

> ... the very foundation stone of our position is that capital ... namely, capital in the hands of those who are not workers ... has no rights at all. Its existence – in such hands – is itself a wrong, demanding instant remedy ... in labour disputes, we are always on the side of the workers ...
>
> (*The Labour Elector*, 8 June 1889: 12)

In this context, Champion switched the focus of his attention away from the match girls[58] and on to Brunner, Mond and Co, analysis of which became a major feature of *The Labour Elector*. Brunner, Mond and Co. was a chemical company located at Northwich, North West England. It especially captivated Champion from 1888 for a number of reasons, including a factor that fitted well with a message of Champion's new journal. It was a capitalistic business with a similar history to Bryant and May. The company had risen from a small partnership of relatively humble origins to a listed limited company recording huge financial success even in the depressed conditions of the late nineteenth century. The further significant point was that John Tomlinson Brunner, a founder and the continuing head of the company, was the Liberal MP for Northwich. In strongly advocating that labour be represented by an independent labour party, Champion was keen to undermine the mainstream Liberals of the time. Here was an opportunity to mobilise criticism of a Liberal MP and point to the affiliation of mainstream Liberal and capitalistic anti-labour interests. Moreover, Brunner, Mond had already been the focus of Champion's critique some two years earlier when, in a letter to *The Star*, he had attempted to expose its 'inhuman conditions of labour' (see *The Labour Elector*, August 1888: 2). His efforts in this line are reflected in an 1889 commentary of *The Echo* as follows:

> For some months past Mr. H. H. Champion ... has issued a little weekly paper
> called THE LABOUR ELECTOR. Apparently it chief purpose is to attack
> capitalists who happen to belong to the Liberal Party. For example, it has
> fastened upon Mr. J. T. Brunner with the pertinacity of a sleuth-hound.
>
> (*The Echo*, 8 June 1889: 12)

Champion continued apace to mobilise accounting publicity to his cause. Integral
to Champion's concern to make visible what he saw as the exploitative and unjust
practices of Brunner, Mond was his detailed analysis of publicly available accounting
disclosure, disclosure usually understood as of interest only to shareholders and potential investors. Champion's history of Brunner, Mond unfolds through analysis of the
company's prospectus and published accounts. Indeed Champion points out that
because the business had been a partnership in the first eight years of its existence 'its
transactions were not open to the public view' and hence these years had to be passed
over (*The Labour Elector*, 15 November 1888: 4). The story begins on the front page of
The Labour Elector of 1 November 1888 with an announcement that reflects
Champion's concern to focus upon Brunner, Mond so as to indicate unjust capitalistic practice more generally as well as to undermine Brunner's mainstream liberalism:

> We propose in this and following issues, to give at some length the story of the
> origin and growth of one of the most commercially successful of the monopolies
> which are at present extracting tribute from the long suffering workers of this
> country. The facts here given have been carefully verified, and may be taken as
> absolutely accurate. We venture to think that a study of this history will prove
> instructive as well as amusing, or, besides the personal application of the facts,
> they throw a good deal of light on debated economical points. He who remembers
> and repeats what will be here recorded will be furnished with the most complete
> answer possible to many a hackneyed argument used against the emancipation
> of Labour from the thraldom of Capital. ... since the head of the firm is, on polit-
> ical platforms, an ardent democrat, an enemy of monopoly, and general "Friend
> of Man", who uses his money to buy a seat in Parliament, to subsidise the Liberal
> party, to keep at his heels a pack of fawning "Labour representatives", and to
> employ Irish journalists to write up the woes of the unfortunate tenantry with
> whose grievances the Liberal party are now bound up, it becomes very instruc-
> tive to learn how these riches have come into his hands, and to follow his
> commercial history.
>
> (*The Labour Elector*, 1 November 1888: 1–2)

The Labour Elector informs its readers that Brunner had been employed as a clerk
in a chemical works at Winnington, Northwich. Here he teamed up with Ludwig
Mond, a chemist at the works, to patent a method of alkali manufacture. They established their own alkali manufacturing works at Winnington in 1872. It is stressed
that by the late 1880s, after the business had become a limited company, Brunner

and Mond had accumulated and continued to accumulate enormous financial wealth from this enterprise. Champion points out that additionally Brunner and Mond acted as Managing Directors and received £1,500 each for their services. The article emphasises that the wealth and income manifested within the short period of sixteen years and questioned how this had been possible:

> ... [they] held between them no less than 29,391 of the ordinary shares of the company. On the 22nd October last the market value of each such share was £35 13s. 4d. Consequently the stake that these two gentlemen own today in the business they commenced in 1872 with borrowed capital, amounts to £1,048,279!...The last half-yearly balance sheet of the company shows it is paying a dividend of 25% out. This, on the capital held by Messrs. Brunner & Mond, 29,391 £10 shares, represents an income of £73,477 10s a year between them! ... wealth also may be honourable. But, when there is a sudden jump from poverty to wealth, the matter wants looking into, and that is what we are doing with the wonderful adventures of Mr John Tomlinson Brunner, once the impecunious clerk at Widnes, and now the millionaire MP for Northwich.
>
> (*The Labour Elector*, 15 November 1888: 4)

Champion begins a more detailed analysis with a focus upon the 1881 prospectus. The price Brunner and Mond asked for the business that 'they had started previously under the humble condition we here described' was £200,000. This was a 'modest' sum 'squeezed out of the labour of their white slaves in eight short years'. He suggests that 'one or two comparative calculations' of interest 'especially to our workmen readers' would clarify that it was not possible for a worker to save such a sum over even a lifetime (*The Labour Elector*, 15 November 1888: 4):

> Let us, for example, assume that the advocates of thrift are right. These gentlemen practice what they preach, for they seldom give away anything but advice. Suppose that advice were taken by a couple of men working for Messrs. BRUNNER, MOND & Co. at 18s. per week, and that, with a view to amassing wealth for old age, they practiced self-denial to the extent of keeping themselves and their families on 13s. a week, and put away 5s. a week each in the Savings' Bank. How long would these two working men take to amass £200,000 [ie. £100,000 each]? Just seven thousand six hundred and ninety-two years and sixteen weeks. Clearly then Messrs. BRUNNER & MOND found a much more speedy way of obtaining capital than is afforded by practising the virtue of abstinence.
>
> (*The Labour Elector*, 15 November 1888: 5)

Having referred to the workers as 'white slaves', Champion added to the picture of contrast by pointing out that a trade union delegation had asked for a rise of two shillings in the wages with the result that Brunner, Mond not only refused the rise but simply sacked every union member. Champion points in this context to what he sees as the hypocrisy of Brunner who was proclaiming continuing support of Irish tenants to form associations similar to trade unions. Such a contrast in fortunes,

Champion suggests, was scarcely reported in the public realm because Brunner had 'bought the silence of the great Liberal party and the Liberal press' (*The Labour Elector*, 15 November 1888). Meanwhile, as *The Labour Elector* of 16 February 1889 was to report, Brunner proclaimed the great and 'honest' financial success of the company at the AGM:

> I am very pleased to meet you here to-day again, and to congratulate you and ourselves on the continued prosperity of this concern. You see we are enabled to pay the handsome dividend of 35 per cent per annum, and to carry forward the large balance of £29,647 8s. 5d. I can say, as I have said before, that this dividend is honestly earned, and there is every prospect of the future prosperity of the Company being equal to the past.
>
> (*The Labour Elector*, 16 February 1889: 4)

On 15 December 1888 (13), *The Labour Elector* printed the first half-yearly balance sheet of the new limited company. Champion analysed the balance sheet to question further the appropriateness of the £200,000 paid to Brunner and Mond to effect the transfer of the business.[59] One of the constituent items was some £126,000 for factory works. According to the prospectus, this was the cost to the vendors. Champion points out that no evidence had been given to support this statement. And he notes that details of the valuation constituting the remaining £74,000 were absent. He also draws readers' attention to the increasing size of equity (or, equivalently, increased assets) in the balance sheet – increasing in spite of the high dividend due to earnings retention and the attracting of capital to the business. Champion also highlights that of the gross profit for the half-year, interest, Directors' salaries and fees and 'the lion's share' of the dividend were paid to Messrs. Brunner and Mond. He concludes that 'the transformation of the business from the private concern of these two gentlemen into a limited liability company was quite a success, so far as *they* were concerned' (*The Labour Elector*, 15 December 1888). The returns to the owners and owner-directors are again contrasted with employee experience:

> And their workmen? their white slaves, whose arduous and unhealthy toil made all that wealth, they thought also of them in this their hour of prosperity? Well, no, not exactly; or, if they did, it was only to devise fresh schemes whereby the toil being made yet more arduous and unhealthy, the dividends on the beloved Ordinary Shares would mount higher and higher. And mount they certainly did, in an astonishing degree; but the how and the why we must defer to our next issue.
>
> (*The Labour Elector*, 15 December 1888: 13)

Champion noted that his objective of publicising the story beyond *The Labour Elector* was very soon successful. The *Evening News*, in a leader, published a story about the treatment of the workmen at Northwich, citing *The Labour Elector*. The article asks *The Star*, Mr Brunner's paper (in that he was the major shareholder)[60] to respond. Champion reports that criticism of Brunner, Mond was made in Parliament. This prompted T. O'Connor, MP, an ally of Brunner, to launch there a counter-attack, portraying Brunner as a good employer and suggesting that that was why he was MP for Northwich. Champion took the opportunity to retort:

> Mr. O'CONNOR's next plea on behalf of his master, is that "Mr. BRUNNER is concerned with the financial part, and the financial part alone, of the firm." That is to say that, so long as the men work so as to give him his 50 per cent dividend, he does not much mind how they do it. "He has never employed, he has never dismissed one solitary man in the works." Why should he? Has he not got managers and foremen at Northwich, as well as an editor in London, to do his dirty and unpleasant work? Why should he do it himself?... If an election took place tomorrow in Northwich, Mr. Brunner would have to fight hard to keep the seat at all; if it took place after we have finished his history in the Labour Elector, Mr. Brunner will probably decline to stand.
>
> (*The Labour Elector*, 15 December 1888: 14)

The next issue of *The Labour Elector*, of 5 January 1889, published the accounts of the company for the half-year ending 31 December 1881. The profits were again contrasted with the poor working conditions. Champion calculates, with reference to the published accounts, that the cost of introducing an eight-hour day at Brunner, Mond, assuming the workers were paid the same amount for the shorter shift as the longer, would be small relative to the profits:

> GRANTING that such work must be done, unhealthy though it be, there is no reason (but expense) why the 12 hour shift should not be changed to 8, fresh men being set on to work the fresh shift. A man *might* live through the 8 hours shift; he is now being killed, more or less swiftly, by the 12. Well, what be the cost of the fresh batch of men? Three hundred men, say, at a pound a week (the present workers are receiving about 18s.), would be £15,600 in the year. The present profits of the company are about £200,000 a year. From such a sum £15,600 would be scarcely missed, and £185,000 would still remain to be annually divided between Messrs. BRUNNER, MOND & Co.
>
> (*The Labour Elector*, 5 January 1889: 7)

Such an analysis was aimed at countering the 'most effective opponents of the Eight Hours' Day at the present time... officials of Trade Unions who protest that such a reduction of working hours would reduce employers' profits to vanishing point, and thus lead to the closing of their mills and factories and the dismissal of their "hands"' (*The Labour Elector*, 15 June 1889: 6). In seeking to counter the opponents of the eight-hour day, Champion went beyond his analysis of Brunner, Mond:

> We have ... taken the accounts of Limited Liability Companies in various trades, and carefully analysed them, with a view to discover what would be the precise effect of an Eight Hours' Day on the profits of capital in those trades. The results

of these investigations we shall from time to time give to our readers, and think they will prove very useful to all who argue the Eight Hours' question in public or private. The first industry we have selected for examination is cotton spinning, as of that industry, perhaps more than of any other, we hear it said that a reduction of hours without lower wages would lose England the foreign markets to which so large a proportion of our cotton goes.[61]

(*The Labour Elector*, 15 June 1889: 6)

One analysis of the Albany Spinning Company Limited which maintained that a reduction in the return on share capital from 13.5 to 8.5 per cent would be the effect of paying the same wage to employees for an eight-hour shift as was currently paid for a nine-hour shift – an acceptable reduction for Champion – gave rise to a response from one of the readers of the paper to the effect that Champion's analysis had been too generous to the employers:

I think your practical exemplification of the result of the Eight Hour movement is likely to be very useful, but it occurs to me that you have made your calculation on the wrong basis with the result of making the case worse for the employer than it would be in fact. There is nothing in the fact of shorter hours being worked to reduce the demand for goods, but exactly the reverse, more men being employed and having money to spend. Consequently, instead of *deducting* one-ninth from sales on one side, and cost of raw material and sundries on the other, I think you should simply *add* one-ninth of item for wages, which would have the profit balance £840 instead of £696.

(*The Labour Elector*, 22 June 1889: 10)

In mobilising accounting data, Champion could bring out contrasting experiences very succinctly in the case of a variety of companies. Thus, in an analysis of gas companies in the context of developing industrial tension:

… every Gas Stoker has the satisfaction of knowing that while he is earning 2s. 8d. in wages, he is making 12s. 4½d. for Capital. It will be well for the stokers, while they are at their work, to remember that they fill three mouthpieces for the shareholders' benefit, and only the fourth for their own. Could there be any stronger proof that the only cause of poverty and overwork is that the workers have to keep the idlers? But if the Gas Stokers keep on at their agitation they will soon be able to say with BYRON –

I have seen the people, like o'er burdened asses,
Kick off their burdens, meaning the upper classes.

(*The Labour Elector*, 29 June 1889: 11)

On 19 January 1889 the half-yearly accounts to 31 December 1882 of Brunner, Mond are discussed at great length (8–10), the published accounting profit figure of £133,000 being linked to the number of men producing it. If, according to Champion, one assumed 2,000 employees at Winnington then they would have created a value of £127 each. Given £60 for wages this would leave £67 'confiscated by Messrs. BRUNNER & Co.'[62] Champion analyses the balance sheet as at 31 December 1883 and argues that a reserve fund was being built up as an alternative to paying out even higher dividends that might have attracted unwanted publicity. By 1883, the company was paying a dividend of 35 per cent on the nominal value of ordinary shares. He had made a similar point earlier in referring to the build up of assets and here highlights the significant increase in the figure for patents on the balance sheet (*The Labour Elector*, 26 January 1889: 9). Champion went on to develop his theme:

> BUT, strange to tell, even these extraordinary efforts to absorb the wealth produced by Mr. BRUNNER's white slaves were found to be inadequate, and a device was invented which is, we think, unique in the history of Limited Liability Companies. It may be that it was legal; most probably it was; for your BRUNNERS are always, or almost always, sharp enough to keep within the law. But surprising as our revelations concerning BRUNNER, MOND & Co., have been up to this point, that which we have now to tell reduces by comparison all that has gone before to mere commonplace. The operation belongs to the half-year succeeding the one we are now considering; therefore we will say no more about it until next week.
>
> (*The Labour Elector*, 26 January 1889: 9–10)

Having hinted at this device for hiding or deflecting attention from the high profits of Brunner, Mond, Champion attempts to negotiate with Brunner through the pages of *The Labour Elector*. If Brunner agreed to introduce the eight-hour day, proclaims Champion, 'we will stay our pen at this point and never write another line either against his political actions or his administration of the Winnington works' (*The Labour Elector*, 26 January 1889: 10). With Brunner failing to respond to this, the next issue of the paper brings attention to the dilution of share capital via a bonus issue to reduce the dividend as a percentage of the nominal value of shares issued (*The Labour Elector*, 2 February 1889: 1–4). Later, Champion notes that his interpretation of the share issue had not been questioned (*The Labour Elector*, 16 February 1889: 4). The balance sheet as at 30 June 1884 constituted the accounts immediately preceding the capital increase. After printing this, Champion notes:

> As the above set of Accounts are those immediately preceding the "act of transformation" by which Mr. BRUNNER, by a stroke of the pen, doubled the amount of his capital in the company, it is interesting to know what was exactly the rate of profit produced for him during those six months by the exhausting toil of men … As the Accounts show, the profit made during the half-year was £69,282. Deducting the £6,288 required for the Preference Shareholders we have £62,994 left for the Ordinary Shareholders. This represents no less than 56 per cent … No wonder Mr. BRUNNER thought it high time to adopt the expedient of doubling the nominal amount of his Shares, so as to endeavour to conceal the enormous profit …
>
> (*The Labour Elector*, 2 March 1889: 5)

Champion also questions the appropriateness of a further share issue with reference to the balance sheet as at 31 December 1884 (*The Labour Elector*, 9 March 1889: 5). And – problematising the status of the chartered accountant in the process – he criticises an accounting practice of aggregation which he suggests is aligned to the capitalist's concern to disclose minimalist information:

> This practice of including two separate things in one item may be, for the Directors, a convenient system of account keeping but we are surprised at its receiving the sanction of any auditor who signs himself a chartered accountant.
> (*The Labour Elector*, 9 March 1889: 5)

In *The Labour Elector* of 23 March 1889 (5) Champion returns to the increases in reserves and the issues of shares:

> It was only wanted [ie. the transfer to reserves and the issues of shares] by Mr BRUNNER and Mr MOND, the promoters, first, for its own sake; second to hide the shame of their monstrous dividends; and third to get others to share the anxieties and responsibilities of the concern with them. But, we repeat the money was not required for the business. The profits already yielded were more than enough to provide for all additions, developments and expansions. But these profits were taken away to other investments, and fresh capital was created, and thenceforward that fresh capital has to get its profits and its dividends just as if it has been necessary to the industry. Thus Capital is always adding to the load which is first placed upon the shoulders of Labour.
> (*The Labour Elector*, 23 March 1889: 5)

He points out that in spite of such increases, Brunner was still not prepared to introduce the eight-hour shift (*The Labour Elector*, 23 March 1889: 5). In *The Labour Elector* of 27 April 1889, Champion again points to the continuing increase in assets/equity in spite of the high dividends being paid, with reference to the accounts of the half year ending 31 December 1885.[63]

Champion also used the accounts in the context of exposing Brunner's monopolistic and 'protectionist' practice. Referring to an item in the balance sheet in respect of Mersey, Salt and Brine Co., Champion went on to reflect the particular nature of the benefit to the company entailed therein by citing Brunner's statement to the extraordinary general meeting of August 1884:

> Your Directors are of opinion that the safe way to maintain this monopoly is to enlarge your works. With this object in view, the Directors have entered into an agreement with the Mersey Salt and Brine Co. The essence of this agreement is that they grant to us the monopoly of the use of their pipes so far as the carriage of brine for the manufacture of Ammonia Soda is concerned.
> (*The Labour Elector*, 2 March 1889: 6)

In the 26 January 1889 issue of *The Labour Elector*, Champion adds to his exposure by noting that not only did the company pay low wages and have the employees work in conditions that destroyed their lives and happiness, it also impacted negatively by polluting a river by pumping it with brine (8).[64]

By 19 January 1889, Champion had felt able to report that the publicity he was giving to Brunner, Mond was bringing about some changes for the better, encouraging him to disclose more:

> With respect to the conditions of the workmen – the object of all our thoughts – we hear from our friend Mr Litster that our blows are beginning to tell, and that signs of improvement are appearing here and there. But they are so trifling to be hardly worth mentioning, and they certainly will not cause us to abate our efforts one jot.
>
> (*The Labour Elector*, 19 January 1889: 10)

The publicity had resulted in the employees incurring less fines:

> The evils of the worst feature of the science of profit-making as carried on by Mr. BRUNNER – the 23 hours "shift" – has been materially reduced ... Add to this, that since we began to take the firm seriously at hand *not a single fatal "accident"* has occurred at Winnington, and our readers will agree that the Star is right in saying that a newspaper "can bring to bear the force of public opinion on natures that would otherwise defy with impunity every power, human and divine".
>
> (*The Labour Elector*, 27 April 1889: 3)

The journal reprints a report of a public meeting held in Appleby that had initially appeared in the *East Cumberland News*. This discusses working conditions at Brunner, Mond and the impact *The Labour Elector* had on changing them:

> But since Mr Champion had made his exposure the men had been allowed to go off after working 10½ hours, instead of doing the double shift. They had also dispensed with the fining system, and also the fines of the shiftmen for losing three-questers during the week. Mr Brünner had admitted to him personally, Mr. Champion had done a deal of good to the employes of Brünner, Mond and Co.
>
> (*The Labour Elector*, 18 May 1889: 10)

In once again claiming that the publicity was having a positive impact and in the context of a further death of one of 'Brunner's white slaves', Champion re-iterates that yet more pressure had to be brought to bear:

> It is true that since our exposure of the atrocious system maintained at Mr. BRUNNER's works, many improvements have been made in the conditions of

labour to which the workmen are subjected. Fines – known by Mr. BRUNNER to be illegal – have been discontinued; at some of the most dangerous places the machinery has been fenced; and several other evils have been remedied, and abuses stopped, which would, undoubtedly, have been still flourishing to-day, but for our intervention and exposures. But it was not to be expected that every grievance would be remedied, and every danger removed. The leopard does not change his spots, though he may before the moment cowed ...[65]

(*The Labour Elector*, 25 May 1889: 1)

Consistent with such reported impacts, Champion attracted supportive comment from his readers. According to one correspondent, formerly employed at Winnington, Champion had understated the degree of exploitation in his analysis (*supra*) because in 1882 less than 2,000 people had been employed and when the number of employees did rise to 2,000 over £200,000 a year of profits were being generated (*The Labour Elector*, 26 January 1889: 3). Champion, referring to the increasing numbers of friends who sent in reports of the 'villainies of capitalism' (*The Labour Elector*, 26 January 1889), asked readers to recognise that space was 'limited as well as our time' but added that 'we are very glad to receive the information that is pouring in upon us, and will deal with one case after the other as rapidly as possible'. He declares in this respect that his concern was to 'select those cases in which exposure, besides relieving the condition of the workers, teaches a great political lesson and economic truth' (*The Labour Elector*, 26 January 1889).[66] Any texts that could be interpreted as responses by Brunner to the criticism were also further taken up in the pages of *The Labour Elector*. Champion again typically mobilised the accounts to defend his position. After Brunner had written in *The Star* that the 'average dividend for the last four years has not exceeded 18 percent', Champion used the published balance sheets to argue that dividends for the last four years averaged 22.5 per cent (*The Labour Elector*, 16 March 1889: 7).

Champion was eventually pursued in a similar manner to Besant. On 20 April 1889 *The Labour Elector* informed its readers that Champion had received a letter from solicitors acting on behalf of Brunner informing him that they had been instructed to 'commence an action against [him] for the libels published by [him] of [Brunner]'.[67] Champion's counter was to continue his campaign: '... Mr. BRUNNER, although he may have fled to the arms of Mr. GEORGE LEWIS [lawyer] for protection, is still the callous, greedy, slave-driving owner of "the slaughter-house" Northwich' (*The Labour Elector*, 25 May 1889: 1).[68] Champion maintained: '... we did not make these charges lightly, nor without satisfying ourselves of their absolute truthfulness, and we do not intend to say anything in the shape of either their withdrawal or qualification' (*The Labour Elector*, 1 June 1889: 1). On 8 June 1889, *The Labour Elector* printed the counter allegations brought against Champion by Brunner, including in respect of how Champion had tried to indicate, through analysis of the accounts, how Brunner had enriched himself. Champion departed for Melbourne, disillusioned with political activism in Britain, and this brought this particular battle to an end. Champion continued his radical activism in Australia with similar disappointments (Whitehead 1977).

Emancipatory dimensions and possibilities of ambiguous accounting: reflections upon our analyses

Many critical appreciations of accounting understand the practice as a capitalistic and repressive servant of problematic hegemonic forces. Most critical appreciations of accounting in effect displace attention from accounting's emancipatory dimensions and even from its emancipatory possibilities. In an earlier study, we contributed to redressing this by attempting to theorise emancipatory dimensions of accounting in action through an analysis of accounting's emancipatory effects in the crisis context of Germany during the first World War and its aftermath (Gallhofer and Haslam 1991). This earlier study furnished a number of insights. Attention was focused upon the social perception, or aura, of accounting in German society. Accounting was typically seen as a neutral and authentic professional expertise and was perceived to be supported by a state and its law that were taken to be legitimate. Accounting's powers to create a 'harmonising illusion', and to reflect and constitute 'repressive familiarity' in a way supportive of the status quo, were bolstered by such an aura (see Gallhofer and Haslam 1991: 489–93). Developments in a crisis context helped to shatter much of this aura. Accounting could here be used by radical political forces to counter problematic hegemonic forces and came to function in an emancipatory way. By exploring various dimensions of accounting's functioning in late nineteenth century Britain, we can further develop our theoretical argumentation so as to gain additional insights for an emancipatory praxis involving accounting. Reflecting on our case analysis here, we can appreciate aspects of accounting's functioning that pertain to quite general contexts as well as explore dimensions specifically associated with the quite particular contextual developments we have elaborated in our analysis.

Accounting can be appropriately seen as a social practice that is communicative and a system of informing. As such it can be seen as functioning so that at any given moment some of its effects, in the complexity of society, are emancipatory, while others are repressive. Accounting practice always has some emancipatory dimensions, including having emancipatory effects, albeit that throughout much of its history in modern society its repressive effects have had the greater weight and significance. The social manifestation of communicative practices and systems of informing such as accounting implies an interactive process in which repressing and repressed forces are mutually involved. While such a process engenders and reflects power relations in society, repressive forces can never absolutely control such practices. Such a state of affairs is reflected in our case analysis. Further, as indicated, while the critical theorist today can reasonably maintain that accounting functions repressively in terms of its overall effects,[69] accounting has the potential to function so that its emancipatory effects come to constitute the greater force. This, hinted at above, has also in effect been suggested in a number of critical texts (e.g. Tinker 1985, Lehman and Tinker 1987, Gallhofer and Haslam 1991).[70] In terms of accounting's overall consequence in its social context one can, more generally, thus conceive of a continuum along which accounting can be perceived to substantively move in accordance with its emancipatory or repressive tendencies. Accounting's positioning on this continuum, a dimension of accounting's ambiguity, will reflect trajectories of its broader historical context. Our case analysis in effect traced a movement along this continuum in the emancipatory direction. By reference to this continuum, we can also point to contradictory elements that actually stifle movement in the direction of a repressive tendency. Where accounting is mobilised by repressive forces, this also engenders countervailing forces of emancipatory effect, so that in some respects a contradictory development occurs (see Gallhofer and Haslam 1991: 490). Hegemonic forces can in general be undercut in mobilising what they take to be, often quite unambiguously, consistent with hegemonic interests. Repressive power can engender resistance – supplying, moreover, that resistance with ammunition. In a modern capitalistic society it is the case that relatively powerful repressive agents can come to perceive gains in actions which subsequently have the consequence of aiding the repressed. In our case analysis, the accounting facts that came to be valued, and valued as exposed or visible accounting facts, came to the service of radical socialist movements in a particular context. Critical research has theorised more generally the ostensible promotion of practices of mass production, education and democracy in this way. The particular manifestations and visibilities associated with such practices and the rhetoric by which they have to be legitimised (e.g. the claims of the accountancy profession to serve the public interest and to provide assurances in respect of a 'True and Fair View'[71]) can come to counter hegemonic forces. Critical historical research that we have engaged in has brought out accounting's location as an ambiguous Enlightenment praxis which can come to disturb the status quo. As a systemic communication and practice of informing, including through exposing and making visible, accounting can come to serve radical democratic forces aiming to challenge and go beyond the status quo to effect emancipatory change (Gallhofer and Haslam 1993, 1994b, 1997a). Such a possibility has been integral to a radical Enlightenment discourse influencing accounting's formation as a modern institution and practice.[72] Systems of informing and communicative practices in the public sphere always include a threatening element for relatively powerful but relatively illegitimate forces. Again, the extent or significance of such contradictory development is influenced by trajectories of the broader historical context.

Our case analysis illustrates some further contradictory developments that have affinity with those discussed so far. For instance, accounting can be understood in our case analysis as embracing a particular content and form, which renders a number of dimensions of business operations visible, because of the pressures of shareholders on management to disclose information.[73] While much secrecy is preserved in the public realm and albeit that the visibilities are shaped so as to reflect the power relations of the socio-political order, this still furnishes material for an alternative mobilising of accounting disclosures. Similarly, in our case analysis, the mass media is used to promote capitalistic interests, including through accounting disclosures, but these very disclosures are mobilised by the radical socialist forces, including through journals aimed at a mass audience. Indeed, even though the socialistic intervention transformed how accounting was perceived in the context focused upon, some of the power of accounting was maintained in this way.[74] Our argumentation here recognises that socially repressive forces do not absolutely capture practices such as accounting. For instance, we have suggested that accounting is situated in a field of social tension and that it has no necessary class belongingness (even if its overriding allegiances at a given moment may be evident).[75] Again, this is borne out by our case analysis. Another reason why accounting is not captured absolutely is that it is also often situated in a context that is very complex, dynamic and uncertain. This adds to the difficulty facing anyone or any particular forces concerned to capture accounting, even in the event of a deliberative strategy to capture it being deployed. Our case analysis illustrates dimensions of complexity, change and uncertainty that made it difficult for hegemonic forces to control accounting's social functioning with assurance. One dimension here is that accounting was functioning in a context in which a number of things could not be taken for granted. Amongst these was the affiliation of particular agents in social struggle: the figure of Champion, if nurtured to serve the status quo, comes to align with radical forces. Another dimension is illustrated in our analysis of the character of the dynamic interlinkages between practices functioning in what can be understood as particular and differing 'micro-contexts'. On the one hand, there was a 'conventional' accounting functioning in a particular localised micro-context delineated by the capitalistic relations between business managers and financiers and the communications pertaining thereto. On the other, there was a mobilisation of 'facts' in radical socialistic praxis. Developments in the context led to the former accountings being re-deployed as facts in the latter critical praxis. This particular dynamic interaction, which engendered emancipatory developments, brings out the inextricable positioning of accounting in the field of tension of its wider context, no matter how non-controversial the practice may come to appear. It is also reflective of the possibilities of complex interactive social processes. A further factor to be stressed in exploring why accounting is not amenable to absolute capture is that, more generally, accounting, no matter the extent of its capture at a given moment, can come to float relatively free of its socio-historical constitution and signify different things for different interpreters and users in different contexts, with differing effects. In our case, for instance, the accounting came to mean something different to the socialist activists than it did to capitalistic investors and financiers.

The detailed analysis in our empirical study permits exploration of how the change in accounting that was indicated as a possibility and potentiality in the above largely general argumentation actually manifested in a specific context in practice. If accounting is to change or function differently in terms of its consequences, it appears that the form, content, aura or usage of accounting, or a mixture of these dimensions, must change. What changed in our case analysis so that accounting could function on behalf of a relatively oppressed group as a more emancipatory force? And what made such change possible or even likely? In one sense, accounting's content scarcely changed in the particular cases explored in that the actually existing accounting disclosures that had become conventional business practice were mobilised by the socialist activists. A change, however, was that as a result of the investigative journalism, the content of accounting disclosure was expanded to include the disclosure of wages and working conditions. What about the aura of accounting? In our previous study (Gallhofer and Haslam 1991) we suggested that a context of crisis engendered developments helping transform accounting's aura. In the cases discussed here, the sense of crisis, albeit present, is not as strong. There is, however, a situation where some businesses were making enormous profits – which they were proud to publicise – and severely exploiting and repressing labour in a context of economic stagnation. Further, there was an increasing and quite generally held recognition of a need for social change, notably in terms of the need to do something in respect of the conditions of the poor and an extension of the franchise. The figure of Champion manifests to some extent as a contingency. Here was a socialist activist who felt confident enough to challenge and mobilise the then conventional accounting disclosures in the context of socialist struggle. Accounts are not so 'distant' from Champion in consequence, for instance, of their professional and expert status. Rather, because of his own background, he can make them central to his critical praxis. At the same time, Champion was in part a reflection of the re-invigorated socialist movements of the time. In the context, socialism was attracting a range of supporters including those, like Champion, who one might have expected to enter politics formally through affiliation with the mainstream liberal and Tory parties, and including some, again like Champion, who were exploring ways in which socialism could be 'practically' effected. So perhaps it was not only possible but to some extent likely in these circumstances that an intervention such as that of Champion would occur. In the event of its occurrence the aura of accounting was disturbed in the social dynamics. It was no longer 'preserved' in a particular historical set of conditions (cf. Benjamin 1973). A view that accounting was a quite technical, neutral and mundane practice that operated, as it were, outside of the 'grand' political struggles of the day, was modifed. Accounting could be seen to be politically aligned in such struggles. It could in this context come to be seen as contestable in relation to such struggles in that it was a practice, for instance, that could be manipulated in accordance with the perceived interests of wealthy and powerful capitalists. Accounting was becoming central to radical ways of seeing the functionings of the capitalistic enterprises of the time, ways of seeing that disturbed rather than re-inforced the status quo. Socialist activists also felt themselves able in our analysis, largely because of the experiences of their engagements, to promote new accountings that would disclose information in the interests of the employees. This included their promoting disaggregated accounting disclosures, incorporating non-financial elements, so that local activities could be rendered more accountable to labour. Thus, radical perceptions of accounting's potentiality emerged and were promoted in this context. At the same time, the notion that accounts could equate to objective, hard facts and figures beyond the manipulation and mystification remained.[76] In our case analysis the facticity of the accounting numbers was, indeed, used by the socialist activists to bolster their campaigns. This is consistent with the influence of a discourse in which facts, especially if numerical and financial, had considerable weight. Socialist movements and their activists were clearly influenced by this discourse. They held perspectives on publicity and making things visible echoing Bentham's views to some extent re-iterated in the work of Adolphe Quetelet, John Stuart Mill and the Victorian statistical movement (see Cullen, 1975). The socialists sought, aside from organising strikes, to mobilise journalism and education for their purposes. They mobilised 'facts' in their argumentation to reflect the discourse shaped by Benthamite forces (and acknowledged in these terms by Sydney Webb), and Champion and Besant were prominent amongst those socialist activists who saw accounting as equating to such facts. A clear change that occurred in our case analysis is in the usage of accounting. There is a sense in which this also entails a change in accounting's form. Accounting, even in part an actually existing accounting, is mobilised by socialist activists.[77] This usage was in the context of struggles aligned to 'unskilled' women workers and labour in general and a critique and engaged praxis focused upon companies deemed to be making very high profits but paying very low wages and offering poor working conditions to the labour force. Such companies were treated by the activists as micro-organisational reflections of the wider social struggle. The juxtaposition of conventional, actually existing, accounting alongside the information about wages and working conditions in a radical socialistic and journalistic text is in effect a modification of the form of accounting disclosure beyond what was conventional – even if it made use of the weighty 'conventional accounting logic' to re-inforce its message.

Our case analysis here does suggest that at least some emancipatory effect was engendered by the accounting mobilisations. Greater potentialities were hinted at. Our analysis points to particular changes in the content, form, aura and usage of accounting that engendered emancipatory developments. These changes occurred, it should be recognised, in a context that made these things possible and even to some extent likely and, again we should stress, the changes took place in a context that made other things not possible or less likely. The analysis here also particularly encourages critical praxis in and through accounting.

Our analysis indicates a more general potentiality of accounting, the potential to offer critical reflection upon the socio-political order. We have seen that we may move towards this potentiality through a focus upon a particular aspect of the socio-political order, if from a location within it (Gallhofer *et al.* 2000b). There is clearly scope for further studies that explore accounting in action through the theoretical frame of reference we have mobilised here. We have especially come to recognise how few studies have sought to articulate the ambiguous involvement and not necessarily dominant class belongingness of accounting in the context of social struggle.[78] Specifically, we have noticed a lacuna as far as study into accounting's interface with the activities of radical political movements is concerned.

4 Is social accounting the soul of justice?

Towards a critical appreciation with emancipatory intent

> ... it is the reform and further development of accounting which offers the most hopeful prospect of resolving many of the most pressing problems of our societies.
>
> (Gambling 1974: 201)

How can we better align accounting and emancipation today? To help contribute further insights so as to inform reflection upon this question, we here focus upon an accounting phenomenon of relatively recent times. Building upon existing contributions in the literature and reflecting on-going work, we seek, through a set of brief analyses, to gain some further critical appreciation of a 'social accounting' phenomenon that has manifested over the last 40 years. These last 40 years have witnessed something of a take off, followed by a subsequently interesting trajectory, in the idea and practice of a social accounting (Gray 1999). This social accounting has been characterised as challenging conventional accounting, involving a fusion of concerns about accounting's content, form and social role. And, on the face of it, it has been constituted in efforts to go beyond a narrow instrumentalism towards an appreciation, informed by critical reflection, of 'what really matters' to people, including in the governance of social organisations. What can we learn from this social accounting phenomenon? The question is a rhetorical one. How can one respond to the challenge to learn everything that there is to learn? The challenge is a substantive one. The social accounting phenomenon refers to a vast set of episodes and developments that have manifested throughout the world. Furthermore, we must consider what attempting a substantive critical theoretical appreciation – informed by various theoretical advances, including postmodern insights – involves. On the one hand, it properly involves explorations of these episodes and developments that delve into the specificities, complexities and ambiguities of the various social accounting manifestations in relation to the wider context of which they are part. On the other, if one is to avoid the sort of myopia that can problematically manifest in focusing upon the particular and the specific, it involves recognising key structural forces and seeking to develop a substantive critical thematisation that is also contextually informed. No wonder relatively little has been done by way of responding to the challenge referred to. In respect of this area, a limited number of social analyses and overviews of accounting in action have at least touched upon some aspects of episodes involving social accounting. For instance, Burchell *et al.* (1985) is an especially notable contribution (see also Hopwood *et al.* 1994, Robson 1994), and Gray *et al.* (1995a, 1996) and Gray and Bebbington (2001) summarise a wealth of insight. Yet clearly this is only scratching the surface in relation to what can potentially be done. And in this regard the existing studies acknowledge the difficulties of constructing the dimensions of a substantive critical appreciation (see Gray 1999: 15). Thus, we can only make a very partial contribution here towards filling the gap. In spite of the partial character of prior studies, we can build upon previous appreciations in the literature − re-interpreting and extending them − to a much greater extent than in the empirical analyses of our earlier chapters. Yet we must eschew, in the context of the limited available space, the elaboration of something akin to the recent history of social accounting in critical theoretical terms. Nevertheless, our concern here is in some ways to extend critical appreciation of a number of key episodes and developments from the late 1960s onwards involving the mobilisation of social accounting. Our selection of episodes and developments for analysis and re-appraisal, from the vast and rich tapestry that has manifested, has been informed by existing literature on social accounting. The selection has been made with a view to offering some key insights and stimulating further research and engagement towards the realisation of social accounting's emancipatory potential.

Before overviewing the episodes and developments reviewed here, we can elaborate and substantiate more explicitly why we believe, given an interest in better aligning accounting and emancipation, that episodes and manifestations helping make up the social accounting phenomenon of relatively recent times form a worthy focus of analysis. As we have already mentioned, social accounting has been mobilised as an accounting challenging conventional accounting and, on the face of it, as an accounting reflecting a concern to go beyond a narrow instrumentalsim (cf. Lehman and Tinker 1997). Thus, the mobilisation of social accounting is suggestive of accounting being aligned with the idea of emancipation as understood here. Further, a number of discourses and movements have promoted the notion of social accounting more evidently as emancipatory and indeed some have done so explicitly, including mobilising the construct of emancipatory accounting in this context (Tinker 1984a,b, 1985, Gray 1992, 1999: 3, 12−13, Owen *et al.* 1997, Bebbington 1999, 2001). Further, commentators see the phenomenon of social accounting in relatively recent times to be a significant one. Social accounting's take off period has been characterised as the 'heyday' of social accounting and even as constituting the emergence of 'the social accounting movement'[1] (Zadek and Evans 1993, Gray *et al.* 1996, Zadek *et al.* 1997, Owen *et al.* 2000: 81). There are also broader contextual factors that help justify the analysis of social accounting we are concerned to contribute to here. The take off in social accounting in the late twentieth century − around the late 1960s and in the 1970s − was in respect of the business organisation in particular (Gray *et al.* 1996). This is suggestive of a number of negative and positive potentialities for the broader context that are appropriately explored. For instance, this increased attention given to business could have displaced attention from other entities or activities, thus potentially posing an obstacle to emancipatory work through social accounting in these other fields. Or, the increased emphasis given to business here could properly have reflected the significance, or increasing significance, of business organisations in the world, so that attempts to transform them through accounting may have had particular emancipatory promise. Another factor is that, as we shall elaborate, the context of social accounting's take off and subsequent trajectory has been one of interesting and significant socio-political tensions and dynamics. For us, then, the manifestations of social accounting and the struggle to capture social accounting in this context constitute focuses that are fertile for the gaining of insights and inspiration towards the furtherance of an emancipatory project involving accounting's mobilisation today.

We seek here to bring out emancipatory and repressive dimensions of social accounting in a number of key differentiated and overlapping episodes and manifestations from the relatively recent historical context. We are concerned initially to gain some insights from an analysis broadly contrasting counter information systems type interventions mobilising social accounting – taking pressure group and social activist interventions as exemplars – with the mobilisations of social accounting by business organisations. We build into our comparative analysis an appreciation of the contextual dynamics of recent decades. Thus we also seek to gain and convey a sense of discontinuities as well as continuities in respect of both counter systems type activity and business interventions over the period from the 1970s to very recent times. With regard to counter information systems type activity, particular attention is given to the work of Counter Information Services (CIS), a group of social activists operating in the UK in the 1970s with ostensibly a strong radical orientation and critical emancipatory intent. In respect of business interventions, we summarise key insights for the period of interest. And we offer brief commentary upon aspects of the recent work of the Institute of Social and Ethical Accountability (ISEA) and the Global Reporting Initiative (GRI), apparently collaborative but strongly business orientated mobilisations of social accounting in the 'globalisation' context of today. We are then concerned to gain insights from a review of mobilisations of social accounting by government and the accountancy profession. Here, we overview the profession's mobilising of *The Corporate Report*, and parallel government activity, again in the UK in the 1970s. Further, we go on to seek to learn from an assessment of certain aspects of academic interventions in respect of social accounting over relatively recent times. The focused, if brief, explorations, here, are prefaced by an overview, integral and geared to the subsequent analyses, of key contextual characteristics and developments and by further introductory elaboration upon social accounting's delineation in this context. The relative emphasis upon the UK in our choice of interventions here reflects in part our geographical location, but also our view that the UK has witnessed key contextual dynamics and some key episodes and interventions involving manifestations of social accounting that are also reflective and to some extent illustrative of more global developments (cf. Gray *et al*. 1996).

Contextual dynamics: an overview

A number of features of the contextual landscape are of relevance in elaborating what was something of a take off in social accounting in the late 1960s and in the 1970s.

In the UK, as throughout the Western world, one can reasonably suggest that hegemonic forces strove for greater legitimacy and also control in the face of what were perceived as increasingly threatening counter hegemonic forces. Governments and established institutions, including the large and monopolistic business corporations whose influence was significant – if it was to later reach greater heights – were pressurised and threatened by a number of factors. Notable, in this regard, were the high expectations of the populace. These expectations in part had been fuelled by a range of social, economic and technological developments, some of which the state had earlier encouraged and mobilised. The public's expectations had grown in the post Second World War context. In the aftermath of the reversal of an explicit Fascism that had assumed significance over the previous quarter century and in the context of the Cold War with the ostensibly communist Soviet Union, Western institutions had felt pressurised to assume responsibility for the delivery of economic progress, a greater sharing of benefits from continuing technological advance, better conditions, more social justice and an enhancement of democracy and openness. Social legislation was enhanced (Hobsbawm 1995). Concerns to manage the economy especially came to the fore (Hopwood *et al.* 1994: 219). Further, control was extended over a variety of businesses. That interventions were apparently at least promising increased the pressure for more of such steering. And, in this regard, the UK government was then understood as a relatively more significant, if declining, centre of power when compared with the situation in the global context today (see Bailey *et al.* 1994, Monbiot 2001).

By the late 1960s, there was a growing frustration about the performance of society's institutions. Political tensions and social trajectories engendered a radical questioning, of increased intensity, of established practices and institutions. This bolstered radical progressive forces in the context. Clifford (2001: 6), reflecting on his own experience, characterises the late 1960s and early 1970s as a period of revolutionary ferment, a period of 'idealism and hope, when the old structures of authority and dominance seemed to be crumbling, a time when those of us who believed, and continue to believe, in the absolute necessity of alternative forms of government and personal relations could profoundly believe that history was on our side' (see Gray 1999: 3). There was a growth in the number of people identifying with the notion of radical progressive development and believing it possible in the context, for instance through the mobilisation of the widespread and developing communicative technologies, to increasingly realise substantive social change. This was an age of significant radical activism. Radical movements, variously democratic, socialistic and anti-establishment, gained support. Support for pressure groups took off. There was diversity here, reflecting what for some was a context of value re-appraisal towards a more holistic way of thinking. Ullman (1976: 71) refers in this respect, for instance, to a 'noticeable shift in public opinion concerning the relative importance of economic goals in relation to other aspects of life'. New social movements were constructed with reference, as notable instances, to ethnicity, gender, sexual orientation, nuclear war and environmentalism. The late 1960s witnessed a significant radical students' movement and a proliferation of political protests and campaigns. In some countries, notably in France, strong alliances were forged between radical students and workers, with capitalistic business a target of attack (Ali and Watkins 1998).

The position of labour itself was deemed an increasing threat to the established order, including in Britain, as the power of the unions was understood to be on the increase. Again, labour's influence had been encouraged to some extent by government. In the post Second World War context, many Western states embraced versions of social democratic politics. A feature, in Britain (see Middlemas 1983) and in Europe more generally, was that trade unions and labour representatives were brought by government into the arena of social and economic policy-making in an enhancement of a corporatist system of industrial relations, a form of organising capitalistic society that had been practiced in various countries prior to the War. By the late 1960s and early 1970s, labour representatives' ostensible involvement in the practice of government had reached something of a zenith. The trade unions were beginning to take their role in government for granted, if there were some moves to enhance further the unions' involvement in economic management and formal politics at the national level. Hopwood *et al.* (1994: 216, 223) note that in the 1970s there was a perceived growth in the militancy and power of the trade union movement, with strikes coming to be measured and being found to be increasing. Trade unions enhanced their struggle for better conditions and higher wages for their members through national bargaining arrangements.[2] Further, the trade unions pushed for an extension of public ownership and supervision, a large-scale re-distribution of income and wealth and an extension of industrial democracy. A liaison committee of the unions and the opposition Labour party committed Labour to such measures in 1973. In *Labour's Programme* 1973 there was a plan for the state takeover of 25 large British companies.[3] Albeit with some reluctance, the nationalisation thrust was supported by the Labour leadership. While the mainstream union movement was not especially radical in respect of industrial democracy, campaigns for it were backed by some senior members of the Labour party and key union figures (Powell 2001: 63).

In the social dynamics, business had to give further attention to the need to attain social legitimacy. A movement of significance here was that grouping around the theme of business ethics and corporate social responsibility from the 1950s and especially the 1960s in the US. Paralleling developments elsewhere in the Western world, the US experienced a crisis more particularly in the 1960s as a number of episodes, including political assassinations and the Vietnam conflict, as well as economic problems, destabilised the US public's 'expectations of a benevolent domestic environment ... Criticism of established institutions and norms developed, culminating in the conflicts of 1968' (Puxty 1986: 102). As Puxty (1986) suggests, these social dynamics led to overt public criticism of business – and subsequently accounting, with a number of 'accounting scandals' being highlighted in public debate. Debates and tensions about the social responsibility of business subsequently became more obviously global, gathering pace with some impact in Britain in the 1970s (Drucker 1965, Hopwood *et al.* 1980, Tinker and Lowe 1980, Gray *et al.* 1996: 92). A number of questions were raised in this context. Was a commitment to the maximisation of profit or shareholder wealth appropriate or sufficient in the context? Should organisations have wider social responsibilities and goals, including in respect of the ecological environment? Should they not be responsible to the public at large beyond the shareholders? Were business organisations, especially given their increasing power (see Bowen 1953), being as socially responsible as they might reasonably be? Such questions helped constitute a challenge for accounting including in the more global context. In the UK too, for instance, various accounting scandals were highlighted (Lowe and Tinker 1977). Moreover, 'social accounting' was on the agenda (Hopwood 1985: 362–3).

Later in the 1970s and by the 1980s, such questioning carried less weight, except in relation to growing concerns about the ecological environment. Writing in 1985, Hopwood could argue of a committee meeting in the 1970s:

> Of course, the committee met at a time when the social was more visible and legitimate. Explicit attempts were being made to produce new intersections of accounting and the social. Effort was being devoted to reforming accounting in the name of the social. All too clearly the situation is very different today. The legitimacy of the social apparently is not so great. The economic has once again monopolized attention and action.
>
> (Hopwood 1985: 375)

The late 1970s witnessed the oil crisis – a restriction of oil supplies leading to a substantial increase in energy costs – and a recession of worldwide impact. This exacerbated the profits squeeze that was associated with the perceived power of labour and the unions, with wage rises recorded as outstripping high levels of inflation and disruptive strikes being recorded as on the increase. Hegemonic forces, reflected in the media and the transition of Western states, exchanged a social democratic and corporatist polity for a more aggressively capitalistic neo-liberalism. Emphasising the formal political orientation, Stuart Hall (1983) refers to 'The Great Moving Right Show' in depicting this contextual change, a change enhanced by the formal ascendancy of Thatcher and Reagan and buoyed in the 1980s by the Cold War victory (Hobsbawm 1995; see also Lehman and Tinker 1987). The unleashing of relatively enhanced market pressures was now seen as the better mechanism for disciplining labour, rather than the subtle interventionist building of industrial harmony and co-ordination. An even freer hand was given to business, as hegemonic forces pushed to reduce the power of the unions, advance privatisation programmes and role back state commitments and interventions, including through a reduction in legislative and quasi-legislative control restricting business.[4] Stress was placed by hegemonic forces in the Western capitalistic context on the need to compete in global markets and such a policy was supported by interventions such as equating to a greater, if still strategic, liberalisation of global markets. The repressive state could increasingly appeal to global structural conditions and the pressures of world competition to justify poor labour practices and inadequate legislative and quasi-legislative standards and regulations. The same sort of rhetoric was also put out by apologists for the huge salaries of some corporate directors and for lax tax regimes: it was a rhetoric that in all these cases could have been seriously deflated by the mobilising of substantive global as opposed to local regulations. Democracy, crudely in one of its popular senses as the exercising of power by the people, a continuing threat to relatively powerful established interests, was not just heavily manipulated, it was increasingly suppressed. A less fettered global capitalism gave relatively more power to global, transnational business in relation to nation state governments, if some of the more powerful governments (notably the US) appeared to welcome aspects of this as an aid to polity geared to maintaining and enhancing current structure (Bailey *et al.* 1994, Monbiot 2001). In the absence of a properly functioning world parliament, this context of globalisation equated to a constraining of democratic forces (Held and McGrew 2000, Monbiot 2002). Monbiot (2001) refers here to the corporatisation of Britain and much else besides: that is, the pervasive influence of business organisations in this context. Political dependencies and interdependencies, global business influence and the functioning of global hegemonic forces became increasingly apparent. The potential for acts at one location of the global system to impact at another some distance away has been enhanced (Held and McGrew 2000). Monbiot (2001) suggests that large transnational corporations recently accrued a tremendous influence on supra-national bodies such as the World Bank and the World Trade Organisation. The United Nations, long criticised for being dominated by powerful interests of the status quo, has been seen as increasingly coming to collaborate with big business in this regard.

If the immediate post Second World War context fostered the social democratic in the West, the late twentieth century tended to enforce a more capitalistic polity. If labour, the unions, new social movements and even democratic socialistic forces were gaining influence of significance in the late 1960s and early 1970s, by the 1980s these forces had been significantly weakened. More and more people were, it seems, susceptible to the dynamics of big business interventions in shifting politico-economic contexts. Concerns to protect people and even to provide basic social and economic security were attacked. One force with strong counter hegemonic dimensions that continued to grow in spite of the broader political changes, bolstered by the weight of scientific opinion, was environmentalism, particularly in terms of a focus on sustainability. Capturing many people's attention, to some extent this exerted a similar kind of pressure on business and governments to that engendered by the earlier social responsibility and related movements. The problematic actual and potential ecological impacts clearly cut across the boundaries of given nation state contexts, notably in the case of global warming. Thus developments and movements were further encouraged to think and act globally (Gallhofer and Haslam 1997b). As some forms of environmentalism and sustainability also stressed the case for wider social responsibility, these broader concerns began to return to a higher level on the agenda (Gray and Bebbington 2001).

What is social accounting? Deliberations in the historical context and some critical reflections

We have suggested that, in the late 1960s and in the 1970s, business organisations and social institutions in general perceived themselves to be pressurised and threatened. In the case of business organisations, the issue of corporate social responsibility was here a key one. The sort of questioning of business we have referred to translated in part into calls for more openness and transparency, coming to pressurise government and the accountancy profession (*subter*) as well as business. The discourse and polemics helped to advance a 'social' accounting on the agenda: calls for more openness and transparency were in part being translated into calls for social accounting. In the introduction to this chapter, we introduced our social accounting focus by characterising it as ostensibly an accounting challenging conventional accounting. We there suggested that this challenging includes deeming conventional accounting deficient vis-à-vis concerns that social responsibilities be better fulfilled in the name of the enhancement of social well-being or, put differently, deeming it deficient in not reflecting everything that matters to society or to various key groups within society. This characterisation, or delineation, constitutes the social accounting we focus on in the analyses of this chapter. In this section, we are concerned to provide a summary overview of this delineation as manifesting in the historical context of recent decades. Such an overview helps to clarify the character of the particular manifestations of social accounting that are focused upon in our subsequent analyses. And reflection upon our overview here already can suggest the criteria by which these manifestations can be evaluated in those analyses.[5]

A basic notion of social accounting that still circulates in the discourse is constituted by a simple dichotomous differentiation between conventional and social accounting. Conventional accounting is here reduced to financial economistic accounting in general, with the latter conceived of in terms of its emphasis upon the numerical and the monetary (e.g. Hopwood and Burchell 1980) or the economic (e.g. Gray 1999: 2). The reduction of conventional to financial economistic accounting thus makes possible delineation by a single criterion. Albeit that conventional accounting is here reduced to financial economistic accounting, the image of conventional accounting here corresponds typically, as in most constructions, to the narrowly financial economistic substance of mainstream financial accounting practice. That is, it typically corresponds to taken for granted and adopted accounting practice with its influential emphasis upon depicting the stock and flow of an entity in financial terms.[6] This basic notion of social accounting seems to us to remain influential, although it has been problematised and has been largely surpassed by an approach that allows some types of financial economistic accounting to be categorised as social accounting. In what is in effect a more complex way of seeing social accounting, social is here distinguished from conventional accounting by reference to a range of criteria. It is the character of these criteria and how they have come to be applied in the constitution of social accounting, on the one hand, and conventional accounting, on the other, that have rendered both social accounting and conventional accounting more complex constructs, reflective of a compromised fusion of ideas. A factor here is that, while an accounting manifestation can satisfy all the criteria of relevance, there are points of inconsistency, as well as overlap, between these criteria. Accountings have been understood as 'social' where they have satisfied all or some of these criteria and by reference to the *extent* they have satisfied these criteria. That is, the criteria applied in constituting social and conventional accounting have involved relational rather than dichotomous conceptualisations: the labelling of a particular accounting as social has reflected a subjective assessment of the emphases involved. The more complex way of seeing is exemplified by social accounting's application to the case of the business organisation, the application that has come to assume particular prominence in relatively recent times. The range of criteria by which social and conventional accounting have been delineated in this context can be summarised as follows. Social accounting, as in the case of the basic way of seeing, is demarcated as an accounting going beyond the financial economistic, notably in the assessing of business performance. It is differentiated from an accounting constrained to reflect what are conventionally assumed to be the interests of the shareholders. Social accounting here reflects a presumption, at least on the face of it, that the goal of the business organisation properly goes beyond the narrow and conventional focus upon profit or financial wealth maximisation in current or envisaged contexts. Social accounting goes beyond an accounting for the use of shareholders only, with other users, including the public at large, and hence multifarious usages, being envisaged. And, as indicated, it is an accounting that to some extent satisfies one or more of these criteria.[7] That these criteria involve inconsistency and contradiction can be illustrated. For instance, an accounting orientated to a group beyond the shareholders, such as one orientated to the employees, can focus on the financial economistic at least to some extent: it can, for example, be an accounting analysing the different pay received by different categories of workers, with a view to securing greater justice for labour. In focusing on the financial economistic, such an accounting scarcely well satisfies the criterion of going beyond financial economistic accounting. In effect, as we have already indicated, the discourse of social accounting in such instances has deemed it unnecessary for an accounting to satisfy all the key criteria elaborated to be named as social accounting. What is taken or not taken to be social accounting – or, conversely, conventional accounting – has predominantly come to reflect an assessment of the extent to which one or more of the range of criteria are satisfied. That is, it has come to be a matter of emphasis in these terms.

Social accounting has been delineated as something of a compromised fusion. Writers such as Milne (1996) have in this respect characterised the fuzzy relationship we have elaborated upon here in terms of overlapping sets. While, in the basic way of seeing social accounting, the dominant differentiating characteristic is understood in terms of *content* and *form*, in the more complex way relatively more weight is given to the envisaged *role* and *purpose* of social accounting. Both of these ways of seeing, in finding conventional accounting deficient, have been mobilised ostensibly to give social accounting a progressive edge. Indeed, both of these ways of seeing social accounting are not only promoted by concerns about social responsibility but also promote such concerns themselves. The more complex way of seeing social accounting, however, by placing greater stress on the role and purpose of accounting, arguably constitutes a more positive alignment to the progressive. This complex way of seeing, as the literature of social accounting illustrates (Gray *et al.* 1996), has especially come to dominate the social accounting discourse over recent decades – in the context of social accounting's take off and relatively high-profile trajectory. This last point emphasises the mutability of social accounting and, since conventional accounting moves in tandem, the mutability of conventional accounting too.

Reflecting on the mutability of accounting, and social accounting in particular, we can more clearly envisage the potentialities of social accounting in terms of its emancipatory as well as repressive possibilities. In our subsequent analyses of social accounting in action we can helpfully draw upon a schema that differentiates our social accounting focus, already seen as variously progressive, into broad types of social accounting that are demarcated by reference to their radical orientation or the extent to which they are emancipatory in intent. The radicality of the orientation is thus reflected in the envisaged role, content and form of the social accounting and, for instance, shapes whether the 'challenging' of conventional accounting involved in its constitution is seen more as opposing, or working alongside, or even enhancing, this accounting. Our schema, which we introduce below, to some extent draws from related attempts to appreciate the notion of different social accountings that one finds in especially academic discourse (for instance, Gray *et al.* 1988, Tinker *et al.* 1991). The schema is mobilised in all of our subsequent analyses, taking on a particular resonance in our critique of the academic discourse given that related, if differing, categorisings of social accounting are features of this discourse. Such a schema involves simplification. As Chapter 1 helps us to see, social accounting manifestations of practice will share commonalities and be located on a continuum rather than fall into absolutely distinct categories. Particular manifestations will be mixtures of the different types rather than correspond to the ideal–typical categories. Nevertheless, an appreciation of the notion that a social accounting might be more or less radical should helpfully inform and enhance our analyses and later reflections.

A critical theoretical appreciation of complex and consequential manifestations of social accounting in our view recognises the sense in which they constitute a range of forces that are neither properly theorised as purely emancipatory nor as purely repressive and recognises at the same time how these manifestations can be located on a continuum which summarises their functioning in terms of an overall emancipatory or repressive tendency. A 'radical social accounting' in our view is more explicitly concerned to contribute to a radical critique of the socio-political order, including its business organisations and their activities, and to strive for radical democratic and socialistic development. Consistent with Tinker (1980, 1984a,b, 1985, Tinker *et al.* 1982, 1991), a Marxist orientated advocacy of radical social accounting for business organisations is concerned to challenge financial economistic dimensions of existing accountings as well as to go beyond these accountings. Such a perspective emphasises problematics of an abstracted neo-classical perspective of value, which largely, if imperfectly, informs much conventional accounting and substantively mainstream current accounting practice (Tinker 1980, 1984a, 1985, Tinker *et al.* 1982).[8] It challenges an accounting that functions in conformance with the neo-classical tendency to abstract from a context of significance and to unquestioningly accept in this regard the distorted valuations that manifest in a problematic context – including the giving of even no value to things not priced by the market, irrespective of their substantive value for society. At the same time, a radical social accounting for us is characterised also by a strong concern to go beyond the narrow conventional accounting. If it makes sense to conceive of a radical social accounting it also in our view makes sense to conceive of the possibility of a 'counter radical' social accounting. This, for us, is a type of social accounting that might formally satisfy the criteria for categorisation as social accounting (*supra*) – but that is, however, substantially captured by problematic forces intent on countering the push towards radical progress. Such social accounting is conceived of as having gone beyond the conventional but with an orientation towards the preservation or enhancement of the current socio-political order rather than something akin to an emancipatory intent. Given these two opposite orientations – very broad classifications but reflecting the key concern to theorise alternative social accountings aligned with alternative politico-ethical stances – one can conceive of a variety of positions in between the 'radical' and the 'counter radical'. One such type elaborated in the literature – a type emerging substantively in the context of the late twentieth century take off in social accounting and the relatively high profile trajectory of social accounting that ensued – has been accused of metaphorically falling down the hole in the 'middle of the road' between different political orientations. It has been termed 'mainstream social accounting' by its proponents as well as opponents (see Tinker *et al.* 1991, Gray *et al.* 1996, Owen *et al.* 2000). This type of social accounting, while arguably highly prone to capture by hegemonic forces – the real connotation of 'falling down the hole' – is arguably better theorised as 'mildly progressive' than as 'middle of the road' in terms of the above schema. It is, however, one of the varieties in between our two more 'extreme' tendencies and academic proponents of mainstream social accounting have variously expressed alignment to 'liberal democracy' and to anti-revolutionary, pragmatic and gradualist orientations to differentiate themselves from more radical approaches that go beyond alignment with mainstream social accounting (see Gray *et al.* 1996). If mainstream social accounting at a general level of resolution has much in common with at least some versions of radical social accounting, it has been characterised typically by its less radical orientation to the socio-political order (see Gray *et al.* 1987, 1996, Tinker *et al.* 1991).

Publicity at the service of different masters: towards a comparison and contrast of the social accounting interventions of pressure groups and social activists with those of business organisations

Here we are concerned to contribute to a comparison and contrast between counter information systems type mobilisings of social accounting and the mobilising of social accounting by business organisations. On the face of it, the intent of the former is radically orientated while that of the latter is especially suspect from a critical theoretical perspective.

Of the myriad of social accounting interventions from the late 1960s onwards, amongst the ones that are on the face of it most suggestive of radical orientation and emancipatory intent are those involving the mobilising of social accounting by pressure groups and social activist groups, especially those with radical aims. In the context of these relatively recent times, a number of such groups have in effect identified with the view that the social responsibility of business ought to go beyond maximising profit or shareholder wealth. And some have identified with the promise of a social accounting that would engender more openness in respect of the matters they have deemed relevant. Thus, as well as there having been interest expressed in a more expansive accounting beyond the conventional on the part of unions and labour, to which we turn our attention later, some pressure groups and social activists have been particularly interested in such accounting too. Indeed, a take off in the radically orientated 'social auditing' was noticeable in the UK (Hopwood 1985: 362, Owen *et al.* 2000). Amongst those seeing a value in such forms of social accounting have been The Institute of Workers Control, groups of academic activists, Friends of the Earth, Greenpeace, The Consumers Association, critical journalists, various ethical consumer and investment groups, local authorities, The New Economics Foundation, Environmental Data Services, Corporate Watch, CorpWatch, Essential Action, Indymedia and Schnews. Let us focus in initially upon the social accounting interventions of CIS, a social activist group operating in the UK in the 1970s.

Of those pressure groups and social activists groups taking an interest in social accounting, some engaged in what we can properly call counter information systems type activity, activity echoing Bentham's advocacy of unofficial publicity systems that would challenge official publicities and raise questions in society (Bentham 1843a: 592, cf. Mack 1962: 182, Peters 1993). Some even came to make the provision of information to the public, including to other pressure groups and activists, their main *raison d'être*. For these, the stress placed on the role of information and audit in bringing about social betterment and justice was such that the mobilisation of these systems dominated their *modus operandi* and helped to give them their names. Prominent instances in the 1970s were Social Audit Ltd and CIS. Social Audit Ltd, which still operates today – concentrating its focus on pharmaceutical companies under the continuing direction of Charles Medawar (see Medawar 1976, Gray 1999: 12) – had as one of its objectives 'to illustrate the feasibility of progress towards the day when reasonable safeguards of economic democracy will be embodied in law and social audit universals' (Gray *et al.* 1996: 266).[9] This group held social accounting and audit – in the more expansive and evaluative sense – to be key safeguards in this context and produced accounting reports on government, specific industries and also on particular business organisations. They always attempted to build the latter reports in co-operation with the business concerned. Often failing to gain or retain this co-operation, they nevertheless pressed ahead while taking the opportunity to highlight the lack of co-operation and call for greater legislative control, thus further antagonising the organisation's management (Gray *et al.* 1996: 267, 271). The reports were constructed in part to show what could be done within existing laws and with a view to stimulating substantive social accounting and auditing prescription, including in terms of more 'independent' disclosures – beyond a trusting in business. A typical report analysed the financial accounts, including value added statements, the competitive character of the organisation's environment, wages, job conditions, job security, equality, health and safety and motivation, record in respect of consumers, advertising policy and practice, environmental impact against standards and local community impact. The form of the reports went beyond that of accounting reports as conventionally envisaged. Highly detailed and lengthy, reports were mainly narrative, with photographs, cartoons, compliance with standard summaries, and quantitative/statistical summaries including tabulated financial data (see Gray *et al.* 1996: 267–71). While many of the practices of Social Audit Ltd. evidenced similarities to those of CIS, the latter embraced, on the face of it, a more radical stance and emancipatory intent. For Gray *et al.* (1996: 274), the CIS 'Anti-Reports' or counter accountings were 'important as a … somewhat rare, example of a "radical" approach to reporting, produced on a regular basis'.[10] Our focus upon CIS here consequently reflects a number of factors. It reflects our view that there are continuities and discontinuities in the interface of pressure groups and related groups with social accounting from the time of this earlier intervention through to today. And the choice also reflects our assessment, vis-à-vis our concern to gain general insights for praxis today, of the significance of this particular intervention in terms of the nature of the activity involved as well as the context in which it was located. We discuss below apparently positive dimensions of the activities of CIS in relation to emancipatory concerns. We also bring out some problematic aspects of CIS and limitations to CIS's operations given its context. In this regard we make the point that CIS is not alone in mobilising social accounting and indeed is engaged in a struggle, notably with business organisations, to capture this practice. We broaden out upon this point to elaborate upon business interventions in respect of social accounting to constitute a comparison and contrast with counter information systems type mobilisings of social accounting. Shifting the focus more towards today, we go on to compare interventions and struggles of very recent times, comparing the interventions of today's social activists with the apparently collaborative but business orientated interventions of ISEA and the GRI.

In line with Champion in the late nineteenth century, CIS, financed by the Transnational Institute, the Joseph Rowntree Social Services Trust and the sale of its publications, was a collective of journalists dedicated to bringing about action to effect radical social change by highlighting, through its reporting, injustice, especially capitalistic exploitation, repression and alienation. The group produced reports referred to as 'Anti-Reports', reports focusing upon a number of areas that reflected the diversity of the group's radical interests. For instance, *Cutting the Welfare State: Who Profits?* (1975) aimed at exposing the interested nature of the public spending cuts. It sought to provide information to those dependent on welfare services and to public sector workers. *Women under Attack* (1976) was aimed at making visible the extent of women's dependency on anti-anxiety drugs in battling with stress (Ridgers 1979: 229–31). CIS reports also focused upon specific business organisations (including Rio Tinto Zinc, General Electric Company, British Leyland, Courtaulds, Unilever and Ford). A particular feature of the CIS approach was an explicit concern to enroll the workers in a form of immanent critique of capitalistic management and governance. One of the CIS collaborators, Ridgers (1979: 326), articulates the group's goals as 'providing information resources for workers engaged in specific struggles and exposing the nature of the social and economic system which is the cause and content of these struggles'. The CIS Anti-Report *Where is Lucas Going?* (CIS 1975), a report produced in the mid-1970s upon Lucas Ltd, is a good illustration of a report focused upon a particular business, that mobilised a radical form of social accounting. Analysis of this report allows us to elaborate upon aspects of CIS's mode of critique, some of the themes CIS pursued, the social accountings CIS mobilised, the ways in which CIS mobilised these social accountings and the problematics of and limits to CIS's activity.

The basic way in which the report seeks to raise especially workers' awareness of the injustices of business operations is through a mode of immanent critique reflected in all the themes it pursues. The report contrasts the business management's representation of Lucas and its broader context, which basically amounts to portraying the company and the socio-political system as good in ethical terms, with an alternative account indicating a counter view. In developing the critique, workers are given a voice in the counter reporting. This is not just a strategy but a basic principle shaping CIS's vision (Ridgers 1979). The report uses the employees' own words to emphasise how Lucas management held themselves out as good employers: 'We are told that Lucas has always done its best for us – "a job at Lucas is a job for life". Our welfare, our safety, our feeling of oneness has always been the company's major concern' (CIS 1975: 3). Similarly, the report brings out how the company portrays itself as struggling on behalf of the workforce and community in the face of what the company holds out to be unavoidable financial pressures. The image of a caring company in difficult financial times is contrasted with the view that the company was treating the employees unreasonably in spite of what was actually financial success (see Ridgers 1979: 311). The report counters the view that Lucas was having financial difficulties by highlighting (CIS 1975: 6) that the company had benefited from the oil crisis as a result of an acceleration in the demand for diesel engines, noting Lucas's relatively healthy indebtedness and detailing the firm's impressive stock market performance – the market being described as 'electrified' by the 'near record half-yearly trading profit for 31 January 1975' (CIS 1975: 4). In elaborating upon Lucas's financial success, the authors of the CIS report are able to refer to broader concerns about what was possible given the character of the socio-economic context. For instance, the report points to how Lucas had secured a strong position in the motor industry by eliminating competitors through takeovers and cartels. In elaborating aspects of the problematic way Lucas treated the workers, CIS is concerned to contrast its critical observations with Lucas's rhetoric and disclosures in its own employee reporting or social accounting as well as in its accounting more generally. The Lucas Anti-Report suggests that the company's approach to reducing costs had engendered more hazardous and dangerous working conditions. One woman is reported as summarising factory conditions by stating that: 'You freeze to death in winter and heat knocks you out in summer' (CIS 1975: 5). The report contrasts such observations with the company's own policy or mission statement: 'It is the company's policy to provide safe and healthy working conditions and to ensure that the conduct of its affairs is not harmful to the health of its employees or the general community' (CIS 1975: 19). The Anti-Report also draws attention to problematic working conditions in the South African and Brazilian factories, internationalising their concerns. A particular feature of the CIS reporting on working conditions and health and safety issues is that the impact upon the local community, in particular upon the children of those working in the factories, is stressed and broadened to some extent into a general concern about pollution:

> Reddings Lane runs alongside the Lucas Formans Road battery factory. Huge acid tanks tower over the houses in Reddings Lane, families in the road suffer the fumes day and night. The McCrellis family say their kids choke when they're trying to get to sleep and always have headaches and have dizzy spells. In the

same street a three year old boy killed several of his pets for no reason. His father works in the Lucas battery factory. A baby from Reddings Lane has been taken into Selly Oak Hospital because it keeps getting sick. All these children had a high concentration of lead in their blood.

(CIS 1975: 19, 21)

The Lucas report also reflects CIS's concern to expose aspects of the multiplicity of experiences of repression of the workers. Particular attention is given in the report to the experiences of women workers. The low wages paid to women in the workforce, who were mainly part-time, are highlighted, as are the higher bonus rates paid to men relative to women for doing the same job. One female worker is reported to have the following views in respect of her experience of assembly line work:

Lots of the women are trained to do mindless jobs and many of them are very intelligent. Operators start feeling like cabbages. On the assembly line you get so dulled that your mind slumps; you don't bother to respond to people when they talk to you and you don't answer questions. It doesn't seem worthwhile, you just can't be bothered. I think assembly work effects your brain. It's so boring.

(CIS 1975: 5)

Another female worker is reported as reflecting on her working experience as follows:

I'm older now. I've got used to it ... Some of the women though, I don't know how they manage. I think eight out of ten of them are on tranquillisers. They worry about getting to work in the morning if they're on early shifts. They worry about the kids getting to school. They worry about the piecework, then they go home and have to worry about getting the housework done. I've seen them line tranquillisers and pills up alongside their plates in the canteen like rows of dolly mixtures.

(CIS 1975: 5)

These two citations are aimed at raising awareness about the impact of alienating working practices on spiritual well-being and at highlighting aspects of the several types of repression experienced by women given the various roles, including that of worker and mother, society expects of them.

The Lucas Anti-Report also explicitly discusses strategies on the part of business management to divide the employees of the company. For one worker, Lucas was trying to 'maintain fragmentation, union by union, area by area, product group by product group' and to divide Lucas companies and workers of different skills: 'There's no communication between the groups and the areas and Lucas knows it and loves it' (CIS 1975: 27). The Anti-Report draws attention to a job evaluation system encompassing twenty nine grades that were vaguely distinct, rendering plant and national level negotiations extremely difficult: 'The workforce is the victim of this chaos. It is a management scheme, management administered, and its end result is a multi-graded workforce often incapable of any sort of solidarity or cohesive activity'

(CIS 1975: 27). Throughout the year, it was further reported, senior union stewards attended special courses on industrial relations run by Lucas that were described by the workers as 'a concentrated Lucas public relations and indoctrination exercise' (CIS 1975). According to the report, the company especially tried to ensure that workers' representatives were loyal to the company through participation in Lucas committees. CIS, in pursuing its critical themes in the Lucas Anti-Report, mobilise various accountings, in various ways, including adopting a range of strategies. The CIS reporters here indicate, à la Champion, a degree of sophistication in respect of their usage of conventional accounting. They make the point, for instance, that the company's accounting was known to be cautious in respect of profit and that, even given this, Lucas were nevertheless reporting near record high accounting profits in 1974–5, the year focused upon (CIS 1975: 8). While thus mobilising the company's financial accounting, the CIS team also shows technical sophistication in mounting a critique of this accounting. They therefore buttress their argument through, and at the same time render their report a vehicle for, the mobilisation and critique of the actually existing accounting. They criticise associate company accounting, transfer pricing practice, aggregation of trading figures and a failure to breakdown assets on a geographical basis, suggesting in effect that these practices amounted to distortions and manipulations to help hide actualities from the view of workers and the public (CIS 1975: 9). As well as challenging and making use of Lucas's conventional accounting, CIS also challenge and at least in this sense make use of Lucas's own social accounting and employee reporting, for example, referring to the dubious public relations' character of the latter in the following:

> In recent years it has apparently been management's policy to further conceal what is actually going on, despite the gloss of the Report to Employees. British subsidiaries ... used to report separately to Companies House ... and anyone could go along there and see their accounts ... These figures are now not available ... you cannot tell which subsidiary sold what anymore.
>
> (CIS 1975: 9)

The report critically reflects upon what was at stake in the change: 'This, as Lucas apparently boasted in a letter to banks and finance companies, serves to conceal the actual performance of each of the individual product groups from "interested parties" – particularly the workforce' (CIS 1975: 9). Through a sophisticated usage and critique of accountings, CIS thus aimed to help strengthen their reporting in relation to their concern to create an awareness of the company's failings vis-à-vis the welfare of the workers.

As well as mobilising a financial economistic accounting which in part made use of Lucas's own reportings, the Lucas Anti-Report embraces the use of narrative. The CIS group attempt here, at least, to tailor the narrative to reach a wide audience and especially the Lucas workforce. Including narratives of experience is seen as helping to bring attention to repressive practices. We have already in effect illustrated this usage of narrative above. In elaborating upon employee conditions, where a concern to counter Lucas's own employee reporting is evident, a mainly narrative style is adopted. Narrative is especially used to elaborate upon divisive management practices and to suggest that Lucas care little about their local community. The concern to reach a wide audience is explicitly suggested by Ridgers (1979: 327), for whom 'dissemination of information is ... central to effective counter-information'. By transforming at least aspects of the role, scope, content, form and aura of conventional accounting in their own reporting practice, CIS arguably facilitate alternative ways of seeing to the mainstream. They thus on the face of it better challenge problematic forces and align with the relatively oppressed and projects with emancipatory intent. According to Ridgers (1979: 327), workers were brought together by the intervention in respect of Lucas. Questions of content and form were explicitly considered by CIS as a matter of strategy. For Ridgers (1979: 331), 'counter-information is no neutral artefact: its form and content need to be tailored to the political task in question'. The Lucas Anti-Report reveals usage of a particular format or layout to emphasise the form of immanent critique (cf. Gallhofer and Haslam 1996a). It is a format that very much echoes Champion. Reports of financial success and 'rational' business plans are sharply juxtaposed against workers' experiences and concerns. Left-hand pages summarise the company management's position. Right-hand pages – in a different typescript, emphasising the contrast – give the counter.

Counter Information Services put together their elaborations upon the situation, strategies and practices of Lucas partly through the creative and innovative usage of annual reports, newspapers and other publicly available information and partly through the collecting of data and construction of information beyond that already publicly available. Instances of the latter involved the CIS reporters talking with the employees and the local community and reflecting interviewee opinions. Again this echoes the practices of the nineteenth century socialist agitators discussed earlier. The enrolling of the employees in the collecting and reporting of information is a particular feature of the Lucas Anti-Report. Relatively close co-operation with the employees was secured in the Lucas case. Ridgers maintained:

> ... we sought to make as many contacts as possible with the workforce: the report had to be acceptable and useful to the workers. Their experience and knowledge was an integral part of the generation and organisation of our data, and their active involvement in preparing the report also facilitated its distribution.
>
> (Ridgers 1979: 331)

The Lucas Anti-Report had actually been requested by Lucas shop stewards and there was a reasonably high level of collaboration with the workforce. This approach of CIS whereby employees are enrolled in the project reflects a concern to go beyond a 'privileged knower' stance. An aspect of the potential of avoiding such a stance is arguably indicated in that contact with the workers was maintained after the publication of an Anti-Report. For instance, co-operation over CIS's Anti-Report of GEC led to the founding, in collaboration with CIS, of a company-wide newspaper for employees that sought to expose company malpractices. Giving workers a voice was understood as better facilitating the creation and sustaining amongst the workers of an awareness of exploitative work practices. As well as attempting to go beyond the privileged knower, the Lucas Anti-Report, notably in its concerns to give female workers a voice and relate their own specific grievances, relatedly reflected a type of differentiated universalist stance to the reporting of the experience of repression. A feature of the CIS Anti-Reporting is that it does not shy away from its political alignment. It explicitly seeks to counter injustice and specifically in the Lucas case to aid the workers in their struggle against the threat of redundancy. The report explores business management strategies in terms of a conflict with labour. The rhetoric of Lucas's management is admitted to be effective while being attacked (CIS 1975: 10). The workers are encouraged in the report by some elaboration upon successes they had already achieved as well as given insights concerning the difficulties they encountered in relation to this struggle. The report ends by pointing to the necessity of workers uniting to achieve better conditions: 'Until workers in other divisions combine to make overall strategy a reality, all resistance to Lucas's ruthless company-wide rationalisation will remain isolated' (CIS 1975: 45).

Reflecting on the interventions of CIS as illustrated in the Lucas Anti-Report, and upon counter-information systems activity in general, one can point to some problematic dimensions or limitations of such activity in the context vis-à-vis a project of critical emancipatory intent. One can indicate particular areas and suggest that dimensions of the potentiality of CIS were unrealised. For example, although CIS shows an awareness of the multiplicity of the experience of repression in referring to women, other groups and issues, such as the experiences of different ethnicities, have in effect been silenced. CIS's concern to reflect the multiplicity of experiences could have been extended further into the local and broader community. The focus upon employees displaces attention from others and displaces the possibility of helping other change agents, consistent with the open character of a critical theoretical approach today. In respect to the employees, CIS could have covered more categories of worker to better bring out experiences and impacts, including former workers of Lucas.

One can argue that CIS show in the context what was possible in terms of counter-information. Yet it is worth emphasising that there were limits to what CIS could do in terms of structural impediments to their actions in the context. A specific issue here for counter-information activity is that operating within the law poses its own particular obstacles. For example, there are the difficulties of gaining access, by keeping within the law, to the information on organisations that would be useful for the purposes of putting together an alternative report (Stephenson 1973, Gray 1980, Gray *et al.* 1996: chapter 9).[11] More generally, in drawing from or acting consistently with the practices of the context, especially the established institutional and lawful practices, there is a danger of at least to some extent reinforcing rather than challenging the socio-political order. To argue otherwise is to fail to see the penetration of hegemonic forces in these situated practices. What is possible is not neutral. While we argue that the practices of the social context are not fully under the control of hegemonic forces they are, nevertheless, heavily influenced by them. CIS in effect worked hard to avoid such capture by adopting a deliberately critical stance that was concerned to challenge business management and by giving an opportunity to employees to voice their ethical opinions. Nevertheless, our suggestion is that it is impossible to escape capture absolutely, given the imperfect character of the context. A group concerned to engage in counter-information systems activity is trying to balance working within and against the socio-political order. For instance, it is seeking to work at least typically within the law and at the same time to challenge the law. Engaging in one of these activities may to some extent counter the other or displace it from attention. Choices made in practice inevitably will be imperfect to some extent given the context and the insurmountable tensions involved. Relatedly, if CIS were concerned to avoid the stance of the privileged knower or the professional-expert they could not entirely do so and this, as we have seen, involves some negation, including displacing other interventions (Harte and Owen 1987, Gallhofer and Haslam 1997b). One can point out, in this regard, that CIS were concerned themselves to use aspects of established professional-expert practices in terms of content, form and aura.

Another concern here is that counter-information systems type activity, including CIS, could easily accrue a negative image in the context focused upon and thus come to be more easily dismissed. Diverse, uncoordinated, somewhat marginal and short-lived practices can be labeled as lacking 'standards' and even as eccentric by more established forces and it is difficult to mobilise strategies to counter this. In this regard, the various groups involved in mobilising counter information systems have, on the face of it, scarcely acted in a unified way and a number, including CIS, have failed to survive over a long period of time. Gray *et al.* (1996), albeit reserving positive comments for CIS, echo the negative rhetoric that was possible in terms of standards by describing 'the priorities of some counter reports as being a "good story"' that is 'quite deliberately selective and biased' (273) and by referring to some producers of more radical publicities as 'self appointed' watchdogs (275). They also suggest that publicities like CIS amount to an 'investigative journalism' and compare this unfavourably with their vision of social accounting, arguing that in the reports 'the frequent expressions of writers' opinions could be viewed as defects in the communication process'. In this respect Gray *et al.* (1996: 272) comment on the 'vivid, emotive phraseology' of CIS. If this rhetoric sets or implies an impossible criterion of neutrality for social accounting as well as delimits its potential content and form, it also reflects a powerful established institutional discourse that is mostly difficult for counter information systems type activity to compete with (Gallhofer and Haslam 1991).

Building upon the above points, a key structural and contextual factor that delimits and disturbs the functioning of groups seeking to mobilise social accounting as counter information systems activity is that they are engaged in a struggle with other groups to capture social accounting's possibilities. Furthermore, these other forces and groups are relatively more powerful than pressure groups and social activists. Notably, they manifest in the form of powerful business organisations. From the late 1960s and the 1970s through to today business organisations have expressed an apparent interest in mobilising social accounting. In the UK bodies such as the Confederation of British Industry (see CBI 1973) ostensibly encouraged such activity.[12] From the 1970s onwards there was especially an increase in reporting to employees and in employee-orientated themes in business accounting (Maunders 1984, Hopwood *et al.* 1994). In the 1980s there was a dramatic increase in business social accounting focused ostensibly upon the ecological impact of business organisations

(Gray and Bebbington 2001). Analyses in the literature to date suggest that the number of interventions reflecting substantially positive identifications with broader notions of social responsibility, and embracing substantively progressive versions of social accounting that would challenge the status quo have been small. Inconsistent with the basic capitalistic tenets of the business system, serious instances have been the practices of organisations akin to charities, some of these explicitly distancing themselves from profit-orientation, such as Traidcraft in recent times (see Zadek and Evans 1993, Gray *et al.* 1995a: 285–7).[13] Moreover, the literature suggests that even these limited efforts of business to mobilise something akin to an at least mildly progressive social accounting diminish in the face of policy initiatives to re-inforce conventional behaviour and at times of financial crisis. In this respect the oil crisis and recession of the late 1970s impacted negatively upon some aspects of social accounting's promotion (Hopwood and Burchell 1980: 14, see also Maunders 1981, 1982a,b, Gray *et al.* 1995a, 1996: 93, 116, Mathews 1997: 482). Some of the more positive interventions, especially in the 1970s, appear to have reflected the pressures upon business – the threats posed, for instance, by a deteriorating public image of business, a shift towards interventionism in respect of legislative or quasi-legislative regulation and ethical consumerist and ethical investment activity.[14] Most business social accounting disclosure, whether pressurised or not, has constituted, however, a counter radical social accounting. This is broadly to agree with the weight of substantiated argument in the literature. Much theorising of social accounting practice has properly emphasised the tendency of business organisations over recent decades to hijack social accounting for their own public relations' purposes and to mobilise it to counter more progressive social accounting possibilities. In practice and in proposals, social accounting has been watered down by business or problematically steered. It has been made integral to a public relations exercise of the more dubious variety: the telling of good news rather than bad news, the countering of bad news, a practice of the larger company that could most afford it and put it better to their advantage, and a justification for the functioning of business operations within the existing or within some other envisaged minimal framework of legislative or quasi-legislative control. Social accounting practice has exhibited great diversity (see Gray *et al.* 1995a) but most theorising of it indicates that across this diversity much of it has been problematic in the above terms.[15] Hopwood (1978: 56) suggests that corporations may have seen social accounting as a means of establishing and reinforcing their claim to social legitimacy. In doing this, however, businesses have been problematically manipulative and deceptive doing more to reproduce and enhance rather than to challenge and counter the problematic socio-political order. Puxty (1986: 99–100) cites Burchell *et al.* (1985) in suggesting in effect that a counter radical social accounting has functioned more intensely and effectively than conventional accounting in this regard (see also Hopwood 1978). Many would agree that, even while mobilising their social accountings, the substantive opposition of business to legislative or quasi-legislative interventionism in this area helps to reinforce the point.[16] In this regard, some business managers have explicitly and officially opposed interventions threatening their discretion. Gallhofer and Haslam (1997) cite a few illustrative and recent management views in respect of environmental accounting.

For Buck (1992: 38), of the Institute of Directors, business should aid the environment but 'these are matters for the company – not for government legislation' (cf. Blaza 1992: 34). It seems that business spokespersons have rarely felt they had to justify their anti-interventionism, albeit occasionally pointing to motivational arguments and the crudeness and/or costliness of a legislative approach. They have often drawn from a popular rhetoric as if the case was self-evident, some expressing the view that management needs to be trusted for results (see Cannon 1994, Gallhofer and Haslam 1997: 155–6). Where discretion has been possible, most businesses have not had their social accounts attested substantively and independently from business management and owners (Gray *et al.* 1995a: 48). Even in the unlikely event that most of those seeking to protect their discretion do so with appropriate intentions, uncoordinated micro-organisational responses fail to re-assure. The pronouncements do not constitute an argument against more substantive regulation that would seemingly give further re-assurance (see Tinker 1985, Hines 1991b, Maunders and Burritt 1991: 23–4, Gallhofer and Haslam, 1993, Semple 1993). It appears that given the contextual pressures to pursue the conventional financial goals and conform with hegemonic preferences, there are incentives to avoid engaging in social accounting or to embrace its more counter radical varieties (see Owen 1992b: 7, see also Bronner 1994: 347). Hall's (1991) suggestion that strong capitalistic structures have never willingly reduced business profit materially in the general interest is pertinent here. Further, for Bronner (1994) the concern to capture disclosures can constitute a strong motivation for intervention on the part of the relatively powerful in this context: powerful established forces feel especially threatened by the possibilities of democracy and the potential power of the masses and are quick to see the downside of openness.

Business interventions, then, have typically reflected instrumentalist concerns to manage public relations and to secure further control, consistent with a conservatism or the enhancement of problematic hegemonic forces. In these business strategies, the wider context has basically been viewed from a narrow, instrumentalist perspective on what is best for business and in effect from a position aligned to the reproduction and enhancement of wider structures. Even the more positive interventions have substantively overlooked problematic structures and forces of the context. Such interventions have typically been aligned with mildly progressive forces while largely displacing attention from obstacles to substantive change. The more influential impact of business interventions in respect of social accounting has reduced to efforts that, rather than progressively emancipate, seek to deceive, distort, manipulate and problematically control. In the main, the interventions amount to a cynical mobilising of both unofficial and official information. And here it should again be noted that the more official disclosures of business, with their powerful aura, can lend some support to their unofficial ones (Gallhofer and Haslam 1991). Business managers have typically led and shaped interventions in respect of social accounting and some pressure has been exerted to preserve or enhance managerial discretion. Even the more positive interventions are scarcely integral to a more holistic progressive strategy. The structural forces are such that little more than this can be expected from business organisations, in the absence of more interventionist regulation. In this regard, the billionaire investor, George Soros, in advocating at least a degree of interventionist regulation in this area, reflects on especially today's competitive context in commenting: 'If individual companies did it (i.e. disclosed more), they would suffer a competitive disadvantage against others that don't do it' (cited in Denny 2002: 28). Further, in the interventions of business, principles equating to a concern to problematise the role of a privileged knower and to embrace a differentiated universalism that is respectful of diversity have been distorted. Business organisations monitor and research their stakeholders in terms of their diversity so as to manipulate and control them rather than give them a voice, in effect reinforcing problematic hegemonic forces (Owen *et al*. 2000). On balance, business social accountings on the face of it are suggestive of an activity to engender more repressive than more emancipatory movement. As public relations' exercises they can be dangerously seductive and mollify advocates of potentially more radical emancipatory accounting possibilities in society in the process.

In more recent times, a number of trends are observable in respect of business disclosure on the one hand and counter-information systems on the other. The shift in the socio-political context towards an anti-interventionist neo-classical polity has meant that social accounting is perceived even less as a threat by the business world (cf. Bailey *et al*. 1994, Gray *et al*. 1995a: 62–3, Monbiot 2001). Business increasingly has seen social accounting as a public relations opportunity in an age where increased emphasis has been placed on business image. As global communication in cyberspace has taken off, social accountings have manifested increasingly on the World Wide Web. From the 1980s onwards, business has reflected the increasing concerns about the ecological environment in their social accounting, displacing other social accounting concerns to some extent (Owen *et al*. 1997, 2000, Gray 1999: 9). If environmental accountings have in some cases intermeshed with wider social concerns – a tendency that is marked in some forms of sustainability reporting (see Elkington 1998) – such social accounting in practice has continued to be disappointing. Environmental and sustainability accountings may have become increasingly evident in practice but critical analysts sum up the way they are seen by using expressions such as public relations' 'greenwash' to summarise their status (Greer and Bruno 1997, Karliner 1997, Gray and Bebbington 2001).

A number of business organisations today take the public relations' possibilities of social including environmental accounting very seriously, spending substantial sums of money on it. Transnational corporations like Shell and BP have joined the Co-operative Bank and the Body Shop as major investors in social accounting. The reports they have produced, often in addition to the legally required annual report, are significant documents, ostensibly communicating the impact of the company's operations on the community and the environment to a range of different stakeholders, evidencing continuities in the latter regard with the stakeholder models pushed in the 1970s. Indeed, the social reports of transnational companies such as Shell and BP are similar in terms of their form to bodies such as Traidcraft (Owen *et al*. 2000: 82). This similarity of form is on the face of it powerful in creating an aura through which the company is able to hold itself out as socially responsible. The reports differ, however, from Traidcraft in terms of their orientation. Commentators on and critics of this type of social reporting by business have pointed out that these reports contain little of value to stakeholders. Indeed, the way companies portray themselves in their social reports amounts to what has again been called a public relations 'whitewash' or 'greenwash'. As in the social accounting manifestations of the late 1960s and early 1970s, the emancipatory potential of social accounting has been displaced whilst social accounting has been mobilised for counter radical and systems preserving purposes. Although there is more social accounting, with the phenomenon of the World Wide Web of note in this regard, close critical analysis indicates that it has come even more evidently to typify the output of the public relations department (Greer and Bruno 1997, Karliner 1997).

The increased power of transnational business, including relative to many nation state governments today, and the tightened grip of financial pressure within the context of a markets orientated globalisation, has in our view enhanced the control of business over social accounting even further (see Bailey *et al.* 1994, Monbiot 2001). If pressure groups and counter-information systems type activists have shifted more of their focus to a more global level, in part a positioning that has enhanced challenges to business, business attempts to displace and transform these initiatives have also been strengthened at the global level. As we have seen, transnational corporations have invested much in social, especially environmental, accounting – whether as integral to annual reports, in 'stand alone' reporting, in websites or in other media – that has aimed at mollifying social criticism and legitimising business activities (see Gray and Bebbington 2001: 250). Recognising the potentiality of more global regulation of the various quasi-legislative or context-pressurised types, business has sought to stay ahead of the game and sought to soften the impact of such regulation and minimise any prescription (see Gallhofer and Haslam 1997b). Interesting case studies here are the involvements of business in recent times in initiatives to mobilise and give professional or quasi-official status to social accounting at a global level. Reflecting their power, business interests have been working in co-operation with a variety of different agencies, most notably the United Nations, groups concerned with ethical investment, academics and professional accountancy bodies, in respect of such initiatives. The presence of business in initiatives implicating social accounting is so pervasive today that – parallel to what Monbiot (2001) observed to be a corporatisation of the state – one can describe more recent developments in social accounting as the corporatisation of social accounting. The manifestations of the ISEA and the GRI are here worth exploring.

In part, out of frustration over the disappointing interventions of the established accountancy professions in respect of social accounting, ISEA was set up ostensibly as a new and global professional accounting body aiming at the global mobilising of forms of social accounting that would render business organisations socially and ethically accountable (ISEA 2002b). Its aim continues to be to function as a body producing social accounting standards and providing education and training programmes to develop professionally qualified social accountants. While a global social accounting profession and practice suggests much potential, there are aspects of ISEA that severely restrict the realising of this. For instance, the founding membership of ISEA includes business organisations along with 'non-profit' corporate responsibility organisations, consultancies, business ethicist groups and business school faculty. Indeed, the constitution of ISEA's governing body indicates a significant input from business (ISEA 2002b,c). It is thus not surprising that the tone of ISEA pronouncements is one of trusting and engaging in experiments or 'trialing' with business organisations (see Zadek *et al.* 1997: 56). Relatedly, ISEA's recommendations in respect of social accounting are much nearer to a mainstream approach than they are to a radical. Current social structures and institutions are scarcely challenged and critique of conventional accounting is somewhat sidestepped (see Owen *et al.* 2000: 82). Advocacy of a legislative interventionist stance is largely eschewed and substantially countered, ISEA's pronouncements arguably evidencing the influence of a business rhetoric aimed at 'business friendly regulation':

> The adoption of AA 1000 [ISEA's foundation standard in social and ethical accounting, auditing and reporting] can play a part in encouraging governments to *acknowledge the self-regulating processes that organisations are following* to improve accountability and performance. As a reflection of practical and useful best practice, AA 1000 may also help to ensure that any future regulation in the field is viable and meaningful [emphasis in original].
>
> (ISEA 1999: 5)

Critics suggest that, in seeking to gain acceptance from business, ISEA's social accounting fuses with the watered down and problematic versions already found as 'voluntary' public relations exercises in practice (Owen *et al.* 2000). There are many aspects of ISEA's interventions that indicate a displacement and appropriation of the emancipatory and radical possibilities of social accounting. For instance, although ISEA advocates reporting to a whole range of different stakeholders, it gives considerable power to business management to influence the terms of reference for the participation of stakeholders. The danger here is that a narrow instrumentalism will thus shape the engagement with stakeholders. The way in which ISEA elaborates the aims of stakeholder engagement in its foundation framework Accountability 1000 (AA 1000) is of note in this respect. The executive summary of AA 1000 states that stakeholder involvement 'can be at the heart of a virtuous circle of [financial] performance improvement' (ISEA 1999: 20) Owen *et al.* (2000: 82, 85) in their insightful critique of what they call the 'new social audits' – implicating initiatives such as ISEA – comment critically in this respect on the 'managerial slant to the practice of social auditing'.[17] AA 1000's mobilising of emancipatory concepts parallels the problematic rhetoric of the empowerment literature in management more generally in that it appropriates radical terms and renders them consistent with a conventional and instrumentalist business strategy. The rhetoric here is powerful, downplaying social conflict and displacing concerns about the operations of capitalistic organisations and social conflict.

Another recent development illustrating the pervasiveness of the presence of business in social accounting interventions today is the GRI, an example of what can be understood as the recommending of a quasi-official social accounting on a global level. Launched in 1997 by the Coalition of Environmentally Responsible Economies (CERES)[18] in co-operation with the United Nations' Environmental Programme (UNEP), the GRI implicates social, with emphasis on environmental, accounting. It explicitly refers to being concerned to 'elevate sustainability reporting practices worldwide to a level …[equivalent]… to financial reporting' (GRI 2002e). It published *Sustainability Reporting Guidelines* in 2000 after these, echoing conventional accounting standards setting procedure, had gone through an Exposure Draft stage a year earlier (GRI 2000a). The GRI sought that all organisations adopt a 'triple bottom line' approach to accounting whereby duties to economy, society and the environment – considered the three facets of sustainability – would all be reflected.[19] Organisations were encouraged to use the Guidelines as a framework to demonstrate conformance with the UN's Global Compact principles (The Global Compact 2002a,b). The latter principles, proposed in an address by Kofi Annan, the UN Secretary General, to world business leaders at the World Economic Forum, Davos, 31 January 1999, were aimed at involving business in a compact with society and the environment. In his address, the Secretary General suggested to business leaders that they should 'help build the social and environmental pillars required to sustain the new global economy and make globalisation work for all the world's people'. The Global Compact was aimed at disseminating 'good practice based on universal principles' and focusing upon human rights, labour and the environment (The Gobal Compact 2002a,b). The GRI Guidelines, which seek to impact in part through the Chief Executive Officer's Report or its equivalent, promote reporting on employee welfare and also require statements in respect of profile, vision, strategy, policies and organisation and management systems (GRI 2000a). The universality of the Guidelines, aside from plans to develop approaches to meet the specific needs of smaller organisations and industry-specific supplements, is explicitly emphasised. On the face of it, GRI is suggestive of a progressive development of enormous potential. In our world today, the idea of a global social accounting is a very positive one. Radical movements are increasingly recognising a need for democratic and socialistic world governance (Monbiot 2002). A global social accounting goes hand in hand with such a vision. It can potentially play its part in radical and emancipatory projects on a global scale. The possibilities for a global social accounting are also enhanced today given the technological advancements facilitating co-operation and communication on a global level (Gallhofer and Haslam 1997b). Membership of GRI's Charter Group, which has provided strategic, financial and operational support to GRI, since its inauguration as a permanent, global and independent institution in April 2002 (GRI 2002c), includes representatives from pressure groups such as Amnesty International, Greenpeace, Friends of the Earth, Oxfam and Human Rights Watch, the World Bank group, The Association of Certified Chartered Accountants, accountancy firms such as KPMG and PricewaterhouseCoopers and transnational corporations such as General Motors, Ford, Nike and Shell (GRI 2002f). The GRI has also been able to attract significant financial backing not only from the UN and the US Environmental Protection Agency but also from several business-funded bodies (GRI 2002d). Given the strong representation and influence of business it is thus not surprising that much of what GRI proposes parallels that of ISEA in terms of its radicality. Proposals reflect at best mildly progressive initiatives of business organisations in the social accounting arena and facilitate more public relations whitewash. The substantive involvement of big business in social accounting interventions, in the context indeed of UN initiatives to address problems that business has helped to engender and build up, does much to displace and contradict their emancipatory potential and adds to claims about the captured status of the UN (Owen *et al*. 2000, Monbiot 2001).

Initiatives such as ISEA and GRI, in summary, have significant potential to displace more radical social accounting initiatives. They exhibit a limited vision and substantively end up aligning social accounting with hegemonic forces, thus promoting a form of counter radical social accounting. Owen *et al*. (2000: 82) point here to the danger of social accounting manifestations such as ISEA displacing the 'democratic ideals of the founding fathers of the [social audit] movement'. Further, global accounting initiatives implicating business today have strong imperialistic tendencies in reflecting a problematic rather than legitimate world governance. In this respect, these initiatives are continuous with previous imperialistic mobilisings of accounting (see, e.g. Gallhofer *et al*. 1999, 2000a, Annisette 2000, Davie 2000, Gibson 2000, Greer and Patel 2000, Jacobs 2000, Neu 2000). They have promoted a social accounting exhibiting a strong universalistic stance that displaces difference in terms of cultural values and privileges Western ways of doing instead. Aside from repressing valued particularism, such a stance displaces possibilities for the West – and for the global or universal – to learn from particular 'other' cultures. In this regard, Gallhofer *et al*. (1999, 2000a) point, in relation to accounting, to the emancipatory possibilities of learning about the philosophy and culture of indigenous peoples. Culturally, globalisation is suggestive of a problematic Western universalism that threatens to swamp local valued particularism (Held and McGrew 2000).

In the light of the corporatisation of social accounting, counter information systems activists today face a challenging struggle. Yet, aided by the possibilities of global and electronic communications technology, a number of activist groups (e.g. Corporate Watch, CorpWatch, Schnews and Indymedia) continue to try to mobilise a social accounting that is much more recognisable as a radically orientated accounting with critical emancipatory intent. Such activities more especially indicate that the capture of social accounting by business, if stronger today than earlier, is not complete. Indicative interventions constituting counter information systems activity today are those of the activist group Corporate Watch. Oxford-based Corporate Watch describes itself as a 'radical research and publishing group' (Corporate Watch 2002a). Set up initially in late 1996 by anti-roads activists who were interested in gaining insights into the construction and road building industry, Corporate Watch soon embraced a more global orientation by including the exposure of transnational corporations in their range of activities. The aim of the group is 'to support grass-roots and direct activism against large corporations, particularly multinationals' (Corporate Watch 2002a). The group is a workers' co-operative and receives the majority of its funds from charitable foundations and radical trusts – examples include Greenpeace and London Reclaim the Streets – for its contract research. The group's activities are, however, not restricted to the stated interests of such organisations. The group explicitly stresses its aim to be independent from those who provide funding and in this regard carries out work beyond specific funded contracts (Corporate Watch 2002a). Echoing CIS, Corporate Watch also provides detailed 'counter' reports on companies which are available on the their website. These reports – for example focusing on Shell and some of the large supermarket chains – reflect the expertise of the group in the food, agricultural and oil industry. In addition to these reports the group also publishes a bi-monthly newsletter which is 'jam-packed with news of anti-corporate activism from around the world, and cutting-edge research into corporate misdeeds and cover-ups' (Corporate Watch 2002a). The radical orientation of Corporate Watch is indicated in their description of the approach they take in their analyses:

> Our approach is to investigate, corporate structures and the system that supports them more broadly, rather than solely criticising the individual companies for bad behaviour. We are committed to ending the ecological and social destruction wrought by the corporate profit motive.
>
> (Corporate Watch 2002a)

Again this echoes CIS, including in terms of its focus on the repressive character of capitalistic structures and institutions. Corporate Watch, however, reflecting the shift in the context, embrace the global electronic communications technology. And they form alliances with various activist groups and grassroots movements to reflect a more global orientation and a more remarked recognition of a multiplicity of potential change agents shaped by a multiplicity of experiences (see, e.g. Corporate Watch 2002b). These latter reflections and recogntitions refine and enhancce *Corporate Watch's* version of a radical social accounting in today's 'globalisataion' context.

Our summarised review has here offered some comparison and contrast of counter-information systems type mobilisings of social accounting and business interventions in respect of social accounting and pointed to continuities and discontinuities in both kinds of activity. Both of these interventions are suggestive of progressive as well as regressive dimensions. They manifest in the same context and share things in common. Their orientations and intentions, however, suggest different, indeed conflicting and opposing, emphases. If both interventions can be located on the same continuum in terms of orientation to the current socio-political order, the characters of their activities locate them towards differing extremes of this continuum. The radical activist groups attempt to mobilise social accounting in order to destabilise current repressive structures and engender emancipatory change. Business attempts substantively to displace this emancipatory potential of social accounting through a counter radical social accounting that is geared to the protection or enhancement of a repressive socio-political order. If social accounting can be mobilised by hegemonic as well as counter hegemonic forces it cannot, it seems, be fully captured by either. Nevertheless, it is heavily shaped by the relatively powerful hegemonic forces. The efforts of counter hegemonic groups to mobilise social accounting in this respect constitute an especially challenging project of struggle in today's context.

On the interventions of government and the established accountancy profession in respect of social accounting: further insights into the ambiguity of social accounting in action

Including in the guise of business and business dynamics, hegemonic forces are confronted in effect with issues of governance, including the problems of how to maintain and how to enhance legitimacy. On the face of it, a counter radical social accounting helps hegemonic forces to deal with such issues, including mollifying and transforming the problem of legitimacy. On the one hand, in part through their counter radical social accountings, relatively wealthy and powerful business owners and managers in effect convey the message that not only do they care about things beyond the narrow financial economistic instrumentalism that is their conventional scope but that they are also even benevolent in their actions in respect of such matters. On the other, in the context of each individual business, or in some sub-group of businesses (such as all the businesses located in a particular nation state), these owners and managers, also in part through their accountings, emphasise at the same time the pressures upon them to succumb to such an instrumentalism, pressures which they portray as emanating from a system that they in effect naturalise, take-for-granted and de-politicise, depicting it as 'economic' rather than 'socio-political' and even seeing it as something like the best of all possible worlds. Dynamic contextual factors, such as changing pressures upon business, render the capacity of business to deal with such issues mutable, but we have indicated the strength of business in dealing with these issues over a relatively long period. In the guise of government, hegemonic forces also face related issues, including problems of legitimacy. The precise character of these issues and how challenging they are for government are matters that also in principle are mutable, influenced by broader contextual dynamics. Given an acknowledgment on the part of people of the power of transnational business in a context of globalisation, an appreciation in part fostered by the media, many nation state governments claim a sort of legitimacy – if it is one that ironically highlights their weaknesses and encourages apathy in respect of formal democratic practices of the national system – by reference to this global context, as it can provide excuses for actions or inactions that otherwise could be regarded as unethical and irresponsible. If in an earlier context such excuses were less easily made, nation state governments arguably faced, in at least this respect, a more intense legitimacy crisis. If seen as a relatively powerful player, a nation state government could hardly blame a systemic context it was meant to be responsible for and in control of. In the guise of the established accountancy profession, there are also governance issues, including again issues of legitimacy. Some of these issues will resemble or fuse with those of governments: the profession can, in some respects, where it is not already a state body, be seen as a 'privatised' branch of government that, as a profession, legitimises its activities by reference to the government-like explicit claim to serve the public interest. Other issues will resemble or fuse with those of business. The profession has been seen as a sort of club representing the interests of the profit-making accountancy firms, including the larger transnational ones. The accountancy profession can itself be seen as helping make up a business system that is substantively at the service of hegemonic forces (see Willmott 1990, Sikka *et al.* 1991, 1995, 1999, Cousins and Sikka 1993, Willmott *et al.* 1993, Sikka 1994, 2000, Sikka and Willmott 1995, 1997, Dunn and Sikka 1999). There are particular complexities and intricacies here. For example, in some contexts it has arguably been perceived to be in the interests of established forces for the accountancy profession to be seen as 'private' or 'independent'. This creates very particular governance, including legitimacy issues. For instance, the profession has in this context to be concerned about legitimising the regulatory framework or space within which it functions and it has to be concerned to legitimise involvement of its members in particular activities in the face of competing alternatives. There are legitimacy problems vis-à-vis particular as well as general interests. Again, these governance issues are mutable in the contextual dynamics of their location. For example, to the extent that government is relatively powerful vis-à-vis corporations and the international market orientated system, one would expect to see a correspondence between government and professional interventions that is substantively fashioned by government. To the extent that the government is relatively weak in this regard, or captured by a business oriented policy, one would expect both the government and the profession in accounting interventions to be pursuing parallel paths strongly influenced by business.

So, what of mobilisations of social accounting by government and the established accountancy profession in the UK? Over several decades there have been calls for legislative and/or quasi-legislative interventions. One recent call was reported in *The Guardian* on 13 June 2002:

> Growing frustration about lack of progress on corporate responsibility has led to the launch of a private members bill in the House of Commons ... It calls for social, financial and environmental reporting to be made mandatory ... is backed by a coalition of non-governmental organisations such as Amnesty and Save the Children, but was immediately shot down by business leaders [claiming that excessive intervention risks stifling innovation]... the prime minister had called on the UK's top 350 companies to produce social and environmental reports by 2001 ... over 75% of firms ignored the challenge.
>
> (Macalister 2002: 24)

'Growing frustration' is the appropriate, indeed understated, expression. The private members bill echoes initiatives going back over especially the period since the late 1960s, when concerns about corporate responsibility and social accounting took off in quite a significant way. The response of business reported here substantially echoes what has been the typical business response over the same period. Businesses have expressed preference for the sort of 'voluntary' approach that is here encouraged by the prime minister, albeit that it is an approach that allows them to do very little or to mobilise counter radical accounting in accordance with what suits their perceived interests. Also recently, an attempt to introduce environmental accounting standards has been formulated by the European Union (see The Commission of the

European Communities 2001). We shall have to wait to learn of the success or otherwise of these recent initiatives as they manifest and impact in practice. We cannot, however, be confident of a substantive progressive mobilisation of social accounting based on experience. In especially recent times, governments, including the UK government, have succumbed to business demands and displaced moves to engender any substantive progress in this area. Our focus here is upon some mobilisations of social accounting in the UK in the 1970s, paralleling interventions in other nations states at the time, in which on the face of it the government and the accountancy profession were moving to intervene more directly and substantively. Analysis suggests that there are considerable ambiguities in respect of these social accounting interventions. On the one hand, given contextual pressures and political currents, they reflect progressive potential in terms of possible alignment between social accounting and emancipation. On the other, in line with business, both the government and the profession appear here to seek to capture and transform social accounting's progressive potential, arguably embracing a counter radical accounting.

In the 1970s, papers were produced by both government and opposition suggesting the substantive expansion and enhancement of social accounting. Following the recommendations of the 1968 Donovan Report and the 1969 White Paper 'In Place of Strife', employers were obliged to disclose more to unions for the purposes of wage bargaining by the Industrial Relations legislation of 1971. The Industrial Relations Code of Practice published by the Department of Employment in 1972 reinforced this message (Robson 1994: 51). The 1973 Company Law Reform White Paper elaborated the responsibilities of the directors to 'employees, investors, government and the customer' (Robson 1994: 53). The Labour government's Industry Bill,[20] approved by cabinet in August 1974, and associated debates long continuing thereafter, promised an accounting that would yet better serve employees and trade unions (Jackson-Cox et al. 1984). Labour and the Trades Union Congress (TUC) were working towards a plan to involve trade union representatives on company boards (Robson 1994: 53). The report of the government commissioned inquiry (in 1975) into industrial democracy, chaired by Lord Bullock, published in 1977, reflected and helped constitute government policy aimed at a broad intervention in industrial relations, including through worker representations on the board and accountings aimed at employees (Cmnd 6706). Also reflecting this policy, the Health and Safety Act of 1974 and the Employment Protection Act of 1975 (which replaced the 1971 Industrial Relations Act) involved the mobilising of social accounting (as understood here) in legislation. The former act gave employee representatives the right to access information in respect of health and safety. The latter, as well as echoing the 1971 legislation it replaced, gave statutory form to the Advisory Conciliation and Arbitration Service, a body that issued a Code of Practice on the disclosure of information to trade unions (Hopwood et al. 1994: 223). Labour's opposition Green Paper of January 1974, The Community and the Company (Labour Party 1974), with its proposal to set up a Companies Commission for the regulation of companies and financial institutions, promised to extend government regulation of accounting in a way consistent with the promotion of some social accounting (Hopwood et al. 1994: 218) and had also proposed worker representation on company boards (Robson 1994: 54). The consultation document of the Department of Trade, *Aims and Scope of Company Reports*, issued on 9 June 1976, underscored the recommendations of the accountancy profession's *The Corporate Report* (*subter*) – its very title echoed the discussion paper – with a legalistic prescribing of some key statements recommended therein. The Department's subsequent Green Paper, The Future of Company Reports, appearing in July 1977 (Cmnd 6888), promoted social accounting in a way that closely paralleled the intervention of the accountancy profession, proposing the disclosure of the value added statement, one of the statements also advocated by the profession (*subter*). These moves by the government in the 1970s towards prescribing social accounting type disclosures were a degree weightier than had earlier been the case (Hopwood 1985: 362, Gray *et al.* 1996: 93). These interventions in our view had progressive dimensions. Reflecting the social democratic and corporatist polity and the perceived pressures and threats of the time, the developments explicitly promoted an accounting for employees in the context of calls for a type of industrial democracy. This promised the potential mobilising of a social accounting for employees that would raise awareness consistent with a broadly emancipatory project. The government's intervention also raised the profile of social accounting type disclosures.

The established UK accountancy profession intervened in a way that paralleled the government's own concerns. For instance, they mobilised a type of social accounting and gave particular emphasis on the face of it to developing accounting for employees. The mobilisation of the value added statement in this context is especially bound up in government policy. The profession set up a working party in 1974, the Boothman Committee, and charged it with the task of re-examining 'the scope and aims of published financial reports in the light of modern needs and conditions' and concerning itself 'with the public accountability of economic entities of all kinds, but especially business enterprises', and identifying 'the persons or groups for whom financial reports should be prepared, and the information appropriate to their interests' (ASSC 1975: 1). The committee's discussion paper, *The Corporate Report*, was produced in August 1975 (ASSC 1975). The mainstream social accounting literature hails *The Corporate Report* as a significant development in social accounting. For Gray *et al.* (1996: 100) it contributed to 'an excellent bank of thinking and ideas on the whole spectrum of social accounting and accountability', for Gray (1999: 4) it 'remains, the most radical re-statement, from the accounting profession, of how organisational disclosure, needed to be enhanced by social and environmental accounting' (cf. Bedford 1976, Renshall 1976), while for Mathews (1993: 28) it 'was the most significant of the conceptual frameworks (for socially responsible accounting) produced by committees and working groups on behalf of major accounting organisations'. We are thus here particularly interested to take a closer look at *The Corporate Report* and the way it is intertwined with UK government policy.

The Corporate Report constituted a blue print of an accounting that would be consistent with more socially responsible business. It recommended a corporate reporting practice equating to the promotion of some of the key tenets of a mainstream social accounting. We can again articulate much in *The Corporate Report*, a significant departure for the accountancy profession, in terms of positive and progressive proposals or recommendations. If in a not too coherent way, the discussion paper ostensibly reflected and even in some senses enhanced contextual pressures for an accounting beyond the narrow accounting of convention towards one reflecting orientation to a wider corporate social responsibility. A point of departure for the social accounting proposals of the discussion paper was a critique of conventional accounting, especially its overemphasis on profit, and, relatedly, its emphasis on an accountability on the part of management to the owners of the business, namely its shareholders:

> ... economic entities compete for resources of manpower, management and organisational skills, materials and energy, and they utilise community owned assets and facilities. They have a responsibility for the present and future livelihood of employees, and because of the interdependence of social groups, they are involved in the maintenance of standards of life and the creation of wealth for and on behalf of the community.
>
> (ASSC 1975: 15, 1.3)

According to *The Corporate Report*, it was this 'custodial role ... in the community' that gave rise to the responsibility to 'report publicly' and to satisfy 'public accountability' (ASSC 1975, 1.3). The discussion paper therefore highlighted obligations to a variety of stakeholders, beyond if including the shareholders, of a financial and non-financial nature. All organisations, including the business organisation that constituted the report's main focus, were to be accountable to the public and were to properly satisfy reasonable demands for or 'rights to' information in respect of the organisation (ASSC 1975: 17, 1.8). Aside from equity-investors, loan creditors and business contacts, the report delineated employees, local/national governments and a catch-all group actually termed 'the public' (explicitly including taxpayers, rate payers, consumers and community or special interest groups such as environmental protection groups, regional pressure groups and political parties) as stakeholders in the business organisation having a reasonable 'right' to information (ASSC 1975: 17, 1.9). Thus even pressure groups on the face of it were to be catered for. Further, there was an explicit commitment to making accounting more comprehensive to these envisaged users. New statements promoted included statements of future prospects (covering employment levels), corporate objectives and value-added, and an employment report (ASSC 1975: 48, 6.5).[21] A broadening of the auditor's role and of what the phrase true and fair view was to connote were promised. With the call for more research into social accounting, the paper gave a stimulus to accountings that would measure and report upon stakeholder, for instance employee, satisfaction (Renshall 1976, Hopwood *et al.* 1994). Later, *The Corporate Report's* commitments would come to look more astonishing as the profession's interest in social accounting waned.

The proposals made in *The Corporate Report* point to an accounting with the potential to increase visibility of aspects of the operation of a business organisation that would help stakeholders other than the owners of the business to assess its impact on their own lives and well-being in particular and its impact upon the community more generally. An especially significant departure in *The Corporate Report* was the attention ostensibly given, consistent with government policy, to accounting for employees, if it also reflected as well as helped stimulate an already expanding employee reporting practice (*supra*, see also Hussey 1978, 1979, Purdy 1981). This attention to employees was emphasised in the paper's frank acknowledgment of 'the way in which employees are almost totally ignored in the present Companies Act and in corporate reports' (ASSC 1975: 51, 6.12). The discussion paper maintained that employers had a duty to report to and about employees who were deemed materially dependent on the business. Employees and unions were to be provided with information that would facilitate 'assessing the security and prospects of employment and ... collective bargaining' (ASSC 1975: 21, 2.16). Matters deemed of interest to actual and prospective employees were the ability of the employers to meet wage demands, the financial viability of the bargaining units and other parts of the firm as well as of the whole of the firm, the pay and conditions of employees by group, prospects regarding employment levels, locations and conditions, and employees' divisional contributions (ASSC 1975: 21–2, 2.17). The employment report advocated in the discussion paper was to inform about a number of matters of interest to employees and those concerned about employees, including the size and dynamics of the workforce, the age and gender distribution of the workforce, employees' functions and locations, major closures, disposals and acquisitions made, working hours, fringe benefits, pensions, names of unions representing workforce and membership details, health and safety and some employment ratios (Gray *et al.* 1996: 196). Such disclosures promised to create or re-inforce awareness of matters of social concern, consistent with the promotion of a social accounting with a progressive intent.

Of the new statements of reporting advocated in *The Corporate Report*, the value added statement is of particular interest here as it was also specifically promoted in government policy in the broad area of industrial relations (*subter*). Value-added accounting ostensibly reflected a stakeholder and especially employee orientation by embracing and fostering a new way of seeing the relationship between the company and its stakeholders, including its employees. For Morley (1978), this way of seeing reflected the dynamics of the social context of the time, in which corporatist thinking was still very influential: government, employees and shareholders and other financiers were portrayed as partners in the business, sharing in the distribution of the new 'value added' bottom line.[22] Employee remuneration was thus, significantly, not depicted as a cost, as in what had become the conventional profit and loss account, but as a distribution of the value added to a partner stakeholder (ASSC 1975: 49–50, 6.7–6.11). For Binder *et al.* (1978), the advocacy of value added was consistent with an open management style that would ' "open the books" and welcome the increased questioning ... and promote a more participative and less autocratic way of getting results'. The TUC (1974) were convinced enough by value added to suggest its appropriateness as a performance indicator in disclosure to employees. And they demanded further openness to facilitate the system's acceptance where it was to be linked to remuneration. That the profession, as well as the government (*subter*) saw value added and related disclosure as facilitating industrial democracy suggested greater employee interaction with accounting (Robson 1994: 50), indicating more radical possibilities in terms of employee usage of accounting (Hopwood *et al.*

1994: 219, 221). In this respect, commentators point to how value added accounting may make more visible the social character of production and in some contexts help raise issues about the justice of distributions made (Stolliday and Attwood 1978, Gray and Maunders 1980, Hopwood *et al.* 1994: 214–5). For Gray *et al.* (1987: 51), 'showing the comparative share received by each stakeholder group may ...[high-light]... the antagonistic nature of such relationships, as an increased share for one group is associated with a corresponding reduction for others'. Ammunition of sorts was here supplied to radical groups. And value-added accounting potentially could become more explicitly contested and a focus of struggle in recognition that some value addeds might favour counter-hegemonic forces more than others. The social accounting of *The Corporate Report* thus had the potential to be mobilised in more radical interventions and to thus be conflict-enhancing rather than conflict-resolving for problematic hegemonic forces (cf. Hopwood *et al.*, 1994). The public criticism of the recommendations in *The Corporate Report*, notably from business and often expressed in a blunt and forceful rhetoric, in part can be taken as indicating aspects of *The Corporate Report's* radical possibilities. For a spokesperson for The Guardian Exchange Group:

> The Corporate Report does nothing to increase profits but will impose further statistical demands on industry: the details in these statistics will be used to further sectional interests within the community and I fear in some cases the use would be mischievous. It is essential therefore that corporate reporting should be confined to those who have – in the case of companies – provided the capital ...
>
> (Comments on *The Corporate Report* on public record at the ICAEW library)

The Young Chartered Accountants Group noted that some of its members saw the discussion paper as 'socialist clap trap' and suggested that it appeared to be a 'sop to the current socialist climate', indicating that some perceived the social accounting proposals as potentially radical in character and challenging to the status quo (Comments on *The Corporate Report* on public record at the ICAEW library). Similarly, the suggestion in *The Corporate Report* that employees had a 'right' to information was considered by commentators as a threat (see comments on *The Corporate Report* of The Law Society's Standing Committee on Company Law and the Management Sub-Committee of the Manchester Technical Advisory Committee, Comments on *The Corporate Report* on public record at the ICAEW library). The perceptions of some of the commentators thus point to the emancipatory potential of *The Corporate Report*: its social accounting had the potential to help radically construct ways of seeing the injustices of the operations of business and capitalistic economy and society.

If the intentions of government and the profession in the 1970s had apparently progressive dimensions, was there also a downside? A number of regressive dimensions can be suggested. One point it is worth making here is that the interventions displaced more radical possibilities. It is of interest that the profession itself, if it suggested it 'tempting to propose that entities disclose information which will show their impact on, and their endeavours to protect society, its amenities and environment'

(ASSC 1975: 57, 6.45), declared many social accounting possibilities impractical due to a lack of generally agreed 'measurement' techniques and simply called for further research. Relatedly, *The Corporate Report's* tendency to continue to promote conventional and technocratic accounting practice threatened to seriously oversimplify the task of disclosing on the business organisation in more socially holistic terms. The discussion paper's proposals also amounted to a narrowing down or displacement of radical social accounting possibilities and an overly close alignment to conventional accounting in terms of perceived role, content, form and aura. The emphasis in *The Corporate Report* was upon a financial economistic accounting, albeit through a more expansive stakeholder perspective. The working party's terms of reference, for instance, stipulated that it 'seek to establish a set of working concepts as a basis for financial reporting' and consider 'the most suitable means of measuring and reporting the economic position, performance and prospect of undertakings for the purposes and persons identified ...' (ASSC: 1). *The Corporate Report* ironically displaced attention from the need to critically evaluate conventional accounting. The latter was granted too prominent a status in the discourse, with alternatives seen as very supplementary to this core practice. Conventional accounting was interpreted as in many ways basically a mature and sound practice that just needed adding to a little in spite of the hints in the discussion paper that it was narrow and instrumental, even reflective of a system giving too much weight to the assumed narrow financial economistic interests of capitalistic owners and the interests of the socio-political order in an economic materialism in general. Too much of the proposal, irrespective of whether it is seen as an expert technology of procedural rationality, is captured by the conventional. It thus displaces broader questions and depoliticises controversy. Attention is displaced from injustices of the wider socio-political context (see Tinker 1980, 1985, Power 1991: 30–1). Hopwood and Burchell (1980: 14), reflecting on the seventies, thus see the push for broader disclosure orientated mainly to employees as giving 'rise to an expansion of the scope of traditional accounting rather than the provision of alternative means of assessment'. *The Corporate Report* is largely consistent with this analysis. The emancipatory potential of the accounting under construction was constrained and displaced. Some protagonists in debate over *The Corporate Report* even promoted the view that 'social accounting' was outside of the realm of conventional accountancy, a deliberate restriction on the scope of accounting. The Leinster Society of Chartered Accountants of the Institute of Chartered Accountants in Ireland put it as follows: 'The majority of members seem to accept at a personal level that public accountability and social audits are acceptable and desirable values. There was, however, a reluctance to accept that the accountancy profession as such should be a leader in the development of these values' (Comments on *The Corporate Report* on public record at the ICAEW library).

A problematic of *The Corporate Report* that served to enhance the above regressive dimension was that it was overly influenced by a professional-expert rhetoric and imagery. While there are positive dimensions to social accounting's assuming a professional-expert status (see Hines 1988, Gray 1990a,b, see also Gorz 1989), there are also a range of negative dimensions, as has been suggested in the literature (see Power and Laughlin 1992, Gallhofer and Haslam 1997b). These negative dimensions pertain to a weakening of social accounting's emancipatory potential by rendering it more easily captured by problematic hegemonic forces. A professional-expert practice, in its search for rules and regulations, can problematically oversimplify (see Hines 1988, Gorz 1989, Gray 1990a,b, Power 1991). Once established it can come to be difficult to change (see Gray and Laughlin 1991, Gray 1992, Power 1992). It can accrue an aura that helps place it beyond a critical questioning and people may in any case come to trust it and see it as fulfilling a noble social role. They may come to see it as professional, neutral and beyond politics, an institution recognised and valued by the state, the law and their affiliates and as something that might substantively be taken-for-granted. While an accounting may be close to the people in terms of its pervasiveness and the significance of its impact, it can thus come, in spite of its claim to serve the people, to be overly distant from them (Gallhofer and Haslam 1991). Power (1991) in this context expresses concern about the potential extension of the power of accountants through the capture of social accounting. He fears the extension of existing modes of accounting regulation that he takes to give too much influence to 'self-appointed experts such as accountants' (cf. Perks and Gray 1979, 1980). Further, in this regard, *The Corporate Report* reflected the tendency discernible in many professional accountancy interventions in respect of social accounting to elaborate a professional-expert accounting technology prior to even arriving at any firm consensus over social accounting's purpose. This is even if such an elaboration can be very problematic, for instance, in unduly influencing the very construction of relations of accountability (see Puxty 1986, 1991, Power 1991). The professional-expert stance thus threatens to be one of the overly confident 'privileged knower'. Indeed, the initiatives of the profession as well as the government that mobilised social accounting appear to have reflected fairly minimal concern to consult with different social groups and rather assumed a privileged authority status, although the working party on *The Corporate Report* did get involved in some broad consultation as in their survey of directors. *The Corporate Report* very much promoted existing professional practice and the profession's preferred 'self-regulatory' *modus operandi* where it maintained that 'the responsibility to report publicly ... is separate from and broader than the legal obligation to report' (ASSC 1975: 15, 1.3). Several commentaries on *The Corporate Report* also promoted a social accounting strongly integrated with existing professional practice and the existing self-regulatory framework. The Association of University Lecturers in Accounting saw a case for extending 'the deliberations of the ASC' (the Accounting Standards Steering Committee having become the Accounting Standards Committee) to the area of social accounting. The East Anglian Society of Chartered Accountants' Technical Advisory Committee called for a code of *Fundamental Social Concepts* to parallel *Fundamental Accounting Concepts* (Comments on *The Corporate Report* on public record at the ICAEW library). Such ideas are not without merit but they do risk the overly confident expansion of professional accountancy expertise into a broader domain.

A further problematic dimension of the mobilising of social accounting by the accountancy profession can be located in the government policy initiative it helps reinforce. The social accounting of *The Corporate Report*, from the broad stakeholder approach to the mobilising specifically of the value added statement – with the profession, indeed, emphasising the latter by including it on its accounting standards' agenda – broadly fused with the government's own promotion of social accounting and the associated policy initiative. Thus, the accountancy profession's intervention fused with a concern to discipline labour and manage industrial relations in the context of a subtle corporatist control strategy. In the 1970s, corporatist governance encouraged the view, especially under Labour from 1974 (Robson 1994: 53), that increased co-operation between workers and management, a system of disclosure orientated to employees and the linking of wages to productivity could work together as elements in a strategic policy of disciplinary control and control of inflation (cf. Robson 1994: 50).[23] The accountancy profession was ostensibly supportive of employee orientated accounting in a number of initiatives and the rhetoric of promoting harmony between the stakeholders, notably between employees and managers, was evident in *The Corporate Report* (Renshall 1976, Hopwood *et al*. 1994: 217–18). The social accounting type disclosure bolstered in the working paper, with its employee and stakeholder emphasis, blended with the thrust of government policy. At least, the ambiguities and possibilities of the social accounting promoted in *The Corporate Report* facilitated its mobilisation in ways consistent with this policy. Hopwood *et al*.'s (1994) study of value added, focusing upon its mobilisation in a number of arenas in the 1970s, including in that of the accountancy profession's regulatory project, here contains much detail and suggests a number of insights (Burchell *et al*. 1985).[24] In portraying the employees as a partner in the creation and sharing of the value added, value added accounting came to be understood to promote harmony and goal congruence. Value added was an ambiguous term that could 'stand in' for profit, thus usefully switching emphasis from a concept that was understood to involve conflictual relations. The value-added statement did little to question the conventional business goal and scarcely highlighted issues in respect of the fairness of the wage. If we have noted its radical potential, it is much more obviously a device for making visible how much profit is reduced by wages and how 'little the shareholder receives': it is much more evidently part of a wage restraint strategy (see Vickers da Costa, cited in Burchell *et al*. 1985). As Puxty (1986: 100–1) points out, most value-added statements made use of a classification scheme that suggested the understatement of distributions to shareholders (see also Hird 1978, cf. Burchell *et al*. 1981).[25] If the TUC endorsed value added, we should stress that employers very much advocated it too. The government was concerned to promote value added as a way of enhancing wage restraint through linking wages to productivity. It saw disclosure as securing greater harmony in industrial relations and facilitating industrial democracy. This in turn would help achieve the goal of a disciplined and efficient workforce. The ambiguities of value-added accounting – and, we would suggest, social accounting more generally – facilitated its functioning here as a subtle force of control that helped capture a variety of agents in a web reflecting and reinforcing social relations (Hopwood *et al*. 1994). The government – with support from other quarters, including from academia – was in this regard also concerned to give business flexibility in its operationalising of value added accounting. The suggestion is that both the government and the profession here were engaged in a problematic hegemonic practice. And in this context the desire of the profession to remain influential and prosperous aligned it, beyond any claim made to neutrality, to hegemonic forces (see Cooper 1992, Power and Laughlin 1992).

Consistent with the above argumentation pointing to a problematic aspect of the mobilising of social accounting by both the government and the accountancy profession, neither business nor government appear to have been especially committed to social accounting's potential as a system of informing that renders accountable and responsible. The proposals of both very much failed to reflect recognition of any conflicting interests of stakeholder groups. They were at best only mildly progressive and we have seen that they were bound up in a more problematically interested policy. The point is underscored in that in the context of the 'great moving right show', neither government nor the accountancy profession have shown a great deal of interest in prescribing social accounting. From the late 1970s, discourse over social accounting severely reduced in state and professional arenas. Hopwood *et al.* (1994: 229–31) elaborate in this regard how specifically interest in value added accounting waned from the early 1980s. Constructing a positive relation between democracy and efficiency was no longer seen as very relevant in a context where industrial relations were being managed differently. Value added also moved from the agenda of the accountancy profession's standards' setters. The social accounting that emerged to function on behalf of hegemonic forces in the changing context became less employee-orientated and less reflective of corporatist governance. The profession's support of the more radical ideas in *The Corporate Report*, including the call for the development of non-financial performance indicators, has been very disappointing since the mid-1970s and has largely regressed (see Hopwood *et al.* 1994, Gray *et al.* 1996). It is also striking that most of the government proposals as well as *The Corporate Report* were never formally implemented. Hopwood (1985: 362) indicates that *The Corporate Report* was never approved by the profession's leadership.

Another insight helps to problematise the accountancy profession's mobilising of *The Corporate Report*. It seems that a major factor motivating the profession's intervention was not so much a strong identification with a social accounting project, but a concern to protect its own influential status in the prescriptive and regulatory framework of accounting. The profession was very concerned about the possibility of increased government involvement in its affairs – there was, in the context, relatively weighty debate about even the nationalisation of accountancy. Relatedly, the profession was concerned about the threat of being displaced by others in relation to its own inter-professional struggles.[26] The profession appears in the context to have been worried about being sidelined too often by the government. For instance, when the previous Conservative administration had set up the Sandilands committee in the early 1970s, to advance reform in the context of inflation, this had been done over the heads of the accountancy profession, which was even working on its own ideas (see Robson 1994: 45). Further, Labour's opposition Green Paper of January 1974, *The Community and the Company*, proposed a setting up of a Companies Commission that threatened substantial government intervention in accountancy (Whittington 1993, Hopwood *et al.* 1994: 217–18). The implication is that the accountancy profession was scarcely committed to anything like a substantively radical social accounting. In pursuing its own interests it rather embraced the principles of a counter radical social accounting.

In summary, it seems that the interventions by the government and the accountancy profession reviewed here indicated emancipatory possibilities that were, however, largely displaced and transformed. The interventions on the face of it equated to an effort to mobilise an at least mildly progressive social accounting. Indeed, we suggest that the developments in the 1970s, in which both government and the profession were pressurised and in which a social democratic polity was influential, did help to positively advance and encourage an accounting that was a step forward. Nevertheless, the initiatives were also governed by forces that tended to mobilise these social accountings towards the counter radical typification. The correspondence to the interests of business helps to reinforce this point. The visions of those involved in the interventions, their appreciations of the context and the general strategies they pursued were consistent with an instrumentalism supportive of hegemonic forces.

Social accounting and the academic

Academics cannot stand outside their context. They cannot absent themselves from the socio-political struggles of the context of which they are part. Their practice and discourse cannot be neutral in this regard. In effect, academics take sides, even if their allegiances may be in varying degrees subtly understated (Tinker 1991). Thus academics can intervene more or less to positive effect or more or less to negative effect in interacting with the phenomenon of social accounting. They may variously progress social accounting towards the realisation of its emancipatory possibilities or even variously regress it to more repressive possibilities. Furthermore, academics can have a substantial impact on society through their various activities, including through their various engagements with social accounting. While there are strong anti-intellectual currents in society – stronger in some societies than in others (see Puxty 1993) – academics nevertheless possess a cultural capital that gives them some social influence.

In respect of social accounting, radical and especially mainstream social accounting interventions by academics have been influential. Mainstream academic texts such as Gray *et al.* (1987, 1993, 1996), Mathews (1993) and Gray and Bebbington (2001) and the more radical texts of Tinker (1984a, 1985) have facilitated the development of educational programmes. A significant number of academics have contributed material in the form of articles and books that has stimulated interest and advanced social accounting on the agenda. Rob Gray and Dave Owen, much of whose work is of the mainstream school as seen above, have been especially notable chroniclers of and contributors to a social accounting literature that took off in the late twentieth century. Gray's Centre for Social and Environmental Accounting Research (CSEAR), again a more 'mainstream' institution, has played a key role in encouraging social accounting research worldwide. Academic journals have encouraged engagement with social accounting. *Accounting, Organizations and Society*, from its very first issue in 1976, has promoted an interest in social accounting and additional journals, emerging with a social analysis emphasis, notably *Accounting, Auditing and Accountability Journal, Accounting Forum, Critical Perspectives on Accounting* and *Advances in Public Interest Accounting* have been especially keen to give space to analysis of social accounting. Today, a whole variety of accounting journals have opened their pages to social accounting too: social accounting has become much less marginal in the accounting literature. Academic discourse on social accounting not only reflects wider discourse in this field but also helps shape it.

In our view, through their writings and educational inputs, as well as through other interventions – for instance, through their efforts to change practice more directly[27] – academics of both the mainstream and more radical persuasions have had some positive impact. They have raised the profile of a social accounting promising forms of emancipatory development. And they have added to the pressure for such an accounting. We should also stress that, on the face of it, the intentions of academics have been progressive, consistent with a concern to advance an emancipatory accounting through exposing the unethical and through informing about what matters to people from a more holistic and emancipatory perspective.

While acknowledging these progressive dimensions of academic interventions, we here want to explore these more critically with a view to gaining insights into how academics can better contribute to the realisation of social accounting's emancipatory possibilities. Our main if not our only concern here is to indicate dimensions of the academic discourse of social accounting that have at least threatened to weaken social accounting's emancipatory possibilities in one way or another: the displacing and silencing of a radical social accounting in some of the rhetoric of mainstream and even radical social accounting texts; the mollifying, beyond appropriate refinement of social accounting in mainstream and radical discourses reflecting dimensions of recent developments in social theorising; the positive identification in the mainstream discourse of a narrow and delimited social accounting; some other narrowings of social accounting in the general academic discourse on social accounting and some problematic constructions of the image of social accounting in academic discourse.

Some of the rhetoric of texts promoting mainstream social accounting has threatened to displace or silence more radical social accounting. By highlighting elements of this problematic rhetoric here we are concerned to counter its influence. Gray (1999: 1) exemplifies a rhetoric displacing radical social accounting where he maintains that 'social accounting, at its best, is designed to open up a space for new accountings between the "conventional" accounting literature and practice and the "alternative" critiques and theorising' (see also Owen *et al.* 1997: 176–7).[28] As in this citation, the word 'mainstream' has typically not been used in the discourse promoting it. Consistent with an imperialistic universalism, mainstream social accounting has in effect often been characterised as *the* social accounting through the exclusion of reference to any other type of social accounting. The notion of a radical social accounting, as again is evident in the above citation, has also been displaced in the rhetoric by reference to a radical or alternative analysis or theorising of accounting, a reference that stands in place of mentioning the possibility of a type of radical social accounting, which it thus helps to silence. Such rhetorical moves help to establish social accounting as a universal and undifferentiated category (contra Gray 1999: 2) that excludes radical social accounting from the agenda and thus delimits the emancipatory possibilities of social accounting. Other ways in which radical social accounting has been displaced in the discourse promoting mainstream social accounting are through its being denied an accounting identity and through its being labeled as very extreme. The interventions of CIS have been portrayed as not really involving accounting at all but an investigative journalism lacking in professionalism and allegedly prioritising the production of a ' "good story" ... quite deliberately selective and biased' (Gray *et al.* 1996: 273). And attention from Tinker's (1984a, 1985) suggestions towards a type of social accounting he sees as emancipatory are somewhat displaced by reference to the alleged extremes of Tinker's politics (Gray *et al.* 1988: 8, 1996). Since Tinker's (1984a, 1985) positive advocacy of a radical social accounting is unusual amongst critical writers and since, as Gray *et al.* (1996) suggest, CIS's approach is something of a rarity, once these interventions are suppressed there remains only a much depleted array of substantial manifestations of radical social accounting as idea and practice left to displace. It is sometimes as if mainstream discourse is seeking to suppress the more radical positions that would challenge the mainstream school – and potentially divide it, given that the mainstream school arguably incorporates a variety of positions of quite differing degrees of radicality (cf. Gray *et al.* 1988: 8, 1996, Guthrie and Parker 1989a, Parker 1989, 1991, Gray 1992, 1999, Bebbington 1997, 1999, 2001, Owen *et al.* 1997: 180–1, 183, Bebbington *et al.* 1999).

We should not exaggerate these displacements of radical social accounting. Reading mainstream social accounting texts more comprehensively, there have been a number of occasions where a type of radical accounting has been hinted at (see dimensions of Gray *et al.* 1986, 1988, Gray 1999). Further, in very recent times there have been some especially positive signals towards a bridge-building between mainstream and radical orientations at some general level, influenced positively, according to Owen *et al.* (2000) by texts such as Gallhofer and Haslam (1997), Power (1997) and Lehman (1999, see also Rubenstein 1992, Lehman 1995, cf. Owen 1990, Arnold and Hammond 1994, Gray *et al.* 1995a, Bebbington 1997, Owen *et al* 1997, Gray 1999). Nevertheless, it remains the case that the dimensions of the rhetoric of the mainstream discourse that we have touched upon here do to some extent close off possible pathways towards a more radical social accounting and render it more difficult to envision the realisation of the emancipatory possibilities of social accounting.

Ironically, it seems, some radical or critical writers have in effect buttressed that rhetoric of the mainstream discussed above that has helped displace the idea of a radical social accounting. They have thus also weakened social accounting's emancipatory potential. Puxty (1986) and Cooper (1992) are here interesting cases for analysis (see also Hines 1991a, Puxty 1991, Tinker *et al.* 1991). Puxty (1986: 106–7) states that 'moderate critique has developed a call for social accounting'. This appears to inextricably intertwine social accounting with the notion of the 'moderate'. The position is not clarified by Puxty's elaboration that 'more radical critics of capitalist society have been more concerned with the broader issues [which are] of accountancy and accountants within that society' (Puxty 1986: 107). His text here parallels the mainstream discourse in seriously underplaying differentiation within the category social accounting: it threatens to reduce social accounting to mainstream social accounting and to displace the possibility of a radical social accounting. Both Puxty (1986) and Cooper (1992), the latter a study drawing from the feminist theorising of Cixous and Kristeva, appear to make a quite general call not to advance accounting in the name of the environmental or the social. In their view mobilising accounting in this way is even to risk engendering more sophisticated social repression or contributing further to environmental problems (Puxty 1986, Cooper 1992: 35–7, cf. Burchell *et al.* 1985, Roberts and Scapens 1985, Hines 1988, 1989, 1991a,b, Arrington 1990, Laughlin and Gray 1991, Maunders and Burritt 1991: 23–4, Gray 1992: 412). For Puxty:

> ... insofar as conventional accounting is infused with the problematic characteristics of the social context within which it operates, social accounting in fact is only a truer reflection of that context ... to the extent that it legitimates and reproduces class relations, social accounting is only a more effective way of doing so.
>
> (Puxty 1986: 99–100)

For Cooper:

> Accounting cannot change society, it is not on the 'outside', it is an intricate part of the existing masculine political economy. Without a change to society, there is no way out of this. In the present symbolic order accountants should not attempt to account for the environment.
>
> (Cooper 1992: 35)

Cooper (1992: 36) goes on to suggest that mobilising 'green' accounting in the current context would 'make matters worse'.[29] Thus at least rhetorical elements in Puxty (1986) and Cooper (1992) appear to challenge and indeed to dismiss social accounting in general and with this to displace and suppress the idea of a radical social accounting. Such a reading of Puxty (1986) and Cooper (1992) is at least in effect embraced in that rhetorical dimension of the mainstream discourse that constitutes a suppression of radical social accounting. Owen *et al.* (1997: 183) can even accuse critical accounting of restricting their 'activities to critique rather than actively seeking to reform practice ... [to] pose a minimalist threat to current orthodoxy'.[30]

Recent developments in social theorising threaten to impact upon the academic discourse of social accounting and social accounting regulation and thus upon practice in such a way as to weaken social accounting's potential vis-à-vis projects of emancipation. Postmodern theorising has especially stressed the uncertainties of the contemporary context, problematising and restraining a policy discourse that would intervene for substantive change. The danger here is that too much respect is in effect given to the status quo. Žižek (2000a,b) worries about a tendency in radical as well as neo-liberal stances to argue against substantive interventionism, the latter all too often being deemed to lead to something worse – such as 'authoritarianism' and 'totalitarianism' (see Žižek 2001). Bronner (1994: 325) conveys a similar message to Žižek when he suggests that not intervening is abdicating responsibility to others, who surely will intervene and not necessarily democratically or benevolently: 'refusing to make a practical judgment in the name of resisting the "domination" supposedly implicit in such a choice, is merely an abdication of responsibility'. If one can make out the case for a substantive interventionism mobilising a radical social accounting as idea and practice in critical theoretical terms (Gallhofer and Haslam 1997b), this case is not seen as an especially strong one by many of today's more mainstream and more radical theorists. Both mainstream and critical discourses of social accounting, influenced by recent theoretical developments, have been expressing increased caution about social accounting interventions (Power 1991, 1992, cf. Gray *et al*. 1987, Harte and Owen 1987, Maunders and Burritt 1991, Gray 1992). Power (1992: 489) cites Dobson (1990) in articulating Gorz's (1989) position vis-à-vis developments in environmental policy discourse that emphasise the uncertainty, or even the ignorance, of our situation, developments that are taken to conceivably impact upon environmental accounting: 'The ... impossibility of knowing enough is crucial to the Green suggestion that we adopt a hands-off approach to the environment'. Can we ever know enough? This is problematic.

In that discourse explicitly identifying a notion of mainstream social accounting (e.g. Gray 1999: 6), this notion is constituted as a problematically narrow and weakened version of social accounting. To the extent that this mainstream social accounting is prominent and displaces possibilities, the emancipatory potential of social accounting is again delimited. We can illustrate this problematic dimension of the academic discourse of social accounting with reference to some academic texts. Mathews articulates his version of the mainstream middle ground as follows:

> ... it must be stated that this book is based upon existing socio-economic conditions of a managed mixed economy and is evolutionary rather than is revolutionary in orientation. The position argued is that a more socially responsible accounting may be justified and should be implemented, not to radically change society but to modify and improve our present system by including measurement and reporting relationships which are currently excluded.
>
> (Mathews 1993: 6)

Giving themselves more scope, but similarly, Gray *et al*. (1988: 8) ambiguously hold that most writings on corporate social reporting are of 'the "middle ground" in which the status quo is accepted (although variously interpreted) and explicit, and overt ambition is neither to destroy capitalism nor to refine, deregulate and/or liberate it ... It is on this "middle ground" that we wish to concentrate'. Mathews (1993: 6) is here explicitly concerned to delimit social accounting and to distance it from a notion of radically changing society. Gray *et al*.'s (1988: 8) reflections on a middle ground position to which they are aligned similarly does not threaten to stray far beyond envisioning a social accounting that would fuse with the restraining forces of the socio-political order. The mainstream social accounting constructed and defended in the discourse has accrued at best a mildly progressive character (see Gray *et al*. 1987, 1988, 1996). The liberalism, pragmatism and middle of the road positioning of the mainstream has constituted the subject matter of critique for more radical writers. For Tinker *et al*. (1991), a 'middle of the road' positioning is problematically unprincipled: 'the middle ground is a contested terrain that shifts over time with social struggles and conflicts'. In the context of the debate the embracing of liberal democracy is suggestive of an acceptance of much of the status quo and a concern at best to bring about relatively moderate improvement rather than aspiring to more radical change, threatening to reduce to a kind of cosmetic surgery (see Žižek 2000a,b). Tinker *et al*. (1991: 28) emphasise the mainstream's commitment to a broadly capitalist and problematic polity implied in their liberal democratic frame-work, its failure to take sides in social conflict and its overlooking of much of the oppression and exploitation associated with the unequal wealth and power distribu-tions in society. For Tinker *et al*. (1991), the pluralism inherent in liberal thinking counters any possibility of radical systemic change. A problem for the mainstream in responding to the critique is that one can seek to bring about radical change, includ-ing through radical social accountings, gradually and pragmatically. Albeit that in very recent times alliances are being constituted at a general level between mainstream and radical actors,[31] it is still the case that the restraints upon social accounting in some branches of the mainstream discourse constitute a narrowing of the phenomenon that distances it from a radical social accounting and weakens its emancipatory possibilities. As the mainstream form of social accounting is the promi-nent notion shaping discourse and practice, this is a significant negative dimension of the academic discourse of social accounting (see Lehman and Tinker 1997).

Another factor threatening to suppress social accounting's emancipatory potential relates to how social accounting has been delineated from conventional accounting. Mainstream social accounting has sometimes been portrayed as something like a 'side-dish' to conventional accounting's substantial fare. Albeit that the mainstream discourse is critical of conventional accounting in various ways, implicitly and explic-itly, it has delimited critique of conventional accounting as well as delimited social accounting's possibilities in conveying the impression that financial economistic matters are irrelevant or adequately dealt with through conventional accounting. Gray *et al*. (1987: ix) are consistent with the majority view when they state that 'corporate social reporting' involves extending accountability 'beyond the traditional role'. The category 'economic', however, appears often to be in effect dropped from social accounting's scope in this and similar delineations. Yet one can properly indicate through accounting publicity a concern, for instance, about productive efficiency, the ethics of the very practice of profit-making, the extent of monopolistic or oligopolistic power exercised, the distribution of wealth and the reproducing of material poverty. Not to challenge conventional accounting in this context renders social accounting more susceptible to its influence and thus enhances the grip of problematic hegemonic forces upon it.

Overviewing the academic discourse of social accounting more generally, there are a whole range of rhetorical emphases that arguably weaken social accounting in the sense of constraining its emancipatory potential.[32] We merely give a flavour of some emphases of concern in what follows. Amongst these rhetorical emphases is the artic-ulation of social accounting's role as the reporting of consequences or effects of the business organisation upon society (for instance Mobley 1970: 762, Epstein *et al*.

1976: 24, Gray *et al.* 1987: ix). In this context, if seeing business organisations as socially significant in this way is not without merit, it may displace some potential visibilities that could be pursued and thus restrict emancipatory possibilities. If, for example, the business organisation and its characteristics are themselves viewed as a consequence or effect of government policy, social pressures or the general functionings of the social context, business social accounting can assume a broader scope. For instance, one can disclose the educational background of company directors, a disclosure that goes beyond the scope of many mainstream delineations of social accounting.[33] More generally, there are dangers that a promotion of *business* social accounting as idea and practice can displace other possible social accountings in respect of individuals, groups intersecting across several organisations and the macro-social (see Gallhofer and Haslam 1993). A related rhetorical emphasis that is problematic is the emphasis upon the responsibilities of organisations, corporate bodies, entities or enterprises (see for instance ASSC: 15, 25, Gray *et al.* 1987: ix). The entity's personification threatens to displace attention from the people involved. People can somehow become uncoupled from key social actions as responsibilities come to be invested in fictional entities. People can hide behind a corporate veil constituted by capitalistic law. It is important that people are seen in terms of the roles they play as well as in terms of their well-being if social accounting is to have a broad and positive emancipatory consequence. The rhetoric of the academic discourse of social accounting has also reinforced the public–private dichotomy that we ought to be questioning and going beyond (cf. Arrington and Watkins 2002). Mobilising this dichotomy can help delimit the social accounting we might properly apply to 'private' as distinct from 'public' sector operations. This threatens to counter a dimension of the rationale for business social accounting, which is meant to reflect the public or social character of business from a more holistic perspective. The potential applicability in the 'private' sector of control and accounting standards from the 'public' sector can be displaced. Where social accounting is dominated by business social accounting, as it has been over recent decades, mobilising or taking for granted a public–private dichotomy can also displace the 'public' sector from attention, although there is some academic work that constitutes a significant negation of this possibility (Broadbent *et al.* 1991, Broadbent 1995). Whereas Mobley's (1970: 762, *supra*) delineation of social accounting extended to 'public' and 'private' organisations that are categorised but ostensibly given equal attention, such an orientation is now rare, with the mainstream focus being business. Gray *et al.*'s (1987: ix) delineation of corporate social reporting (CSR), which refers to an accounting for corporate entities and 'particularly companies', if located in a text quite explicitly demarcating CSR from social accounting in general, in effect has come to be the mainstream delineation of social accounting. Yet it makes good sense to conceive, for instance, of a social accounting for schools, hospitals, the police and local councils. It would be appropriate to challenge the dichotomy public–private so as to open up further the possibility of comparing and contrasting the accountings including social accountings of a variety of organisations, whatever be their legal structure of ownership. Writing in the 1970s, Robertson (1976: 98) observed a breaking down of the dichotomy between private and public sector in part through social accounting: 'The erosion of profitability as the single, dominant indicator of company performance and the accelerating trend towards social accounting in the private sector, has narrowed the conceptual gap between it and the public sector' (Robertson 1976). This trajectory, which would see all organisations as being partly public and private in character, has not continued as one might have hoped. Related to the public–private dichotomy is reference in discourse to externalities (see Gambling 1974, Tinker 1985). Given the basic thrust of the capitalistic legal structure, with the particular weight it gives to the notion of a business making profits for private owners, it is an advance to recognise externalities in respect of the business organisation even if externalities are often labeled as such in general discourse so that they can be ignored. Yet, externalities emerge out of a structure of a socio-economic system already problematically structured by capitalistic politico-economic forces (see Tinker 1985: 199–200). It is important that the problematics of this socio-political system are not displaced into notions of externalities (see also Lehman and Tinker 1997, Lehman 1999).

Social accounting has had a poor image relative to conventional accounting. Many business managers and accountants have not seen it as accounting at all (Bebbington *et al.* 1994). There are a number of ways in which the academic discourse of social accounting has conceivably contributed to this poor image and thus weakened social accounting's possibilities. One illustration is the way social accounting is proclaimed as 'new' in the discourse when it can be perceived as having centuries of history: Gray *et al.* (1996: 124) suggest that it manifested in ancient civilisations. Hopwood and Burchell (1980), in an overview article on social accounting, offer 'an explanation of the scope, intentions and practical applications of this new discipline' and stress that 'it has been argued that some form of wider accounting must emerge to complement the narrowly focused financial accountings of the past'. They suggest that it was in recent history that 'early social accounting experiments originated in the United States' (12). Conventional accounting meanwhile is generally understood as 'traditional', as in Gray *et al.*'s (1987) influential definition of corporate social reporting. Yet, as indicated, social accounting has a long history. In modern history, interventions in Europe centuries ago that fused 'statistics' and 'accounting' (cf. Burchell *et al.* 1980), and aimed at mobilising accountings in the name of social betterment, can be understood as social accounting interventions. One can delineate this type of intervention in the context of seventeenth century rationalism and its eighteenth century legacy (see Gallhofer and Haslam 1995). We have elaborated how Bentham's project is especially of note. Bentham envisaged that an accounting rationalised in its limits would serve well the duty to humanity. This is recognisable as a mode of 'social accounting' in today's terms. His linking of social accounting to democracy, control, enlightenment and wisdom are also echoed in more recent interventions. Further, Bentham advocated and encouraged 'counter' accounting. There are also numerous examples from before the twentieth century of various social accounting type practices being pursued, for instance by businesses and religious communities (see Davidoff and Hall 1987, Guthrie and Parker 1989a,b, Gallhofer and Haslam 1995). If placing stress on newness can be positive – an envisaged break with repression may be emphasised and some may be inspired by a sense of being involved in something new – it is also the case that, the longevity of an institution and practice can add to its value in many cultures, including in Britain. De-emphasising social accounting's historical continuities threatens to conceivably delay or render overly cautious its adoption or make it easier to pull out of if adopted. One can more easily characterise social accounting as immature, marginal, amateur and/or eccentric. To displace attention from how old an idea is can reduce its weight. Conveying the sense of there having been calls for a social accounting for a long time and arguing that by now many might have benefited from its adoption could bolster the case for it. To conceive of social accounting as new may lead one to overlook the insights that one can gain from historical study. Best (1995) in this regard suggests that radical dimensions of philosophers such as Bentham and Kant are often overlooked in sweeping and dismissive treatments of their texts today (including, ironically, in some postmodern interventions). Promoters of social accounting can positively mobilise the insight that the struggles for a democracy to inform and empower the people in respect of the functionings of social institutions, and for a 'social accounting' that would be emancipatory, have a long history.[34]

Aside from mobilising academic discourse in various problematic ways, we should also add here that various other aspects of the interventions of academics in general can equally be problematised. For example, we have already indicated that in getting involved with campaigns to promote social accounting, academics have often problematically given legitimacy to dubious practices. Further, a cursory review of academic interventions indicates their lack of co-ordination. And social accounting's presence on educational syllabi is still disappointing. Gray *et al*.'s (2001) survey, focused upon environmental but also giving attention to social accounting education, echoes earlier disappointing findings (Owen *et al*. 1994, Humphrey *et al*. 1996, Watt 1998). Gray *et al*. (2001: 87–8) report a move from focusing upon social towards environmental accounting, albeit that they also find a move towards the coverage of social audit and acknowledge that the term 'environmental' has sometimes incorporated the social (see Vidal 2002). For Gray *et al*. (2001: 101): 'Students and teachers would appear to be overly influenced by the professional syllabi and are exceptionally reluctant to step outside the notion of "accounting" as represented by those syllabi'. Recent concerns on the part of professional bodies to develop programmes to enhance communicative and intellectual skills may be taken as encouraging focuses upon phenomena such as social accounting. The general picture is disappointing, however, in spite of some positive signs.

With critical emancipatory intent: summary reflections on our analyses

Our analyses of some key instances of social accounting in action in recent decades are brief and elaborate points of a vast problematic. Nevertheless, we can bring out in broad terms how they are suggestive of insights for a project concerned to mobilise an emancipatory social accounting today. We can briefly outline insights that can be located in relation to prior work and in relation to the further extensive work that we hope to stimulate and encourage. Our analyses confirm in general that one needs to be suspicious of any accounting that is held out as being in the service of people and the environment. All such social accountings, along with conventional accountings, are located in a context that is imperfect and problematic. They are all to some extent corrupted and their influences are to various degrees corrupting. Nevertheless, unless we strongly accept the status quo and its dynamic, our analyses suggest that it is appropriate to seek identification with forms of radical and progressive accountings and these can at least intersect with some types of social accounting. Various key social accounting manifestations over recent decades have indicated both progressive and regressive dimensions. One can positively identify to some degree with a whole range of different types of social accounting. Our analysis suggested at the same time that it is possible to differentiate between social accountings that have manifested in terms of their apparent intent, their various characteristics and their likely consequences.

We can elaborate emergent insights in terms of the broad themes of our socio-historical analyses. Efforts by pressure groups and activists to mobilise counter information systems have been variously radically orientated, some strongly and explicitly so. The success of such groups in terms of emancipatory impact is influenced by the context. We have suggested that these groups can influence their success, it would seem, by switching at least emphases of their strategies as contexts change. There is a need to respond contextually and strategically to the shifting frameworks of power and resistance. Today's context represents quite a challenge to counter information systems type activists. If these activists work on a global level with advanced communicative technology, they face a frighteningly powerful set of global hegemonic forces that are very difficult to shift. By maintaining a vision of an accounting that can expose repressive practices and can help bring about an envisaged better world, by being concerned to work with and listen to the relatively repressed, by constantly questioning conventions, by trying to build up a positive reputational effect and by shifting strategies in the changing context towards global collaboration, counter-information systems activists can hope to maintain an alignment between their form of radical social accounting and emancipation and move along the continuum that summarises dynamics in an emancipatory direction (cf. Lehman and Tinker 1997, Neu *et al*. 2001). Consistent with a questioning of conventions, activists can make use of existing official and unofficial information as well as construct their own information. The need to develop and maintain a reputation and positive image requires a balanced approach that is sensitive to the contextual dynamics. The substance of actions taken, the way activities are presented and their perceived relative maturity are amongst the factors involved in shaping the public image (Neu *et al*. 2001). Should counter-information systems type activists be concerned to manage image by reference to existing conventions and official practices, they run the risk here, as do others, of emerging with a professional expert aura that distances them from the repressed groups they are ostensibly meant to serve. We should also stress that deliberative attempts to go beyond the 'privileged knower' – a seeking to give a voice to, and to listen to, others – and to embrace a differentiated universalism, constitute approaches that help preserve, refine and enhance a radical approach today. Indeed they take us beyond a crude totalising imperialism that would silence 'other voices' (Mouck 1995). Where counter information systems activity is suppressed by the state's law, the activists are left with a dilemma the response to which is appropriately influenced by the context and the possibilities it offers for substantive change.

Our critical explorations have here indicated that those seeking to promote a more radical or at least progressive social accounting can in some contexts be undermined when forming alliances with business and government. There is a great danger, in this act, of legitimising and supporting a system that one is concerned to problematise and challenge. Our analyses suggest that, on the face of it, business and government can be pressurised to introduce some progressive measures and we have suggested that some contexts are more facilitative of this strategy than others. At the same time, we have seen that initiatives of business and government ought to be especially treated as suspicious. We have indicated that the phenomenon of hegemonic capture, in the shape of variously counter radical social accountings, exists. Indeed, it can be somewhat subtle, involving a mix of programmatic interventions by government, the profession and business, as in the case of the mobilising of social accounting in the 1970s. At the same time, manifestations of social accounting do not reflect an absolute hegemonic power. Rather, the ambiguous character of social accounting, and the tensions that run through it, make possible its alignment with various social forces, counter hegemonic as well as hegemonic: social accounting has no necessary class belongingness. Critical research indicates that the capture of social accounting is a matter of the outcome of a socio-political struggle. We have seen how various key agencies and institutions have had a shifting hold over social accounting. Out of the conflicts of the 1960s, business looked to have in large part found a winning strategy in its efforts to control social accounting's development but subsequently the counter-information systems type activity that was stimulated appears to have gained some increased influence. Later, business substantially reappropriated social accounting. We have pointed to how accounting trajectories can set in motion processes that undermine the intentions and strategies apparently behind them. These counter tendencies also create opportunities for the various protagonists in the struggle. In respect of the accountancy profession, we have indicated how it needs to have some sort of alliance with both business and government, if it might shift the relative emphasis of its alliance with one over the other in differing or changed contexts. In addition, we have elaborated how an accountancy profession that stands at least ostensibly (especially in the public realm) some distance from both government and business has its own particular agenda. We have seen that this helps to raise questions about its interventions. Awareness of the motivations and tensions involved in interventions of the accountancy profession and their shifting pattern could be a considerable aid to activists seeking to develop counter information type contributions to debate in the public realm. The emancipatory project must be concerned to struggle against those forces that oppose it. It can mobilise counter-information systems that help counter the accountings of the relatively powerful agencies and institutions. And it can seek to advise and steer these bodies towards a radical orientation and expose their response to such pressure. Interventions here have to deal with complexity and ambiguity. For instance, in a dynamic context in which strategies need to be constantly re-worked, there are a number of themes to pursue, a number of repressed groups to give attention to as well as a number of agencies and institutions to variously challenge and interact with. The existence of such matters to attend to suggests the need in the current context to collaborate across national boundaries and to develop ways to align the various change agents or emancipatory struggles. Emancipation is about creating new values, new forms of co-operation and new types of collectivist praxis and the mobilising of accounting with emancipatory intent has to manifest in this frame of reference. Since serious engagement with accounting is also serious engagement with the context of which accounting is part, and the dynamics of that context, these issues have to be faced up to (Tinker 1999). If life is difficult, messy and awkward with no easy pristine solutions, we have to engage in a praxis that can implicate the fostering of an emancipatory accounting (Arrington and Watkins 2002). We indicated how academics could play a significant role in the successful and radical mobilising of social accounting through the various texts they construct, through their educational activity and through their more general strategic interventions. Studies expressing disappointments in respect of the latter, and more general reviews of accounting academics and praxis, are usefully being published to stimulate thought and practice (see, e.g. Willmott *et al.* 1993, Puxty *et al.* 1994, Sikka *et al.* 1995, Lehman and Tinker 1997, Sikka and Willmott 1997, Gray 1999, Tinker 1999, *Neu et al.* 2001; see also Garnham 2000). We need more appreciations of and reflections upon praxis just as we need more social analyses of accounting as praxis. Such appreciations and reflections, as well as the analyses, are not straightforward. In understanding the contextual embeddedness of the phenomena there are considerable complexities to face up to. Over time, however, we can aim to build up useful insights (Gray 1999, Neu *et al.* 2001). Academics cannot detach themselves from the wider struggles and issues of the social context (Lowe and Tinker 1977, Hopwood 1985, Tinker 1985). In general, that accounting is not a practice beyond but is rather interwoven in politics is not to be regretted but acted upon. Academics have the possibility to contribute in their educational programmes by, for instance, giving recognition to the struggles that manifest between various radical and counter radical social accountings and more generally by developing appreciation of the situated character of accounting practice (cf. Gallhofer and Haslam 2002). Academics can make possible the embracing of perspectives beyond the mainstream (see Panozzo 1997). They can also point to parallels between education and accounting (see Gallhofer and Haslam 1996b, Gray 1999: 15). They can educate for praxis in, for instance, giving recognition to the significance of libel laws, the relevance of which to various parties (not least to counter-information systems type activists) has been insightfully highlighted by Hopwood (1978). Contemporary struggles with the law and concerns to police systems of informing are well articulated in this context by Mitchell *et al.* (2001) (see also Herman and Chomsky 1994, Finn 1996, Mitchell *et al.* 1998, Evans 2002, cf. Sikka 1994, Puxty and Tinker 1995). Our analysis, furthermore, suggests that attention needs to be given by academics to the careful delineation of social accounting from conventional accounting and in relation to accounting in general. We have indicated that a key conceptual contribution that academics can make is to seek to evaluate accounting *in general* by reference to the criterion of whether it is in the service of society – the criterion by which accounting is socially legitimised, indeed in explicit terms by professional bodies of accountants.

Such a holistic perspective, which academics could aim to promote in the public realm, would only break up or differentiate accounting into, for instance, 'financial', 'social' or 'environmental' accounting, as a matter of practical convenience: striving to realise the relationship of these elements in a holistic perspective would emerge as a crucial aspect of academic and broader praxis (cf. Elkington 1988, Owen *et al.* 2000: 84, 91).[35] We should add that, in radical discourse, to serve society is to engender emancipatory change. We have seen that academics as well as other groups can be undermined, even with good intentions, by a failure to give sufficient attention to the character and consequences of the discourses they engage with. Our analysis suggests that it remains important for accounting academics to recognise the value of their educational practice and to keep striving to engender improved insights through this interaction. Further, it appears to be important for academics to take particular care with whom they form alliances in accounting interventions as their involvement may in various ways enhance what amounts to a disappointing and even counter radical practice. Academics need to strive to maintain a questioning and critical approach that takes not only 'social' but also 'conventional' accounting seriously, seeking to transform both of these in the name of a holistic emancipatory accounting (see Tinker 1999). We hope that critical engagement with the insights that we have suggested from our analyses here can stimulate further work. In relation to social accounting as we have understood it here, there is a lot to do in terms of the 'size' of the phenomenon and in terms of critical reflections upon praxis (Lehman and Tinker 1997, Gray 1999). If there are obstacles to overcome, the potential for bringing about emancipatory change is significant. We are thus hopeful that future work can move us further towards the realisation of accounting's emancipatory possibilities, or the realisation of Bentham's vision of an accounting publicity that would be the soul of justice.

5   Epilogue

Accounting, emancipation and praxis today

You Can't Be Neutral On A Moving Train
Title of a book by
Howard Zinn (1994)

The analyses of this book point to relevant insights for the project to better align accounting and emancipation today. Nevertheless, ending here would feel like leaving the train too early. We hope we can advance a little further or make more emancipatory progress. Maintaining engagement in the struggle, we seek here, informed by the insights of the above theoretical and empirical discussions and analyses, to reflect further upon the possibilities of an emancipatory praxis implicating accounting today. Our elaboration upon accounting, emancipation and praxis here builds upon our theoretical intervention in Chapter 1 where we were concerned to elaborate the possibility of a positive alignment between accounting and emancipation. Indeed, it helps us to see that theoretical intervention, the interventions in the form of historical analyses that followed it (Chapters 2–4) as well as the intervention of this chapter itself, as all instances of praxis. Our commentary can only be partial and unfinished, raising questions and encouraging further work rather than providing final answers. What we offer is a kind of sketch (Bronner 1994) of a notion of emancipatory praxis implicating accounting rather than a blueprint. As a sketch, it can, we suggest, encourage others to engage in a 'differentiated universalist' and emancipatory struggle and can restrain tendencies towards an approach that is at once problematically universal, dogmatic and over burdened by the even detailed prescriptions of a 'privileged knower'. It is a sketch that speaks to our concern, in summary terms, to advance accounting and its context along the continuum towards a more emancipated state.

Sketching an emancipatory praxis implicating accounting

Critical theoretical and holistic praxis is here the struggle to progress towards the emancipated state.[1] It responds to concerns about how we are to achieve this progress or what is to be done. Locating accounting in praxis thus is to ask what is the role of accounting in progressing emancipation and how can we mobilise it to realise its potential. This involves understanding accounting contextually, going beyond a perception of the practice as static and technical and envisioning progressive emancipatory development. And it involves an envisioning of an emancipatory accounting and a whole range of further interventions in interaction therewith to help engender emancipatory progress, whether implicating more direct challenges to accounting or the more indirect opening of possible pathways for accounting's development.

A critical theoretical appreciation or re-construction (see Tinker 2001: 84–5) of the context and of accounting embedded in this context constitutes a key dimension of praxis implicating accounting. That is, a key intervention involves gaining theoretical understanding of the problematic contextual dynamics and of the functioning of accounting as an integral and thus problematic and dynamic element thereof. Such theorising helps point to the transformative significance of accounting and indicates opportunities for strategic emancipatory intervention. For Tinker (2001: 81), in this regard, in theorising accounting contextually 'we must find a way to grasp, assimilate, and render intelligible case experience in a manner that retains or parallels its own internal relations, that is: its own (self) transformative dynamics'. The reconstructing of experience in terms of a dialectical analysis that privileges change in phenomena can actively intensify contradictions and constitute 'potentially, a transformative and revolutionary episteme ... that may highlight the transformative possibilities in our experience' (Tinker 2001: 82).[2] In this regard, a critical theoretical analysis of accounting pursues critical themes, including, for instance: delineating the dynamics and trends of accounting; indicating the contradictory and conflictual character of accounting and the sense in which it reflects social instabilities; elaborating the repressive dimensions of accounting's functionings today and in the past; exposing how accounting is captured by problematic hegemonic forces; bringing out accounting's role in supporting an unjust and exploitative socio-political and economic order;[3] detailing particular as well as universal effects of accounting's functioning; gaining insights into how accounting is perceived in society and how this delimits its potential and enhances its negative functioning; arriving at new radical insights for accounting in practice in different cultures and historical contexts;[4] tracing accounting's role in relation to practices and processes functioning as instigators of radical change; and elaborating emancipatory dimensions of accounting's functioning[5] (see Gallhofer and Haslam 1997a). Understanding context and accounting in this way is a form of intervention that is itself a struggle. It involves striving to appreciate our own dynamics as people and being concerned to realise emancipatory development in selves and others (Gramsci 1971, Adorno 1973, Ollman 1976, Jameson 1991). Given substantively entrenched ways of seeing accounting and the world (see Lehman 1999, Tinker 2001: 86), it involves a striving to achieve a critical perspective in the sense of embracing a far-reaching analysis that questions norms otherwise restrictive of inquiry and that challenges the socio-political order. For Tinker (2001: 82): 'A phenomenon's presence or surface is a limit, boundary, or barrier in the sense that it stands in opposition from the outset to the phenomenon's infinite expansion to change into "what it is not" (Ryan 1982). It is the "is" that precludes the "other" (Marx 1973: 31)'. A critical contextual appreciation can thus implicate the analysis of various accountings in practice – accountings for various entities or focuses, accountings assuming various forms and accountings having various contents, users and usages – in radical and innovative ways so as to open up new ways of seeing. Accounting can in this respect be conceived of, for instance, as fusing with the notion of 'system of informing' in general (like the stat(e)istics with which it has had such a strong interface, cf. Burchell *et al*. 1980, Gallhofer and Haslam 1995) or as an element in or dimension of the communicative structure of society. Likewise, its broad interface with the law can be delineated as can its interface with the multifarious socio-political and cultural forces involved in its regulation.

As elaborated in Chapter 1, we conceive – informed by our contextual understanding – of the possibility of emancipatory development along a continuum. This involves the envisioning of a better world, including a better accounting, an envisioning that is in itself an aspect of praxis. Again, a struggle is involved here. Our contextual location is such that the imagining is less than perfect. We struggle to gain a critical distance from the current context and the instrumentalist reasoning that threatens to engulf us (see Held 1980, Lehman 1999, Tinker 2001). As we struggle to attain a better world we anticipate changes to our vision, including the possibility of clearer visions as progressive moves are made and emancipatory forces gain relative to repressive ones. The notion of progression towards a better world suggests the idea of utopia, an idea that Bronner (1994) helpfully elaborates in relation to the critical theoretical project. Visions of better worlds – with better accountings in them – may be thought of as 'utopias' in the context in which they are imagined. Any vision of a utopia in an ultimate sense is, however, in accordance with our theory, very speculative. It could only be constructed as the vaguest of sketches. The same goes for any vision of a utopian accounting in an ultimate sense, saving that such an accounting would be basically concerned to maintain and reproduce the ultimate utopia achieved. Substantively, what matters in engaging in praxis is the envisioning of a better world that we can reasonably imagine in our admittedly imperfect context. Even this vision has to be something of a sketch if we are to intervene consistent with the principles elaborated in Chapter 1. On the one hand, having to recognise our imperfect location suggests caution. On the other, we should properly embrace openness to theoretical refinement through the adoption of alternative perspectives (Gallhofer and Haslam 1997a: 81). It is, however, important to have a critical vision and one that goes beyond the instrumentalist reasoning that is so influential. This is a position appreciated by a number of critical writers in accounting who have called for a clarification of goals, values and politico-ethical stances, prescriptions for emancipatory design, the adoption of a target critical practice and an institutional or political stance consistent with a critical perspective (see, e.g. Cooper and Sherer 1984, Moore 1991, including his critique of legal realists: 768, Neimark 1994, Neu *et al*. 2001).

Chapter 1 elaborated the possibility of an emancipatory accounting that can move us in a positive dimension along the envisaged summary continuum. Since one of the objects of the envisioning of a better world is accounting itself, we should stress that we here foresee the mobilising of an emancipatory accounting to help us move to a better world that will also feature a better accounting. This notion of mobilising accounting – an emancipatory accounting – to in part progress accounting itself, may at first appear curious. Its logic, however, follows our argumentation concerning progress along a continuum. The concern of critical holistic praxis is to overcome alienation, repression, discrimination, injustice and exploitation and to achieve openness, justice, the control of people over government and the state through a participative democracy, a balanced relationship between humanity and nature and, in short, emancipation, fulfillment and well-being (see Ollman 1976, Arthur 1986, Benton 1994). An emancipatory accounting is therefore shaped by these aims and this vision.[6] Thus, the mobilising of a range of emancipatory accountings in relation to the contextual dynamics creates awareness of problems to be addressed, hence exposing alienation, repression and injustice in our world, and suggests potentialities for emancipatory development (see Held 1980, Bronner 1994: 340–7, cf. Puxty 1991: 37). Emancipatory accounting reflects a concern to express a critique of the social structure, to counter the institutional constraints and to draw attention to negative dimensions of social and organisational functioning that inhibit exposure of the interests of the exploited (cf. Bronner 1994: 327). Such an accounting gives people key insights, including into the potential role of at least some aspects of mainstream accounting in an emancipatory praxis as well as into the role of mainstream accountings in the reproduction of repressive activities. Emancipatory accountings monitor what matters to people whether material or non-material, financial or non-financial. They reflect what people pushing for emancipation would want disclosed from a holistic perspective rather than getting overly bound up in an obsessive instrumentalism whether organisation-centred or otherwise (see Nelson 1993, Lehman 1999). Such accounting helps build community and environmental awareness and buttresses solidarity as well as takes more seriously a concern to foster personal development and growth. Emancipatory accounting, reflecting social needs and wants, also provides re-assurance and acknowledges what matters to the community. A holistic approach pursues the construction of systems of informing in respect of a wide range of focuses, individuals, micro-organisations and societies. Emancipatory accountings are shaped by the interests of repressed groups and communication with and learning from these groups. Such accountings reflect concerns to cater to these particular as well as more universal interests. At the same time, emancipatory accounting should reflect the critical activist's concern to exercise the responsibility of having an opinion (see Bronner 1994). Thus, there is, for instance, the need to take seriously the possibility of satisfying accountability to groups that cannot easily speak for themselves, something evident in the case of accounting for the child (Haslam 1991, Gallhofer and Haslam 1997a, cf. Gaa 1986, 1988). Emancipatory accounting has a broad scope and goes beyond accounting's conventional norms.[7] Various forms as well as contents of accounting can be experimented with. Counter accountings are thus mobilised in a variety of different forms available, forms which have no necessary class-belongingness (see Tinker 1984a–c, 1985, 2001, Gallhofer and Haslam 1996a). In respect of form, technological change creates opportunities. The Internet currently in some ways facilitates global communication including through accounting's mobilisation (see Arrington and Puxty 1991, Arrington and Francis 1993, Puxty 1993, Moore 1991: 782, Laughlin 1995, Gallhofer and Haslam 1997a, cf. Spender 1995, Žižek 2001: 256). Another important feature of an emancipatory accounting reflects a concern to treat seriously the issue of the openness of accounting itself, especially given the possibility of accounting's capture by problematic hegemonic forces, including by an aligned professional expert rhetoric (Mirvis and Lawler 1983, Butterworth *et al.* 1989, Tinker 1991, Arrington and Francis 1993).

From the above, an emancipatory accounting enables people to contribute to progressive development, a role for accounting recognised in strands of the critical theoretical literature. Bronner (1994: 322) is amongst those giving it a significant weight in general praxis, in including accountability amongst his list of categories necessary for translating theory into meaningful forms of emancipatory practice. His analysis is influenced by Habermas' stress on the potential of the communicative structures of society, a stress influenced by a radical dimension in Bentham, as we have seen (Chapter 2). Following the logic of Bronner's (1994) argument, it is thus consistent with praxis to mobilise an accounting for empowerment and institute a practical fulcrum for making judgments concerning democracy (335–6). This accounting helps fulfil the practical need of the disadvantaged to equitably adjudicate their grievances, overcome their lack of unity and develop a sensible view of those institutional conditions that would foster their well-being (cf. Bronner 1994: 326). It gives the poor a voice and in doing so enables them.

Beyond the delineation of emancipatory accounting, praxis today embraces multifarious interventions, including some that correspond more obviously with the project of how in practice we might mobilise or realise an emancipatory accounting. Of these possibilities, a number have been pursued, although one can question how well. Choices and emphases in respect of where to intervene and how ought properly to be contextually informed. One can, informed by contextual specificities, challenge accountings and construct alternative accountings. There is the possibility of engagement with more official and indeed more unofficial accountings, for example, by bringing pressure to bear on these, including by proposing new alternative official publicities. This may be strengthened by being backed by a global radical accounting body. Consistent with Gramsci's (1971) view that one has to be versatile, flexible and pragmatic in forming alliances at an historical juncture, interventions can be more or less pragmatic. In this respect, recognition of the possibility of progress along a continuum is consistent with a view that there is something to be rescued in the institutions and practices of modernity, even with post-Nietzschean recognition of the problematics thereof (*supra*, Connolly 1988, Gallhofer and Haslam 1994b, 1995) and the concern to go beyond existing practices and existing structures (Ridgers 1979, Moore 1991, Tinker 1991, Gallhofer and Haslam 1996c, 1997a: 84–5, Reiter 1994, 1995). Critical intervention should in any case reflect caution about the problematics of an overly sweeping approach (see Moore 1991: 781, Giddens 1994). Where one is attempting to engender emancipatory development through collaboration and organisation it can be sensible to opt for a pragmatic compromise. Even if they have different preferences in respect of an emancipatory accounting, a broad church of progressive individuals or groups can thus be appropriately included in a movement to develop accounting progressively. Yet interventions should always be radically orientated. In this regard, while engaging with an official accounting through a pragmatic approach has its merits and its appeal, a question to take seriously is whether this increases the likelihood of capture by problematic hegemonic forces.

In intervening one can attempt to change accounting more directly or more indirectly. Intervention to change accounting more indirectly involves efforts to transform dimensions of the context of accounting's location that promise to then impact upon accounting. Some 'indirect' interventions can be in areas that are relatively close to accounting. An instance would be an intervention in accounting education (see Gallhofer and Haslam 1996a) with the aim of promoting new ways of seeing accounting, creating awareness of the potential of an emancipatory accounting amongst the accountants of the future, developing critical appreciations of accounting's contextual location, mobilising critical accounting research – which several researchers suggest has scarcely been reflected in accounting education (Lewis *et al*. 1992, Day 1995, Gray 1995, Gallhofer and Haslam 2002) – and developing immanent critique (see Puxty *et al*. 1994). Other indirect interventions can be in areas on the face of it more distant from accounting. For example, one can be active in a project to change institutional and governmental structures – such as a project seeking to create a world parliament (Monbiot 2002) – following the logic that this will then open up pathways for accounting's development. It is possible to engage with a multiplicity of agencies, general or particular instances of government, business, the accountancy profession, pressure groups, labour and the 'public at large', whether challenging or working with them. Thus, ways of trying to shape more official accountings more directly – with the aim, for example, of bringing about the disclosure of well audited information to facilitate emancipatory progress – include trying to pressurise or work with a relevant part of government, the accountancy profession (or some part or fraction thereof, see Briloff 2001) or with business organisations. One can bring concerns to the attention of these agencies, pursue a form of immanent critique – mobilising, for example, the profession's quite explicit claim to serve the public interest (see Held 1980) – and aim to enrol them in progressive accounting initiatives. An approach that has potential here is to locate and challenge the attitudes of different groups (see Bebbington *et al*. 1994). One can conceivably pressurise a variety of agencies through forms of accounting itself, most obviously through mobilising forms of counter accounting that expose an agent's culpability in relation to current problematic practices. Further, ways of trying to shape unofficial accountings directly include getting involved with academic pressure groups, social activists, the unions or political parties in the construction of counter accountings that pressurise business and government. This type of intervention, also advocated by Bentham (*supra*), remains one of the most legitimate for radical emancipatory praxis given that its explicitly radical orientation can often sharply distinguish it from problematic hegemonic forces. There are a vast number of more local and more global areas or sites of possible intervention for praxis. One might engage in a particular site of conflict involving a particular business or other micro-entity or in the struggles of a global movement. For Bronner (1994: 337): 'Opening the various sub-systems of society to public pressure can only occur by contesting the various hegemonic interests embedded within them'. As well as reflect a concern to acknowledge particularism, a specific or local intervention should properly have a global orientation to avoid the danger of embracing an overly parochial interest. Research is also an element in praxis focused upon accounting and critical researchers should be concerned to critically reflect upon their research as praxis. Consistent with this, Cooper and Tinker (1994: 3) encourage critical accounting research from as well as on behalf of oppressed groups. Critical writers also point to the range of methods that can be mobilised in critical interpretive research to support praxis (Gallhofer and Haslam 1997a). All these possible interventions are properly made consistent with the principles elaborated in Chapter 1. Of particular note here is the need to go beyond reliance on the privileged knower and to embrace a differentiated universalism.

The struggle continues

Accounting – and the accountant – can potentially function more benevolently as instruments of social well-being or welfare: they can potentially better align with the emancipatory project. Realising this potential, however, involves quite a struggle. Throughout our theoretical discussions and empirical analyses, we have developed and maintained the argument that the adoption of a radical accounting, as an element in a contextually informed emancipatory praxis, together with the development of a range of strategic interventions, does, however, hold out some hope (see Arrington and Puxty 1991, Broadbent *et al.* 1991, Tinker 1991, Reiter 1995). We have been concerned in this book to articulate the sense in which we can still justifiably seek to align accounting and emancipation. Our analyses have brought out progressive and regressive dimensions of manifestations of accounting in the name of emancipatory endeavour. They have located accounting in the context of struggles between hegemonic and counter hegemonic forces and indicated, encouragingly, how accounting has not been fully captured by the latter. We have elaborated how accounting can be conceived of as a radical force and indicated that the manifestation of such a way of seeing has a long history to give emphasis to and draw upon, with the notion of accounting as an instrument of social progress being notably reflected in the discourse of the Enlightenment. Our analyses have articulated how accountings of various types can be mobilised by and on behalf of relatively oppressed groups to counter the accountings of the relatively powerful. Here, the example of CIS in the 1970s points to the possibilities for emancipatory praxis of using existing conventional accounting practices as well as developing new accountings. Interventions by Henry Hyde Champion and Annie Besant in the late nineteenth century indicate that where little accounting is available publicly, alternative radical accounts that expose repressive practices can be produced. The absence of well established and substantively hegemonically captured accounts can create space for the development of support for alternatives even if at the same time the failings in disclosure also constrain the radical activists. We have indicated that a range of actors and institutions can be involved in accounting interventions, reflecting a multiplicity of interests. An insight of our analysis is that we should be highly cautious about forming alliances with relatively powerful actors in the name of progressive accountings, albeit that in some contexts this seems more likely to be effective than in others. We have argued that the content, form, aura and practical usage of accounting are key dimensions of accounting's manifestation. Our critical explorations have brought out how all accountings have repressive dimensions and possibilities but that this is more especially the case where they have been mobilised by relatively powerful and established agencies or actors and institutions. Our research has highlighted the ambiguous and contradictory dimensions of accounting in action. We have stressed the importance of contextual contingencies and dynamics, which can change the precise character of radical envisionings but also impact upon the degree of success of various strategies of intervention. Today, some of the contextual conditions of possibility have improved the prospect for a project that would mobilise accounting with emancipatory intent. Technological change has been important here. With the – in some respects – increased and cheaper access to information, possibilities to design counter information systems have been variously extended. Technological advancements have enhanced the possibilities of disseminating counter information globally and quickly. At the same time, the challenges facing those concerned to mobilise a radical accounting today are strong. The struggle is at a global level against relatively powerful forces. Our analyses have confirmed the relevance, it seems to us, of a critical and holistic praxis that appreciates accounting contextually and that seeks to transform and mobilise it through more direct interface with it and through more indirect contextual interaction. We have highlighted the shifting character of this praxis and indicated some of the complexities and subtleties involved. It remains the case, however, that a vision of a better world, with a better accounting, and correspondingly the critical questioning and challenging of current accounting practices, is a key element of such praxis. Much work has to be done if accounting publicity is to realise more of its potential to function as the soul of justice and emancipatory development. The obstacles to realising progress here should not be understated. For Bronner (1994), the concern to capture disclosures can constitute a strong motivation for intervention on the part of the relatively powerful in this context: powerful established forces feel especially threatened by the possibilities of democracy and the potential power of the masses and are quick to see the downside of openness (see Lehman and Tinker 1997). The struggle continues.

Notes

1 Accounting and emancipation: developing and promoting an alignment

1 We adopt a critical theoretical perspective influenced by German Critical Theory (see Held 1980, Kellner 1989, Alway 1995). As in the work of, notably, Best and Kellner (1991, 2002), Kellner (1988, 2002a–d), Agger (1991, 1992, 1998), Bronner (1994) and Calhoun (1995), it is open to reconstruction and refinement through engagement with developments in philosophical discourse that variously challenge it, such as in the critique of modernity. We continue to adopt a critical theoretical emphasis, labelling our approach a critical theoretical perspective rather than opting for an alternative term such as critical postmodernism (see Gabardi 2001). Our perspective, as critical theoretical, is supradisciplinary. It finds problematic the notion of, as it were, operating within the confines of particular 'disciplines' as a mode of praxis. These disciplines, constituted historically by different focuses, ways of seeing and methodological approaches, albeit that they foster specialist insights of value, can pose obstacles to a deeper, more holistic and more substantially relevant critical appreciation. Further, they can assume an elitist and anti-democratic expert character. A concern is to counter these problematics (Kellner 1989). For instance, borders that might be conceived as delineating self-contained disciplines such as 'Accounting' and 'Politics' need to be transgressed in both directions in critical supradisciplinary engagement.

2 The aura of accounting is understood here as how accounting is socially perceived in society in terms of the various dimensions of its image (see Gallhofer and Haslam 1991).

3 A number of texts are here illustrative (see Cooper 1980, Tinker 1980, 1984b, 1985, 1991, Tinker et al. 1982, Neimark 1983, Cooper and Sherer 1984, Ogden and Bougen 1985, Hopper et al. 1986, Neimark and Tinker 1986, Knights and Collinson 1987, Lehman and Tinker 1987, Tinker and Neimark 1987, Tinker et al. 1988, Bougen 1989, Willmott 1990, Gallhofer and Haslam 1991).

4 Social analyses of accounting influenced by postmodernism have contributed insights, several going beyond the almost exclusive focus upon labour and production in many previous social analyses of accounting, while not necessarily displacing these dimensions altogether (see Hoskin and Macve 1986, 1988, Hopwood 1987, 1988, Miller and O'Leary 1987, Robson 1993, 1994, Puxty 1993, Cooper and Puxty 1994, Hopwood and Miller 1994). Some have fused with feminist and postcolonial critique (see Cooper 1992, Gallhofer 1992, Shearer and Arrington 1993, Gallhofer and Chew 2000, Gallhofer et al. 2000a). Inspite of their multifarious contribution, a dimension of many social analyses of accounting influenced by postmodernism that has been disappointing is that they have often manifested as crudely oppositional to neo-Marxist approaches. Analyses have often in effect suffered from a problematic conservatism (see Moore 1991). On the other hand, it is for us also somewhat disappointing that, perhaps influenced by such analyses, critical accounting writings of a neo-Marxist and/or Habermasian genre have tended to distance themselves somewhat from postmodernism (see also Laughlin 1987, 1988, Broadbent et al. 1991, see commentaries in Puxty 1993, Gallhofer and Haslam 1997a, Laughlin et al. 1994, Broadbent and Laughlin 1997). Albeit that the last mentioned analyses have also in

many ways been insightful, they run the risk of missing the radicalism of postmodern insights. Neo-Marxist and/or Habermasian and postmodern perspectives in accounting have more recently come to influence each other in a more positive way. We are concerned to advance this tendency, which mirrors what Gabardi (2001) overviews as the emergence of a critical postmodernism out of antagonism between postmodernism and critical theory.

5　Below, we refer to the critique of modernity/emancipation in terms such as the challenging philosophical discourse, the philosophical critique or simply the critique for ease of expression.

6　Alvesson and Willmott (1992) is a key text elaborating the linkages between management and emancipation.

7　Views that amount to replacing emancipation by another term for strategic reasons are for us less easy to dismiss. There are views, including views informed by the critique, that suggest that the term emancipation has so many negative and problematic associations that it ought to be abandoned and to some extent, at least, be replaced by another term. Laclau (1992) wonders, for instance, whether we should displace the term emancipation and promote the term liberation (see also Foucault 1984, Giddens 1991, Gabardi 2001). We believe that the still continuing positive associations of emancipation can be re-vitalised. For us, what amounts to in part a clarification of the concept of emancipation that draws from the better insights of a now long-existing critical theoretical discourse – including the appreciation of dialectics – and in part a refinement of the concept, can provide for its rescue.

8　While 'Marxist' understandings of emancipation have been subjected to problematic critique that has set up its target as something of a 'straw-man' (see Benhabib 1986), Laclau (1992) has carefully articulated the view that problematic conceptions of emancipation have left substantial traces in varieties of Marxist, neo-Marxist and critical theoretical discourse. Problematic conceptions of emancipation are clearly located in Enlightenment conceptions of emancipation more generally.

9　Weeks (1993: 205) goes on to articulate the problematic of linking particular and universal in pessimistic terms, relating his perspective explicitly to other themes of the discourse challenging emancipation: '… the belief that there can be a single moment of emancipatory transformation, led by the preordained agent of history, can no longer carry weight in a world confronted by a multitude of emancipatory claims. The politics of emancipation, however appealing, has been no more able than the discourse of rights to provide a common set of values for coping with difference'. A way of coping with difference, of articulating differences, has to be attempted in a discourse of emancipation that must thus be duly sensitive to the problematics involved.

10　In the citation here, accounting could be considered a key institution or feature of modern society or it could in some respects be considered part of the mundane detail. For our purposes it is the former both actually and potentially, albeit that one can also consider it to involve or possess what might be termed 'mundane detail'.

11　The move beyond dichotomous thinking that we advocate can be seen to impact upon an attempt to delineate an accounting that would embrace dimensions of accounting 'as it is' and 'as it should be', and even 'as it might be'. It can in our view help resolve some tensions in previous interventions, tensions that have likely contributed to problematically narrow delineations even through critical lenses, such as those delineations that in mobilising notions of 'economic calculation' risk involving departure from wider notions of accountability and the rendering of an account. The reader is referred to various struggles to delineate accounting in the literature (see Power and Laughlin 1992, Puxty 1993, Gray *et al.* 1996, see also Hopwood 1985, 1990).

12　The notion of emancipation as a process has in effect been embraced in several emancipatory movements, and has been given more emphasis in the context of a greater appreciation of complexity. Many have placed emphasis upon the notion of emancipation as in the first instance an awareness and an understanding of social conditions that can enable resistance and bring about emancipatory change in the sense of transformation and structural change (see Fay 1987: 23, Nederveen Pieterse 1992: 13). Alvesson and Willmott (1992: 449), in re-thinking emancipation, acknowledge the processual nature of emancipation in distinguishing between questioning, incremental and utopian approaches to emancipation and between focuses upon means, social relations and ends.

13 Nederveen Pieterse (1992: 25) refers to a discontinuity in epistemology as Marxism is refined by engagement with poststructuralist, postmodern and post-Marxist critique. For Alvesson and Willmott (1992: 440, 446), reason's capacity to question practices should be considered contextually limited and contingently variable in its significance.

14 Nederveen Pieterse (1992: 21), accepting that 'there is no longer a privileged subject for radical collective action' (and that 'revolution as total rupture is abandoned') here favours placing stress on 'expanding civil society as against state and market along with structural reform'.

15 Accountings can reflect the various particular interests involved. They can also constitute instances of communicative social practice aiming to aid negotiations to align particulars. Alvesson and Willmott (1992: 448, see also p. 454) articulate Habermas' advocacy of rational communicative praxis (which could involve as well as be about accounting) in these terms.

16 In this regard, for Butler *et al.* (2000: 3) 'universality is not a static presumption, not an apriori given ... it ought instead to be understood as a process'. And, as suggested, interests, identities and rationalities can change in social interaction including in struggle, reflecting their socially constructed character. That this construction involves diverse and contradictory discourses and practices, unconscious forces and even the functionings of oppressive forces (Fraser and Nicholson 1988, Biesta 1995), further indicates the need for a cautious and self-critical approach in emancipatory praxis.

17 Any view that agency is completely determined by structure problematises the very act of formulating it and is problematic in its implications. Laclau (1990) maintains that he has never 'taken the position that the subject is passively constructed by structures', rather seeing the subject to be precisely located as a lack of the structures.

18 Laclau's 'great myths' here include 'emancipation' (as well as 'universality' and 'rationality'). As we have already seen, however, this follows Laclau's displacement of the term emancipation in favour of 'liberation' rather than the clarifying and refinement of it that is preferred here and that is consistent with Laclau elsewhere (see also Arrington, 1990: 3).

19 Agger (1998: 6–7) still recognises in this context people's capacity for co-operation, indicating the possibility of aligning emancipatory struggles against capitalistic, patriarchal and racist repression.

20 Alvesson and Willmott (1992: 438) point out that poststructuralism retains a commitment to questioning what appear to be incontrovertible truths that help constitute subjectivity. In stressing the 'ambiguous, open quality of seemingly fixed, taken for granted structures' it is 'in sympathy with the emancipatory project of Critical Theory'. But this questioning is not in itself enough. Relatedly, Nederveen Pieterse (1992: 11) cites Hall (1988: 237) in support of a call to go beyond an overly constrained defensiveness: 'Socialism has been so long on the defensive in Britain that it has by now acquired a permanent negative posture'. One might articulate this in terms of the need to go beyond resistance although resistance can imply something quite positive in character.

21 Poststructuralism's emphasis on the ambiguity of texts aims at subverting controlled systems. For Harland (1987: 124, cited in Puxty 1993), this involves being 'true to the real being of the Sign'.

22 One can here begin to appreciate how accountings can be integral to such 'wars of interpretations' in the context of radical democratic social struggles.

23 Nederveen Pieterse (1992: 25) refers to a discontinuity in the Marxist project, the latter being seen no longer in terms of 'the future dictate of the subaltern but of inclusive democratisation'.

2 Jeremy Bentham, accountant: a radical vision of an emancipatory modern accounting

1 In writing to the British government concerning his Panopticon plan, Bentham, entrusted with government funds in relation to the plan, signs his letter with 'Queries submitted by the Accountant, Jeremy Bentham, to the Audit Board' (see UC, cxxii: 31–105, Audit Office, Correspondence: 160–266, cf. 267–328). UC designates University College, the mode of referencing used for documents located in the Bentham archive at University College, London (UCL).

2 The term denotes the equivalent of ethnocentrism in cultural analysis (see Cousins 1987: 127).

3 A less constrained reading of the past beyond any tendency to excessive dogmatism is facilitated in taking up the challenge. A radical dimension of a contextual approach sensitive to difference is also found in theorising mutability. This can disturb taken for granted fixity in respect of current discourses and practices and stimulate change (Haslam 1991). Another critical dimension of analysis equates to appreciating the contingency of forces constituting past discourses and practices. These forces may now be muted. What would this imply? In this respect, some discourses and practices of today cannot be understood adequately without historical analysis. Grew (1990: 205) argues this for the task of understanding the vocabulary of social science (see Edwards 1989 on financial accounting). Appreciating accounting as a social and communicative practice necessarily bound up in the political – a practice consequential, contingent, mutable, controllable and both actually and potentially of social significance – can enrich the insights we can gain through delving into ways of seeing and rationales of accounting in context (see Laughlin 1984, Haslam 1991).

4 Here we are countering Singleton-Green's view of history. Singleton-Green (1993) dismisses critical exploration of Bentham's texts on accounting on the grounds that these texts were written in the late eighteenth and early nineteenth century.

5 Accounting, broadly conceived, has been a focus of critical attention and prescriptive exposition for centuries – constituting, albeit discontinuities, attempts to link it to ethical systems having some affinity with emancipatory concerns. Indeed, key texts of Christianity and Islam can be read as promoting particular types of accounting to help discharge the accountability of various social, including organisational and business activities. Plato and Aristotle, enormously influential upon Western institutions of learning for centuries and major contributors to Western philosophy, focused to some extent upon issues of accountability and accounting in their texts (see Gambling and Karim 1986, Gray *et al.* 1996: 124). A wealth of material upon accounting can be found globally in the ancient world – we cannot do it justice here. One can more generally legitimately seek insights from analysis of any accounting text, as well as any accounting practice, whenever and wherever it manifested. We stress here the case for analysis of Bentham on accounting.

6 The late eighteenth and early nineteenth centuries can be thought of as a crystallisation of modernity not only in Europe but on a more global scale. Developments in the eighteenth century brought more people under European influence and increased interactions between different peoples. Western reason was fostered as universal, coming to dominate particularity (Horkheimer and Adorno 1972). Anti-traditionalism was promoted through printed text communicated widely. A push for democracy gathered pace (Hume 1981). There was an increased confidence in mathematics, a furtherance of an epistemological optimism and a prevailing of secular and positivistic science over religious orthodoxy, tradition and superstition (see Habermas 1974, 1987a,b, 1992).

7 See Lamare (1729), von Bielfeld (1760: ii, iii, chapters 1–3, 174–6, 263, 282, 288), Mildmay (1763), Necker (1785: i, lv-xi, 363), Bonvallet des Brosses (1789: 32–3), Turgot (1913–23: iv, 568–628), Catherine the Great (1931), Hume (1981), Forrester (1990), Haslam (1991), Hood and Jackson (1994), Gallhofer and Haslam (1995), cf. the work of Richard Price, discussed in Cullen (1975), and, John Howard, discussed in Hume (1981),

see also Polanyi (1945), Hume (1951), Burchell *et al.* (1980) and Davidoff and Hall (1987).

8 The modern state here, for Habermas (1974, 1987, 1992), more emphatically pursued a bureaucratic rationality and reflected the pursuit of civilization and certainty (more of cognition than of sanctity). A concern to administer and police a dynamic and in some ways threatening society was becoming more evident (see Polanyi 1945, Foucault 1977a,b, Hume 1981). Scientific materialistic reasoning was enhanced through those interacting episodes often understood as the French and Industrial Revolutions (see Hobsbawm 1962, Evans 1983).

9 We are not maintaining that an accounting 'profession' in no way existed in Bentham's context but that it differed significantly from those professional bodies of accountants formally organised around a particular construct of expertise in the second half of the nineteenth century. Different forces influenced 'accounting' in Bentham's context. The earlier accounting was, for instance, integral to a pragmatic political economy discourse from which it later became more distinct, including in consequence of the particular trajectory of economics and the emergent professional expert character of accounting (see Paul 1979, Haslam 1991, Gallhofer and Haslam 1995).

10 More recently, theorists such as Bauman and Latour, influenced much by Foucault, have enhanced the negative reception of Bentham's Panopticon (see Boyne 2000).

11 Marx, with many, is influenced by a caricature of Bentham as narrow and negative that can be read into Mill, Carlyle and Dickens – if an in-depth reading of these commentaries indicates more of a balanced view often overlooked (see Fraser *et al.* 1999, cf. Blake 1997). Distortions of Bentham – for some a radical threat to the established order, we must remember – were already numerous in Marx's context. A belated obituary of Bentham linked him to specifically bourgeois interests: '... the changes [in society] which have been made ... [are] ... not the work of philosophers, but of the interests ... of large portions of society recently grown into strength ... But ... Bentham gave voice to those interests' (Anonymous 1838). There are more texts of Bentham available today than were available to the earlier critics. Mill's negativity in respect to Bentham is not so easy to fathom but there are several possible explanations. In some ways Mill equated the philosophy of his father James to that of Bentham, thus overlooking much in Bentham. Bentham angered Mill in disputes. Mill saw Bentham as being too radical in several respects (see Mack 1962: 270). Critchley (2001) notes Mill's psychological crisis as a possible factor.

12 Some of the insights of Foucault in basic terms are actually paralleled or anticipated in some ways in other influential work, notably Himmelfarb (1965).

13 The extent to which 'Panopticism' is now descriptive is debated. Latour (1998) and Bauman (1999) appear to almost wish to abandon the term (see also Deleuze 1995). Others suggest it be retained as an analytical type that still usefully clarifies dimensions of various systematic practices (see Boyne 2000).

14 McKinlay and Taylor (1998: 175), cited in Boyne (2000: 294) thus were led to comment that '[b]eguiled by Foucault's Panopticon metaphor a number of labour process writers have ... produce[d] gloomy analyses of emerging ... carceral regimes and omniscient surveillance'.

15 If influenced by Foucault, only a few of these researchers might properly be characterised as Foucauldian in overall emphasis.

16 We acknowledge that academics such as Hopwood, Power (personal communications) and Hoskin and Macve (1986) have indicated the potential of a close reading of Bentham on accounting. One can argue that a negative Panopticism became more important in the twentieth century and that Foucault, in bringing attention to this, has (in some sense ironically?) stimulated at least some further work on Bentham even while displacing some possibilities. This positive tendency has still not impacted widely in the accounting literature.

17 Loft (1988) is also influenced by the inspiring Bahmueller (1981). Again, however, this is a negative portrayal. In the main text we shall indicate how our own reading differs from

that of Loft. Hoskin and Macve (1986) also briefly comment on Bentham's accounting texts. We return to this later.

18 See Hobsbawm (1962), Mack (1962: 217), Russell (1962), Letwin (1965), Hume (1970, 1981, Lyons (1973, 1984, 1991), Foucault (1977), Roberts (1979)), Griffin-Collart (1982), Rosen (1982, 1983), Taylor (1982), Evans (1983), Habermas (1987a), Dinwiddy (1989), Twining (1989), Pitkin (1990), Haslam (1991), Semple (1993), Gallhofer and Haslam (1994a,b, 1995, 2000b), Hoskin (1994), Crimmins (1996), Harrison (1996), Schofield (1996), Akinkummi and Murray (1997) and Blake (1997). For Hume (1970: 30), Bentham on accounting was scarcely influential. While underplaying the influence, he underscores how Bentham's vision remains an unrealised potentiality. And where Bentham's influence is discernible, distortions and repressions of the more positive possibilities of his ideas are typically evident (Haslam 1991, Gallhofer and Haslam 1994a, 1995).

19 Peters (1993) even expresses the view that Boralevi's work actually indicates an affinity between Bentham and Foucault (cf. Blake 1997).

20 Foucault's critique of modernity is subtle and complex. He theorises resistance as functioning within the most problematic modern control systems (cf. McKinlay and Taylor 1998, Boyne 2000: 295, 302). And he refers to the Panopticon in a way indicating an awareness of its positive as well as negative dimensions (see Foucault 1977b: 205, see also Boyne 2000: 288, 299, who also hints at a less one-sided position in this respect, e.g. p. 302). We acknowledge that such hints at balance manifest in a treatment especially sharply emphatic of the negative.

21 Habermas focuses especially upon one Bentham text, whereas the principle of publicity features in several. The link to accounting is still discernible in the former text (see Gaonkar and McCarthy 1994: 554).

22 What follows is a possible interpretation of Bentham's radicalism helping us to appreciate insights for today in his work. We should stress that we are aware of the controversies surrounding Bentham and appreciate Pitkin's (1990) view that Bentham is especially 'slippery'.

23 Bentham saw himself as a citizen of the world. He is understood to have introduced the word international into British and French (Harrison 1983: 276). He sought a universal as well as perpetual peace (see Conway 1989). One of his views was that 'Nations are associates and not rivals in the grand social enterprise' (Kayser 1932). As Bentham sought to knock down all man-made obstacles in the pursuit of general happiness, one could argue that his approach is consistent with the move towards world government, with differentiated sub-governments as and if desired.

24 Godwin was thus led towards a communistic theory of property. For Bentham, caution was necessary to preserve security but, within this, progress towards equality could be made (Boralevi 1984: 97–8).

25 Bentham actually used the term emancipation in reference to particular campaigns (e.g. when challenging colonialism, slavery or the restriction on particular groups to practice their religion; see Bentham's '*Emancipate Your Colonies!*', Boralevi 1984: 179–80, 184). At the same time, as Boralevi (1984) suggests, Bentham had in effect a broader notion of emancipation corresponding to his social aims.

26 We discuss Bentham's advocacy of an extensive democracy later when discussing his mode of intervention.

27 Here as stated, Bentham once more follows Helvétius. If a sexual act could reasonably be shown to have at least no negative consequences in terms of general happiness he had nothing to write against it. Thus, for instance, he was (again in unpublished works) a defender of homosexuality. It might be emphasised that, in matters sexual, Bentham placed a high value on privacy (see Semple 1993).

28 In this regard, in his own lifetime he was accused of fostering a society of robots rather than people. His provocative-sounding reply was that so long as the 'robots' ('call them what you will') were happy (i.e. genuinely happy) it did not matter (Gallhofer and Haslam 1994b).

29 This helps us to further appreciate Bentham on liberty. It was deemed reasonable to intervene within or through the law to override forms of 'liberty'. For instance, when an individual (irrespective of age) is lying on the pavement in apparent pain, it would often be appropriate for someone to take that person even against that person's stated will and try to help them and such an act might be properly prescribed in law. This can be 'reasonably' seen to benefit not only the general community but also the individual. Bentham is willing to waive sensitivities about government powers that have tended to paralyse liberal thought. He was a strong proponent of parliamentary sovereignty (Mack 1962, Peardon 1974: 127). Bentham sees 'rights' as constituting desiderata that people might reasonably strive for in pursuing general happiness rather than as something that might be properly denoted 'natural' (see Mack 1962).

30 Mack (1962: 110), referring to Bentham's work on D'Alembert's encyclopaedic tree, argues of Bentham that he 'hoped to show men the interdependence of everything they did, in order to persuade them of the wide and interrelated range of better things they might do'. Science, art, thought and action were all inseparable. All human enterprises were deemed interconnected (Mack 1962: 136).

31 Mack (1962: 296) indicates Bentham's concern to 'look after people' citing him as follows: 'A shepherd knows every sheep in his flock, though he have 2000 of them. Are men and Christians less worth knowing to their Pastor than sheep?' While such sentiments have their dangers, the concern to understand and look after people is of merit and overly suppressed in our problematic times. The sense in which Bentham is concerned to enhance the well-being of the poor in his pauper management is argued by Quinn (1994). For Taylor (1982), Bentham's schemes were humane, selfless and enlightened. Bentham emphasises the role of publicity in looking after people by linking it to security, seen by him as the first subordinate end of good government: '... the grand security of security is *publicity*: – exposure – ... whatever is done by anybody, being done before the eyes of the universal public' (cited in Mack 1962: 313).

32 It seems incongruous that Bentham received the patronage (for a short period after 1781) of someone becoming a British Prime Minister – Lord Shelburne (William Petty, first Marquis of Lansdowne, 1784). Having noted this, Shelburne was a patron of progressive movements (broadly understood). He has been described as 'a Whig in name ... a radical democrat out of season' who witnessed the French Revolution with sincere delight (Mack 1962: 384, see also 391–3). In any case, Bentham did not widely disclose the extent of his radicalism. Further, Shelburne was Prime Minister for a very short period. In spite of his wealth, given his own radicalism it remains surprising that he became Prime Minister at all (see Mack 1962: 370–93).

33 This text was dictated by Bentham. We are most grateful to Philip Schofield of the Bentham Project UCL for helping us to decipher the manuscript here.

34 The location of accounting publicity in Bentham's wider conception of publicity is articulated in Fraser *et al.* (1999). Earlier more fragmented articulations can be found in Gallhofer and Haslam (1993, 1994a,b, 1995). We here draw from these works to concisely elaborate the linkage.

35 Hume (1970), in separating out the financial economistic accounting writings of Bentham (focusing indeed upon 'internal' accounting systems) from those on publicity more generally, follows Cumming (1961) in failing to appreciate the significance of accounting in Bentham's scheme (in part corrected in Hume 1981).

36 A question mark in the citation indicates that we have been unable to decipher the original text.

37 As Mack (1962) suggests, Bentham was not very open about his views in his repressive context. His concern to educate the people (including the poor and prisoners) had been evident from relatively early works. His radical leanings were not as explicit however as they might have been. His Chrestomathic education programme (Bentham 1816, 1817) was styled 'for the use of the middling and higher ranks of life'. Yet the plan can be located in a broader more radical educational movement. Contemporaries appreciated this.

Henry Brougham was encouraged by *Chrestomathia* to commit himself to the extension of education very widely (cf. Grobel 1932). James Langham complained that Bentham's Chrestomathic plan was objectionable 'in as much as the low terms of admission ... throw open to the lower classes of society an establishment which makes provision for the extension of science far beyond what is necessary or expedient for the purposes of ordinary life ... students with a great acquisition of general knowledge will aspire beyond their real situation in life ... minds thoroughly capable of enduring the drudgery of manual labour must inevitably be ...[prone] ... to disappointment and misery' (UC, clxv: 14, letter of Langham to Joseph Hume, Secretary of the Chrestomathic project, 19 April 1816). Concerns in critical work on accounting today to have more disclosed respecting disadvantaged or oppressed groups have an affinity with Bentham (see Tinker 1984a, 1985, Sikka *et al.* 1999, cf. Lyons 1973, Boralevi 1984).

38 This is consistent with a critical approach that would challenge what can become problematically instrumental obsessions that introduce distortions and obstacles to a more progressive or emancipatory focus (see Held 1980, on the related concerns of a more sophisticated German Critical Theory). One can point to some resonances with a Bentham re-constructed through a critical theoretical lens in projects in accounting and management today concerned to problematise objectives and link practices to enlightened conceptions of goals (cf. Laughlin 1984, 1987, 1988, Forester 1985, 1992, 1993).

39 Bronner (1994: 336), following a similar line of reasoning, gives particular emphasis to such advocacy today.

40 Bronner (1994) again echoes this perspective. A concern to protect against possible abuses and to make abuses visible, involving a distrustful dimension, is not inconsistent with a critical theoretical approach with practical intent (see Gallhofer and Haslam 1997b). Making visible abuses and protecting the people against their possible manifestations is one of the contributions a critical approach is concerned to make as a way of stimulating rational and critical debate.

41 It would be problematic and tend to chronocentrism to believe that Bentham's view here was absolutely isolated or unique in his context. Yet it was apparently unconventional in his time (see Cooke 1950, Forrester 1980, Kistler 1980, Haslam 1991, Gallhofer and Haslam 1994b, n30, 1995). As far as the need to check for different threads in Bentham's argument and to try to reconcile them is concerned, Bentham scholars will recognise this common problematic in attempting to unravel his argumentation. Bentham's work was vast in scope and contains a lot of detail. It is not always easy to reconcile different aspects of this work and one can reasonably claim Bentham's texts to contain contradictions. Our interest is not so much to make these reconciliations (if we might suggest them) but to gain critical insights for the present.

42 In *Nicholas Nickleby*, Dickens (1839) gives us an insight into what can happen in the absence of publicity to the world in respect of the treatment of the disadvantaged. Nicholas is concerned, as is Dickens (see Fraser *et al.* 1999), to expose the goings on in such institutions as the 'Yorkshire Schools' depicted in the book, thus pursuing Bentham's principle. Behind 'closed doors', such schools are depicted, based on real world events, as tyrannical and cruel regimes. Accounting publicity can, for Bentham, help counter such manifestations.

43 Hume (1970), as Gallhofer and Haslam (1994a,b) indicate, is concerned to elaborate upon the similarities between the approach of Bentham and his brother Samuel here.

44 Critical work today reflecting concerns that conventional accountings promote a narrow materialism has some affinity with Bentham (see Haslam 1991, Power and Laughlin 1992, Gallhofer and Haslam 1993, 1995).

45 The idea of moral book-keeping was not original, although Bentham adopted it emphatically (Davidoff and Hall 1987, Walsh and Stewart 1988, Haslam 1991, Gallhofer and Haslam 1993). Robert Owen's 'Parallelogram', influenced by what was then Bellers' more than 120-year-old plan for colleges of industry, shares especially with the Panopticon the concern to improve morals (Polanyi 1945: 11). The 'serious Christian' movement sought

to improve the lot of the poor including their 'morals' (Davidoff and Hall 1987: 421). For Davidoff and Hall (1987: 203), the drive in the eighteenth century towards regular account keeping was influenced by this strict religion: 'the force necessary to make man operate within this artificial paper mould primarily comes from the dictates of serious Christianity, the fundamental place within Protestantism of "casting up accounts" with God'. Much of the non-orthodox religion of non-conformist sects, a strong cultural force in the seventeenth and eighteenth centuries, was especially compatible with Bentham's moral book-keeping (Cullen 1975, Davidoff and Hall 1987). Arthur Young, friend of and influence upon Bentham who also enthused about book-keeping (Hume 1970: 26, cf. Young 1797), was a proponent of serious Christianity (Gallhofer and Haslam 1994a). For serious Christians, as for the aristocratic, there was a scrupulous emphasis on diary-keeping. An emphasis on New Year's resolutions and on birthday books fused with an annual casting up of accounts before God (Davidoff and Hall 1987: 88). The following poem of Jane Biddell, an Ipswich farmer's wife, written in the 'spiritual accounts book' given to her daughter, makes a strong link between record-keeping and moral behaviour for betterment: 'The Memorandum, brief yet clear/The record of each hour so dear/Spent as the conscience best can tell/On which remembrance loves to dwell/That the ensuing year may tell/That thou hast spent the period well/Little will thou avail the time/Allotted in this nether clime/If true improvement marks each year/And fits us for a nobler sphere/' (cited in Davidoff and Hall 1987: 88). Davidoff and Hall (1987: 88) point out that such meticulous 'overlooking' of self and children was extended in serious Christian practice, in the context of the congregations, to the overlooking of members' personal and business concerns. The serious Christians saw the religious body as having a public character and thus understood it as being appropriately rendered open and visible. Public accountability was a principle that many religious bodies as well as scientific societies at least ostensibly followed as well as advocated (Davidoff and Hall 1987). And when Jeremy Bentham proposed a Chrestomathic day school he drew up accounting provisions whereby the school was to produce a report and accounts to an annual meeting, three auditors were to be chosen from non-managing subscribers, and, within three weeks of the annual meetings, accounts were to be sent to subscribers (UC, clxv: 13). For Davidoff and Hall (1987), serious Christians sought to establish coherence through the careful regulation of life that would bring psychic and other rewards. They report one serious Christian writing regretfully that there had been few opportunities for making a memorandum on religious progress and the state of her individual soul. And they report another expressing an awareness that human life 'is but a loan to be repaid with use (meaning interest)' and asking of God 'when he shall call his debtors to account' (Davidoff and Hall 1987: 89).

46 For Bentham, a system giving responsibilities to individuals, and the making of practices visible in accordance with this, would contribute to enhancing well-being (see Bentham 1816, 1817). His separate-exhibition principle adjoined what he termed the 'separate work principle' (UC, cliiia: 165). Given difficulty in applying the latter, Bentham came more pragmatically to place greater emphasis on collective solidarity (see Hume 1981: 158, 163).

47 Critical writers today stressing the potential of visibility through accounting implicitly or explicitly concur with dimensions of Bentham here (see Morgan and Willmott 1993, Broadbent 1995, Broadbent *et al.* 1997). Tinker's usage of the term emancipatory accounting, refined by neo-Marxist affinities, also has affinities with Bentham's call for publicity. Studies such as Mitchell *et al.* (1994), Cousins *et al.* (1998), Dunn and Sikka (1999), and, Sikka *et al.* (1999) call, quite properly in terms of a critical perspective, for more light – or accounting publicity – as an element of what they are seeking to achieve through political struggle. Sikka *et al.* (1991: 18) explicitly refer to openness and accountability as safeguards for the public interest and seek some regulatory intervention respecting these matters. More generally, if as such analysis in accounting and management indicates (see, for instance, Laughlin 1984, 1987, 1988, Forester 1985, 1992, 1993, Arrington and Puxty 1991, Broadbent *et al.* 1991, Puxty 1991, 1993, Power and Laughlin 1992,

Broadbent 1995), the constructs and concepts of a critical approach inspired much by German critical philosophy, cast something of a shadow on any equivalent in Bentham, there are still aspects of Bentham that are stimulating for a critical theoretical project and which give a historical weight to the latter's concerns.

48 Mack (1962: xii) points out that by 1790 Bentham had become a full-fledged democrat and parliamentary reformer. There is a controversy here in Bentham studies with some suggesting that Bentham kept changing his mind on the issue of democracy in the late eighteenth century (Polanyi 1945: 10, Dinwiddy 1989). Many commentators point to an increasingly evident radicalism after around 1808 and his particular acquaintance with James Mill (see Cumming 1961). Bentham came to pursue the right of women to vote but he felt it would damage his wider progressive aims to widely publicise that view in his context (Mack 1962, Boralevi 1984).

49 Bentham believed that through education, knowledge, time and experience, democracy would come to be more effective. He believed that individuals had a 'social sympathy' (a necessary view to give some validity to his own stance) but that it was useful to enhance this through institutional including democratic mechanisms and forces (Peardon 1974: 122–4). Bentham may to a degree be somewhat naive, but a struggle for a radical democracy is central to many critical perspectives today.

50 The following citation from Roger North, writing some one hundred years before Bentham, is apposite: '... by accident the author fell in love, and ever since has been enamoured with them [merchant accompts]... this gave the author a great curiosity to find out, wherein this wonderful virtue of a regular accompt consisted ... [some are] ... blinded and bambouzled by the mists that artful men raise up before their Eyes, with Estimates, as they call 'em, a Representation of Values... listen to the Jargon, as if it were Coptick or Arabick' (North 1714, cited in Murray 1930: 262–4).

51 Patrick Colquhoun, an associate and friend of Bentham (Mack 1962), was helped by Bentham in the drafting of a police revenue bill. The draft obliged licensed dealers to record their transactions in a set of books and in a form that would facilitate inspection (Hume 1981: 154, UC, cl: 147).

52 Gallhofer and Haslam (1994a) note Bentham's concern, towards the end of his life, with the aid of the 1797 *Encyclopaedia Britannica* (3rd edition, Edinburgh, vol. III: 367–91) and Robert Hamilton's (1788) *Introduction to Merchandise*, to elaborate a more general critique of double-entry book-keeping. This project intersected with his intervention, with Samuel, in debate over public accounting (cf. Goldberg 1957, Hume 1970). By then both Benthams had long been critics of the 'Italian mode' (see Bentham 1816: 63–4, for more detail). The passage indicates the location of Bentham's critique in his general critique of fictions (see Mack 1962). Harrison (1983: 131) points out that in Bentham's poor-house plans he typically found current book-keeping to be full of fictions and took time out to invent a new system, specifying various account books. Rather than referring to taking time out we should perhaps regard this focus of Bentham as reflecting and being integral to one of his major principles.

53 Thus, Bentham believed that the management of more successful administrative units could more easily be replicated as something like model practice elsewhere (see UC, cli: 309–10, 352, 448, cliib: 361, cxlix: 241, Hume 1970, cf. Polanyi 1945: 124, Bahmueller 1981: 188, 193, Hume 1981: 160–1, Brundage 1988: chapter 1).

54 For Bentham, in his pauper management system: '...everything is comparative; under every head, the management in each house presents an object of comparison to the management of every other ... [there is a much higher] ... chance of being advanced to the highest possible pitch of perfection. To profit by this advantage, it is necessary that the system of book-keeping should in each house exhibit, with the utmost precision and in the utmost detail what the management *is*: – as for example – under the head of pecuniary economy, what the rate of *expence* is on each of the articles *consumed*... and what the rate of *receipt* or *profit* is, as well as the rate of expence, on each of the articles produced: that it may be seen in which of all the houses the management, in relation to each of those heads, is most

advantageous upon the whole; and thence with a view to practice, that the management of the most successful house may be taken in each instance for a pattern and copied in every other ...' (Bentham 1797: 102–3). And, the principle of publicity: '... strengthens power ... by enabling each of the component establishments to receive instruction not only from any other of its fellow establishments but from the enlightened part of the public at large. It shows to each what there is good and bad in every other: that the good may everywhere be adopted and the bad avoided' (UC, cliiia: 154).

55 Jeremy's brother Samuel was also concerned to correct book-keeping in its language. Samuel focused most of his critique upon double-entry book-keeping (see Bentham 1830: 4–5). For Samuel, 'the language [of accounts] should be the most intelligible of all description' (Bentham 1830: 8) and it was 'essential that [accounting] be intelligible and instructive [and moreover] that mode of book-keeping [is to be preferred] which has the fewest technicalities, if it be as good in other respects' (40, see also 41, 45, 49). For Samuel Bentham (1830: 41–2), the language of double-entry book-keeping was 'a language ... the more objectionable, as the terms employed being in common use for expressing other ideas, require, on this occasion their signification to be changed, before they can be made to render the facts intelligible' (see 42–4, 46).

56 We have elsewhere construed this as questioning the unit of account, interpreting that construct broadly (see Gallhofer and Haslam 1993).

57 Samuel considered that mystifying expertise might have been embraced by mercantile men to effect concealment of their affairs, 'a material object in private mercantile transactions; but in regard to public concerns, no such motive seems justifiable'. Further, the experts would have gained by dint of the demands for their peculiar as opposed to more ordinary talents (Bentham 1830: 42–4). Jeremy was more broadly concerned to critique the means, including the problematic promises, slogans, myths, symbols and rhetoric by which the relatively powerful remained powerful in spite of their corruption (see Mack 1962, Peardon 1974: 121). This is another concern that overlaps substantially with later critical theoretical positions.

58 This critical theoretical theme has influenced critical writers on accounting today (see Power 1991, Power and Laughlin 1992, Morgan and Willmott 1993, Mitchell *et al.* 1994, Dunn and Sikka 1999).

59 Through the construction of a uniform administrative unity, facilitating openness and involving book-keeping, all the poor houses would be connected together under and visible to one authority, making each 'as transparent in the figurative sense, as each House, if constructed in the Inspection Architecture principle, would be in the literal sense' (UC, cli: 361, Bahmueller 1981: 190). At times Bentham advocates the idea of a one best practice for all (see UC, cliiia: 153).

60 Samuel was keener than Jeremy to make a distinction equating more to that made today between public and private bodies. In the pecuniary realm Samuel refers to private bodies being concerned to make profits while public bodies were concerned to reduce costs. He felt that private concerns justifiably had to conceal some of their affairs from the world (Bentham 1830: 42–4). He appreciated (see Bentham 1830: 20) a sense in which public concerns 'however desirable it may be that money value should be set upon them' can seldom be expressed in money. Jeremy, although occasionally slipping into Samuel's dichotomy (see UC, cliiia: 154, Bahmueller 1981, chapter 5) had a notion of there being different types of organisations but in his view all organisational bodies and their activities should contribute to public well-being and in this respect had a public character. Further, Jeremy elaborates his notion of the duty to humanity as well as economy as a universal principle, not one confined to a particular type of organisation or activity.

61 Kayser (1932: 23) points out that Bentham is interested in particularity as well as universality in the governance of nations.

62 Relatedly, there may be a tendency, in mobilising a vision consistent with Bentham, to underplay the significance of formulating a strategy for realising the vision. Complexities such as the potential benefits of aligning a myriad of dynamic social interests and identities to further such a radical intervention can be overlooked to far too great an extent.

The desideratum of reflecting a sense of an emancipatory dimension that is multiple may be seriously neglected.

63 This is the case even if Bentham may have wanted to emphasise the common factor that all the institutions referred to are all to be mobilised for the furtherance of well-being. Regarding the word 'amusements' here, Bentham was concerned to emphasise on a number of occasions that his own exhaustive efforts were not a sacrifice but what his own happiness dictated. Following Helvétius (1809), he maintained that no greater happiness could alight on an individual than that gained through seeking to enhance the happiness of others.

64 In the pamphlet referred to in note 59, the Chrestomathic programme is praised for having been 'proved so wonderfully to augment the power of superintendence' (3).

65 Yet the control of people over people is an on-going dimension of the social. In our world it includes the Mafia and drug dealers. Bentham, to the extent that he was concerned to democratise and render accountable social practices aimed at well-being, needs to be assessed by comparison to alternatives that might be suggested.

66 In terms of its possible distortion and problematic capture, much of the negative (as well as positive) potential of Bentham-like scheming in his own context and then later does appear to have been realised in practice (see Hobsbawm 1962, Himmelfarb 1968, 1984, Foucault 1977a,b, Bahmueller 1981: 123, 160–3, Evans 1983, Ignatieff 1984, Berg 1985, Loft 1986, Haslam 1991, Gallhofer and Haslam 1995). In respect of the mobilisation of Bentham-like schemes today, there remain many possibilities for distortion and problematic capture.

67 Munro, an ex-paymaster of the Royal Navy, is consistent with Bentham where he refers in his guide to farm book-keeping (Munro 1821: xi, cited in Davidoff and Hall 1987) to a 'love of good order and the gratification of a thorough knowledge of his own affairs ... regularity and precision should be as much expected'.

68 Bentham advocated that capitalistic activity be a focus of social and democratic control to be administered by the general happiness principle. Yet his context was one of the development of a more uniform legal framework that served to promote a relatively more unfettered capitalistic practice and that manifested in the event in an often crude and extremely exploitative form, a form that Bentham in his pursuit of social control, would have challenged. His context was one in which capitalistic activity was rapidly growing outside of much in the way of any significant social and democratic control through substantive and co-ordinated interventionism. The increased capitalistic and bourgeois influence, steered by a bourgeois–aristocratic alliance and encompassing enhanced processes of commodification (including the treating of people as commodities) and monetarization, was equating wealth more and more with power (Hobsbawm 1962, Evans 1983).

69 Elsewhere, Bentham hints at an integrated, more holistic approach and is concerned to supplement commercial book-keeping in respect of economistic concerns. For instance, he sought to record and disclose financial outcomes against targets, he was concerned that good management practices be discernible and he wanted to expose monopolistic practice (Gallhofer and Haslam 1993, 1994b).

70 We have mentioned, however, the need to appreciate the context (a context in which many saw no need to help the poor or the prisoner in any way at all and actively resisted such notions). We have already noted that Bentham switched to preferring a state-run pauper management system.

71 See also Samuel Bentham's (1830: 39) reference to accounting as 'professional' in this respect.

3 Accounting and emancipatory practice: the mobilising of accounting by socialist agitators of the late nineteenth century

1 This is the William Booth of the Salvation Army. The work was produced in collaboration with W. T. Stead (Hattersley 1999: 323), suggesting that Stead was the main author

but acknowledging Booth's significant influence on the wider project of which this was part.

2 See also *The Globe*, 24 July 1888: 1, which reports Reverend Barnett's consistent figures from the Metropolitan Poor Law Guardians.

3 There was also a concern about the fantastic difference between the wealth of the materially rich and poor. *St. James's Gazette* of 5th July 1888 comments, for instance: 'It may well be for a country to have a certain number of rich people; but to endow a single individual to the extent of four millions sterling is an act of very doubtful benefit to the state'.

4 Disraeli's Tory government had also appointed a Royal Commission to investigate the agricultural depression in 1879 (Hopkins 1995: 138–41).

5 This emerged out of the reorganisation of the Democratic Federation set up 3 years earlier.

6 There was a view that morals could also be improved by publicity, strongly influenced by Bentham (see Gallhofer and Haslam 1993, 1994a,b).

7 Such a stance was typically a philosophical emphasis rather than a rigorously worked out philosophy. Comtean positivism (by which we mean the complex nineteenth century political phenomenon – latterly this has been problematic narrowed giving rise to conceptualisation in methodological debates) had some influence on the Fabians and other socialist agitators in at least that a social realism that stressed the benevolent power of observation and facts was embraced. As such, this positivism fused and overlapped with lots of influences pointing in this direction.

8 The common law implicitly required companies to keep business records by dint of its principle that dividends not be paid out of capital (see Edwards 1989: 177).

9 Champion was a keen propagandist (Mann 1923) and Hyndman (1911: 345) recalled his frequent 'very good' orations in open air meetings in London parks. He gave numerous lectures and was involved in several public debates on socialism. Several of his contributions were published (including *Facts about the Unemployed, Wrongs that Require Remedies, The Theories of Socialism* and *Co-operation versus Socialism*, a debate with Benjamin Jones that took place at Toynbee Hall, all of which were published by or during 1887).

10 The publications of the Socialist League, the Fabian Society, Besant, the social reformer and liberal MP Bradlaugh (associated with land reform), Hyndman (leader of the SDF) and Aveling were all advertised, along with Champion's own publications.

11 *Common Sense* cited the *Women's Union Journal* to evidence the low wages paid to women.

12 *Common Sense* (15 May 1887: 14) prints the following citation from Thomas Carlyle: 'Liberty I am told is a divine thing. Liberty when it becomes the "liberty to die by starvation" is not so divine'. And the journal (15 July 1887: 1) prints the following from John Stuart Mill: 'The restraints of communism would be freedom in comparison with the present condition of the majority of the human race'. In Champion's own journalism, the desirability of socialistic state intervention is more explicitly stated.

13 *Common Sense* often deploys a Benthamite language. The word 'felicity', associated with Bentham, is used (1 January 1888: 27). A citation echoing Bentham is put into a Queen's speech reflective of an imaginary socialist government: 'I earnestly commend to you the sense of Justice, in the certain response of which to the cry of oppressed people lies the only safeguard of order, prosperity and stability' (*Common Sense*, 15 July 1887: 46; see Gallhofer and Haslam 1993, 1994b; see also *Brotherhood*, 24 June 1887: 118–9, which reports on a Champion speech of similar sentiment). On 15 July 1887: 43, *Common Sense* printed the following rhetoric, closely associated with Bentham: 'THAT government is the best which in practice produces the greatest happiness of the greatest number'.

14 *Common Sense* cites Porter's *Progress of the Nation* and Bevan's *Industrial Classes and Industrial Statistics* as useful sources of information on, for example, wages, echoes the Fabian Society's *Facts for Socialists: Compiled from Political Economists and Statisticians* and makes use of the work of the Statistical Society.

15 It should also be recognised in this respect that as someone running a business himself (he was joint owner of the publishing firm Modern Press) he could well have worked with

accounts. Whatever the source, his analyses in the late 1880s, especially in respect of the case of Brunner, Mond and Co., discussed later, indicate something of a working knowledge.

16 The company came to have a very dominant position in the British match-making industry. By the end of the first decade of the twentieth century the firm's Fairfield works became one of the largest factories in London and employed some 2,000 women and girls (Beaver 1985: 61). Another possible factor explaining Champion's focus was that the match girls had built up something of an image as a group that might protest from an earlier notable episode. When the government moved to impose a match tax in the 1870s, the girls working at Bryant and May staged a demonstration, marching to Parliament. The tax was abandoned (Beaver 1985).

17 After the death of his father in 1874, Wilberforce Bryant, the eldest son, became senior partner. The subsequent death of one of the Bryant brothers and withdrawal of another (if Theodore continued to work in various capacities for the firm) is reported to have determined Wilberforce and Frederick to form a limited liability company (Beaver 1985). With the subsumption of other match-making companies into Bryant and May, Trummer, Pace and Dixon joined the Bryant brothers as the first directors, with Carkeet, a cousin of the Bryants, taking the position of company secretary. References prefixed DB/BRY are to holdings of the Bryant and May Ltd records at Hackney Archives, London. Where a document is referenced in the text it is not repeatedly so until a new item is referenced. The Minutes of Directors' Meetings are in the following referred to as MDM (DB/BRY/1/2/13). The Secretary's Diary (DB/BRY/1/2/77) is in the following referred to as SD.

18 On the transfer of the various businesses to the company, the two Bryants and those with ownership stakes in the subsumed businesses received one-third of an issue of 60,000 shares (the nominal value being £5 per share), together with a significant share of a sum of £150,000 constituted by debenture stock plus cash (MDM 24 June 1884) (it appears that they received £40,000 of debentures each – the two brothers were paid this plus a 5 per cent premium on January 22nd 1886, an early redemption date). The directors were to receive remuneration at 2 per cent of the issued capital at nominal value (i.e. initially £6,000 per annum) subject to the dividend being 10 per cent of the same (i.e. initially £30,000). The directors, it seems, also held company accounts involving interest (see e.g. DB/BRY/1/2/264, 22 October 1886) and also occasionally seem to have paid themselves to do various tasks. According to the books of 1886, payments appear to have been made to the Bryant directors in respect of 'accountancy and legal work'. Each was paid £329 8s 11d. This figure in itself is over six times the annual wage of even the better paid amongst the women and girls working for Bryant and May (*subter*). Some shares were allotted to Department Heads and to long-serving employees. The firm's travellers and some of the best customers were offered shares (Beaver 1985: 61–2). This policy did not extend to the bulk of employees, however.

19 The more cautious side of the firm is seen in its coming to hold a significant reserve, invested in relatively safe investments, to serve as a fighting fund against competitors. The more aggressive stance is seen in the reference to acquisition activity reported in many MDM – while decisions to close particular works, although it is difficult to perceive the substance, are reported shortly and sweetly (MDM, e.g. 25 November 1885, 26 September 1887).

20 We should note also that by the time Champion was preparing to write about Bryant and May in *Common Sense*, Clara Collett had already begun surveying the match-making industry in the East End, paying several visits to Bryant and May, to prepare an article for Charles Booth's *Life and Labour of the People of London*. She was to report that poor wages were continuing (Collett 1889).

21 When Champion (and later Besant) highlighted dividends they likely also had in mind accounting profits (equated to business profits). Dividends and accounting profits often corresponded very closely, as they did at Bryant and May (Table 3.1). That the directors'

remuneration was dependent upon dividends is equated by the directors as linking it to profit (MDM 12 June 1884). Wilberforce declared at an extraordinary meeting that 'in recommending a dividend at the rate of 15% for the half year we do so with much confidence and pleasure, because, when we put before you the report and accounts ... we have earned not only 15% but a little more'. The notion that a high dividend, close to the profit, had to be paid was strong. Shareholders hesitated to expand the capital as this imposed a 'permanent burden on the company' (MDM 2nd March 1885). Directors were pressured towards a dividend policy distributing most of the profits. When the company decided to put aside a provision for 'premises: plant and goodwill' they struggled to defend themselves (especially once admitting that the 'real value' of this item had not fallen) (see MDM 10 February 1886). A provision in the Articles allowed the board to 'cause to be ... retained in a separate account or for reserve, or depreciation ... or guarantee fund ... to make good falling asset values ... to equalising dividends ... or any other purpose of the company' (Article 88, DB/BRY/1/2/1). Yet, while retained profits were available for future distribution, only relatively small amounts were carried forward (see MDM 10 February 1886). Champion's analysis of Brunner, Mond and Co. (discussed later) made extensive use of accounting profit disclosures. This all tends to support the view that in the match girls' case the term dividends used in argumentation is virtually a proxy for accounting profits.

22 The greater part of this was constituted by what would later be called share premium, being a premium created in the latter half of 1885 on the issue of additional share capital.

23 This is an unusual offer, albeit consistent with the commitment to openness. It is arguably dangerous for the person exposed. We have found no evidence that this offer was taken up.

24 Indeed, according to *Common Sense*, Bryant and May had a positive public image that had to be shattered. The following citation from the journal of 15 July 1887: 42 is intended to be ironic: 'In "Wyman's Jubilee Album" appears some pictures of the factory and an eulogistic notice winds up "It is a question whether there is another match factory in the world so admirably conducted, and so well known by all classes of society, as that of the highly esteemed and old established firm of Bryant and May" '.

25 Here an error appears to be made. The 20 per cent is calculated on the nominal value of share capital issued. It is the case that someone holding the shares from the company's formation is in one sense making 20 per cent return on the original cost of the shares. Reference to fictitious capital is surely a reference to the market value of the shares being to all intents and purposes based on an overly optimistic appraisal of future returns. Since the share price fluctuated around $2^1/_2$–4 times the nominal value in the period focused upon it is difficult to believe that the article was suggesting that even the nominal value was to some degree 'fictitious', although this is possible (the company had a monopolistic presence but this was threatened). These calculations do not take into account the significant capital gains involved. It is possible that the calculation in *Common Sense* is more sophisticated than we suggest (see Champion's analysis of Brunner, Mond and Co. later) and based on a combination of dividend, gain and market value. We suspect the figure is simply the 20 per cent cited at the AGM. But Champion is also likely hinting (awkwardly) here at the sizeable capital gains.

26 A warning of his intention to bring up the subject at the Church Congress had been given in *Common Sense* as early as 15 July 1887 (42).

27 Champion actually understated the number of ministers of religion involved in the company. Around the time of the emergence of the controversy in the public eye, roughly 120 ministers of the Church had shares in Bryant and May (holding some 2,200 of 80,000 shares issued). This reflects the positive image the company had. It is also interesting to note that around 835 women held some 13,100 shares on 5 June 1888, one month prior to the match girls' strike. By this time the company's shares were quite widely held, even if the major shareholders continued to be the directors, with there being over 2,200 shareholders (SD 5 June 1888).

28 The record of the speech also mentions the exploitation of the tram workers (91). It seems that Champion wanted to also confront some of the business practices of the church newspapers while he had the opportunity to do so quite directly. In discussion of Champion's speech at the Congress, Reverend Headlam, a Christian Socialist and friend of Champion, intervened to note that Champion had asked him to mention that some of the church newspapers were printed at 'unfair' rates of wages, that is, under trade union prices (92).

29 The firm did respond to this: it came up with a figure of 11s 2d, later used in the match girls' strike (see the retrospective in *St. James' Gazette* 13 July 1888: 12).

30 A consequence was that Bryant and May came to search out criticism and monitor it. It was almost as if the firm was becoming paranoid. An instance suggesting this is that when Reverend W. Adamson (St Paul's, Old Ford) gave evidence to the House of Lords' sweating commission, Bryant and May's board assumed he was talking about them and a delegation (Carkeet and Bartholomew) was sent to see Adamson at the vicarage (SD 8 May 1888). It does not seem to have been easy for Adamson to persuade them then that no criticism of Bryant and May had been made (see *The Times'* letter pages on 9 May and 11 May 1888; see also SD 12 May 1888). The firm also sought to get full details of Adamson's evidence from the Sweating Commission so that it might provide its own counter publicity. A letter from Mr E. Thesiger on behalf of the Commission (opened on 12 May 1888, SD) reports that it was to consider a request by the company to disclose to it Adamson's full evidence. This effort was not successful as Thesiger later informed the company that this action was deemed impossible (15 May 1888).

31 Besant and Champion knew each other well. Aside from the fact that Champion advertised Besant's works, both were members of the same circles. This included that they were both members of the socialist dominated Charing Cross Political Debating Society along with Reverend George Allen, S. D. Headlam, S. Olivier, George Bernard Shaw, Graham Wallas and Sydney Webb (*Common Sense* July 15th 1887: 44).

32 In her autobiography, Besant suggests that this was the first time the match girls' case had been brought to her attention (although this may be a problematic recollection).

33 Champion's resolution, its acceptance by the Fabian meeting and Besant's assignment is noted in the secretary's diary. An article of *The Star* of 16 June 1888 printing the resolution is filed therein (SD 16 June 1888).

34 Stead was editor of the *Pall Mall Gazette* and a campaigner against child prostitution (see Hattersley 1999).

35 The subtitle of the paper was 'servants of men'.

36 Here Besant is less than accurate in that Theodore Bryant was no longer actually a director (although he was still active for the company). It was some time previously that the directors had spent company money on the 'statues and parks' referred to (a statue of Gladstone was erected in the Bow).

37 The Truck Act, steered through Parliament by Bradlaugh, the radical liberal MP and colleague of Besant, made illegal various systems of fines and payment systems (see *St. James's Gazette*, 9 July 1888: 11).

38 Besant and Burrows asked readers to contribute to a fund so that the wages of the dismissed girls could be covered until they had found alternative employment.

39 Carkeet had a very abbreviated style.

40 After news had broken about the threat of legal action against Besant by Bryant and May, a number of girls had sent a letter (details published in *The Link*, 7 July 1888: 3) re-assuring her by declaring '... dear lady, you need not trouble yourself... because you have spoken the truth, and we are very pleased to read it' and declaring that the girls would not be forced by the company to sign a declaration to the effect that Besant's information was false. The letter also indicated that, after refusing to sign the declaration the girls went on strike. The directors maintained that the girls were sacked after refusing to follow a foreman's important safety instructions. Many women and girls came out in support of their dismissed colleagues and the directors shut down the factory (see *St. James's Gazette*, 9 July 1888, *The Link*, 7 July 1888). Whatever were the immediate factors bringing about the

strike, Beaver (1985: 67) suggests that the dismissal notices were withdrawn but by then over one thousand women and girls had left work and the factories were closed.

41   According to the secretary's diary he had lunch with the former director Theodore Bryant (SD 6 July 1888).

42   Besant and Burrows also sought to raise funds to support the girls. Some girls subsequently received 4–5s a week in strike pay. It is appropriate to add here that they were concerned themselves to disclose weekly audited statements of the strike fund. Those supporting the strike included Reverend Headlam, Cunninghame Graham, MP, Clementina Black and George Bernard Shaw. Champion, having helped instigate the process, was turning attention to other radical projects (*subter*).

43   A public meeting at Regents Park also passed a resolution to boycott Bryant and May matches (*St. James's Gazette*, 9 July 1888: 11).

44   If we take some of the figures Besant herself uses in giving publicity to the company (a share price of around £18 and a dividend of around 20–23 per cent) combined with our understanding that the price of the shares 1 year previously fluctuated around £15 (and approached a figure nearer to £14) this does imply a return on such an opening market value of around 38 per cent.

45   Cunninghame Graham spoke at the Mile End Waste meeting citing Bryant and May as sweaters. He attacked most fellow MPs for their 'supineness and cowardice ... because they grovel before the rich'. No doubt with reference to the clergy investing in Bryant and May, he was reported as having declared that: 'Our morality, Christianity and system of commerce [are] one gigantic fraud'.

46   Rix was a senior manager at Bryant and May.

47   The letter is signed by four people, two giving an address at Toynbee Hall.

48   The letter elaborating the firm's response reported that according to Theodore and Frederick Bryant the fillers received 1d and not 10d per 100 coils. They also suggested that younger girls were employed these days because the work was lighter. They denied that the machines broke down more frequently and they argued that the 6d for the brushes was necessary in order to prevent wastage. In response to the complaint of the cutters down they pointed out that the racking out process was now done by machinery and this is why the rate had come down to 2/34d per gross. The children were discontinued once the women had got used to the new machinery at the women's own request. They suggested that the match girls could earn more money under this arrangement. With regard to the packers, they argued that a charge of 3d for children to fetch the paper had been long discontinued and that a deduction of 2d for booking was an arrangement that the girls had made themselves. They also argued that the stamping arrangement was enforced in the girls' own interest to protect the innocent from the accusation of bad packing. They maintained that fines were only imposed for wilful firing and the deliberate wastage of matches. They denied that girls were fined for arriving late in addition to the loss of half a day's pay (but did not deny imposition of the latter penalty). They suggested that the total amount of fines over the last three months was only £8 and they argued that the girls could complain about the deductions and fines and have them explained to them if they wanted. The firm (vaguely) denied that the wax-match makers received an 'appreciable higher wage than the rest of the workers' (*St. James's Gazette*, 12 July 1888: 4). From Collett's (1889) figures, the Toynbee Hall team had the better argument about the average – significantly less than half the girls were earning 11s or more just before the strike.

49   According to the Toynbee Hall investigators, while it was the case that the fillers received 1s per hundred coils rather than 10d it was still the case that less wages were earned with the new machines.

50   The day after the strike had begun, various newspaper reporters were received by the Board of Bryant and May, including from *The Star, Pall Mall Gazette, East London Observer, Daily Telegraph* and the *Evening News* (SD 6 July 1888). Such papers, with wider circulation than *The Link* or *Common Sense*, also printed letters from Besant and Burrows in which the authors attempted to get support for the match girls, including of a financial kind.

51 This was in spite of their history as a company that had put great effort into and spent lots of money on building an image. Some historical episodes are of interest. The MDM of 6th August report a financially motivated dispute with one of the company's travellers. The traveller had made his grievances public and the company had been concerned to counter his story. On Thursday 25th February, 1885, an extraordinary general meeting was called in respect of the articles of association. One reason for calling the meeting appears to have been to dispel rumours. According to Wilberforce Bryant: '... the shareholders occasionally received anonymous communications and they liked to be able to meet the directors and have them explained' (see *Railway News*, 27 February 1885). Another attempt to counter damaging publicity was when the company secretary circulated shareholders that a claim from a competitor 'that matches can be produced at 1/3 the present price is simply ridiculous' (MDM 11 August 1886). An example of a rebuff to someone querying an accounting figure came at the AGM of 9 February 1887. *The Investors Guardian* of 12 February 1887 reports the following statement from a Board member to the shareholders: 'Now, in reference to this cash in bank, the ridiculous question has been asked: "How can you get £45,000 with which to pay the dividend out of £13,000?" (Laughter)'. It is possible that such an approach to more critical questions may have dissuaded some from raising queries (MDM 12 February 1887). Bryant and May after the strike as well as before and during it were at various times criticised by shareholders and the financial press in respect of the way the accounting of the company was seen to be less than open. At the AGM of 29 January 1889, Herbert Hope, a shareholder, asked how much of an aggregated total of £276,000 on the balance sheet was constituted by the items of goodwill, patent-rights and trademarks. And he complained that the accounts were 'not full enough'. Wilberforce Bryant responded by pointing out that the articles of association from the inception of the company provided that a trading account should not be published (MDM 29 January 1889). *Samuel C. Hatch's Investment Circular* of 1 February 1889 commented: '... it may be observed that the non-publication of any profit and loss account, year after year is hardly calculated to inspire confidence' (SD 1 February 1889). The secrecy in respect of accounts is of interest in the context of the usage of accounting information by radical activists. The same circular continues the theme on 1 July 1889: 'The mysterious suppression of the company's accounts has recently extended even to the meagre and unsatisfactory skeleton described as the "Report", that is so far as the issue of a copy to the public is concerned'. (*Samuel C. Hatch's Investment Circular*, SD 1 July 1889). The same article expresses concern that 'shareholders believe anything said to them'. The filing of this in the secretary's diary indicates a concern about the publicity. The MDM record that once the strike was underway there manifested several instances of concern to manage the public reception of the strike in terms, for example, of letters to the papers and interviews with reporters (e.g. MDM 6 July 1888). The secretary's diary of 9 July 1888 records that the board were seeking to agree a letter to be sent to the papers on the dispute. In his diary, the secretary kept cuttings and notes on the strike from the records (his practice of keeping cuttings from the papers is especially evident during the period of the strike). On 13 July the diary reports: 'See Daily News of this Date for Article on the strike'. A note in the secretary's diary of 13 July is in the form of an aide memoire: 'See leader in Times of today on the strike'. We have already pointed out Bryant and May's concern to respond to the findings of the Toynbee Hall investigators. Other actions during the strike recorded in the secretary's diary indicate the significance of the strike to the directors and to the government: 'F.C.B. [ie. Frederick Bryant] called at the Home Office to see Mr Undersecretary Tushington with reference to the strike and asking that protection may be afforded to the hands who are willing to return to work but are intimidated by others. F.C.B. afterwards interviewed Sir C. Warren, Chief Commissioner of Police at Scotland Yard' (7 July 1888). The view that the company was considering moving its London operations overseas, rumoured at the time (see the retrospect of the *Echo*, 18 April 1889, secretary's diary of same date), is borne out by the following entry in the secretary's diary: 'Alfred Raphael...hearing that we propose

purchasing a match factory abroad, would like an appointment ... as he has one to sell'
(10 July 1888).

52 The second of these had included ten of the girls on strike (SD 17 July 1888).

53 A correspondent of the *St. James's Gazette* wrote on 21 July 1888: 4: 'For the first time, at
least on any conspicuous scale, the Trades Council, representing directly only the aristo-
cracy of labour, the skilled artisans employed in organised and special trades, has undertaken the duty of representing a class of unskilled labour'. The correspondent next looked
forward to the formation of a dockers' union. The London Trades Council also gave vital
financial support to the girls.

54 The surrender stance of the directors was being reported in the *St. James's Gazette* even on
17 July 1888, close to the end of the strike: 'About seventy of the strike girls assembled
yesterday morning round the premises of Bryant and May in the hope of being taken on.
They were informed that the firm could entertain no proposition for compromise.

55 An article in the *Pall Mall Gazette* of 4 April 1889 reflected the theme of ethical
consumerism in respect of the continuing phenomenon of phossy jaw in match making
(cutting in SD). A cutting in the secretary's diary, of 13 April 1889, is from the front cover
of the Salvation Army's *War Cry* and refers to the very poor remuneration of home workers making matchboxes. A cutting from the *Financial News* of 13 August 1889 (consistent
with the *Globe* of this date and the *Railway News* of 17 August) indicated continuing
debate over the directors' remuneration: '... received two proxies from two of the shareholders ... to be used against the board ... proposal to pay five directors 2% of whole
capital ... £8,000 was excessive, and directors' remuneration should be 2% of the amount
available for dividend. It almost amounted to an insult the Chairman remarked for a shareholder to write ... suggesting such a remuneration. Evidently they did not think the board
actually managed the company but even if they were simply directors they could not entertain ... [this] ...'

56 As far as Bryant and May's learning from the experience of the dispute is concerned, they
stepped up their monitoring of any potential agitation against the company. Bryant and
May became very concerned to monitor the activities of, perhaps obsessively, Besant and
other socialists after the strike. Besant's article on 'Labour Statistics' (*supra*), Champion's
article in *The Labour Elector* of 24 August 1888 (*supra*) and an article on ethical consumerism and phossy jaw published in the *Pall Mall Gazette* are amongst a number filed
in the secretary's diary (see 23 February, 4 April, 24 August 1889). The secretary's diary
includes cuttings on her support of William Morris and co-operatives (SD 14 January,
1889; see also 15 January 1889, 24 September 1889). The obsession with Besant includes
collecting reports of her active theosophy (see SD 10 September 1889). The company monitored radical activity more generally. It especially noted the call during the Dockers'
strike in 1889 for a general strike in London, a call supported by Champion (SD 30 August
1889). Champion is also reported as joining together with Clementina Black to propose
the formation of a Women's Labour Bureau and to encourage the unionisation of women
in the East End (SD 2 October 1889). The monitoring of Champion's activities by Bryant
and May extends to his engagement with Brunner, Mond and Company (see SD 16 April
1889).

57 An article 'An Eight Hours day, with Ten Hours pay: How to get it and how to keep it',
authored by James Leatham was commissioned by Champion, appearing in instalments in
The Labour Elector between June and August 1889 (15 June 1889: 13–14; 22 June 1889:
13–14; 29 June 1889: 13–14; 6 July 1889: 13–14; 20 July 1889: 46–47; 3 August 1889:
77–78).

58 Champion did continue to give some publicity to the Bryant and May case. For instance,
in the 9 February 1889 issue of *The Labour Elector*, Champion exposed the sizeable estate
left by Frederick Bryant on his death, as follows. The will is introduced in a way that
invites curiosity: 'Here is one of those innocent-looking common-place announcements
that appear from time to time in the columns of our daily newspapers attracting little or
no attention: "Probate of the will dated and 2nd July, 1888, with codicils of the same date,

and of 21st and 29th November, of the late Frederick C. Bryant, of Bryant and May (Limited), and of Woodlands Park, Surrey, who died on the 16th November last, has been granted. The value of the personalty is £272,321" (9 February 1889: 10).

59   Brunner and Mond both get £40,000 in cash and £60,000 in the shape of 6,000 ordinary £10 shares (*The Labour Elector*, 15 November 1888: 5). Champion argued that it was common for those forming companies to receive excessive amounts (*The Labour Elector*, 15 June 1889: 6).

60   *The Star* was a liberal paper that Champion and other socialist agitators had previously seen as sympathetic.

61   As in the Brunner, Mond case, the paper pointed out that only 'public' companies were investigated as it was not possible to obtain access to the books of private firms. Such analysis is similar to analyses of Benjamin Jones, the leading advocate of co-operatives.

62   Further, Champion concluded: '... when we remember that this has been going on for nearly ten years, it is easy to understand where Mr. Brunner gets the money to run an Irish newspaper in London, to reward election agents, and to generally replenish the depleted coffers of the "great Liberal Party"' (*The Labour Elector*, 19 January 1889: 9).

63   Champion also admitted an elementary error in a previous analysis which did not, however, alter the thrust of his argument when corrected: in discussing the figures for the half year ended 30 June 1885 he had stated the profit to be £108,000, a figure which included a balance of £26,000 brought forward from the previous year. Champion was concerned, he reported, to be fair: 'The fact that we gave the figures themselves correctly at the time, and that we have now spontaneously and gratuitously pointed out our error, is proof – to those to whom proof is necessary – of our scrupulous anxiety to be quite fair to all our enemies, not excepting even Mr. J. T. BRUNNER' (*The Labour Elector*, 27 April 1889: 6).

64   Champion expressed his anger about the company's attempt to convince an enquiry that it had done everything it could to prevent pollution and the company's claim in respect of external attempts to control the pollution that if the 'authority persisted in their oppression, there was no alternative but to stop the works' (*The Labour Elector*, 26 January 1889: 8). Further exposure of Brunner, Mond came in a report in *The Labour Elector* of 25 May 1889 that focused upon the court case arising from the death of a workman employed by the company. Champion questions the practice of appointing a shareholder as coroner. 'The thing is not only an anomaly, it is a shameful scandal. It is as if a wolf were asked to sit in judgment on the killing of a sheep it had itself devoured' (*The Labour Elector*, 25 May 1889: 5). This report gave rise to a question in Parliament by Randell, member of the Gower Division of Glamorganshire: 'Has the attention of the Home Secretary been called to a statement in the LABOUR ELECTOR, of May 25th, to the effect that Mr. Henry Churton, County Coroner, Cheshire, who held an inquest, on May 15th and 22nd, on the body of Joseph Washburne, a workman who was killed at the works of Brunner, Mond & Company, Ltd, Northwich, Cheshire, is a shareholder in the firm of Brunner, Mond & Company, Ltd, and if so will the Home Secretary take steps to prevent the recurrence of such a scandal'? (*The Labour Elector*, 1 June 1889: 2). The Home Secretary did not answer the question as 'he had not had time to ascertain the full facts, but so far as they were known to him he was not aware of anything which disqualified the coroner from sitting in the case' (*The Labour Elector*, 1 June 1889).

65   Other interventions of *The Labour Elector* were granted success. On 30 March 1889 (8) the paper had contrasted increased sales with decreased wages – but increased directors' pay – at *Army and Navy Stores Ltd*. This led, it was reported, to discussion at the AGM resulting in the directors promising to improve matters for the employees. A copy of *The Labour Elector* had been sent to the directors.

66   Apart from the feature story of Brunner, Mond *The Labour Elector* also highlighted the high and increasing profits of other companies, such as the London, Brighton and South Coast Railway and the East India Railway Company, the latter reported as making profits of about 200 per cent on their expenses (*The Labour Elector*, 9 February 1889: 6). Of interest

is also the discussion of the Sovereign Life Assurance Company which was in liquidation in February 1889. The paper questioned various financial accounting items – such as, for example, the valuation of land – and the way profits were made on transactions (*The Labour Elector*, 9 February 1889: 8–9). This subject is discussed on the grounds that it was 'of vital interest to the 4,021 persons who hold policies of life assurance' in the company in particular but also more generally because it was 'of great importance to the hundreds of thousands of other persons who have insured their lives for the benefit of their families' (*The Labour Elector*, 9 February 1889: 8).

67 According to *The Labour Elector* of 27 April 1889, Brunner had got eminent lawyers to work for him. *The Times* reported on this development adding that 'owing to the publicity given to Mr Champion's statements in the press and in the House of Commons the case is expected to excite great interest' (*The Times*, 20 April 1889: 3).

68 As *The Echo* of 8 June 1889 (12) put it: 'Mr Brunner has commenced an action for libel; but so far from being daunted, it [*The Labour Elector*] boldly challenges him to come on, and freely comments upon the inquest held upon another unfortunate man who lost his life in Mr. Brunner's works, as it alleges, through excessive hours of labour'.

69 Many critical appreciations of accounting, while they may reflect a more dichotomous thinking, largely in effect emphasise this state of affairs in perceiving accounting as negative and repressive. Sometimes they do this to the point of extremity whereby the possibility of an accounting with a non-repressive tendency is displaced from perception. Indeed it is as if we ought to be rid of accounting. If we have a broad appreciation of accounting's potentiality, as in the case of a re-invigorated conception of Bentham's construct of accounting publicity, then accounting at a limit blurs into communication in general and the view that we ought to be rid of accounting, itself communicated in academic texts, appears to be contradictory or a reflection of despair. If accounting is absolutely captured by prevailing hegemonic forces then why not all instances of communication – including, indeed, 'radical' texts published in accounting journals? (cf. Haslam 1986, on Lenin's views on accounting).

70 Such analyses appreciate that accounting's relative allegiance to dominant forces can be buttressed by such practices as manipulation of accounting numbers, highly constrained disclosure, mystification and the constitution, preservation and enhancement of auratic properties attaching to accounting (Gallhofer and Haslam 1991). Yet they continue to point to accounting's radical potential.

71 The rhetoric associated with accounting's professionalisation had to some extent matured by the late 1880s (see also Haslam 1991, Gallhofer and Haslam 1995).

72 Indeed, the contradictory and emancipatory dimensions have historically been grasped in this respect in hegemonic policy formations. Key moments in the promotion and formation of modern accounting are in part moments of controversy and tension in which accounting has been understood as a threat to the status quo (see Haslam 1991, Gallhofer and Haslam 1995).

73 In Gallhofer and Haslam (1991) we analysed how tensions between shareholders and managers were linked to subsequent tensions in the wider public realm (see 502–3).

74 In Gallhofer and Haslam (1991: 493) we indicate the centrality of this argumentation to critical theoretical praxis.

75 We have already mentioned that, nevertheless, established accounting practices have substantively served hegemonic forces. Certain types of accounting, such as accounting disclosure in the public realm, may be relatively easier for counter forces to make progress towards capturing than others.

76 This also appears to be the case in our earlier analysis (Gallhofer and Haslam 1991).

77 This substantial point, which needs to be emphasised, is also illustrated in our earlier study (Gallhofer and Haslam 1991). Accounting disclosures were published on the front pages of the socialist newspaper *Vorwärts* and were mobilised by the revolutionary leaders Rosa Luxemburg and Karl Liebknecht (Gallhofer and Haslam 1991: 507, see also 498, 503, 509, 513).

78 The study by Lehman and Tinker (1987) is a notable exception here (see also Walker and Mitchell 1998).

4 Is social accounting the soul of justice? Towards a critical appreciation with emancipatory intent

1 In this period, we do see a take off, if not a beginning, of social accounting. Aspects of it constituted a movement but the term potentially overly simplifies appreciation of significant tensions within the category of social accounting mobilisations as a set of fragmented interventions, some quite radically opposing each other.

2 Average wage rises were to jump over 30 per cent at one point in the 1970s, with inflation rising above 25 per cent in the mid-1970s (Powell 2001: 67).

3 The programme was authored in part by Tony Benn, one of the more radical amongst prominent Labour politicians during the latter half of the twentieth century, who was then shadow spokesperson for industry (Powell 2001: 63).

4 While these changes did effect a disciplining of labour, we should not exaggerate the strength or radical potential of labour prior to them. Already labour's strength had been sapped. Labour was scarcely revolutionary: a factor here was the relative material prosperity of working people after the War. One can also point to changed industrial relations practices. Further, labour and the relatively poor generally were more easily divided (see Hobsbawm 1995: 306–10, Lash 1990: 26, 29–30).

5 Social accounting is equivocal, ambiguous, mutable and controllable. If we treat it properly as such, we should recognise that any logic reflected in its manifest form is thus neither more nor less than that possible for any such construct. Attempts to delineate social accounting can be tempted, against this, into investing social accounting with a different status, such as in classifying it as if classifying natural science phenomena. Social accounting is not a uniform, undifferentiated category: in this respect, a number of different 'social accountings' have manifested in our historical context. We note here that some historical delineations of social accounting go beyond what we are working with here. For example, social accounting has been delineated as accounting for societies – or nation states – with National Income accounting being the typical exemplar (see Hicks 1942). While we should stress that we are concerned to challenge, with others, the breadth of scope and the narrow financial economistic and quantitative form of conventional versions of such accountings beyond the micro-organisation (see also Gambling 1974, Waring 1989, 1999), we do not *delineate* social accounting here as accounting for societies. Also for example, social accounting has been delineated as the universe of possible accountings in society (see Gray *et al.* 1996, Gray 1999: 5). Again, we do not here delineate social accounting in these expansive terms. We should, however, add a few comments here on the latter delineation as this has come to circulate more in the discourse, largely through its articulation in Gray *et al.* (1996). In our view, the intention in delineating social accounting as the universe of all possible accountings is positive, and we return to it later. Nevertheless, as a delineation in relation to current usages it has almost always been confusing, as notions of social accounting that are more constrained and thus inconsistent with the delineation – notions that characterise social accounting as going beyond conventional accounting, for example – are almost inevitably invoked (Gray *et al.* 1996).

6 We should also note here that there are aspects of mainstream current accounting that go beyond conventional accounting, in part a dimension of the sense in which current practice is an unstable compromise between conflicting interests (see Tinker 1984, 1985; Haslam 1991, Gallhofer and Haslam 1995).

7 Compare Gray *et al.*'s (1996: 324) view of mainstream social accounting as 'some combination of . . . accounting for different things [other than accounting strictly for economic events] . . . in different media [other than accounting in strictly financial terms] . . . to different individuals . . . for different purposes'.

8 We refer here to the 'imperfect' character of much conventional and mainstream practice. Similarly, we referred earlier to a notion of the latter reflecting the neo-classical in a 'less than pristine way'. For Tinker (1985), the financial accounting thrust of mainstream current accounting practice has not reflected shareholder interest perfectly. It may, however, reflect assumed shareholder interests very well indeed in an imperfect markets context (see Haslam 1991, Gallhofer and Haslam 1995).

9 Social Audit Ltd was founded in 1971 by Michael Young, later Lord Young of Dartington. Long a prominent member of the Labour Party, Young had earlier contributed to the writing of Labour's 1945 manifesto and served as Research Secretary of the party. He also set up the Consumers Association. Young emphasised a view of people that understood them to be motivated by a broad duty to society. The attack on inequality constituted one of his key focuses and commitments (Brome 2002).

10 This is one of the indications, on the part of mainstream social accounting writers, of the notion of a radical social accounting. We shall discuss their counter indications later.

11 Governments try to legitimise this lack of openness. Recently, Freedom of Information legislation has followed pressure for more openness in society but governments have earlier bolstered laws that counter this in the name of 'confidentiality' and 'privacy' that arguably amount to problematically interested restrictions on disclosure (cf. Gallhofer and Haslam 1997b).

12 There are in this regard a number of overviews of late twentieth century social accounting that report and comment upon corporate management's unprecedented engagement in a variety of social accounting 'experiments' in the 1970s (see, e.g. Lessem 1977, Ernst and Ernst 1976 *et seq.*, Rey 1978, Brockhoff 1979, Schreuder 1979, 1981, Singh and Ahuja 1983, Gray *et al.* 1987, 1995a,b, 1996, Roberts 1990, 1991, 1992, Owen 1992b, Mathews 1993, Guthrie and Mathews 1985).

13 In the absence of laws prescribing this type of behaviour, the instances occurring can reflect possibilities opened up by imperfect market type structural factors such as the divorce of ownership and control and monopolistic business power, both of which have been seen in terms of opportunities for the extension of social accountability. This noted, the instances occurring have in any case been limited.

14 In this regard it is often a misnomer to refer to social accounting disclosure as 'voluntary' in practice even where it is disclosure beyond law or quasi-law. One can suggest that the usage of the term voluntary here may be bound up in a similar ideological rhetoric which refuses to see 'market forces' as a form of regulation.

15 The diversity itself has contributed to some obfuscation (Gray *et al.* 1995a). Most accounts of social accounting in practice have stressed its similarity to a public relations whitewash (see Estes 1976, Dierkes and Preston 1977, Churchill and Toan 1978, Ingram and Frazier 1980, Wiseman 1982, Puxty 1986, Guthrie and Parker 1990, Roberts 1991, 1992, Kirkham and Hope 1992, Owen 1992b: see especially 15, Gray *et al.* 1993: see especially 257, 1995a, 1996, Bailey *et al.* 1994, Gallhofer *et al.* 1996, Gallhofer and Haslam 1997b, Newton and Harte 1997, Neu *et al.* 1998).

16 The opposition has continued so long as business has been able to otherwise keep disclosures to a minimum and/or heavily manipulate them. Where business has not been so able it has on occasions supported legislation or quasi-legislation that itself minimises disclosures (Lester 1992: 47, Owen 1992a,b: 4, Gallhofer and Haslam 1993, 1995, 1997, Gray *et al.* 1993, Cannon 1994: 29).

17 Owen *et al.* (2000) also indicate that a number of other social audit initiatives are likewise problematic. For instance, SA 8000, issued by the Council for Economic Priorities in October 1997, has also fallen substantively to managerial capture (86). The New Economics Foundation, in advancing social audit, stress its business friendly approach (85). Both bodies on the face of it are more committed to a 'radical' approach than ISEA and GRI. But both are also succumbing to managerial capture.

18 CERES was established in 1989 when it formulated the Valdez (later CERES) environmental principles (Gray *et al.* 1993).

19 The GRI here in part reflects the earlier work on standardising national indicators for global sustainable development, encompassing social and environmental indicators of well-being, that was undertaken by the UN's Commission on Sustainable Development (CSD). Projects such as those of the CSD and the then yet to be formally initiated GRI were boosted or encouraged by the Rio de Janeiro Earth Summit of 1992 (United Nations 2000).

20 This was promoted by Tony Benn, now as Secretary of State for Industry.

21 Other statements promoted were geared, seemingly, to highlighting business–government relations and the linkage of micro-organisational disclosure to macro-economic concerns (see Gray *et al*. 1987: 47).

22 The value-added figure was basically higher up the line, prior to items such as taxation, dividends, transfers to retained earnings, interest and wages and salaries.

23 That the government was concerned to strategically mobilise the information in this context is emphasised by the insight that the various government initiatives to ostensibly increase disclosure to employees were riddled with exception clauses available to business (Ogden and Bougen 1985, Robson 1994: 51).

24 Burchell *et al*. (1981) elaborate some historical precedents when the government and the accountancy profession shared a similar concern that accounting be used to 'educate' the employees. Hopwood *et al*. (1994) point out that they focus upon the specifics of value added. While this in any case makes it interesting for us here, we would suggest that at least aspects of their social analysis have a broader resonance in respect of social accounting in the context. While studies such as Burchell *et al*. (1985), Hopwood *et al*. (1994) and Robson (1994), influenced by a postmodern mode of analysis, may be portrayed as 'very different' from neo-Marxist studies such as Lehman and Tinker (1987), in that they do follow differing theoretical perspectives, it is also the case that there is some overlap between these studies in terms of their critical thematisation (see also Miller 1991, Robson 1993, for studies with a similar critical thematisation of programmatic interventions of institutions of governance).

25 In this regard, value added was used in some *profit* sharing schemes. Profit sharing was especially promoted in the context by the Liberal party, courted by Labour in relation to a bid to hang on to government (see Hopwood *et al*. 1994: 224).

26 The Law Society's Standing Committee on Company Law expressed reservations about the regulatory powers of the accountancy profession in this context: 'We believe that a fundamental change in the ultimate legal responsibilities of directors, affecting the rights of shareholders and creditors, is a matter which should be considered on its own merits; and if a change is merited, it should be introduced by statute and not be brought about as a side effect of a change in reporting requirements' (comments on *The Corporate Report* on public record at the ICAEW library).

27 Our analyses of social accounting in action so far have in this regard understated the role of academics.

28 Owen *et al*. (1997: 176) refer to 'the broad programme of social accounting in the truest sense of the term', conveying a particular status upon the mainstream position.

29 These texts resonate in part with the advocacy of a direct revolutionary action that for some reason minimally makes use of systems of informing (see Puxty 1986: 103–9, cf. Mouck 1994), or alternatively a waiting on the margin (Cooper 1992: 35) for liberating change to occur. In the new contexts, an enabling accounting might be possible but, prior to that, accounting in general has at best a very limited role in social progress. Such views problematise Hopwood and Burchell's (1980) suggestion that social accounting 'was appropriated at an early stage by critical rather than managerial groups'.

30 Another reading of Puxty (1986) and Cooper (1992) is possible that does not displace radical social accounting. Substantively, they challenge a particular type of social accounting they see as problematic – indeed, principally mainstream social accounting. For Cooper (1992: 36), the 'introduction of "green accounting", however well thought out, will, *under the present phallogocentric system of accounting* [our emphasis], do nothing to avert today's

environmental crisis. In fact it would make matters worse'. The emphasis is important. Similarly, the environmental accounting that a number of critical writers have been critical of is an accounting with characteristics similar to conventional accounting (see Gray 1990a,b, 1992, Power 1991, 1992, cf. Gorz 1989: 85–6). Such a reading of Puxty (1986) and Cooper (1992) does save them from a tendency to an avoidable contradiction. An argument along the lines that all systems of communicating and informing are counter progressive in a text that itself can be viewed as such a system is somewhat a contradiction. If all such systems are doomed to be captured by problematic forces, how can their own texts escape?

31 Owen *et al.* (1997: 181) suggest in this regard that even in the liberal democratic framework one can still begin 'to develop new more socially and environmentally benign forms of accounting, which have the potential to create a fairer, more just society'.

32 One aspect of this is that debates over and analyses of the efficacy of social accounting have been influenced against the phenomenon by the adoption of narrow notions of social accounting for the purposes of debates or analyses. In this regard, narrowings of social accounting by those seeking to promote the practice, such as its mainstream advocates, will to some extent be self-defeating (cf. Birnberg and Gandhi 1976, Benston 1982, Schreuder and Ramanathan 1984 a,b, Wildavsky 1994).

33 One could make visible more aspects of concern if one has a broad enough vision of what constitutes organisational effects and consequences. For instance, the particular constitution of the board of directors may be understood as contributing to good effects associated with living in a society of equal opportunity – or bad effects of not so doing. But it is probably helpful to think of the organisation in terms of a locus of effects as well as a set of activities that is consequential.

34 *The Corporate Report* reflected the tendency to problematically construct social accounting as new. It gives the impression that things were fine in the past but now something new was needed (ASSC: 1). Official comments on the report caught the tone of novelty and made much of this in their opposition to the report. The Leinster Society of Chartered Accountants of the ICAI refers to a reluctance to be involved in the development of the new values.

35 The idea that all forms of accounting ought to be in the service of society is conceivably the 'thrust' of Gray *et al.*'s (1996) and Gray's (1999) view that the construct social accounting constitutes all forms of possible accounting in society.

5 Epilogue: accounting, emancipation and praxis today

1 For more on critical theoretical praxis and Hegel's key role in its development, see, for instance, Gramsci (1971), Held (1980), Smith (1993), Bronner (1994) and Rasmussen (1996). In accounting, see Tinker (2001).

2 Tinker (2001: 84–5) elaborates Hegel's phases of the appropriation and reconstruction of experience which Hegel understands to reflect the 'immanent principle and soul' (85) of the subject. We would emphasise here hermeneutics' challenge to an overly positivistic empiricism and Critical Theory's problematisation of hermeneutics, rendering these phases somewhat less than absolutely distinct (see Bernstein 1976, see also Tinker 1998).

3 As Tinker (2001) suggests, it is important to recognise the (dynamic) particular, historical specific, unjust and exploitative social relations of the system of production and the socio-political order in theorising accounting.

4 This is consistent with going beyond the privileged knower and with a differentiated universalist philosophy. Researcher and researched, activist and others, constitute a unity even in their particularisms, but the particularisms shape the character of the unity.

5 In this respect, Tinker's (2001: 85) observation is pertinent: '[current, mainstream] accounting practice is itself the object of conflict and an unstable compromise' (see Haslam 1991, Gallhofer and Haslam 1995).

6 Many broadly progressive writers, from Bentham to Bronner, have in effect advocated accounting's role in exposing and transforming. In the accounting literature, cf. Tinker

(1984a–c, 1985, 1991), Moore (1991), Arrington and Francis (1993), Schweiker (1993), Reiter (1995), Gray *et al.* (1996: 2).

7 As well as the social consequences of the organisation one should, in this regard, also be concerned that disclosures assess organisational manifestations as consequence of state policy or the lack thereof. To reference an instance discussed earlier, one would in the current context be concerned that reports disclose on how much the organisation reflects an equal opportunities policy (see Adams and Harte 2000).

Bibliography

Accounting Standards Steering Committee (1975) *The Corporate Report: A Discussion Paper Published for Comment*, London: ICAEW.

Adams, C. A. and Harte, G. (1998) 'The changing portrayal of the employment of women in British banks' and retail companies' corporate annual reports', *Accounting, Organizations and Society* 23, 8: 781–812.

——(2000) 'Making discrimination visible: the potential of social accounting', *Accounting Forum* 24, 1: 56–79.

Adams, P. (1977) *Fatal Necessity: British Intervention in New Zealand, 1830–1847*, Auckland: Auckland University Press.

Adorno, T. W. (1973) *Negative Dialectics*, New York: Continuum Publishing Company.

Agger, B. (1991) *A Critical Theory of Public Life: Knowledge, Discourse and Politics in an Age of Decline*, London: The Falmer Press.

——(1992) *The Discourse of Domination: From the Frankfurt School to Postmodernism*, Evanston, IL: Northwestern University Press.

——(1998) *Critical Social Theories: An Introduction*, Boulder, CO: Westview Press.

Akinkummi, A. and Murray, K. (1997) 'Inadequacies in the Mental Health Act, 1983 in relation to mentally disordered remand prisoners', *Medicine, Science and the Law* 37, 1: 53–7.

Ali, T. and Watkins, S. (1998) *1968, Marching in the Streets*, London: Bloomsbury.

Almond, B. (1994) 'Liberal and totalitarian morality', *Filozof Istraz* 14, 2/3: 283–93.

Alvesson, M. and Willmott, H. (1992) 'On the idea of emancipation in management and organization studies', *Academy of Management Review* 17, 3: 432–64.

Alway, J. (1995) *Critical Theory and Political Possibilities: Conceptions of Emancipatory Politics in the Works of Horkheimer, Adorno, Marcuse and Habermas*, Westport, CT: Greenwood Press.

Amernic, J. H., Aranya, N. and Pollock, H. (1979) 'Is there a generally accepted standard accountant?', *CA Magazine*, October: 34–42.

Annisette, M. (2000) 'Imperialism and the professions: the education and certification of accountants in Trinidad and Tobago', *Accounting, Organizations and Society* 25, 7: 631–59.

Anonymous (1832) *An Address to the British Public by the Saint Simonian Missionaries*, London: Rolandi; Bossange, Barthes and Lowell; Effingham Wilson.

Anonymous (1838) Article xi, 'The Works of Jeremy Bentham: now first collected under the Superintendence of his executor John Bowring, Parts 1–4, Edinburgh: Tate, 1838', reviewed in *London and Westminster Review*, April–August.

Arendt, H. (1958) *The Human Condition*, Chicago, IL: University of Chicago Press.

Arnold, P. and Hammond, T. (1994) 'The role of accounting in ideological conflict: lessons from the South African divestment movement', *Accounting, Organizations and Society* 19, 2: 111–26.

Aronowitz, S. (1988) 'Postmodernism and politics', in Ross, A. (ed.) *Universal Abandon? The Politics of Postmodernism*, Edinburgh: Edinburgh University Press.

Arrington, C. E. (1990) 'Intellectual tyranny and the public interest: the quest for the holy grail and the quality of life', *Advances in Public Interest Accounting* 3: 1–16.

Arrington, C. E. and Francis, J. R. (1989) 'Letting the chat out of the bag: deconstruction, privilege and accounting research', *Accounting, Organizations and Society* 14, 1/2: 1–28.

——(1993) 'Giving economic accounts: accounting as cultural practice', *Accounting, Organizations and Society* 18, 2/3: 107–24.

Arrington, C. E. and Puxty, A. G. (1991) 'Accounting, interests and rationality: a communicative relation', *Critical Perspectives in Accounting* 2, 1: 31–58.

Arrington, C. E. and Watkins, A. L. (2002) 'Maintaining "critical intent" within a postmodern theoretical perspective on accounting research', *Critical Perspectives on Accounting* 13, 2: 139–157.

Arthur, C. J. (1986) *Dialectics of Labour: Marx and His Relation to Hegel*, London: Blackwell.

Asher, G. and D. Naulls (1987) *Maori Land*, Wellington: New Zealand Planning Council.

Bacon, F. (1944) *Novum Organum*, New York: Willey Book Co.

Bahmueller, C. F. (1981) *The National Charity Company: Jeremy Bentham's Silent Revolution*, Berkeley, CA: University of California Press.

Bailey, D., Harte, G. and Sugden, R. (1994) *Making Transnationals Accountable: A Significant Step for Britain*, London: Routledge.

Barlow, C. (1994) *Tikanga Whakaaro*, Oxford: Oxford University Press.

Barr, H. (1994) 'Towards a bicultural education system: the experience of New Zealand', *Phi Kappa Phi Journal National Forum* 74, 1, Winter: 12–15.

Baskin, J. B. (1988) 'The development of corporate financial markets in Britain and the United States, 1600–1914: overcoming assymetric information', *Business History Review* 62, 2: 197–237.

Bauman, Z. (1999) 'On postmodern uses of sex', in Featherstone, M. (ed.) *Love and Eroticism*, London: Sage.

Beard, V. (1994) 'Popular culture and professional identity: accountants in the movies', *Accounting, Organizations and Society* 19, 3: 304–18.

Beaver, P. (1985) *The Match Makers*, London: Henry Melland.

Bebbington, J. (1997) 'Engagement, education and sustainability: a review essay on environmental accounting', *Accounting, Auditing and Accountability Journal* 10, 3: 365–81.

——(1999) *Accounts of and Accounting for Sustainable Development*, unpublished PhD thesis, University of Dundee.

——(2000) 'Sustainable development: does it add up?, *Readings from the 1999 Conference*, CGA Accounting Research Centre, University of Ottawa.

——(2001) 'Sustainable development: a review of the international, business and accounting literature', *Accounting Forum* 25, 2: 128–57.

Bebbington, J., Gray, R., Thomson, I. and Walters, D. (1994) 'Accountants' attitudes and environmentally-sensitive accounting', *Accounting and Business Research* 24, 94: 109–20.

Bedford, N. M. (1976) 'The Corporate Report: a discussion', *Accounting, Organizations and Society* 1, 1: 111–14.

Bellich, J. (1986) *The New Zealand Wars*, Auckland: Penguin.

Benett, M., James, P. and Klinkers, L. (eds) (1999) *Sustainable Measures: Evaluation and Reporting of Environmental and Social Performance*, Sheffield: Greenleaf Publishing.

Benhabib, S. (1986) *Critique, Norm and Utopia: A Study of the Foundations of Critical Theory*, New York: Columbia University Press.

——(1992) *Situating the Self: Gender, Community and Postmodernism in Contemporary Ethics*, Cambridge: Polity Press, in association with Oxford, Blackwell.

——(1994) 'In defense of universalism – yet again! A response to critics of situating the Self', *New German Critique* 2, Spring/Summer: 173–89.

Benjamin, W. (1973) 'The work of art in the age of mechanical reproduction', in Arendt, H. (ed.) *Illuminations*, translated by H. Zohn, London: Fontana.

Benston, G. J. (1982) 'Accounting and corporate accountability', *Accounting, Organizations and Society* 7, 2: 87–105.

Bentham, J. (1797) *Pauper Management Improved: Particularly by Means of an Application of the Panopticon Principle of Construction*, London (first published 1797 in Arthur Young's Annals of Agriculture, first published separately, 1812, London, from which citations are taken).

——(1816) *Chrestomathia*, London.

——(1817) *Chrestomathia*, Part II, London.

——(1843a) ' "Of publicity", in an essay on political tactics', in Bowring, J. (ed.) *The Works of Jeremy Bentham*, vol. 2, Edinburgh: Simpkin, Marshall & Co.

——(1843b) 'Draught of a new plan for the organization of a judicial establishment in France', in Bowring, J. (ed.) *The Works of Jeremy Bentham*, vol. 4, Edinburgh: Simpkin, Marshall & Co.

——(1993) *Official Aptitude Maximised Expense Minimised*, Schofield, P. (ed.), Oxford: Oxford University Press.

Bentham, S. (1830) *Financial Reform Scrutinized in a Letter to Sir Henry Parnell, Bart, MP*, London.

Benton, T. (1994) 'Biology and social theory in the environmental debate', in Redclift, M. and Benton, T. (eds) *Social Theory and the Global Environment*, London: Routledge.

Berg, M. (1985) *The Age of Manufacturers, 1700–1820*, London: Fontana.

Bernstein, R. J. (1976) *The Restructuring of Social and Political Theory*, Oxford: Blackwell.

Besant, A. (1938) *An Autobiography*, 2nd edition, London: Fisher Unwin.

Best, S. (1995) *The Politics of Historical Vision: Marx, Foucault, Habermas*, New York: Guilford Press.

Best, S. and Kellner, D. (1991) *Postmodern Theory: Critical Interrogations*, Basingstoke: Macmillan.

——(2002) 'Postmodern politics and the battle for the future'. Available at http://www.uta.edu/huma/illuminations/kell28.htm (20 June 2002).

von Bielfeld, J. F. (1760) *Institutions Politiques*, Paris.

Biesta, G. (1995) 'Postmodernism and the repoliticization of education', *Interchange* 26, 2: 161–83.

Binder, Hamlyn and Fry Co. (1978) *Added Value as a Concept*, London: Binder, Hamlyn and Fry Co.

Birnberg, J. G. and Gandhi, N. M. (1976) 'Towards defining the accountant's role in the evolution of social programs', *Accounting, Organizations and Society* 1, 1: 5–10.

Blake, K. (1997) 'Bleak House, Political Economy, Victorian Studies', *Victorian Literature and Culture* 25, 1: 1–21.

Blaza, A. J. (1992) 'Environmental reporting – a view from the CBI', in Owen, D. (ed.) *Green Reporting: Accountancy and the Challenge of the Nineties*, London: Chapman & Hall.

Bolt, C. (1993) *The Women's Movement in the United States and Britain from the 1790s to the 1920s*, New York: Harvester Wheatsheaf.

Bonvallet des Brosses, S. J. L. (1789) *Moyens de Simplifier la Perception de la Comptabilité des Deniers Royaux*, Paris.

Booth, C. (1889–1903) *Life and Labour of the People of London*, 17 volumes, London.

Booth, W. (1890) *In Darkest England and the Way Out*, London.

Boralevi, C. L. (1980) 'In defense of a myth', *The Bentham Newsletter*, May: 33–46, reprinted in Parekh, B. (ed.) (1993) *Jeremy Bentham: Critical Assessments*, London: Routledge.

——(1984) *Bentham and the Oppressed*, Berlin and New York: de Gruyter.

Boston, S. (1987) *Women Workers and the Trade Union Movement*, London: Lawrence and Wishart.

Bougen, P. D. (1989) 'The emergence, roles and consequences of an accounting–industrial relations interaction', *Accounting, Organizations and Society* 14, 3: 203–34.

——(1994) 'Joking apart: the serious side to the accountant stereotype', *Accounting, Organizations and Society* 19, 3: 319–35.

Bowen, H. R. (1953) *Social Responsibilites of the Businessman*, New York: Harper and Row.

Bowring, J. (1877) *Autobiographical Recollections of Sir John Bowring with a Brief Memoir by Lewin B. Bowring*, London: Henry S. King.

——(ed.) (1843) *The Works of Jeremy Bentham*, Edinburgh: Simpkin, Marshall and Company.

Boyne, R. (2000) 'Post-Panopticism', *Economy and Society* 29, 2: 285–307.

Brecher, J., Brown Childs, J. and Cutler, J. (1993) *Global Visions: Beyond the New World Order*, Boston, MA: South End Press.

Briggs, A. and Macartney, A. (1984) *Toynbee Hall: The First Hundred Years*, London: Routledge and Kegan Paul.

Briloff, A. J. (1986) 'Accountancy and the public interest', *Advances in Public Interest Accounting* 1: 1–14.

——(1993) 'Unaccountable accounting revisited', *Critical Perspectives on Accounting* 4, 4: 301–35.

——(2001) 'Garbage in/garbage out: a critique of fraudulent financial reporting: 1987–1997 (The COSO Report) and the SEC accounting regulatory process', *Critical Perspectives on Accounting* 12, 2: 125–48.

Broadbent, J. (1995) 'The values of accounting and education: some implications of the creation of visibilities and invisibilities in schools', *Advances in Public Interest Accounting* 6: 69–98.

——(1998) 'The gendered nature of "accounting logic": pointers to an accounting that encompasses multiple values', *Critical Perspectives on Accounting* 9, 3: 267–97.

Broadbent, J. and Laughlin, R. (1997) 'Evaluating the "new public management" reforms in the UK: a constitutional possibility?', *Public Administration* 75, 3: 487–507.

Broadbent, J., Ciancanelli, P., Gallhofer, S. and Haslam, J. (1997) 'Enabling Accounting: The Way Forward?', *Accounting, Auditing and Accountability Journal* 10, 3: 265–75.

Broadbent, J., Laughlin, R. and Read, S. (1991) 'Recent financial and administrative changes in the NHS: a critical theory analysis', *Critical Perspectives on Accounting* 2, 1: 1–29.

Brockhoff, K. (1979) 'A note on external social reporting by German companies: a survey of 1973 company reports', *Accounting, Organizatons and Society* 4, 1/2: 77–85.

Brome, V. (2002) 'Lord Young of Dartington', *Obituaries, The Wednesday Review, The Independent*, 16 January: 6.

Bronner, S. E. (1994) *Of Critical Theory and its Theorists*, Oxford: Blackwell.

Brundage, A. (1988) *England's Prussian Minister: Edwin Chadwick and the Politics of Government Growth, 1832–1854*, University Park, PA: Pennsylvania State University Press.

Bryer, R. A., Brignall, T. J. and Maunders, A. R. (1982) *Accounting for British Steel*, Aldershot, Hants: Gower Publishing.

Buck, J. (1992) 'Green awareness: an opportunity for business', in Owen, D. (ed.), *Green Reporting: Accountancy and the Challenge of the Nineties*, London: Chapman & Hall.

Burchell, S., Clubb, C. and Hopwood, A. G. (1981) '"A message from Mars" – and other reminiscences from the past', *Accountancy* 92, October: 96–8.

——(1985) 'Accounting in its social context: towards a history of value added in the United Kingdom', *Accounting, Organizations and Society* 10, 4: 381–413.

Burchell, S., Clubb, C., Hopwood, A. G., Hughes, J. and Nahapiet, J. (1980) 'The roles of accounting in organizations and society', *Accounting, Organizations and Society* 5, 1: 5–27.

Butler, J, Laclau, S. and Žižek, S. (2000) 'Introduction', in Butler, J., Laclau, E. and Žižek, S. (eds), *Contingency, Hegemony, Universality: Contemporary Dialogues on the Left*, London: Verso.

Butler, J. (2000) 'Competing universalities', in Butler, J., Laclau, E. and Žižek, A. (eds), *Contingency, Hegemony, Universality: Contemporary Dialogues on the Left*, London: Verso.

Butterworth, B., Gray, R. and Haslam, J. (1989) 'The local authority annual report in the UK: an exploratory study of accounting communication and democracy', *Financial Accountability and Management* 5, 2: 73–87.

Calhoun, C. (1995) *Critical Social Theory: Culture, History and the Challenge of Theory*, Oxford: Blackwell.

——(ed.) (1992) *Habermas and the Public Sphere*, Cambridge, MA: MIT Press.

Calinescu, M. (1986) 'Naming and difference: reflections on "modernism versus postmodernism" in literature', in Fokkema, D. and Bertens, H. (eds) *Approaching Postmodernism: Papers Presented at a Workshop on Postmodernism*, 21–23 September, 1984, Utrecht: University of Utrecht.

——(1987) *Five Faces of Modernity*, Durham, SC: Duke University Press.

Callaghan, J. (1990) *Socialism in Britain since 1884*, Oxford: Blackwell.

Cannon, T. (1994) *Corporate Responsibility: A Textbook on Business Ethics, Governance, Environment: Roles and Responsibilities*, London: Pitman.

Catherine the Great (1931) *Documents of Catherine*, Reddaway, W. F. (ed.), Cambridge: Cambridge University Press.

Champion, H. H. (1983) 'Quorum pars fui: an unconventional autobiography', *Bulletin of the Society for the Study of Labour History* 47: 17–35.

Cherns, A. B. (1978) 'Alienation and accountancy', *Accounting, Organizations and Society* 3, 2: 105–14.

Churchill, N. C. and Toan, A. B. (1978) 'Reporting on corporate social responsibility: a progress report', *Journal of Contemporary Business*, Winter, 5–17.

Clayton, J. (1926) *The Rise of Socialism in Great Britain, 1884–1924*, London: Faber & Gwyer.

Clifford, J. (2001) 'Entrances, stage left', *The Guardian*, S2 Weekend, 11 August: 6–7.

Cmnd 5391 *Company Law Reform* (1973), Green Paper, London: HSMO.

Cmnd 6706 *Report of the Committee of Inquiry on Social Democracy* (1977a), Chairman Lord Bullock, London: HSMO.

Cmnd 6888 *The Future of Company Reports: A Consultative Document* (1977b), Green Paper, London: HSMO.

Coalition for Environmentally Responsible Economies (CERES) (2002) 'CERES: Network for Change' Available at http://www.ceres.org (20 June 2002).

Cole, G. D. H. (1961) *The Common People: 1746–1946*, 4th ed., London: Methuen.

Collett, C. E. (1889) 'Women's work', in Booth, C. (ed.) *Life and Labour of the People in London, 1st Series: Poverty IV, The Trades of East London Connected with Poverty*, London.

Commoner, B. (1972) 'The social use and misuse of technology', in Benthall, J. (ed.) *Ecology: The Shaping Enquiry*, London: Longman.

Confederation of British Industry (1973) *The Responsibilities of the British Public Company*, Final report of the Company Affairs Committee, endorsed by the CBI Council on 19 September 1973, London: CBI.

Connolly, W. E. (1988) *Political Theory and Modernity*, Oxford: Blackwell.

Conway, S. (1989) 'Bentham on peace and war', *Utilitas* 1, 1: 82–101.

Cooke, C. (1950) *Corporation, Trust and Company*, Manchester: Manchester University Press.

Cooper, C. (1992) 'The non and nom of accounting for (m)other nature', *Accounting, Auditing and Accountability Journal* 5, 3: 16–39.

Cooper, C. and Puxty, A. G. (1994) 'Reading accounting writing', *Accounting, Organizations and Society* 19, 2: 127–46.

Cooper, D. J. (1980) 'Discussion of: towards a political economy of accounting', *Accounting, Organizations and Society* 5, 1: 161–6.

Cooper, D. J. and Hopper, T. (eds) (1990) *Critical Accounts*, London: Macmillan.

Cooper, D. J. and Sherer, M. J. (1984) 'The value of corporate accounting reports: towards a political economy of accounting', *Accounting, Organizations and Society* 9, 3/4: 207–32.

Cooper, D. J. and Tinker, T. (1994) 'Accounting and praxis: Marx after Foucault', *Critical Perspectives on Accounting* 5, 1: 1–3.

Corporate Watch (2002a) 'About us'. Available at http://www.corporatewatch.org.uk/pages/aboutus.html (20 June 2002).

——(2002b) 'Corporate Watch'. Available at http://www.corporatewatch.org.uk/ (20 June 2002).

CorpWatch (2002a) 'Campaigns: Greenwash Awards'. Available at http://www.corpwatch.org/campaigns/PCC.jsp?topicid = 102 (20 June 2002).

——(2002b) 'Greenwash Fact Sheet'. Available at http://www.corpwatch.org/campaigns/PCD.jsp?articleid = 242 (20 June 2002).

Counter Information Services (1975) *Where is Lucas Going?*, Anti-Report no. 12, London: CIS.

Cousins, J. and Sikka, P. (1993) 'Accounting for change: facilitating power and accountability', *Critical Perspectives on Accounting* 4, 1: 53–72.

Cousins, J., Mitchell, A., Sikka, P. and Willmott, H. (1998) *Auditors: Holding the Public to Ransom*, Basildon: Association for Accountancy and Business Affairs.

Cousins, M. (1987) 'The practice of historical investigation', in Attridge, D., Bennington, G. and Young, R. (eds) *Post-structuralism and the Question of History*, Cambridge: Cambridge University Press.

Crimmins, J. E. (1994) 'Bentham's political radicalism reexamined', *Journal of the History of Ideas* 55, 2: 259–81.

——(1996) 'Contending interpretations of Bentham's utilitarianism', *Canadian Journal of Political Science – Revue Canadienne de Science Politique* 29, 4: 751–77.

Critchley, S. (1997) 'What is continental philosophy?', *International Journal of Philosophical Studies* 5, 3: 347–65.

——(2001) *Continental Philosophy: A Very Short Introduction*, Oxford: Oxford University Press.

Cullen, M. J. (1975) *The Statistical Movement in Early Victorian Britain: the Foundation of Empirical Social Research*, Hassocks: Harvester Press.

Cumming, I. (1961) *Useful Learning: Bentham's Chrestomathia with Particular Reference to the Influence of James Mill on Bentham*, University of Auckland, Bulletin No. 56, Ed. Series No.3.

Daly, H. E. and Cobb Jr., J. B. (1990) *For the Common Good: Redirecting the Economy Towards the Community, the Environment and a Sustainable Future*, London: Greenprint.

Daunton, M. (2000) 'Society and economic life', in Matthew, C. (ed.) *The Nineteenth Century, The British Isles: 1815–1901*, Oxford: Oxford University Press.

Davidoff, L. and Hall, C. (1987) *Family Fortunes: Men and Women of the English Middle Class, 1780–1850*, London: Hutchinson.

Davie, S. S. K. (2000) 'Accounting for imperialism: a case of British-imposed indigenous collaboration', *Accounting, Auditing and Accountability Journal* 13, 3: 330–59.

Davis, K. R. (1992) 'Kant's different "publics" and the justice of publicity', *Kant Studien* 83, 2: 170–84.

Day, M. M. (1995) 'Ethics of teaching critical: feminisms on the wing of desire', *Accounting, Auditing and Accountability Journal* 8, 3: 97–112.

de Lucas, J. (1987) 'Anotaciones sobre el principio Kantiane de publicidad', *Dianoia* 33: 131–48.

Deleuze, G. (1995) 'Postcript on control societies', in Deleuze, G. (ed.) *Negotiations, 1972–1990*, translated by Joughin, M., New York: Columbia University Press.

Denny, C. (2002) 'Fellow traveller: an interview with George Soros, founder, Quantum Group of Funds', *The Guardian*, 15 June 2002: 28.

Department of Trade (1976) *Aims and Scope of Company Reports*, London: HMSO.

Derrida, J. (1978a) 'Violence and metaphysics: an essay on the thought of Emmanual Levinas', in J. Derrida, *Writing and Difference*, translated by Alan Bass, Chicago: University of Chicago Press.

——(1978b) 'From restricted to general economy: a Hegelianism without reserve', in Derrida, J. (ed.) *Writing and Difference*, translated by Alan Bass, Chicago, IL: University of Chicago Press.

Dickens, C. (1839) *Nicholas Nickleby*, London: Chapman & Hall.

Dierkes, M. and Preston, L. E. (1977) 'Corporate social accounting reporting for the physical environment: a critical review and implementation proposal', *Accounting, Organizations and Society* 2, 1: 3–22.

Dinwiddy, J. (1989) *Bentham*, Oxford: Oxford University Press.

Dobson, A. (1990) *Green Political Thought*, London: Unwin Hayman.

Donzelot, J. (1979) *The Policing of Families*, London: Hutchinson.

Doornbos, M. (1992) 'Foreword', *Development and Change* 23, 3: 1–4.

Drucker, P. F. (1965) 'Is business letting young people down?', *Harvard Business Review* 43, November/December: 49–55.

——(1969) *Preparing Tomorrow's Leaders Today*, Englewood Cliffs, NJ: Prentice Hall.

Dunn, J. and Sikka, P. (1999) *Auditors: Keeping the Public in the Dark*, Basildon: Association for Accountancy and Business Affairs.

Durie, E., Taihakurei, Latimer, G. T. and Temm, P. B. (1986) *Finding of the Waitangi Tribunal Relating to Te Reo Maori and a claim lodged by Huirangi Waikerepura and Nga Kaiwhakapumau Te Reo Incorporated Society*, Wellington: Government Printer, also published in Smith, G. (ed.) *Nga Kete Wanaga: Akonga Maori: Maori pedagogy and Learning*, Auckland: Auckland College of Education.

Edwards, J. R. (1989) *A History of Financial Accounting*, London: Routledge.

——(1992) 'Companies, corporations and accounting change, 1835–1933: a comparative study', *Accounting and Business Research* 23, 89: 59–73.

Elkington, J. (1998) *Cannibals with Forks: The Triple Bottom Line of the 21st Century*, London: Capstone.

Engels, F. (1960) *Correspondence: {of} Friedrich Engels and Paul and Laura Lafargue, 1887–1890*, vol. 2, Moscow: Foreign Languages Publishing House.

Epstein, M. J., Flamholtz, E. and McDonough, J. J. (1976) 'Corporate social accounting in the United States of America: state of the art and future prospects', *Accounting, Organizations and Society* 1, 1: 23–42.

Ernst and Ernst (1976) *Social Responsibility Disclosure*, Cleveland, Ohio: Ernst and Ernst.

Estes, R. W. (1976) *Corporate Social Reporting*, Wiley-Interscience, New York.

Evans, E. J. (1983) *The Forging of the Modern State: Early Industrial Britain, 1783–1870*, 2nd edition, London: Longmann.

Evans, R. (2002) 'The real cost of free speech', *The Times Higher Education Supplement* 21 June: 24–5.

Everett, J. and Neu, D. (2000) 'Ecological modernization and the limits of environmental accounting', *Accounting Forum* 24, 1: 5–29.

Fay, B. (1987) *Critical Social Science*, Cambridge: Polity Press.

Finn, R. (1996) 'Libel concerns are a reality for scientists who speak out in public', *The Scientist* 18, March: 15–16.

Fisher, R. and Murphy, V. (1995) 'A pariah profession? Some students' perceptions of accounting and accountancy', *Studies in Higher Education* 20, 1: 45–58.

Foot, P. (1984) *Red Shelley*, London: Bookmarks.

——(1985) (ed.) *Critical Theory and Public Life*, Cambridge, MA: MIT Press.

Forester, J. (1992) 'Critical Theory: on fieldwork in a Habermasian way', in Alvesson, M. and Willmott, H. C. (eds) *Critical Theory and Management Studies*, London: Sage.

——(1993) *Critical Theory, Public Policy and Planning Practice*, Albany, NY: SUNY Press.

Forrester, D. A. R. (1980) 'Early canal company accounts: financial and accounting aspects of the Forth and Clyde Navigation, 1768–1816', *Accounting and Business Research* 10, 37A: 109–23.

——(1990) 'Rational administration, finance and control accounting: the experience of Cameralism', *Critical Perspectives on Accounting* 1, 4: 285–317.

Foucault, M. (1977a) 'L'oeil de pouvoir', preface to Bentham, J., *Le Panoptique* Paris: Belfond.

——(1977b) *Discipline and Punish: The Birth of the Prison*, Translated by Alan Sheridan, Harmondsworth: Penguin.

——(1980) Power/Knowledge: Selected Interviews and Other Writings, 1972–1977, C. Gordon, (ed.) Brighton: Harvester Press.

——(1984) 'What is enlightenment?', in Rabinow, P. (ed.) *The Foucault Reader*, New York: Pantheon.

——(1991) *Remarks on Marx: Conversations with D. Trombadori*, translated by R. J. Goldstein, and J. Cascaito, New York: Semiotext(e).

Fraser, I., Gallhofer, S., Haslam, J. and Sydserff, R. (1999) 'Dickens and utilitarian accounting: a focus upon *Hard Times*', paper presented at the *Critical Perspectives on Accounting Conference*, New York, April, 1999.

——(2000) 'Dickens and accounting history: towards a critical appreciation', paper presented at the *British Accounting Association Annual Conference*, Exeter, April 2000.

Fraser, N. (1986) 'Toward a discourse ethic of solidarity', *Praxis International* 5, 4: 425–29.

Fraser, N. and Nicholson, L. (1988) 'Social criticism without philosophy: an encounter between feminism and postmodernism', in Ross, A. (ed.) *Universal Abandon? The Politics of Postmodernism*, Edinburgh: Edinburgh University Press.

Fry, R. (1985) *It's Different for Daughters: A History of the Curriculum for Girls in New Zealand Schools, 1900–1975*, Education Research Series No. 65, NZCER, Wellington.

Gaa, J. C. (1986) 'User primacy in corporate financial reporting: a social contract approach', *The Accounting Review* 41, 3: 435–54.

——(1988) *Methodological Foundations of Standard-Setting for Corporate Financial Reporting*, Sarasota, Florida: American Accounting Association.

Gabardi, W. (2001) *Negotiating Postmodernism*, Minneapolis: University of Minnesota Press.

Gallhofer, S. (1992) 'M[othering] view on: "The non and nom of accounting for (m)other nature"', *Accounting, Auditing and Accountability Journal* 5, 3: 40–51.

Gallhofer, S. and Chew, A. (2000) 'Accounting and indigenous peoples', *Accounting, Auditing and Accountability Journal* 13, 3: 256–67.

Gallhofer, S. and Haslam, J. (1991) 'The aura of accounting in the context of a crisis: Germany and the First World War', *Accounting, Organizations and Society* 16, 5/6: 487–520.

——(1993) 'Approaching corporate accountability: fragments from the past', *Accounting and Business Research* 23, 91a: 320–30.

——(1994a) 'Accounting and the Benthams: accounting as negation', *Accounting, Business and Financial History* 4, 2: 239–73.

Gallhofer, S. and Haslam, J. (1994b) 'Accounting and the Benthams: or, accounting's potentialities', *Accounting, Business and Financial History* 4, 3: 431–60.

——(1995) 'Accounting and modernity', *Advances in Public Interest Accounting* 6: 203–32.

——(1996a) 'Accounting/art and the emancipatory project: some reflections', *Accounting, Auditing and Accountability Journal* 9, 5: 23–44.

Gallhofer, S. and Haslam, J. (1996b) 'Analysis of Bentham's *Chrestomathia*: or, towards a critique of accounting education', *Critical Perspectives on Accounting* 7, 1/2: 13–31.

——(1996c) 'No blinkered view: critical reflections on the teaching of a compulsory course component on alternative perspectives on finance', *Accounting Education* 5, 4: 297–319.

——(1997a) 'Beyond accounting: the possibilities of accounting and "critical" accounting research', *Critical Perspectives on Accounting* 8, 1/2: 71–95.

——(1997b) 'The direction of green accounting policy: critical reflections', *Accounting, Auditing and Accountability Journal* 10, 2: 148–74.

——(2000a) 'Bentham on accounting: a summary analysis reflecting on the concept of accountability', in Dahiya, S. B. (ed.) *The Current State of Business Disciplines, Volume One: Accounting*, Rohtak: Spellbound Publications.

——(2000b) 'Bentham, accounting and Critical Theory: encounters in a critical theoretical reading', *Proceedings of the Sixth Interdisciplinary Perspectives on Accounting Conference*, Manchester.

——(2002) 'Accounting education and critical pedagogy', paper presented at the *British Accounting Association Special Interest Group in Accounting Education Conference*, Glasgow Caledonian University, May 2002.

Gallhofer, S., Gibson, K., Haslam, J., McNicholas, P. and Takiari, B. (2000a) 'Developing environmental accounting: insights from indigenous cultures', *Accounting, Auditing and Accountability Journal* 13, 3: 381–409.

Gallhofer, S., Haslam, J., Morrow, S. and Sydserff, R. (2000b) 'Accounting, transparency and the culture of spin: re-orientating accounting communication in the new millenium', *Pacific Accounting Review, Special Millenium Edition* 11, 2: 97–111.

Gallhofer, S., Haslam, J. and Tsen, S.-H. (1996) 'What's wrong with green accounting and auditing prescription? Seeing the wood as well as the trees', *Irish Accounting Review* 3, 1: 69–89.

Gallhofer, S., Haslam, J., Kim, S. N. and Mariu, S. (1999) 'Attracting and retaining Maori students in accounting: issues, experiences and ways forward', *Critical Perspectives on Accounting* 10, 6: 773–807.

Gallhofer, S., Haslam, J., Lowe, T., Mataira, K. and Pratt, M. J. (1995), 'A critical analysis of mainstream texts in accounting and finance: the issue of culture', paper presented to the *Seventh Asian Pacific Conference on International Accounting Issues*, November 8–11, Seoul, South Korea.

Gambling, T. (1974) *Societal Accounting*, London: George Allen and Unwin.

Gambling, T. E. and Karim, R. A. A. (1986) 'Islam and "social accounting"', *Journal of Business Finance and Accounting* 13, 1: 39–50.

Gandy, O. H. (1993) *The Panoptic Sort: A Political Economy of Personnel Information*, Boulder, CO: Westview Press.

Gaonkar, D. P. and McCarthy, Jr., R. J. (1994) 'Panopticism and publicity: Bentham's quest for transparency', *Public Culture* 6: 547–75.

Garnham, N. (2000) *Emancipation, the Media and Modernity: Arguments about the Media and Social Theory*, Oxford: Oxford University Press.

Gibson, K. (2000) 'Accounting as a tool for Aboriginal dispossession: then and now', *Accounting, Auditing and Accountability Journal* 13, 3: 289–306.

Giddens, A. (1981) 'Surveillance and the capitalist state', in Giddens, A. (ed.) *A Contemporary Critique of Historical Materialism*, London: Macmillan.

——(1991) *Modernity and Self-Identity: Self and Society in the Late Modern Age*, Stanford: Stanford University Press.

——(1994) *Beyond Left and Right: The Future of Radical Politics*, Oxford: Blackwell.

Global Reporting Initiative (GRI) (2000a) 'Sustainability reporting guidelines on economic, environmental and social performance, Global Reporting Initiatiative'. Available at http://www.globalreporting.org/GRIGuidelines/index.htm (20 June 2002).

Global Reporting Initiative (GRI) (2002b) 'About GRI'. Available at http://www.globalreporting.org/AboutGRI/Overview.htm (20 June 2002).

——(GRI) (2002c) 'Global Reporting Initiative inaugurated at UN event: a milestone for corporate disclosure and tranparency'. Available at http://www.globalreporting.org/News/PR/Inauguration04-04-02.htm (20 June 2002).

——(GRI) (2002d) 'About GRI-Funding'. Available at http://www.globalreporting.org/AboutGRI/Funding.htm (20 June 2002).

——(GRI) (2002e) 'Global Reporting Initiative and the Global Compact'. Available at http://www.globalreporting.org/AboutGRI/GlobalCompact.pdf (20 June 2002).

——(GRI) (2002f) 'GRI Charter Group'. Available at http://www.globalreporting.org/PermanentInstitution/Charter.htm (20 June 2002).

Goldberg, L. (1957) 'Jeremy Bentham: critic of accounting method', *Accounting Research* 8: 218–45.

Goodman, D. (1995) 'The public and the nation', *Eighteenth Century Studies* 29, 1: 1–4.

Gore, J. M. (1993) *The Struggle for Pedagogies: Critical and Feminist Discourses as Regimes of Truth*, London: Routledge.

Gorz, A. (1989) *Critique of Economic Reason*, Verso, London.

Gramsci, A. (1971) *Selection from the Prison Notebooks*, London: Lawrence and Wishart.

Gray, R. H. (1980) *An Evaluation of the Current UK Practice in External Social Reporting with Special Reference to Social Audit and Counter Information Services*, unpublished MA (Econ) dissertation, University of Manchester.

——(1989) 'Book review: *Models of Democracy* by David Held', *Accounting, Auditing and Accountability Journal* 3, 3: 52–6.

——(1990a) *The Greening of Accountancy: the Profession after Pearce*, Certified Research Report 17, London: Chartered Association of Certified Accountants.

——(1990b) 'Corporate social reporting by U.K. companies: a cross-sectional and longitudinal study – an interim report', paper presented at the *British Accounting Association Regional Conference*, University of Dundee, September 1990.

——(1992) 'Accounting and environmentalism: an exploration of the challenge of gently accounting for accountability, transparency and sustainability', *Accounting, Organizations and Society* 17, 5: 399–425.

——(1999) 'The social accounting project and *Accounting, Organizations and Society*: privileging engagement, imaginings, new accountings and pragmatism over critique?'. Available at http://www.gla.ac.uk/departments/accounting/csear/studentresources/dpsAOSCSR.html (20 June 2002).

Gray, R. H. and Bebbington, J. (2001) *Accounting for the Environment*, 2nd edition, London: Sage.

Gray, R. H. and Laughlin, R. (1991) 'Editorial: the coming of the green and the challenge of environmentalism', *Accounting, Auditing and Accountability Journal* 4, 3: 5–7.

Gray, R. H., Bebbington, J. and Walters, D. (1993) *Accounting for the Environment (The Greening of Accountancy, Part II)*, London: Paul Chapman.

Gray, R. H., Javad, M., Power, D. M. and Sinclair, C. D. (2001) 'Social and environmental disclosure and corporate characteristics: a research note and extension', *Journal of Business Finance and Accounting* 28, 3: 327–56.

Gray, R. H., Kouhy, R. and Lavers, S. (1995a) 'Corporate social and environmental reporting: a review of the literature and a longitudinal study of UK disclosure', *Accounting, Auditing and Accountability Journal* 8, 2: 47–77.

——(1995b) 'Methodological themes: constructing a research database of social and environmental reporting by UK companies', *Accounting, Auditing and Accountability Journal* 8, 2: 78–101.

Gray, R. H., Owen, D. and Adams, C. (1996) *Accounting and Accountability: Changes and Challenges in Corporate Social and Environmental Reporting*, London: Prentice Hall.

Gray, R. H., Owen, D. and Maunders, K. (1987) *Corporate Social Reporting: Accounting and Accountability*, London: Prentice Hall.

——(1988) 'Corporate social reporting: emerging trends in accountability and the social contract', *Accounting, Auditing and Accountability Journal* 1, 1: 6–20.

Gray, S. I. and Maunders, K. T. (1980) *Value Added Reporting: Uses and Measurement*, London: Association of Certified Accountants.

Greer, J. and Bruno, K. (1997) *Greenwash – The Reality Behind Corporate Environmentalism*, Westboro, MA.: Apex Press.

Greer, S. and Patel, C. (2000) 'The issue of Australian indigenous world-views and accounting', *Accounting, Auditing and Accountability Journal* 13, 3: 307–29.

Gregg, P. (1986) *A Social and Economic History of Britain 1760–1980*, 8th and revised edition, Walton-on-Thames: Nelson.

Grew, R. (1990) 'Rethinking the assumptions and purposes of the nineteenth century social science', in Ramirez, F. O. (ed.) *Rethinking the Nineteenth Century: Contradictions and Movements*, New York: Greenwood Press.

Griffin-Collart, E. (1982) 'Bentham: de l'utilité au totalitarianisme', *Revue Internationale de Philosophie* 36, 141: 301–17.

Grobel, M. C. (1932) *The SDUK 1826–46 and its Relation to Adult Education in the First Half of the XIXth Century*, unpublished thesis, University of London.

Guthrie, J. and Parker, L. D. (1989a) 'Corporate social reporting: a rebuttal of legitimacy theory', *Accounting and Business Research* 19, 76: 343–52.

——(1989b) 'Continuity and discontinuity in corporate social reporting: critical case study of BHP reporting 1885–1985', working paper.

——(1990) 'Corporate social disclosure practice: a comparative international analysis', *Advances in Public Interest Accounting* 3: 159–75.

Guthrie, J. E. and Mathews, M. R. (1985) 'Corporate social accounting in Australasia', *Research in Corporate Social Performance and Policy* 7: 251–77.

Habermas, J. (1974) 'The public sphere', translated by Lennox, S. and Lennox, F., *New German Critique* 1, 3, Fall: 49–55.

——(1982) 'A reply to my critics', in Thompson, J. B. and Held, D. (eds) *Habermas: Critical Debate*, Cambridge, MA: MIT Press.

——(1987a) *The Philosophical Discourse of Modernity: Twelve Lectures*, translated by F. Lawrence, Oxford: Polity Press in Association with Basil Blackwell.

——(1987b) *Theory of Communicative Action*, Cambridge, MA: Polity Press.

——(1992) *The Structural Transformation of the Public Sphere: An Inquiry into a Category of Bourgeois Society*, translated by T. Burger with the assistance of F. Lawrence, Cambridge: MIT Press.

Hall, S. (1983) 'The Great Moving Right Show', in Hall, S. and Jacques, M. (eds) *The Politics of Thatcherism*, London: Lawrence and Wishart.

—— (1988) *The Hard Road to Renewal: Thatcherism and the Crisis of the Left*, London: Verso.

—— (1991) 'Das Ökologie-Problem und die Notwendigkeiten linker Politik: ein Interview', *Das Argument* 33,189: 665–74.

Hamilton, R. (1788) *An Introduction to Merchandise*, London.

Hammond, T. (1995) 'Some considerations in attracting and retaining African–American doctoral candidates in accounting', *Issues in Accounting Education* 10, 1: 143–58.

Harland, R. (1987) *Superstructuralism*, London: Routledge.

Harrison, R. (1983) *Bentham*, London: Routledge and Kegan Paul.

Harrison, R. (1996) 'Bentham, Mill and Sidgwick', in Bunnin, N. F. (ed.) *The Blackwell Companion to Philosophy*, Cambridge: Blackwell.

Hart, H. L. A. (1982) *Essays on Bentham's Jurisprudence and Political Theory*, Oxford: Oxford University Press.

Harte, G. F. and Owen, D. L. (1987) 'Fighting de-industrialisation: the role of local government social audits', *Accounting, Organizations and Society* 12, 2:123–41.

Harvey, D. (1993) 'Class relations, social justice and the politics of difference', in Squires, J. (ed.) *Principled Positions: Postmodernism and the Rediscovery of Value*, London: Lawrence and Wishart.

Haslam, J. (1986) 'Towards a Marxian theory of accounting: a comment', *British Accounting Review* 18, 1: 43–57.

—— (1991) *On the Prescribing of Accounting and Accounting Publicity in Early to Mid-Nineteenth Century Britain: Accounting History as Critique*, unpublished PhD thesis, University of Essex.

Hattersley, R. (1999) *Blood and Fire: William and Catherine Booth and their Salvation Army*, London: Abacus.

Held, D. (1980) *Introduction to Critical Theory*, London: Hutchinson.

Held, D. and McGrew, A. (2000) (eds) *The Global Transformation Reader: An Introduction to the Globalization Debate*, Cambridge: Polity Press in association with Blackwell.

Helvétius, C. A. (1809) *De L'Esprit: or, Essays on the Mind*, London: J. M. Richardson.

Herman, E. S. and Chomsky, N. (1994) *Manufacturing Consent: The Political Economy of the Mass Media*, London: Vintage.

Hicks, J. R. (1942) *The Social Framework: An Introduction to Economics*, Oxford: Oxford University Press.

Himmelfarb, G. (1968) 'The haunted house of Jeremy Bentham', in Himmelfarb, G. (ed.) *Victorian Minds*, New York: Knopf.

—— (1984) *The Idea of Poverty: England in the Early Industrial Age*, New York: Knopf.

Hines, R. D. (1988) 'Financial accounting: in communicating reality we construct reality', *Accounting, Organizations and Society* 13, 3: 251–61.

—— (1989) 'The sociopolitical paradigm in financial accounting research', *Accounting, Auditing and Accountability Journal* 2, 1: 52–76.

—— (1991a) 'Accounting for nature', *Accounting, Auditing and Accountability Journal* 4, 3: 27–29.

—— (1991b) 'The FASB'S conceptual framework, financial accounting and the maintenance of the social world', *Accounting, Organizations and Society* 16, 4: 313–31.

Hird, C. (1978) 'Beware of "value added" – a simple device to protect profit', *New Statesman* 96, 2472, 4 August: 142.

Hobbes, T. (1991) *Leviathan*, edited by R. Tuck, Cambridge: Cambridge University Press.

Hobsbawm, E. J. (1962) *The Age of Revolution: Europe 1789–1848*, London: Weidenfeld and Nicolson.

Hobsbawm, E. J. (1964) *Labouring Men: Studies in the History of Labour*, London: Weidenfeld and Nicolson.

——(1995) *Age of Extremes: The Short Twentieth Century*, 1914–91, London: Abacus.

Hohendal, P. U. (1979) 'Critical Theory, public sphere and culture: Jurgen Habermas and his critics', *New German Critique* 16, Winter: 89–118.

Holub, R. C. (1991) *Jürgen Habermas: Critic in the Public Sphere*, London: Routledge.

Hood, C. and Jackson, M. (1994) 'Keys for locks in administrative argument', *Administration and Society* 25, 4: 467–88.

Hopkins, E. (2000) *Industrialisation and Society: A Social History, 1830–1951*, London: Routledge.

Hopper, T., Cooper, D. J., Capps, T., Lowe, E. A. and Mouritsen, J. (1986) 'Financial controls in the labour process', in Knights, D. and Willmott, H. (eds) *Managing the Labour Process*, Hampshire: Gower.

Hopper, T., Storey, J. and Willmott, H. (1987) 'Accounting for accounting: towards the development of a dialectical view', *Accounting, Organizations and Society*, 12, 5: 437–56.

Hopwood, A. G. (1978) 'Social accounting – the way ahead?', in *Social Accounting*, London: Chartered Institute of Public Finance and Accounting.

——(1983) 'On trying to study accounting in the contexts in which it operates', *Accounting, Organizations and Society* 8, 2/3: 287–305.

——(1985) 'The tale of a committee that never reported: disagreements on intertwining accounting with the social', *Accounting, Organizations and Society* 10, 3: 361–77.

——(1987) 'The archaeology of accounting systems', *Accounting, Organizations and Society* 12, 3: 207–34.

——(1988) *Accounting from the Outside*, New York: Garland.

——(1990) 'Ambiguity, knowledge and territorial claims: some observations on the doctrine of substance over form', *British Accounting Review* 22, 1: 79–87.

Hopwood, A. G. (1994) 'Accounting in everyday life: an introduction', *Accounting, Organizations and Society* 19, 3: 299–301.

Hopwood, A. G. and Burchell, S. (1980) 'The idea of social accounting remains an illusive one', *Public Finance and Accountancy*, 7, September: 12–15.

Hopwood, A. G. and Miller, P. (eds) (1994) *Accounting as Social and Institutional Practice*, Cambridge: Cambridge University Press.

Hopwood, A. G., Burchell, J. and Clubb, C. (1980) 'The development of accounting in its international context: past concerns and emergent issues', in Roberts, A. (ed.) *A History and Contempory Review of the Development of International Accounting*, Georgia State University.

——(1994) 'Value-added accounting and national economic policy', in Hopwood, A. G. and Miller, P. (eds) *Accounting as Social and Institutional Practice*, Cambridge: Cambridge University Press.

Horkheimer, M. and Adorno, T. (1972) *Dialectic of Enlightenment*, New York: Herder and Herder.

Hoskin, K. (1994) 'For, against and beyond Foucault in the battle for accounting theory', *Critical Perspectives on Accounting* 5, 1: 57–86.

Hoskin, K. and Macve, R. (1986) 'Accounting and the examination: a genealogy of disciplinary power', *Accounting, Organizations and Society* 11, 2: 105–36.

——(1988) 'The genesis of accountability: the Westpoint connections', *Accounting, Organizations and Society* 13, 1: 37–73.

Hudson, W. (1989) 'Postmodernity and contemporary social thought', in Lassman, P. (ed.) *Politics and Social Theory*, London: Routledge.

Hulse, J. W. (1970) *Revolutionists in London: A Study of Five Unorthodox Socialists*, Oxford: Clarendon Press.

Hume, D. (1951) *Hume's Theory of Politics*, Watkins, F. (ed.) Edinburgh: Edinburgh University Press.

Hume, L. J. (1970) 'The development of industrial accounting: the Bentham's contribution', *Journal of Accounting Research* 8, 1: 21–33.

—— (1981) *Bentham and Bureaucracy*, Cambridge: Cambridge University Press.

Humphrey, C., Lewis, L. and Owen, D. (1996) 'Still too distant voices? Conversations and reflections on the social relevance of accounting education', *Critical Perspectives on Accounting* 7, 1/2: 77–99.

Humphries, B. (1997) 'From critical thought to emancipatory action: contradictory research goals?', *Sociological Research Online* 2, 1. Available http: http://www.socresonline.org.uk/socresonline/2/1/3.html (20 June 2002).

Hussey, R. (1978) *Employees and the Employment Report – A Research Paper*, Oxford: Touche, Ross & Co.

—— (1979) *Who Reads Employee Reports?*, Oxford: Touche, Ross & Co.

Hyndman, H. M. (1911) *The Record of an Adventurous Life*, London: Macmillan & Co.

Ignatieff, M. (1984) *A Just Measure of Pain: The Penitentiary in the Industrial Revolution, 1750–1850*, London: London University Publishing.

Ihimaera, W. (1993) *Te Ao Marama* [The World/knowledge/understanding] – Regaining Aotearoa, Auckland: Reed Books.

Inglis, T. (1997) 'Empowerment and emancipation', *Adult Education Quarterly* 48, 1: 3–17.

Ingram, R. and Frazier, K. B. (1980) 'Environmental performance and corporate disclosure', *Journal of Accounting Research* 18, 2: 614–22.

Institute of Social and Ethical Accountability (ISEA) (1999) *Accountability 1000: A Foundation Statement in Social and Ethical Accounting, Auditing and Reporting*, London: Institute of Social and Ethical AccountAbility.

—— (ISEA) (2002a) 'AA 1000 Series: AA 100 Series home page'. Available at http://www.accountability.org.uk/aa1000/default.asp (20 June 2002).

—— (ISEA) (2002b) 'About Us: The Institute of Social and Ethical Accountability', Available at http://www.accountability.org.uk/aboutus/default.asp (20 June 2002).

—— (ISEA) (2002c) 'About Us: AccountAbility Council'. Available at http://www.accountability.org.uk/aboutus/default.asp?pageid = 19 (20 June 2002).

Jackson, M. (1988) *The Maori and the Criminal Justice System, A New Perspective: He Wahipaanga Hou*, Part 2, Wellington: Department of Justice.

Jackson-Cox, J., Thirkell, J. E. M. and McQueeney, J. (1984) 'The disclosure of company information to trade unions: the relevancce of the ACAS Code of Practice on disclosure', *Accounting, Organizations and Society* 9, 4: 253–74.

Jacobs, J. (1950) *London Trades Council, 1860–1950: A History*, London: Lawrence and Wishart Ltd.

Jacobs, K. (2000) 'Evaluating accountability: finding a place for the Treaty of Waitangi in the New Zealand public sector', *Accounting, Auditing and Accountability Journal* 13, 3: 360–80.

Jameson, F. (1989) 'The politics of theory: ideological positions in the postmodernism debate', in Latimer, D. (ed.) *Contemporary Critical Theory*, New York: Harcourt Brace Jovanovich.

—— (1991) *Postmodernism: Or, the Cultural Logic of Late Capitalism*, London: Verso.

Jay, M. (1993) *Downcast Eyes: The Denigration of Vision in Twentieth-Century French Thought*, Berkely, CA: University of California Press.

Jones, S. and Aiken, M. (1995) 'British companies legislation and social and political evolution during the nineteenth century', *British Accounting Review*, 27, 1: 61–82.

Jones, T. C. (1995) *Accounting and the Enterprise: A Social Analysis*, London: Routledge.

Karliner, J. (1997) *The Corporate Planet: Ecology and Politics in the Age of Globalisation*, Sierra Club Books.

Kawagley, A. O., Norris-Tull, D. and Norris-Tull, R. (1995) 'Incorporation of the world views of indigenous cultures: a dilemma in the practice and teaching of western science', paper presented at the *Third International History, Philosophy and Science Teaching Conference*, Minneapolis, October 29–November 2.

Kayser, E. L. (1932) *The Grand Social Enterprise: A Study of Jeremy Bentham in His Relation to Liberal Nationalism*, New York: Columbia University Press.

Keane, J. (1984) *Public Life and Late Capitalism: Toward a Socialist Theory of Democracy*, Cambridge: Cambridge University Press.

Kellner, D. (1988) 'Postmodernism as social theory: some challenges and problems', *Theory, Culture and Society* 5, 3: 239–69.

—— (1989) *Critical Theory, Marxism, and Modernity*, Baltimore, MD: Johns Hopkins University Press.

—— (2002a) 'Critical theory and the crisis of social theory'. Available at http://www.uta.edu/huma/illuminations/kell5.htm (20 June 2002).

Kellner, D. (2002b) 'Critical theory today: revisiting the classics'. Available at http://www.uta.edu/huma/illuminations/kell10.htm (20 June 2002).

—— (2002c) 'Critical theory, poststructuralism and the philosophy of liberation'. Available at http://www.uta.edu/huma/illuminations/kell7.htm (20 June 2002).

—— (2002d) 'Techno-politics, new technologies, and the new public spheres'. Available at http://www.uta.edu/huma/illuminations/kell32.htm (20 June 2002).

Kirkham, P. and Hope, C. (1992) 'Environmental Disclosures in U.K. Company Annual Reports', *Department of Management Studies Research Paper Series 1692*, University of Cambridge.

Kistler, L. H. (1980) 'The Middlesex Canal: an analysis of the accounting and management', *The Accounting Historians Journal* 7, 1: 43–57.

Knights, D. and Collinson, D. (1987) 'Disciplining the shop floor: a comparison of the disciplinary effects of managerial psychology and financial accounting', *Accounting, Organizations and Society* 12, 5: 457–78.

Kolb, D. (1986) *The Critique of Pure Modernity: Hegel, Heidegger and After*, Chicago, IL: University of Chicago Press.

La Vopa, A. J. (1995) 'Herder's *Publikum*: language, print and sociabilty in eighteenth-century Germany' *Eighteenth-Century Studies* 29, 1: 5–24.

Labour Party (1974) The Community and the Company, London: Labour Party.

Laclau, E. (1990) *New Reflections on the Revolution of Our Time*, London: Verso.

—— (1992) 'Beyond emancipation', *Development and Change* 23, 3: 121–37.

—— (1996) *Emancipation(s)*, London: Verso.

—— (2000a) 'Structure, history and the political', in Butler, J. Laclau, E. and Žižek, S. (eds) *Contingency, Hegemony, Universality: Contemporary Dialogues on the Left*, London: Verso.

—— (2000b) 'Constructing universality', in Butler, J. Laclau, E. and Žižek, S. (eds) *Contingency, Hegemony, Universality: Contemporary Dialogues on the Left*, London: Verso.

Laclau, E. and Mouffe, C. (1985) *Hegemony and Socialist Strategy: Towards a Radical Democratic Politics*, London: Verso.

Lamare, J. de (1729) *Traité de la Police*, second edition, Amsterdam.

Lash, S. (1990) *Sociology of Postmodernism*, London: Routledge.

Lather, P. (1991) *Getting Smart: Feminist Research and Pedagogy With/In the Postmodern*, London: Routledge.

Latour, B. (1998) 'Virtual society: the social science of electronic technologies', CRICT 10th Anniversary Conference, Brunel University.

Laughlin, R. C. (1984) *The Design of Accounting Systems: A General Theory with an Empirical Study of the Church of England*, unpublished PhD thesis, University of Sheffield.

——(1987) 'Accounting systems in organizational contexts: a case for critical theory', *Accounting, Organizations and Society* 12, 5: 479–502.

——(1988) 'Accounting in its social context: an analysis of the accounting systems of the Church of England', *Accounting, Auditing and Accountability Journal* 1, 2: 19–42.

——(1992) 'Accounting control and controlling accounting: the battle for the public sector?', *Discussion Paper*, No. 92.29, Sheffield University Management School.

——(1995) 'Emprical research in accounting: the case for middle-range thinking', *Accounting, Auditing and Accountability Journal* 8, 1: 63–87.

Laughlin, R. C. and Broadbent, J. (1993) Accounting and the Law: Partners in the Juridification of the Public Sector in the U.K., *Critical Perspectives on Accounting*, 4, 4: 337–68.

Laughlin, R. C., Broadbent, J., Shearn, D. and Willig-Atherton, H. (1994) 'Absorbing LMS: the coping mechanism of a small group', *Accounting, Auditing and Accountability Journal* 7, 1: 59–85.

Laurie, A. P., Rogers, A. G. L., Llewellyn Smith, H. and Stevenson, A. G. (1888) 'A letter based on a series of enquiries into industrial conditions of East London', *The Times*, 12 July 1888, reported in *St. James's Gazette* of this date: 11.

Laursen, J. C. (1986) 'The subversive Kant: the vocabulary of "public" and "publicity"', *Political Theory* 14, 4: 584–603.

Lee, H. W. and Archbold, E. (1935) *Social Democracy in Britain*, London.

Lehman, C. R. (1992) *Accounting's Changing Role in Social Conflict*, New York: Markus Wiener.

Lehman, C. R. and Tinker, T. (1987) 'The "real" cultural significance of accounts', *Accounting, Organizations and Society* 12, 5: 503–22.

Lehman, G. (1995) 'A legitimate concern for environmental accounting', *Critical Perspectives on Accounting* 6: 343–412.

——(1999) 'Disclosing new worlds: a role for social and environmental accounting and auditing', *Accounting, Organizations and Society* 24, 3: 217–41.

Lehman, G. and Tinker, T. (1997) 'Environmental accounting; accounting as instrumental or emancipatory discourse?', *Proceedings of the Interdisciplinary Perspectives on Accounting Conference*, Manchester, July 1997.

Leonard, S. T. (1990) *Critical Theory in Political Practice*, Princeton, NJ: Princeton University Press.

Lessem, R. (1977) 'Corporate social accounting in action: an evaluation of British, European and American practice', *Accounting, Organizations and Society* 2, 4: 279–94.

Lester, K. (1992) 'Protecting the environment: a new managerial responsibility', in Owen, D. (ed.) *Green Reporting: Accountancy and the Challenge of the Nineties*, Chapman & Hall.

Letwin, S. R. (1965) *The Pursuit of Certainty: David Hume, Jeremy Bentham, John Stuart Mill, Beatrice Webb*, Cambridge: Cambridge University Press.

Lewis, L., Humphrey, C. and Owen, D. (1992) 'Accounting and the social: a pedagogic perspective', *British Accounting Review* 24, 3: 219–33.

Lister, R. (1997) 'Citizenship: towards a feminist synthesis', *Feminist Review* 57, Autumn: 28–48.

Loft, A. (1986) 'Towards a critical understanding of accounting: the case of cost accounting in the U.K.: 1914–25', *Accounting, Organizations and Society* 11, 2: 137–69.

——(1988) *Understanding Accounting in its Social and Historical Context: The Case of Cost Accounting in Britain, 1914–1925*, New York: Garland.

Long, D. (1987) 'Bentham as revolutionary social scientist', *Man Nature* 6: 115–45.

Lowe, E. A. and Tinker, A. M. (1977) 'Siting the accounting problematic: towards an intellectual emancipation of accounting', *Journal of Business Finance and Accounting* 4, 3: 263–76.

Lowe, E. A., Gallhofer, S. and Haslam, J. (1991) 'Theorising accounting regulation in a global context: insights from a study of accounting in the Federal Republic of Germany', *Advances in Public Interest Accounting* 4: 143–77.

Lowell, J. S. (1982) 'After the match girls strike: Bryant and May in the 1890s', *Victorian Studies* 26, 1: 7–31.

Lyons, D. (1973) *In the Interest of the Governed: a Study of Bentham's Principle of Utility and Law*, Oxford: Clarendon.

—— (1984) *Ethics and the Rule of Law*, Cambridge: Cambridge University Press.

—— (1991) *In the Interest of the Governed: A Study in Bentham's Philosophy of Utility and Law*, revised edition, New York: Oxford University Press.

Lyotard, J.-F. (1984) *The Postmodern Condition: A Report on Knowledge*, translated by Bennington, G. and Massumi, B. Minneapolis, MN: University of Minnesota Press.

Macalister, T. (2002) 'MP leads call for corporate ethics bill', *The Guardian*, 13 June 2002: 24.

Mack, M. P. (1962) *Jeremy Bentham: An Odyssey of Ideas, 1748–1792*, London: Heineman.

MacKenzie, N. (1977) *The First Fabians*, London.

Mann, T. (1923) *Tom Mann's Memoirs*, London.

Marcus, G. and Fischer, M. (1986) *Anthropology as Cultural Critique: an Experimental Moment in the Human Sciences*, Chicago, IL: University of Chicago Press.

Marshall, J. (1993) *Underachievement of Maori, He Kaupapa Whakatikatika {concern to put things right}: a Report for the Foundation for Research, Science and Technology*, Auckland: Auckland University Press.

Martin, D. (1993) 'The joining of human, earth and spirit', in Hull, F. (ed.) *Earth and Spirit: The Spiritual Dimension of the Environmental Crisis*, New York: Continuum.

Marx, K. (1973) *Grundrisse: Foundations of a Critique of Political Economy*, Harmondsworth: Penguin.

Mataira, K. (1994) 'Maori accountability', *Chartered Accountants Journal*, February.

Mataira, K. and Humphries, M. (1992) 'Expatriate managers and local concerns', *Proceedings of the First International Conference on Expatriate Management*, Hong Kong.

Mathews, M. R. (1993) *Socially Responsible Accounting*, London: Chapman & Hall.

—— (1997) 'Twenty-five years of social and environmental accounting research: is there a silver jubilee to celebrate?', *Accounting, Auditing and Accountability Journal* 10, 4: 481–531.

Mathiesen, T. A. (1997) 'The viewer society', *Theoretical Criminology* 1, 2: 215–34.

Maunders, K. T. (1981) 'Social reporting and the employment report', in Tonkin, D. J. and Skerratt, L. C. L. (eds) *Financial Reporting 1981–1982*, London: ICAEW.

—— (1982a) 'Social reporting and the employment report', in Tonkin, D. J. and Skerratt, L. C. L. (eds) *Financial Reporting 1982–1983*, London: ICAEW.

—— (1982b) 'Simplified and employee reports', in Tonkin, D. J. and Skerratt, L. C. L. (eds) *Financial Reporting 1982–1983*, London: ICAEW.

—— (1984) *Employment Reporing – An Investigation of User Needs, Measurement and Reporting Issues and Practice*, London: ICAEW.

Maunders, K. T. and Burritt, R. L. (1991) 'Accounting and Ecological Crisis', *Accounting, Auditing and Accountability Journal* 4, 3: 9–26.

McBarnet, D., Weston, S. and Whelan, C. J. (1993) 'Adversary accounting: strategic uses of financial information by capital and labour', *Accounting, Organizations and Society* 18, 1: 81–100.

McCreanor, T. (1993) 'Pakeha ideology of Maori performance: a discourse analytic approach to the construction of educational failure in Aotearoa/New Zealand', *Folia Linguistics* 28, 3/4: 293–313.

McInerney, D. M., McInerney, V. M. and Roche, L. (1994) 'Achievement goal theory and indigenous minority school motivation: the importance of a multiple goal perspective', paper presented at the *AARE Conference*, Newcastle, New South Wales, November 27–December 1.

McKinlay, A. and Taylor, P. (1998) 'Through the looking glass: Foucault and the politics of production', in McKinlay, A. and Starkey, K. (eds) *Foucault, Management and Organization Theory*, London: Sage.

McNay, L. (1992) *Foucault and Feminism*, Cambridge: Blackwell.

Meacham, S. (1987) *Toynbee Hall and Social Reform 1880–1914: The Search for Community*, New Haven and London: Yale University Press.

Mearns, A. (1883) *The Bitter Cry of Outcast London*, London.

Medawar, C. (1976) 'The social audit: a political view', *Accounting, Organizations and Society* 1, 4: 389–394.

Melucci, A. (1992) 'Liberation or meaning? Social movements, culture and democracy', *Development and Change* 23, 2: 43–77.

Merino, B. and Neimark, M. D. (1982) 'Disclosure regulation and public policy: a sociohistorical reappraisal', *Journal of Accounting and Public Policy* 1, 1: 33–57.

Middlemas, K. (1983) *Industry, Unions and Government*, London: Macmillan.

Mildmay, W. (1763) *The Police of France*, London.

Miller, J. A. (1987) 'Jeremy Bentham's Panoptic device', *October* 41: 3–29.

Miller, P. (1991) 'Accounting innovation beyond the enterprise: problematizing investment decisions and programming economic growth in the U.K. in the 1960s' *Accounting, Organizations and Society* 16, 2: 733–62.

Miller, P. and Napier, C. (1993) 'Genealogies of calculation', *Accounting, Organizations and Society* 18, 7/8: 631–47.

Miller, P. and O'Leary, T. (1987) 'Accounting and the construction of the governable person', *Accounting, Organizations and Society* 12, 3: 235–65.

Miller, P. and Rose, N. (1990) 'Governing Economic Life', *Economy and Society* 19, 1: 1–31.

Milne, M. (1996) 'On sustainability: the environment and management accounting', *Management Accounting Research* 7, 1: 135–61.

Mirvis, P. H. and Lawler III, E. E. (1983) 'Systems are not solutions: issues in creating information systems that account for the human organization', *Accounting, Organizations and Society* 8, 2/3: 175–90.

Mitchell, A. and Sikka, P. (1993) 'Accounting for change: the institutions of accountancy', *Critical Perspectives on Accounting* 4, 1: 29–52.

Mitchell, A., Puxty, T, Sikka, P. and Willmott, H. (1994) 'Ethical statements as smokescreens for sectional interests: the case of the U.K. accountancy profession', *Journal of Business Ethics* 13, 1: 39–51.

Mitchell, A., Sikka, P. and Willmott, H. (1998) 'Sweeping it under the carpet: the role of accountancy firms in moneylaundering', *Accounting, Organizations and Society* 23, 5/6: 589–607.

——(2001) 'Policing knowledge by invoking the law: critical accounting and the politics of dissemination', *Critical Perspectives on Accounting* 12, 5: 527–55.

Mitchell, H. A. and Mitchell, M. J. (1993) *Maori Teachers who Leave the Classroom*, Wellington, New Zealand Council for Education Research.

Mobley, S. C. (1970) 'The challenges of socio-economic accounting', *The Accounting Review* 45, 4: 762–8.

Monbiot, G. (2001) *Captive State: The Corporate Takeover of Britain*, London: Pan Books.

——(2002) 'A parliament for the planet', *New Internationalist*, January/February: 12–14.

Moore, D. C. (1991) 'Accounting on trial: the critical legal studies movement and its lessons for radical accounting', *Accounting, Organizations and Society* 16, 8: 763–91.

Morgan, G. and Willmott, H. (1993) 'The "new" accounting research: on making accounting more visible', *Accounting, Auditing and Accountability Journal* 6, 4: 3–36.

Morley, M. F. (1978) *The Value Added Statement*, London: Gee and Co. for the Institute of Chartered Accountants of Scotland.

Mouck, T. (1994) 'Corporate Accountability and Rorty's utopian liberalism', *Accounting, Auditing and Accountability Journal* 4, 3: 6–30.

——(1995) 'Financial reporting, democracy and environmentalism: a critique of the commodification of information', *Critical Perspectives on Accounting* 6, 6: 535–53.

Mouffe, C. (1993a) 'Liberal socialism and pluralism: which citizenship?', in Squires, J. (ed.) (1993) *Principled Positions: Postmodernism and the Rediscovery of Value*, London: Lawrence and Wishart.

——(1993b) *The Return of the Political*, London: Verso.

Munday, R. (1992) 'Bentham, Bacon and the movement for the reform of English law reporting', *Utilitas* 4, 2: 299–316.

Munro, J. (1821) *A Guide to Farm Book-keeping, Founded Upon Practice and Upon New and Concise Principles*, Edinburgh.

Murray, D. (1930) *Chapters in the History of Book-keeping, Accountancy and Commercial Arithmetic*, Glasgow: Jackson, Wylie.

Natural Resources Unit of Manatu Maori (1991) *Maori Values and Environmental Management*, Manatu Maori.

Necker, J. (1785) *A Treatise on the Administration of the Finances of France*, translated by T. Mortimer, London.

Nederveen Pieterse, J. (1992) 'Emancipations, modern and postmodern', *Development and Change* 23, 3: 5–41.

Neimark, M. (1983) *The Social Construction of Annual Reports: A Radical Approach to Corporate Control*, unpublished PhD thesis, New York University.

——(1986) 'Marginalizing the public interest in accounting', *Advances in Public Interest Accounting* 1: ix–xiii.

——(1990a) 'The King is Dead. Long Live the King!', *Critical Perspectives on Accounting* 1, 1: 103–14.

——(1990b) 'Editorial: Accounting doesn't matter, does it?', *Advances in Public Interest Accounting* 3: ix–xvi.

——(1994) 'Regicide revisited: Marx, Foucault and accounting', *Critical Perspectives on Accounting* 5, 1: 87–108.

Neimark, M. and Tinker, T. (1986) 'The social construction of management control systems', *Accounting, Organizations and Society* 11, 4/5: 369–95.

Nelson, J. S. (1993) 'Account and acknowledge, or represent and control? On post-modern politics and economics of collective responsibility', *Accounting, Organizations and Society* 18, 2/3: 207–31.

Neu, D. (2000) 'Accounting and accountability relations: colonization, genocide and Canada's first nations', *Accounting, Auditing and Accountability Journal* 13, 3: 268–88.

Neu, D., Cooper, D. J. and Everett, J. (2001) 'Critical accounting interventions', *Critical Perspectives on Accounting* 12, 6: 735–62.

Neu, D., Warsame, H. and Pedwell, K. (1998) 'Managing public impressions: environmental disclosures in annual reports', *Accounting, Organizations and Society* 23, 3: 265–82.

Newton, T. and Harte, G. (1997) 'Green business: technicist kitsch?', *Journal of Management Studies* 34, 1: 75–98.

Norris, C. (1993) 'Old themes for new times: postmodernism, theory and cultural politics', in Squires, J. (ed.) (1993) *Principled Positions: Postmodernism and the Rediscovery of Value*, London: Lawrence and Wishart.

North, R. (1714) *The Gentleman Accomptant: or, an Essay to Unfold the Mystery of Accompts, by way of Debtor and Creditor, Commonly Called Merchant Accompts, by a Person of Honour* (R. North), London (reprinted, 1986, Arno Press).

O'Neil, J. (1976) 'Critique and remembrance', in O'Neil, J. (ed.) *On Critical Theory*, New York: Seabury Press.

Ogden, S. and Bougen, P. (1985) 'A radical perspective on the disclosure of accounting information to trade unions', *Accounting, Organizations and Society* 10, 2: 211–24.

Ollman, B. (1976) *Alienation: Marx's Concept of Man in Capitalist Society*, second edition, Cambridge: Cambridge University Press.

Oncina, F. (1994) 'Geheimnis und Öffentlichkeit bei Fichte', *Fichte-Studien* 6: 321–44.

Orange, C. (1987) *The Treaty of Waitangi*, Wellington: Allen and Unwin.

Osborne, P. (1992) 'Modernity is a qualitative, not a chronological category', *New Left Review*, 192, March/April: 65–84.

Owen, D. (1990) 'Towards a theory of social investment: a review essay', *Accounting, Organizations and Society* 15, 3: 249–66.

——(ed.) (1992a) *Green Reporting: Accountancy and the Challenge of the Nineties*, London: Chapman & Hall.

——(1992b) 'The implications of current trends in green awareness for the accounting function: an introductory analysis', in Owen, D. (ed.) *Green Reporting: Accountancy and the Challenge of the Nineties*, Chapman & Hall, London.

——(1994) 'The need for environmental accounting standards', *Accounting Forum* 7, 4: 31–46.

Owen, D., Gray, R. and Bebbington, J. (1997) 'Green accounting: cosmetic irrelevance or radical agenda for change?', *Asia-Pacific Journal of Accounting* 4, 2: 175–98.

Owen, D., Humphrey, C. and Lewis, L. (1994) *Social and Environmental Accounting Education in British Universities*, ACCA Research Report No. 39, London: ACCA.

Owen, D., Swift, T. A., Humphrey, C. and Bowerman, M. (2000) 'The new social audit: accountability, managerial capture or the agenda of social champions?', *The European Accounting Review* 9, 1: 81–98.

Panozzo, F. (1997) 'The making of the good academic accountant', *Accounting, Organizations and Society* 22, 5: 477–80.

Parker, L. D. (1989) 'Accounting for social impact', in Parker, L. D. Ferris, K. R. and Otley, D. T. (eds) *Accounting for the Human Factor*, Sydney: Prentice Hall International.

——(1991) 'External social accountability: adventures in a maleficent world', *Advances in Public Interest Accounting* 4: 23–34.

Parker, R. H. (1990) 'Regulating British corporate financial reporting in the late nineteenth century', *Accounting, Business and Financial History* 1, 1: 51–71.

Patterson, J. (1992) *Exploring Maori Values*, Palmerston North: Dunmore Press.

——(1994) 'Maori environmental virtues', *Environmental Ethics* 16, 4:, 397–409.

Paul, E. F. (1979) *Moral Revolution and Economic Science: The Demise of Laissez-Faire in Nineteenth Century British Political Economy*, Connecticut: Greenwood.

Peardon, T. P. (1974) 'Bentham's Ideal Republic', in Parekh, B. (ed.) *Jeremy Bentham*, London: Frank Cass.

Pelling, H. M. (1953) 'H. H. Champion: pioneer of labour representation', *Cambridge Journal* 6: 222–38.

Perks, R. W. and Gray, R. H. (1979) 'Beware of social accounting', *Management Accounting*, 61, December: 22–3.

——(1980) 'Social accounting: the role of the accountant', *The Accountants Magazine*, May: 201.

Peters, J. D. (1993) 'Distrust of representation: Habermas on the public sphere', *Media, Culture and Society* 15, 4: 541–71.

——(1995) 'Publicity and pain: self-abstraction in Adam Smith's *Theory of Moral Sentiments*', *Public Culture* 7: 657–84.

Pimlott, J. A. R. (1985) *Toynbee Hall: Fifty Years of Social Progress, 1884–1934*, London: Dent & Sons.

Pitkin, H. F. (1990) 'Slippery Bentham: some neglected cracks in the foundation of utilitarianism', *Political Theory* 18, 1: 104–31.

Polanyi, K. (1945) *Origins of Our Time: the Great Transformation*, London: Victor Gollancz.

Postema, G. J. (1988) 'Bentham's equality-sensitive utilitarianism', *Utilitas* 10, 2: 144–58.

——(1989) 'Bentham on the public character of law', *Utilitas* 1, 1: 41–61.

Powell, D. (2001) *Tony Benn: A Political Life*, London: Continuum.

Power, M. (1991) 'Auditing and environmental expertise: between protest and professionalisation', *Accounting, Auditing and Accountability Journal* 4, 3: 30–42.

——(1992) 'After calculation? Reflections on critique of economic reason by Andre Gorz', *Accounting Organizations and Society* 17, 5: 477–99.

——(1997) *The Audit Society: Rituals of Verification*, Oxford: Oxford University Press.

Power, M. and Laughlin, R. C. (1992) 'Critical Theory and accounting', in Alvesson, M. and Willmott, H. C. (eds) (1992) *Critical Theory and Management Studies*, London: Sage.

——(1996) 'Habermas, law and accounting', *Accounting, Organizations and Society* 21, 5: 441–65.

Preston, A. and Oakes, L. (2001) 'The Navajo documents: a study of the economic representation and construction of the Navajo', *Accounting, Organizations and Society* 26, 1: 39–71.

Prokhovnik, R. (1999) *Rational Woman: A Feminist Critique of Dichotomy*, London: Routledge.

Purdy, D. (1981) 'The provision of financial information to employees – a study of the reporting practices of some large public companies in the United Kingdom', *Accounting, Organizations and Society* 6, 4: 327–38.

Puxty, A. G. (1986) 'Social accounting as immanent legitimation: a critique of a technicist ideology', *Advances in Public Interest Accounting* 1: 95–111.

——(1991) 'Social accountability and universal pragmatics', *Advances in Public Interest Accounting* 4: 35–45.

——(1993) *The Social and Organisational Context of Management Accounting*, London: CIMA/Academic Press.

Puxty, A. G. and Tinker, T. (1995) *Policing Accounting Knowledge: The Market for Excuses Affair*, London: Chapman.

Puxty, A. G., Sikka, P. and Willmott, H. (1994) 'Systems of surveillance and the silence of UK academic (accounting) labour', *British Accounting Review* 26, 2: 137–71.

——(1994) '(Re)forming the circle: education, ethics and accountancy practices', *Accounting Education* 8, 1: 77–92.

Quinn, M. (1994) 'Jeremy Bentham on the relief of indigence: an exercise in applied philosophy., *Utilitas* 6, 1: 81–96.

Rasmussen, D. M. (ed.) (1996) *The Handbook of Critical Theory*, Oxford: Blackwell.

Ray, L. J. (1993) *Rethinking Critical Theory: Emancipation in the Age of Global Social Movements*, London: Sage.

Reeves, Sir Paul (1979) *Te Kupu Tuatahi: The First Word*, He Matapuna.

Reiter, S. A. (1994) 'Storytellers, stories and free cash flow', *Proceedings of the Alternative Perspectives on Finance Conference*, Bleed, Slovenia, June 30–July 2.

——(1995) 'Theory and politics: lessons from feminist economics', *Accounting, Auditing and Accountability Journal* 8, 3: 34–59.

Renshall, J. M. (1976) 'Changing perceptions behind The Corporate Report', *Accounting, Organizations and Society* 1, 1: 105–9.

Rey, F. (1978) 'Corporate social responsibility and social reporting in France', in Schoenfield, H. (ed.) *The Status of Social Reporting in Selected Countries*, Urbana, IL: University of Illinois.

Richardson, A. J. (1987) 'Accounting as a legitimating institution', *Accounting, Organizations and Society* 22, 4: 345–55.

Ridgers, B. (1979) 'The use of statistics in counter-information', in Irvine, I., Miles, I. and Evans, J. (eds) *Demystifying Social Statistics*, London: Pluto Press.

Roberts, C. B. (1990) *International Trends in Social and Employee Reporting*, Occasional Research Paper 6, London: ACCA.

——(1991) 'Environmental disclosures: a note on reporting practices in Europe', *Accounting, Auditing and Accountability Journal* 4, 3: 62–71.

Roberts, C. B. (1992) 'Environmental disclosures in corporate annual reports in Western Europe', in Owen, D. (ed.) *Green Reporting: Accountancy and the Challenge of the Nineties*, London: Chapman & Hall.

Roberts, J. and Scapens, R. (1985) 'Accounting systems and systems of accountability', *Accounting, Organizations and Society* 10, 4: 443–56.

Roberts, W. (1979) 'Bentham's Poor Law proposals', *The Bentham Newsletter* 3: 41–2.

Robertson, T. (1976) 'When the name of the game is changing, how do we keep the score?', *Accounting, Organizations and Society* 1, 1: 91–5.

Robson, K. (1993) 'Accounting policy making and "interests": accounting for research and development', *Critical Perspectives on Accounting* 3, 1: 1–27.

——(1994) 'Inflation accounting and action at a distance', *Accounting, Organizations and Society* 19, 1: 45–82.

Rorty, R. (1989) *Contingency, Irony and Solidarity*, Cambridge: Cambridge University Press.

Rosen, F. (1982) 'Jeremy Bentham: recent interpretations' *Political Studies* 30, 4: 575–81.

——(1983) *Jeremy Bentham and Representative Democracy: A Study of the Constitutional Code*, Oxford: Clarendon Press.

Roslender, R. (1992) *Sociological Perspectives on Modern Accountancy*, London: Routledge.

Ross, A. (ed.) (1988) *Universal Abandon? The Politics of Postmodernism*, Edinburgh: Edinburgh University Press.

Rostenreich, N. (1974) 'On Radicalism', *Philosophy of Social Science* 4: 169–82.

Rubenstein, D. (1992) 'Bridging the gap between green accounting and black ink', *Accounting, Organizations and Society* 17, 5: 501–8.

Russell, B. (1962) *History of Western Philosophy and its Connection with Political and Social Circumstances from the Earliest Times to the Present Day*, London: Allen and Unwin.

Said, E. (1996) *Representations of the Intellectual*, New York: Vintage.

Schofield, P. (1996) 'Bentham on the identification of interests', *Utilitas* 8, 2: 223–34.

Schreuder, H. (1979) 'Corporate social reporting in the Federal Republic of Germany: an overview', *Accounting, Organizations and Society* 4, 1/2: 109–22.

——(1981) 'Employees and the corporate social report: the Dutch case', *The Accounting Review* 56, 2: 294–308.

Schreuder, H. and Ramanathan, K. (1984a) 'Accounting and corporate accountability: an extended comment', *Accounting, Organizations and Society* 9, 3 / 4: 409–15.

——(1984b) 'Accounting and corporate accountability', *Accounting, Organizations and Society* 9, 3 / 4: 421–3.

Schweiker, W. (1993) 'Accounting for ourselves: accounting practice and the discourse of ethics', *Accounting, Organizations and Society* 18, 2/3: 231–52.

Semple, J. (1992) 'Foucault and Bentham: a defense of panopticism', *Utilitas* 4, 1: 105–20.

——(1993) *Bentham's Prison: A Study of the Panopticon Penitentiary*, New York: Oxford University Press.

Shearer, T. L. and Arrington, C. E. (1993) 'Accounting in other wor(l)ds: a feminism without reserve', *Accounting, Organizations and Society* 18, 2/3: 253–72.

Shelley, P. B. (1812) 'To a balloon laden with knowledge', in Hutchinson, T. (ed.) (1988) *Shelley: Poetical Works*, Oxford: Oxford University Press.

Sikka, P. (1994) 'The ACCA's preference for darkness revealed', *Accountancy Age* 28, April: 12.

——(2000) 'From the politics of fear to the politics of emancipation', *Critical Perspectives on Accounting* 11, 3: 369–80.

Sikka, P. and Willmott, H. (1995) 'Illuminating the state-profession relationship; accountants acting as Department of Trade and Industry investigators', *Critical Perspectives on Accounting* 6, 4: 341–69.

——(1997) 'Practising critical accounting', *Critical Perspectives on Accounting* 8, 1 / 2: 149–65.

Sikka, P., Wearing, B. and Nayak, A. (1999) *No Accounting for Exploitation*, Basildon: Association for Accountancy and Business Affairs.

Sikka, P., Willmott, H. and Lowe, T. (1991) 'Guardians of knowledge and public interest: a reply to our critics', *Accounting, Auditing and Accountability Journal* 4, 4: 14–22.

Sikka, P., Willmott, H. and Puxty, A. G. (1995) 'The mountains are still there: accounting academics and the bearings of intellectuals', *Accounting, Auditing and Accountability Journal* 8, 3: 113–40.

Simonis, H. (1917) *The Street of Ink*, London: Cassell.

Singh, D. R. and Ahuja, J. M. (1983) 'Corporate social reporting in India', *International Journal of Accounting* 18, 2: 151–69.

Singleton-Green, B. (1993) 'What the researchers found: studies of corporate governance have thrown up some unexpected results', *Accountancy* 112, September: 45.

Smith, G. W. (1989) 'Freedom and virtue in politics: some aspects of character, circumstances and utility from Helvétius to J. S. Mill', *Utilitas* 1, 1: 112–34.

Smith, T. (1993) *Dialectical Social Theory and Its Critics: From Hegel to Analytical Marxism and Postmodernism*, Albany, NY: State University of New York Press.

Solomons, D. (1991a) 'Accounting and social change: a neutralist view', *Accounting, Organizations and Society*, 16, 3: 287–96.

Solomons, D. (1991b) 'A rejoinder', *Accounting, Organizations and Society*, 16, 3: 311–2.

Soldon, N. C. (1978) *Women in British Trade Unions: 1874–1976*, Dublin: Totowa.

Sotto, R. (1983) 'Scientific Utopia and Accounting', *Accounting, Organizations and Society* 8, 1: 57–72.

Spender, D. (1995) *Nattering on the Net: Women, Power and Cyberspace*, Melbourne: Spinifex.

Squires, J. (1993) 'Introduction', in Squires, J. (ed.) *Principled Positions: Postmodernism and the Rediscovery of Value*, London: Lawrence and Wishart.

Stephenson, J. (1973) 'Prying open corporations – tighter than clams', *Business and Society Review*, Winter: 66–73.

Stolliday, I. and Attwood, M. (1978) *Financial Inducements and Productivity Bargaining*, Industrial and Commercial Training.

Sullivan, R. R. (1996) 'The birth of the prison: discipline or punish?', *Journal of Criminal Justice* 24, 5: 449–58.

Taylor, A. (1992) *Annie Besant: A Biography*, Oxford: Oxford University Press.

Taylor, B. (1982) 'A note in response to Itzkin's "Bentham's *Chrestomathia*: utilitarian legacy to English education"', *Journal of the History of Ideas* 43, 2: 309–13.

Teubner, G. (ed.) (1987) *Juridification of Social Spheres*, Berlin: Walter de Gruyter.

Tew, G. (1999) 'What the public thinks about accountants', *New Accountant* 15, 1: 23–4.

The Commission of the European Communities (2001) 'On the recognition, measurement and disclosure of environmental issues in annual accounts and annual reports of companies', *Official Journal of the European Communities*, L156, 13. June 2001: 33–42.

The Global Compact (2002a) 'What it is'. Available at http://www.unglobalcompact.org (20 June 2002).

——(2002b) 'The nine principles'. Available at http://www.unglobalcompact.org (20 June 2002).

Thompson, E. P. (1976) *William Morris: Romantic to Revolutionary*, London: Merlin Press.

Tillett, B. (1931) *Memoirs and Reflections*, London.

Tinker, T. (1980) 'Towards a political economy of accounting: an empirical illustration of the Cambridge controversies', *Accounting, Organizations and Society* 5, 1: 147–60.

——(1984a) 'Accounting for unequal exchange: wealth accumulation versus wealth appropriation', in Tinker, T. (ed.) *Social Accounting for Corporations: Private Enterprise versus the Public Interest*, New York: Markus Wiener.

——(ed.) (1984b) *Social Accounting for Corporations: Private Enterprise versus the Public Interest*, New York: Markus Wiener.

——(1984c) 'Theories of the state and the state of accounting: economic reductionism and political voluntarism in accounting regulation theory', *Journal of Accounting and Public Policy* 3, 1: 55–74.

——(1985) *Paper Prophets: A Social Critique of Accounting*, London: Holt, Rinehart and Winston.

——(1988) 'Panglossian accounting theories: the science of apologising in style', *Accounting, Organizations and Society* 13, 2: 165–90.

——(1991) 'The accountant as partisan', *Accounting, Organizations and Society* 16, 3: 297–310.

——(1998) 'Hamlet without the prince: the ethnographic turn in information systems research', *Accounting, Auditing and Accountability Journal* 11, 1: 3–33.

——(1999) 'Mickey Marxism rides again!', *Critical Perspectives on Accounting* 10, 5: 643–70.

——(2001) 'Paper Prophets: an autocritique', *British Accounting Review* 33: 1: 77–89.

Tinker, T. and Lowe, E. A. (1980) 'A rationale for corporate social reporting: theory and evidence from organizational research', Journal of Business, Finance and Accounting 7, 1: 1–17.

Tinker, T. and Neimark, M. (1987) 'The role of annual reports in gender and class contradictions at General Motors: 1917–1976', *Accounting, Organizations and Society* 12, 1: 71–88.

Tinker, T., Lehman, C. and Neimark, M. (1988) 'Bookkeeping for capitalism: reproducing unequal exchange through professional accounting practice', in Mosco, V. (ed.) *The Political Economy of Information*, Wisconsin: University of Wisconsin Press.

——(1991) 'Falling down the hole in the middle of the road: political quietism in corporate social reporting', *Accounting, Auditing and Accountability Journal* 4, 2: 28–54.

Tinker, T., Merino, B. and Neimark, M. (1982) 'The normative origins of positive theories: ideology and accounting thought', *Accounting, Organizations and Society* 7, 2: 167–200.

Toms, J. S. (1998) 'The supply of and demand for accounting information in an unregulated amrket: examples from the Lancashire cotton mills, 1855–1914', *Accounting, Organizations and Society* 23, 2: 217–238.

Toynbee Hall (1888) *Toynbee Hall: General Information*, London: Penny & Hall.

Tsuzuki, C. (1961) *H. M. Hyndman and British Socialism*, London: Oxford University Press.

Turgot, A. R. J. (1913–23) *Oeuvres de Turgot et document, Le concernant, avec Biographie et Notes par G. Schelle*, Paris: F. Alcan.

Twining, W. (1989) *Reading Bentham*, London: British Academy.

Ullman, A. A. (1976) 'The corporate environmental accounting system: a management tool for fighting environmental degradation', *Accounting, Organizations and Society* 1, 1: 71–9.

United Nations (2002) 'Indicators of Sustainable development'. Available as http: http://www.un.org/esa/sustdev/isd.htm (20 June 2002).

Veron, J. (1994) 'Who is afraid of the linguistic turn – the politics of social history and its discontents', *Social History* 19, 1: 81–97.

Vidal, J. (2002) 'The iceberg cometh', *The Guardian*, 22 March: 21.

Walker, R. (1987) *Nga Tau Tohetohe [The Years of Perseverance]*, Auckland: Penguin.

——(1991) 'Liberating Maori from educational subjection', Working Paper, *Research Unit for Maori Education, Te Tari Rangahau o te Matauranga Maori*, University of Auckland.

Walker, S. P. (1996) 'Laissez-faire, collectivism and companies legislation in nineteenth-century Britain', *British Accounting Review* 28, 4: 305–24.

Walker, S. P. and Mitchell, F. (1998) 'Labor and costing: the employees' dilemma', *Accounting Historians Journal* 25, 2: 35–62.

Walsh, E. J. and Stewart, R. E. (1988) 'Management accounting in the making: two case studies', *Proceedings of the Second Interdisciplinary Perspectives on Accounting Conference*, University of Manchester, vol. 3.

Walsh, E. J. and Stewart, R. E. (1993) 'Accounting and the construction of institutions: the case of the factory', *Accounting, Organizations and Society* 18, 7/8: 783–800.

Waring, M. (1989) *If Women Counted: A New Feminist Economics*, London: Macmillan.

——(1999) *Counting for Nothing: What Men Value and What Women Are Worth*, Toronto: Toronto University Press.

Watt, D. (1998) *A Survey of Environmental Accounting Education in Scottish Universities*, Working Paper, Glasgow Caledonian University.

Weeks, J. (1993) 'Rediscovering values', in Squires, J. (ed.) (1993) *Principled Positions: Postmodernism and the Rediscovery of Value*, London: Lawrence and Wishart.

Wertheim, W. F. (1992) 'The state and the dialectics of emancipation', *Development and Change* 23, 3: 257–81.

Whitehead, A. (1977) 'Champion, Henry Hyde', in Bellamy, J. M. and Saville, J. (eds), *Dictionary of Labour Biography*, vol. 8, London: Macmillan.

——(1983) ' "Quorum pars fui": the autobiography of H. H. Champion', *Bulletin of the Society for the Study of Labour History* 47: 17–20.

Whittington, G. (1993) *Inflation Accounting: An Introduction to the Debate*, Cambridge: Cambridge University Press.

Wildavsky, A. (1994) 'Accounting for the environment', *Accounting, Organizations and Society* 19, 4/5: 461–81.

Williams, R. (1987) *Culture and Society: Coleridge to Orwell*, London: The Hogarth Press.

Williford, M. (1975) 'Bentham on the rights of women', *Journal of the History of Ideas* 36, 1: 167–76.

Willmott, H. (1983) 'Paradigms for accounting research: critical reflections on Tomkins and Groves' "Everyday accountant and researching his reality" ', *Accounting, Organizations and Society* 8, 4: 389–405.

——(1990) 'Serving the public interest? A critical analysis of a professional claim', in Cooper, D. and Hopper, T. (eds) *Critical Accounts*, Basingstoke: Macmillan.

Willmott, H., Puxty, A. G. and Sikka, P. (1993) 'Losing one's reason: on the integrity of accounting academics', *Accounting, Auditing and Accountability Journal* 6, 2: 98–110.

Winiata, W. (1988) *Hapu and Iwi Resources and their Quantification*, The Royal Commission on Social Policy: Further Directions, vol. 3: 791–803.

Wiseman, J. (1982) 'An evaluation of environmental disclosures made in corporate annual reports', *Accounting, Organizations and Society* 7, 1: 53–63.

Wolin, S. (1960) *Politics and Vision: Continnuity and Innovation in Western Political Thought*, Boston, MA: Little Brown.

Yoon, H. K. (1986) *Maori Mind, Maori Land: Essays in the Cultural Geography of the Maori People from an Outsider's Perspective*, Berne: Peter Carey.

Young, A. (1797) 'On the accounts proper to be kept by farmers', *Annals of Agriculture*.

Young, I. M. (1993) 'Together in difference: transforming the logic of group political conflict', in Squires, J. (ed.) *Principled Positions: Postmodernism and the Rediscovery of Value*, London: Lawrence and Wishart.

Zadek, S. and Evans, R. (1993) *Auditing the Market: A Practical Approach to Social Accounting*, Gateshead: Traidcraft / New Economics Foundation.

Zadek, S., Pruzan, P. and Evans, R. (eds) (1997) *Building Corporate Accountability: Emerging Practices in Social and Ethical Accounting, Auditing and Reporting*, London: Earthscan Publications.

Zinn, H. (1994) *You Can't be Neutral on a Moving Train: A Personal History of Our Times*, Boston, MA: Beacon Press.

Žižek, S. (2000a) 'Class struggle or postmodernism? Yes, please!', in Butler, J., Laclau, E. and Žižek, S. (eds) *Contingency, Hegemony, Universality: Contemporary Dialogues on the Left*, London: Verso, pp. 90–135.

——(2000b) 'Holding the place', in Butler, J., Laclau, E. and Žižek, S. (eds) *Contingency, Hegemony, Universality: Contemporary Dialogues on the Left*, London: Verso, pp. 308–29.

——(2001) *Did Somebody Say Totalitarianism? Five Interventions in the (Misuse) of a Notion*, London: Verso.

Index